Malawi
The History of the Nation

B. PACHAI
Professor of History
University of Malawi, Chancellor College

Longman

LONGMAN GROUP LIMITED
LONDON

*Associated companies, branches and
representatives throughout the world*

© Longman Group Ltd 1973

First published 1973

SBN 0 582 64553 0

*Printed in Great Britain by
Western Printing Services Ltd, Bristol*

Contents

iv

Maps

Illustrations

Between pages 20 and 21
Rock carvings near Chapananga's, Chikwawa District
Father Msonthi presenting the Archbishop of York, the Most Reverend
    Michael Ramsay, with an elephant tusk at Nkhota Kota, May 1960
Blantyre Mission Church
Anglican missionaries, 1929

NOTE ON PLACE NAMES
Nyasaland is now Malawi and Lake Nyasa is Lake Malawi.
Cholo is now Thyolo.
Mlanje is now Mulanje.
Fort Johnston has been changed to Mangochi.

Port Herald	,,	,,	,,	,, Nsanje.
Fort Hill	,,	,,	,,	,, Chitipa.
Florence Bay	,,	,,	,,	,, Chitimba.
Deep Bay	,,	,,	,,	,, Chilumba.

These changes have been made at different times and where
the old forms appear in the text they should be understood
to refer to the particular context. Care has been taken to
bring the names in line with current usage and spelling.

NOTE ON CURRENCY

Until early 1971 the currency of the country was in the familiar British
terminology of pounds, shillings and pence. For most of the period
covered in the book this currency was in use and it was decided to
retain the old form in its historical context. The following table
attempts to give a comparative picture as at December 1971, at the
time of the international monetary crisis.

FORMER   PRESENT

British/Malawi	*Malawi*	*British*	*U.S.A.*
Pence	Tambala	New Pence	Cent
Shilling (12 pence)	Kwacha (100 tambala; formerly 10 shillings)	50 New Pence	Dollar (= 80 Malawi tambala and = 40 British new pence).
Pound (20 shillings)	(2 Malawi kwacha = 1 British pound)	Pound	$2.50 = 1 British pound and 2 Malawi kwacha.

Preface

The origin of this book, including its title, was in a series of regular weekly radio talks broadcast by the Malawi Broadcasting Corporation from August 1970 to November 1971. To present almost sixty talks was one form of challenge but to respond to the many requests that the spoken words should be made available in permanent print was a greater one. The publisher first suggested a compilation of some forty thousand words. This was in the early days of the radio series when it was assumed that like similar series elsewhere this one would be confined to a limited time and a limited number. But the demand increased and the supply has turned out to be almost three times the size originally anticipated! The publisher has responded generously to meet the demand. For this I am extremely grateful. I hope the reader will be able to share this gratitude.

The book represents an early instalment of six years of study and research on the history of Malawi carried out in the National Archives of Malawi and in other repositories of information in the country, including the villages and other custodians of so much of the history of the land; in the Public Record Office, British Museum, Royal Commonwealth Society Library and other libraries of various institutions in London; the National Library of Scotland, the University of Edinburgh and the Church of Scotland Library, all in Edinburgh; Rhodes House Library, Oxford; the Library of Congress, National Baptist Convention Library, and various other libraries of universities in the U.S.A.; the National Archives of Rhodesia, Salisbury; and the public libraries of Pretoria, Johannesburg, Cape Town and Durban. Special mention must be made of the National Archives, the Malawi Society Library, the University of Malawi Library at Chancellor College, the Government Printer, Zomba and the Department of Antiquities, Blantyre. To all individuals or officials of the institutions listed I owe a profound debt.

Because of the size of the book few footnotes, bibliographical references or reading list have been included. There is the occasional footnote but no more. The omission is a calculated one and I hope pardonable in the present circumstances. The interested reader is, of course, welcome to write and enquire. I shall be more than happy to oblige. Most of the original material has been retained, for the task is by no means over. This, as I have said above, is only an instalment. Whatever its limitations it is presented to serve as an illustration of what Malawi history is like. It is the Malawian story in compact form, a microcosm if you like. I like to think of it as the story of a nation.

Except for a recasting of part of the first chapter and for the odd omission or extension occasioned by having to transform the spoken word, the textual material is the same as used in the radio talks. Various comments and advice were received from the listening public. These have been of immense benefit. Considerable interest was aroused by both the English instalments presented by myself and the Chichewa version presented by my colleague Mr Alex Kalindawalo, Assistant Registrar. It is hoped that the Chichewa version will be published soon.

In my historical work I have been greatly assisted and encouraged by the kindly professional interest, advice and stimulation that I have received from His Excellency the Life President of Malawi, Dr H. Kamuzu Banda. Because of the personal and professional example of this outstanding man, scholar and statesman, the country's interest in its historical and cultural past has been aroused to greater heights. The historian living and working in Malawi is consequently assisted in his tasks as a result of the upsurge of interest in the country's past. Since I have been on the receiving end of this interest it is impossible to catalogue my thanks to individuals, institutions and to that vast host of Malawian wellwishers who have helped me. I hope they will not take it amiss if I say I am deeply indebted to them all.

I should like to say similar words about the institution which has sheltered me and thus enabled me, through the opportunities given and assistance rendered, tangibly and intangibly, to present this instalment. I owe much to the Vice-Chancellor, Dr Ian Michael, at the top and to others along the line until we get to the bottom. Along the way it is necessary to mention the willing and efficient services of the former Secretary to the History Department, Miss Mercy Kasambara.

My sincere thanks go to those individuals and institutions who gave me the use of their photographs and to my colleague, Mr Alan Cockson, for cheerfully reproducing some of the photographs.

I have my critics, too. Among them the most frequent and most vociferous are the six with whom I live and with whom I share my failures and successes. They are not ordinary critics. By their endurance and goodwill twenty-four hours in the day, at home and in the fields, locally and abroad, patiently listening at all hours to interviews and sermons and radio talks the *History of the Nation* has been possible. To my wife and my five children I owe more than I have ever acknowledged. May they remember Malawi as generously and kindly and permanently as I remember and admire the land, its people and its history.

B. PACHAI
Blantyre, 28 December 1971

Acknowledgments

The author wishes to acknowledge the help received from Father R. Saffroy, w.f. on whose information the map Migration routes of the Maravi and other groups is based.

The publishers are grateful to the following for permission to reproduce photographs: Blantyre and East Africa Company for plate 18; Mrs Daly for plate 4; Inkosana Mopo Jere for plate 14; Rev. Kalilombe for plate 11; Willie Gray Kufa for plate 22; Malawi Department of Antiquities for plates 1 and 30; Malawi Department of Information for plates 3, 5, 6, 13, 16, 24, 28, 31 and for the photograph used on the cover; Malawi Police Headquarters for plates 15 and 21; Rev. Msiska for plate 8; National Archives of Malawi for plates 2 and 12; Rt Rev. J. D. Sangaya for plate 9; Society of Malawi for plate 19; Mr K. Sodagar for plate 17 and the author for plates 7 and 25.

*To my friends, the warm-hearted peoples of Malawi,
among whom I have spent the best years one could hope for.*

i THE PRE-MARAVI PEOPLES

There were three broad periods which characterised the early history of Malawi: the pre-Bantu period, the proto-Bantu period and the Bantu period. These periods refer to the occupation of the country by different physical and cultural groups. The differences include the physical types of the inhabitants, the languages spoken and the domestic and economic occupations, mainly food production techniques.

During the pre-Bantu period man's existence in Africa went back over two million years but it was only over the last half-million years that his cultural advance had been greatest. In Malawi the earliest human remains of this period found so far have been dated to the late Stone Age which started at about 8000 B.C. Stone-Age sites in Malawi have been excavated on Hora Mountain, Fingira, the Livingstonia plateau, Mikolongwe Hill, the Mpunzi Mountain in the Dedza district and elsewhere. The human skeletons as well as the stone tools found in the sites have helped to describe the physical characteristics as well as the possible ways in which these inhabitants lived. Though of pygmoid origin, that is small in stature, Professor Desmond Clark, the leading authority on the Stone Age in Malawi, has said that the physical remains suggest that the skeletons found belong to inhabitants who were larger than the Bushmen (or San) and more robust. They were a hunting people who adapted themselves to a woodland/forest environment. The large number of grindstones, mullers, pestles and mortars found in the sites suggest that they depended quite heavily on vegetable foods which were gathered rather than cultivated. They were hunters, too, and their prey were mainly zebra, wild pig, wildebeeste and hartebeeste. For hunting, they used bows and arrows which had pointed as

1

well as transverse heads. They used heavy stone scrapers, too, for carving wood to be used for spears or for making pointed stakes which were placed in pits dug for catching game. Perforated stone heads might also have been used as clubs for throwing at animals. Traps and nets were also used for hunting animals.

In many parts of Africa various names have been used for these pre-Bantu, Stone-Age inhabitants of hunters and food-gatherers. In Malawi, too, a variety of names are used, including Abatwa, Akafula, Mwandionerakuti and even Ajere and Azimba (the latter are famed as hunters and are so depicted in Nyau pantomimes).

In most Bantu-speaking settlements of central and southern Malawi, oral traditions recall the meeting between these later migrants and the non-Bantu-speaking Stone-Age peoples. The meetings are described as not peaceful. Oral traditions say that many fights took place and that the Akafula were either killed, displaced or absorbed. Where absorption took place this included inter-marriage or patron–client relationships, as well as the possible utilisation of the services of some of the Akafula in ironworking, which was a skill attributed to some of them. The early absorption or displacement of the hunters and food-gatherers in the years following the arrival of Bantu speakers led to the loss of identity of these early inhabitants. Very few survivors remain and these are to be found today in the Lundazi area across the Malawi border and in the swamps of Lake Bangweulu and along the Kafue River in Zambia. A few live near the southern tip of Lake Mweru while some Bushmen are found in South-West Africa and Botswana. They are the lingering remains of the pre-Bantu past. Their more permanent bequests to mankind are the wall paintings in caves found from north to south, from Katanga to Tanzania and from northern Malawi to southern Africa. The designs in these paintings are generally of geometric patterns in certain places such as Zambia, Tanzania and Malawi, and of natural figures and objects in other places like South Africa and North Africa, but they are deemed to be contemporary and of the later Stone-Age period. In Malawi these rock paintings may be seen in Dedza at Mpunzi Mountain and Cencerere Hill as well as at Mikolongwe, not far from Blantyre.

The dim past when Malawi was occupied by small settlements of small people has gone down in legend. Tales are told in villages of gnomes and pixies beating the Drums of Domasi, as well as of strange rock noises. These legends are embedded in fact and fiction. There is no doubt that the pre-Bantu people did exist, even if today they form the subject matter for fancies and fiction.

The second period, of proto-Bantu peoples coming to Malawi,

represents the transition period between the earliest and the latest settlements. They were the advance guard of Bantu-speakers moving from north to south. Like the small men before them, these taller migrants had various names in Malawi: the Pule, the Lenda, the Katanga. Described as tall and well built, this second group of inhabitants were armed with spears, shields, bows and arrows. They were pastoralists and agriculturists. Their broad-bladed spears called *nkalamanga* were used mainly for hunting elephants. As farmers they had a more settled existence and lived in villages. Evidence of their earliest village sites are found in grooves which exist in boulders and on hard rock where they ground their grain. The Maravi people who belong to the third group used smaller and portable grindstones.

Among these pre-Maravi migrants may be classed the Karanga who left the shores of Lake Tanganyika around the ninth century A.D. They migrated southwards with their cattle, choosing the tsetse-free corridor between Lake Malawi and the Luangwa valley. Though the main groups crossed the Zambezi on their march southwards, a number remained in Malawi with their cattle. Traditions among the later Maravi do not generally describe much fighting between them and the cattle farmers and agriculturists already in the country. This was probably because of the smaller numbers involved and because it was easier for the two groups to assimilate because of cultural and economic similarities.

With the arrival of the early farmers also came the Iron Age, or more appropriately it was the other way round. The use of iron in Bantu Africa assisted in the migration of peoples through wooded or forested areas, since from iron more durable tools and implements could be forged, useful for forest clearance and tilling the land as well as for defence and hunting.

In Malawi Iron-Age sites have been excavated in the north between the South Rukuru River in the south and the Songwe in the north (at Karonga, Livingstonia, the Nyika and Lake Kazuni), and in the south in places between Ncheu and Mangochi (formerly Fort Johnston). The earliest Iron-Age date obtained so far from charcoal deposits at Phopo Hill near Lake Kazuni is the third century A.D. while the earliest date in the southern region so far is the fourth century A.D. (at Nkope Bay at Cape Maclear and the Bwanje valley of Ncheu). The conclusion from these dates is that migration took place from north to south. So far, except for a single discovery of a blue glass bead and half a cowrie shell at Matope, about thirty miles from Blantyre, there is no other evidence of trade between the Iron-Age dwellers of the third and fourth centuries A.D. and the coast. On the other hand there is plenty of evidence of coastal trade in northern Malawi from the eleventh century A.D.

One of the relics of the early farmers of the Iron-Age period, and for that matter of all subsequent farmers, is pottery which was used by settled cultivators for storing foodstuffs. Two facts concerning pottery that are of great local interest are: the discovery of Kisi pottery from Bukinga country east of the northern tip of Lake Malawi in the Karonga area and dated to the eleventh century A.D.; and the close relationship between the Gokomere pottery of Rhodesia and the Nkope pottery of southern Malawi. Though it has not been possible to identify all the early Iron-Age peoples, the main later stream constituted the Maravi peoples, some of whom, no doubt, arrived earlier than others and might well have been part of the transition group prior to the arrival of the main Bantu-speaking migrants under their Phiri leaders in the Malawi of old. Since the first phase of the Iron Age in Malawi based on pottery types closes at the eleventh century A.D. it is possible that this century may be reasonably considered to be the watershed between the proto-Maravi and the Maravi proper.

ii THE MARAVI PEOPLES

Between the thirteenth and sixteenth centuries A.D., most of central and southern Malawi was settled by Bantu-speakers who were at first a collective part of the vast and widely settled community of Maravi peoples. The history of this settlement has become complicated by the fact that it is only a small part of a whole. It is the history of a single paramount chief at first (Karonga); then two (Undi) and finally three (Lundu). These paramount chiefs may be likened to senior kings. As the community became enlarged through local quarrels, pressures on land, the adventurous and profitable urge to branch off on one's own, the need to pre-empt good land and also, at a relatively later stage, to control or protect trade goods and trade routes, the Maravi community dispersed: the centre gave way to the parts and a whole host of chiefs or tributary kings emerged, each with a history of his own (Chulu, Kanyenda, Kabunduli, Mkanda, Kaphwiti and Mwase for example). The fluctuating fortunes of these tributary kings, and indeed of the paramounts, too, coupled with the fact that the Maravi settled in a vast geographical area which today straddles three countries, have not helped to minimise the complications.

In the collective story there is, firstly, the account of the migration. The closest and most recent nuclear point of dispersion of most of the Bantu-speakers who settled in Central Africa and neighbouring areas is northern Katanga. Most of the Maravi migrants left this area before the establishment in the sixteenth century of the Luba-Lunda kingdoms which have been responsible for so many of the chiefdoms of Central Africa. Families moved out under family heads; related family heads forged links for obvious reasons under a powerful head who assumed the leadership of his clan. Some clans arrived in Malawi before the emergence of a political leader over the Maravi as a whole. This leadership emerged when the leader of a particular clan, the Phiri, extended his rule over other clans. This development was believed to have taken place along the march to destination Malawi. It was then that the honorific title of Karonga appeared but even at the time not all the names of the different holders of this title were remembered. Mazizi was remembered as the man who led the ruling party out of Congo country. Whether or not he was the first title-holder has been disputed. Then came Chinkhole whose name was certainly associated with it, and who may have been the first Karonga. Then the man Chidzonze was acknowledged as the Karonga who brought his followers to their new home. A place was found in the roll for the Karonga Mazura or possibly Masula, a ruler in the late sixteenth and early seventeenth centuries because of his dramatic involvements with the Portuguese as well as with the Rozwi ruler of the Monomotapa. The early period of the Karonga story closed with the death at the hands of the Yao of Sosola, who was in office in the 1850s and the 1860s when the southern Ngoni and the central Yao were beginning to filter into Malawi.

In accounts of the Maravi migration three main routes were mentioned: the southerly route which speaks of a movement from the Zambezi Valley northwards; the westerly route which includes the passage from the Congo eastwards; the northerly route which describes a general north–south movement. It is reasonable to accept all accounts as possessing some elements of truth. What is interesting in these accounts is that various place names are constant in all of them, not necessarily in the same order of arrival. These are Choma, Kapoche (in present Portuguese East Africa), Kapirintiwa (east of the Dzalanyama range of hills in present Dedza and Lilongwe districts), Msinja, a few miles away, Maere a Nyangu (in the valley of the Upper Shire), Piriulongwe (in present Mangochi district) on to Malawi in the southwestern lakeshore area at Mankhamba near the present site of Kachindamoto's village in the Dedza district. It is inconceivable that most parties passed all of them but possible that some of the important ones did and that a few of those that did not used the names of the sites for other geographic entities. There are, for example, at least four places in Central Africa known by the names Choma and Malawi.

According to one account of the group following the northerly route, the following picture emerges. With a considerable following Mazizi proceeded westwards to Nkhamanga where he settled at Makama close to the Njakwa Gorge. Here he assumed the title of Karonga. With him were his son Kanyenda and his nephew Kabunduli, each with a following of his own. Amongst them were the two principal clans, the Phiri and the Mwali; Karonga and Kabunduli were Aphiri and Kanyenda was Amwali. Kanyenda and Kabunduli were sent to spy out the land and returned with a favourable report, whereupon Karonga set out for Mankhamba. On the way he met a settlement of the Banda clan near Jenjewe Mountain west of Kaning'ina Mountain. Karonga left behind him a number of his followers in small groups such as the Chawinga, Mwachanda, Luhanga, Mkandawire at Hewe, Nkhamanga and Ng'onga. Guided on by members of the Banda clan he proceeded to his destination. In course of time, his nephew Kabunduli crossed the Vipya and settled on the Kakwewa River with his followers who formed the majority of the Tonga people. Kanyenda moved northwards and settled at Nkhunga north of the Dwangwa River.

This testimony contains a wealth of historical leads to Malawi history. For one thing it touches on the historical links between the Maravi (or Chewa) and the Tumbuka who remained in the more northern part of the country to develop their own language and culture. Then, it indicates the relationship between the older settled Banda clan and the more recent arrival of the Phiri rulers. And it also describes the role of the Mwali clan led by Kanyenda and the relationship between the Tonga and the Maravi (or Chewa) through the common link provided by Kabunduli.

From migration and interrelationships we come to issues of terminology. What started off as Maravi ended as Chewa, Mang'anja, Nyanja, Chipeta, Nsenga, Chikunda, Mbo, Ntumba and Zimba. This came about as a result of dispersion and decentralisation, and the various names are no more than regional or geographical designations of people who belonged to the same cultural and language group. Of these, the name Chewa stands out as the numerically strongest group, of whom about 80 per cent live in Malawi and the remaining 20 per cent or so in Zambia and Mozambique. It was only in a Portuguese report of 1831–32 that the name *Chevas* first appeared in print. Various explanations have been advanced to explain its meaning: one of them being that it refers to strangers; the other that it derives, according to the late Professor J. B. Bruwer, from the ancient verb root *chewa* from which the neutral form *ku-ceuka* still survives, though the old form still

Migration routes of the Maravi and other early groups

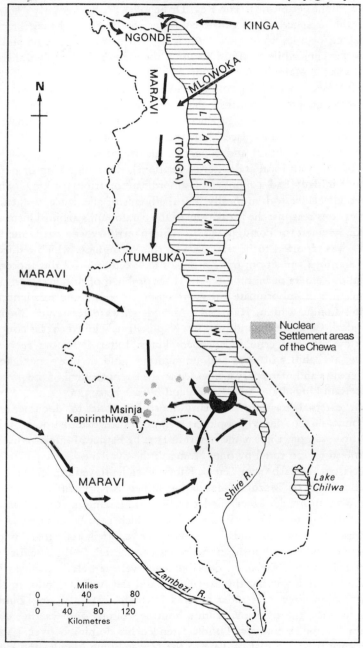

exists in the proverb '*Umcewe mwana angapsye*' ('Look behind you, the child might get burnt'). The Rev. Dr Schoffeleers has recently argued that the presence of different names must be because all the Chewa-speaking peoples were once known by two names, a specific and a generic. Thus while the Phiri group of the Mang'anja described themselves as the Maravi, the non-Phiri called themselves Mang'anja. If the word 'Maravi' stood for an ethnic group or for part of it, it also referred to geographic entities which included the headquarters of the Chewa-speakers near present Kachindamoto's as well as certain ancient settlements or halting-places, hills and royal shrines.

As for the political and economic history of the Maravi peoples (involving both local and external relations), the senior king or paramount initially had a number of subordinate or tributary kings who owed allegiance to him locally. But the bonds of allegiance weakened for various reasons: the breakaway of the paramount's senior kinsman, Undi, who left for Portuguese East African territory westwards and by 1614 was reported to be trading with the Portuguese, which reduced the Karonga's position; the Karonga's failure to control the appointment of holders of high office; the sheer problem of distances and the reluctance of subordinate rulers to submit to economic restrictions. Undi, Lundu, Chulu, Kanyenda, Mkanda, Mwase Kasungu, Mwase Lundazi, Changamire and possibly Kaphwiti developed in the course of time into powerful independent kings. External factors such as trade, availability of arms and ammunition, gold or ivory, navigable waterways and mercenary armies led to the strengthening of the power of certain kings like Undi, Lundu and Mwase Kasungu.

In external relations reference must be made to documentary accounts of the Maravi peoples as well as to their external politics. In the first category there is the report in 1572 by Father Montclaro on the Zambezi region ruled by one 'Mongaz'; the overland journey in 1616 by Gaspar Boccaro from Tete to Kilwa when he stayed for fifteen days at the village of 'Mazura' (Masula), identified as Kaphwiti's village on the Wankurumadzi River; the letter by Luis Mariano in 1624 in which references were made to interior chiefs which may be deciphered as Mwase and Luhanga; and Father Barreto's report in 1667 that Lundu occupied the second position in Karonga's 'empire'. In the category of external politics, the main developments were largely influenced by trade factors involving the Portuguese and the Arabs. Lundu, in the lower Shire area, was most affected by these factors. Using Zimba mercenaries, the overflow from a hunting, mining and warring clan from Tumbuka country, Lundu extended his dominion over a vast territory from the east of Tete to the Mozambique islands, and even northwards along the coast approaching the Mombasa port of East Africa for a while, over a region called Bororo. His expansion was shortlived. A three-sided alliance was formed to curb it. This involved the Karonga, Mazura, the Mwene Mutapa (Gatsi Rusere), the Rozwi king in Rhodesia, and their Portuguese allies. In 1635 it was reported that an alliance of the Karonga and the Portuguese succeeded in defeating Lundu. It was now the Karonga's turn to expand eastwards over the lands of Bororo. It was this period of expansion that provided evidence which led the Portuguese Barreto to write in 1667 that the Maravi had an empire headed by the Karonga and followed by Lundu. But that was perhaps the apogee of the Maravi might. The tide of disintegration which had begun with Undi's defection and with the movement towards decentralisation could not be held in check.

Whereas once there was a single political structure when the settlements were close and the Karonga was at the head, now there were as many political units as there were rulers. Each king, some of whom were more powerful or influential than others, was at the head of a central authority which included both secular and religious duties. The first of these duties involved, among others, the installation of subordinate rulers even if the selection of these rulers was not in the king's keeping; the second involved, also among others, the communication with ancestral spirits. Other responsibilities included the political duty of settling disputes among subordinates, the social duty of ensuring for the security of life and property of his subjects and above all the economic duty of ensuring that his people were not in want. One way to achieve this was to arrange for the exchange or distribution of goods and also by retaining large storehouses of grain based on individual contributions as an insurance against famine.

Though the main language of the Maravi was that of its predominant constituent, namely Chichewa, a language which modern Malawi agreed on 21 September 1968 to proclaim as one of its two main languages, the northern and eastern rump, the Tumbuka and the Tonga, developed their own languages, cultures, political and economic histories to such an extent that they soon become more properly a part of the peoples of northern Malawi.

iii THE PEOPLES OF NORTHERN MALAWI

The area between the Dwangwa River in the south and the Songwe River in the north was the home of many peoples who formed themselves into different groups on cultural lines of language or religion or on economic foundations, such as trade, or who were thrust together

9

by the accident of geography or by the political acumen of a worthy leader.

From south to north these people were the Tumbuka, the Tonga, the Kamanga, the Henga, the Phoka, the Ngonde and the Lambya plus a host of smaller but related groups. The ancestors of the earliest of these peoples came to Malawi over five hundred years ago if we go by dates which have been given to archaeological remains as well as by calculating family trees or genealogies. This early period must, therefore, not be confused with the nineteenth century which brought to all parts of Malawi foreigners from east, west, south and north: the Arabs, the Yao, the Bemba, the Bisa, the Ngoni and the European. This nineteenth-century intrusion forms its own history. The many centuries before form their own too. These we must now consider.

One of the oldest peoples of northern Malawi are the Tumbuka, and one of the oldest clans is the Mkandawire clan, the members of which became known by other family names as movements continued to take place. Some such related clans were the Kachali, the Nyanjagha, the Mwalweni and the Harawa, all direct descendants of one of the oldest clans in northern Malawi. As members of a simple agricultural and pastoral community, the Tumbuka had no pressing need to organise themselves either militarily or politically in defence of their livelihood. Land was plentiful and external threats were few. The necessities of life were few too and were satisfied by internal production or by some measure of internal trade based on exchange of goods. A good example of internal trade—though of a slightly later period—was that between the Hango and the Phoka, the former providing salt, the latter providing hoes.

Where there was no wealth to guard over zealously, land to quarrel over bitterly, or where there were no rulers to keep in office selfishly, the necessity to remember detailed histories was not a pressing one. One significant event in the later history of Tumbukaland radically changed the history of the land and its peoples. This was the coming of external traders about the year 1780. These traders came in peace from the eastern side of the lake, led by one who is referred to as Mlowoka because he crossed over into a new country. This trading party made up of about eight leading men is believed to have crossed the lake at Mtawali in a dhow, a sailing ship with a single mast and made of wood like those commonly used at Zanzibar at the time. The party came to trade in ivory, a commodity which was in abundance then as the country west of the lake extending beyond the Luangwa River teemed with elephants.

Before the coming of the Balowoka, the peaceful peasant and pastoral clans did not appreciate the commercial value of ivory. The elephants provided meat and the ivory was a household commodity used to make seats and bed props. The Balowoka with their knowledge and experience of external trade saw immediately the value of tapping the resources of this area. If they had come with the objectives of buying ivory and returning, the friendly reception coupled with the immense trading potential of the area caused them to stay.

Their bales of cloth, beads of various kinds, and *mphande* shells were in great demand among the local clans. Mlowoka was a shrewd businessman who set about entrenching his commercial position by cheerfully and tactfully extending his influence by distributing gifts and by marrying women from the more influential clans such as the Luhanga and the Kumwenda. In time his wealth and influence transformed his commercial position into a dominant social one. Soon this dispenser of hoes, a valuable implement, was being called Chikuwa majembe which in kiSwahili means 'to carry hoes'. The Phoka, who lived between the Rumphi and Chitimba Rivers before the coming of the Balowoka, supplied Mlowoka with most of his hoes. They called him Chikulamayembe. When the first Mlowoka died, he was succeeded by Gonapamuhanya, his son, who assumed the title of Chikulamayembe. Thus it came to be that the leader of a trading party became the leading light among the people in whose midst he settled.

It remained for Mlowoka to entrench his position further. He sent out the eight leading men in his original party to various parts of the country as his regional trade representatives, firstly to safeguard his trading interests and secondly to spread his influence in any other way. These eight have been listed as Katumbi, Kajumba, Chiwulunta, Kabunduli, Mwahenga, Mwalwene, Mwamlowe and Jumbo. One of these, Kabunduli, is mentioned in tradition as also a member of the earlier Maravi people and his settlement in the Nkhata Bay area is more likely to have been before the coming of the Balowoka.

To what extent a political organisation was created is not quite clear. Some reports say that in the period after 1800 the successors of Mlowoka created a political structure with its headquarters at Nkhamanga village not far from present Njakwa. Whatever the influence and power of this structure it certainly did not extend throughout the territory bounded by the Dwangwa in the south and the Songwe in the north.

Chikulamayembe himself became an important person in Nkhamanga, exacting tribute in the form of a single tusk for every elephant killed there. From how far and wide among his regional representatives tribute reached him is not known.

The southern Tumbuka were certainly more under the influence of the Maravi than of the Chikulamayembe. One other people, the Phoka, who were in the Nkhamanga area before Mlowoka, came into the economic ambit of Chikulamayembe but retained their separate political organisation. One of them, Chaswera Mtimbaluji, was given the name Kachulu by Chikulamayembe in honour of the fact that he had killed an elephant while standing on an anthill. Though Chikulamayembe placed a black turban on Kachulu's head, signifying that he was a chief, the Phoka people continued to maintain their separate organisation until the dawn of the colonial era.

When the Ngoni invaded northern Malawi around the 1850s the sixth Chikulamayembe was in office. The eighth Chikulamayembe, Mujuma, lost his life in the revolt against the Ngoni in 1880. The title was not reinstated until 1907 when the ninth Chikulamayembe, Chilongozi Mlowoka, was restored to the position, thus once again perpetuating the Chikulamayembe title. Chilongozi had in his youth fled from the Ngoni and had taken shelter with the Arabs under Mlozi. Now in the early years of the twentieth century he was a policeman at Chilumba, then known as Deep Bay. He had certainly lived through the hazards of an earlier period to find himself in altogether a new situation. He saw service in World War I and was awarded the King's Medal in 1924.

For Chilongozi the old order had passed. His forefather had come to northern Malawi as a trader. He had settled among such old Tumbuka clans as the Luhanga, Mwachanda, Mkandawire and Nyanjagha. He had married among them and established his headquarters in a village about three miles west of Njakwa Gorge. He had organised trade in a wide area, sometimes called the Nkhamanga empire, but this was not an empire under a single political ruler but rather an area where his commercial representatives spread his influence. Some came under his rule, others retained their independence. But his coming introduced a new dimension in opening up the territory for trade and further publicising its importance.

Like his trading neighbour to the north, the Kyungu, Chikulamayembe was seriously affected by the nineteenth-century invasions of Malawi. But before these are considered, reference must be made to the area further north of Nkhamanga where an older dynasty and a wider trading network existed. This was the area between the North Rukuru River and the Songwe—the land over which Kyungu was an important ruler. This takes us to the northernmost region of present Malawi.

When the ninth Chikulamayembe was installed in 1907, the seventeenth Kyungu was already reigning in Karonga. The Ngonde must have settled in the Songwe area around mid-fifteenth century.[1] Like Mlowoka further south, the Kyungu came with leading men, five in number: Katenga, Mulwa, Kyumba, Mboma and Ngosi.

Just as the Balowoka found older settlements already in existence and clans such as the Mwachanda and the Mkandawire already there, so did the Ngonde find older inhabitants south of the Songwe. Some of these were the Musyani, the Mwenendeka, the Mwenekisindile and the Mwenifumbo. Over them the Kyungu established his overlordship. Giving them headcloths to seal the new relationship he said, in seeking their friendship and support: 'You are the priests, you the indigenous owners of the land, do you pray for me that I, the chief, may sleep in peace.'[2]

The Kyungu needed this support because when he arrived at Mbande Hill, a few miles north of present Karonga town, he found an elephant hunter already there. This was one Simbobwe who was in possession of large stocks of ivory. Perhaps he, too, had come to trade. In any case, the region is known to have dealt in trade long before the first Kyungu arrived. Glass beads found at Mwasampa have been dated to 1190 A.D. and at Mwenepera Hill to 1240 A.D., hundreds of years before the Ngonde were formerly believed to have arrived. Perhaps their arrival coincided with the presence of these beads, in which case the date of their arrival is pushed back to about the thirteenth century and not the fifteenth.

When the first Kyungu, Syora, and his five nobles arrived at Mbande Hill and displaced the elephant hunter, Simbobwe, they too came with trade in mind and a new home in sight. They had travelled a long way. From the country of the Kinga (or from Bukinga) where the Livingstone Mountains are to be found, they had travelled west-wards near Rungwe Mountain, then further westwards until they had reached the country of the Bisa in northeastern Zambia today. They had then turned eastwards until they reached the Songwe River. After further explorations southwards in Tumbuka country they had moved on to Mbande Hill—the end of a long march.

From this rich elephant country ivory was sent northwards through a pass which cut between the Nyika and the Misuku Hills. In return,

---

[1] An earlier date of 1410 ± 80 is now available for Mbande Hill, Karonga, but it is not clear whether this is to be attributed to the Ngonde presence or to pre-Ngonde traders. See M. Wilson, 'Reflections on the early history of North Malawi', p. 140, *Early History of Malawi*, ed. B. Pachai, London, 1972.

[2] G. Wilson, *The Constitution of the Ngonde*, Rhodes-Livingstone Institute, Zambia, 1939, reprinted by Manchester University Press, 1968, p. 11.

cloth, porcelain and metalwork found their way into the country. Slaves or gun traffic did not feature in this early trade. By the time the tenth Kyungu was in office the Ngonde trade had changed its direction. Instead of going northwards the ivory was now being sent across the lake, eastwards.

The control of trade in his region made the Kyungu a powerful ruler. With wealth came religious dominance and together these factors reinforced the power and the position of the Kyungu. In contrast, just north of the Songwe were relatives of the Ngonde, the Nyakyusa, but the Nyakyusa hardly exported any ivory before the Europeans arrived in 1876. The Nyakyusa remained organised in a number of small chiefdoms while the Kyungu to the south was a paramount chief. It was control of trade and of the trade routes that strengthened the Kyungu's position.

One group of people who are sometimes lumped together with the Ngonde are the Balambya. Their homeland is generally traced to Rungwe in present Tanzania. From here they moved to Kasasa on the Songwe River. The leader of the Lambya defeated an earlier inhabitant in the region whose name was Sikwese. From this point onwards the victorious leader was called Mwaulambya and an important group of people in Bulambya lived under him. The common factor, of course, among the Lambya, the Ngonde and the Nyakyusa as for many other peoples in the northern end of Malawi's corridor, is that they all hailed from Bukinga country beyond the northeastern tip of Lake Malawi.

Northern Malawi from the Dwangwa to the Songwe was influenced tremendously later by the Livingstonia Mission which shifted its headquarters from Bandawe to present Livingstonia at Khondowe in 1894. Many mission products became the Kyungus, the Chikulamayembes and the Mwaulambyas of the country. Important court advisers such as the Rev. Edward Boti Manda, one-time adviser to Chikulamayembe, and Charles Chidongo Chinula, one-time adviser to Inkosi Ya Makosi, M'Mbelwa, were trained at Livingstonia Mission. The branch station near Mweniwanda where Dr and Mrs Kerr-Cross and the Rev. J. Bain were posted was a worthy supporter of the Khondowe Mission.

Another important influence was introduced when the African Lakes Corporation opened a branch store at Karonga in 1884. Monteith Fotheringham found himself in the role of a trader and a soldier—a trader in ivory and a soldier against Mlozi, Msalemu, Kopa Kopa and Namakukane, Swahili Arabs whose slave-raiding activities were to create havoc in the area from 1888 to 1895.

CHAPTER 2

Nineteenth-century influences in Malawi

i THE POSITION IN TONGALAND

Sir Alfred Sharpe, Nyasaland's first Governor, once described the Central Angoniland district with its centre at Lilongwe as the Basutoland of Central Africa. This description must have resulted from the fact that the area had mountain ranges and is centrally situated. Taking our cue from this, it would be appropriate to describe Tongaland as the Switzerland of Malawi.

Bordered by the Vipya range of mountains to the west, and extending north and south of the Luweya River, the area was occupied for many hundreds of years before the nineteenth century. Here lived one of the oldest clans in the region, the Nyaluwanga, to which the Kaunda family belongs. Maravi traditions speak of the Karonga sending out his son Kanyenda and his nephew Kabunduli to reconnoitre new lands for settlement. Kanyenda finally settled near the Dwambazi River while Kabunduli moved north of it. Later traditions also connect the first Kabunduli with the Balowoka who entered Malawi from east of the lake in the eighteenth century. But it is clear that Kabunduli's connection with the Maravi is of longer duration.

Tongaland, also known administratively in the colonial days as West Nyasa district, later as Chinteche, and today as Nkhata Bay district, bordered on Tumbukaland to the north and west and Chewaland to the south. Its southern neighbour was Nkhota Kota where Swahili Arab influences were strong in the nineteenth century. When the northern and western neighbours of Tongaland were overrun by the Ngoni invasions of the mid-nineteenth century, the internal and external relations of the Tonga were radically affected. About twenty years after these invasions, the Tonga were bracing themselves to reestablish the old order which had existed for centuries, when Scottish missionaries established a mission station in their area. With Christianity came commerce. Another later factor was the export of migrant labour first to the Shire Highlands and then to other neighbouring and also non-neighbouring areas. All these pulls and pressures, internal and external, made Tongaland, like Switzerland, the meeting ground of various influences.

First something must be said about the Tonga themselves in the nineteenth century. The northern part of Tonga country was settled under Mankhambira and Kangoma; the southern was under Kabunduli with the Phiri mainly in the hill region westwards, and Mlenga Mzoma mainly along the southern lakeshore among the Kapunda Banda. These four chiefs, Mankhambira, Kangoma, Kabunduli and Mlenga Mzoma, were by no means the only chiefs in the area. When the Tonga chiefs and headmen signed a treaty with Her Majesty's Consul, Harry Hamilton Johnston, on 12 October 1889, no Tonga chief north of the Luweya River signed it. It was a treaty negotiated by chiefs and headmen of the middle region of Tongaland. The names of those who signed give some idea about the other chiefs. One was Chikuru Chiweyu Muwamba, the eldest member of the Banda family of chiefs; Marenga Mwale, of the second branch of the local Banda family of chiefs, another of the signatories, was the successor of the Marenga whom Livingstone had met and had written about. Others who signed the 1889 treaty were Sawira, Chikoko, Kasuna, Daambi, Kanyanda, Chenyenta, Longwe, Gombo, Chimuzi, Fuka and Mpimbi.

Many of the Tonga chiefs of old spread out beyond the limits now defined as Tongaland for various reasons such as internal or external disturbances, land shortage and a desire to return to old sites or to other localities of later choice. It is difficult to say, therefore, that the nineteenth-century chiefs in Tongaland were the only important ones at that time.

There is a certain characteristic of Tonga society that is helpful for understanding Tonga political structure, Tonga chieftainships and the reaction of the Tonga to African administration introduced by the colonial government. This may be introduced and illustrated through the use of the words individualism, egalitarianism or equality: that is, every Tonga considers himself able to raise himself to the highest position in his society by hard work and accomplishments. As it is among individuals, so it is among chiefs. It is possible to speak of a senior member in a family of chiefs but not of a paramount chief as such. In this egalitarian society made up of equals a chief is first among equals (or *primus inter pares*).

One point to be noticed about Tonga society is that every individual has two common family names. One is derived from the father and represents his *chiwongo*; the other is derived from the mother and represents his *fuku*. In cases of inheritance or succession it is the latter, or mother's title, that is generally adopted.

In the old days where a cluster of chiefs resided in a particular locality, say south of the Luweya River among the Kapunda Banda, seniority among the chiefs was arrived at by observing in whose *mphara* or public meeting place the initiation rites for girls, or the *nkhole*, were held. Gradually these rites became distributed among all the chiefs and thus the only measure by which seniority was judged ceased to exist, thus adding to the egalitarian nature of Tonga society. (Today in actual practice every village has its own place for these rites. Such places are referred to as *nthanganene*.)

Historical evidence on certain aspects of nineteenth-century Tonga history is provided in an excerpt from a letter written by the Tonga teacher, minister of religion, politician and historian who was baptised at Bandawe by the Rev. Dr Steele on 24 September 1893 and who died on 17 July 1955, the Rev. Yesaya Zerenji Mwasi. He wrote to the Rev. A. G. Macalpine on 7 April 1924:

I am so absorbed in Tonga History. This is rather a passion to me . . . both you Europeans and most of the natives will be much startled to find out that Wiza, Ng'oma, Rungu, Tawa, Bemba are blood related with or are of the same family with aTonga; that Banda and Phiri are the real landowners of Nkhamanga; that Banda on the mother's side and Phiri on the father's side are certainly of one family and I am sure almost all principal men or headmen are identified in a way I did not know before in Tongaland and elsewhere. Now let me state briefly about this relationship.

Mwasi then traces the origins of the Banda and Phiri and comes to the conclusion that their proper tribal designation was Wina Zovu; that at Nkhamanga they were also known as Mwachanda, Chanda being the sister of the first Wemba chief. Yesaya Zerenji Mwasi pursues the argument of origins and connections which serve to illustrate the relationship of the Tonga people with other members traceable to the Banda and Phiri clans; and also that this can be pushed farther in both space and time outside the narrow limits of the present boundaries of Tongaland and to centuries before the nineteenth century.

In the nineteenth century there were many influences which impinged upon Tonga society. The foremost was that of the missionaries of the Free Church of Scotland led by Dr Robert Laws. While the

Nineteenth century arrivals

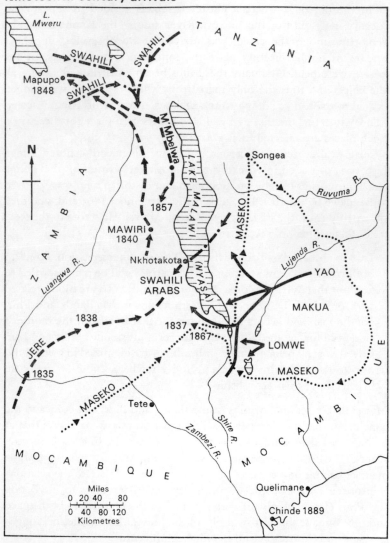

headquarters of these missionaries of the Livingstonia Mission was still at Cape Maclear, the Mission established observation posts at Bandawe and at Kaning'ina (near the present Mzuzu) in November 1878. The objective was to carry the message of Christ and to set up schools among the Tonga and the Ngoni in due course. But before this objective could be realised the missionaries found themselves involved in local Tonga politics: arbitrating in local matters, intervening in the slave trade and acting as a civil authority very much as the Blantyre Mission did at the same time. Dr Robert Laws visited the Bandawe observation post in October 1879 and opposed this practice of intervening in Tonga politics. He said:

> I think there has been shown too markedly a tendency to decide native disputes. When any dispute is brought by the parties to the station for decision, it is right to advise on the matter if possible; but in matters entirely inter-native the executive should be left to themselves.

The policy of Dr Laws was carried out fully only after he himself resumed charge of the Bandawe Mission in 1881.[1]

Local Tonga politics was one thing; Tonga-Ngoni politics was another, and more serious. The observation post set up at Kaning'ina was intended to prepare the ground for eventual entry into Ngoniland. Here the famous Swazi induna, Chiputula Nhlane, guarded and controlled Ngoni interests. Ever since M'Mbelwa I had been installed paramount chief over the Ngoni of northern Malawi about 1857, the Ngoni had been looking around as a united people for crops, cattle and captives from their settlements in the Lunyangwa, Kasitu and Rukuru Rivers. The Tonga to the east and southeast were raided as were other people within raiding distance. A European by the name of Miller and a Xhosa from Lovedale in South Africa, William Koyi, missionary in charge of the Kaning'ina post, were stationed at this tenuous and arbitrary dividing line between the Tonga and the Ngoni. A civil engineer in the service of the Livingstonia Mission, James Stewart, visited this area in December 1879. The following excerpt is taken from his despatch to the Foreign Secretary of the Free Church of Scotland:

> On the 13th [December] I reached Marenga, and there I found Mr John Moir, who was to accompany me. On the 15th we landed at Nkata Bay, having brought on six of Mr Moir's carriers and four

[1] Norman Long, 'Bandawe Mission Station and Local Politics, 1878–1886', *Rhodes-Livingstone Journal*, 32, Dec. 1962.

new recruits. On the 17th we reached Kaningina, and found Mr Miller and William Koyi well. The next day we made our final arrangements, and left Kaningina. The party consisted of Mr Moir and myself, William Koyi and Mapas Ntintili . . . and forty-three natives.

Our road led over the highest point of Mount Kaningina, about five thousand feet above sea level, and was very steep and rough. We camped on its western side, and at mid-day on the 19th reached Chipatula's [sic] village, and were received by the chief in a friendly manner. I told him of the endeavours that Dr Laws had made in the colony to obtain men who might be stationed among them . . . that men were not at present available, but that ere long, we hoped to be able to send a teacher among them. He begged me to go on to Mombera, to give him the same account.[1]

The party called on M'Mbelwa on 20 December 1879 but the chief would not see them. There was a good reason for this. In 1875, many Tonga, chiefly under Chiputula Nhlane near Kaning'ina, who had been incorporated into the Ngoni society forcibly, had broken away and had fled to their former lakeshore homes, finding refuge in the large stockaded villages of Mankhambira and Kangoma near the Chinteche River, Marenga at Bandawe and Katonga southeast of Bandawe. The Ngoni had attempted unsuccessfully to destroy the stockades at Chinteche in 1876–77. Since then relations between the Ngoni and the Tonga were seriously strained, each side striving to avenge old scores. In this atmosphere of bitterness, the Scottish mission observation posts were set up at Bandawe and on the Ngoni borders at Kaning'ina. For the moment the missionaries were in Tongaland exclusively, an arrangement which irritated the Ngoni. James Stewart touched on the core of the matter in his despatch already referred to: 'I have no doubt that they [the Ngoni] were sincere in their desire to make friendship with us; but an exclusive alliance only would suit them. We heard that they were tired of waiting for us, and intended now to take their own way, which, I fear, means war before long.'

The fact that war did not break out as predicted was due solely to the presence of the Scottish missionaries at their now permanent station at Bandawe in 1881 and at their branch station at Njuyu in Ngoniland in 1882.

[1] Livingstonia Mission Shepperson Collection, James Stewart to George Smith, 31 Dec. 1879. The old missionary road from Bandawe to Njuyu which passed Kaning'ina skirted the Kavuzi stream not far from Rosefalls, the residence of Sir Martin and Lady Roseveare in 1971.

1. Rock carvings near Chapananga's, Chikwawa District, probably c. 1000.

2. Father Msonthi presenting the Archbishop of York, the Most Reverend Michael Ramsay, with an elephant tusk at Nkhota Kota, May 1960.

3. Blantyre Mission Church. In the background is the Henry Henderson Institute and in the foreground the cairn showing the site of the first camp set up by Henry Henderson and Tom Bokwito on 23 October 1876.

4. Anglican missionaries, 1929.

Having succeeded in keeping the peace between the Tonga and the Ngoni, the Livingstonia Mission could proceed with its work of education and evangelisation. The names of the earliest African Christians appear in the Livingstonia Mission books. Among them a fair number of Tonga names feature. The first of these were Yuriah Chatonda and Yakobi Msusa Muwamba, who later went on to become the first licentiate of Livingstonia Mission and who died on 22 October 1900 on the day he was due to receive his certificate after completing his studies in Divinity.

Education developed rapidly. For the first five years after the establishment of the observation post at Bandawe in 1878, the only school in Tongaland was the central mission school at Bandawe. In 1883 the chiefs Marenga and Fuka agreed to mission schools being started in their villages. Soon other chiefs followed this example and village schools began to spring up. In 1890 6 open-air schools started at Chinteche. By 1894 there were 18 schools in Tongaland and over 1,000 pupils were in regular attendance. In 1906 there were 107 schools with over 3,500 pupils.

Thus in the early years of Protectorate rule in Malawi, mission-educated Tonga were already receiving a modicum of education which continued to improve in quality and quantity. The results were widespread. The Tonga entered into the service of the African Lakes Corporation and of planters in the Shire Highlands. In 1886 the first party of twenty-five Tonga began service with the A.L.C. as porters. By 1904 over 1,400 of them were working for the A.L.C. in various capacities while over 4,000 were in the employment of planters in the Shire Highlands. In the same year hundreds moved off to work south of the Zambezi, blazing a distinguished trail which was ultimately to bring both distinction and financial benefits to Malawi. Among distinctions achieved abroad, it should be mentioned that the first African District Commissioner in Zambia and the founder of the first trade union movement for Africans in South Africa were both Tonga.

Sir Robert Bell, who conducted a survey of the financial position in the country in 1938, made the following observation: 'In the north the Atonga . . . by their skill and intelligence can earn high wages abroad; the percentage of absentees in their district of West Nyasa is the highest of all, 60.9 per cent.' Yet the casualty rate of migrant labourers who became lost permanently to this country, the so-called Machona, was the lowest in the case of the Tonga, only 7 per cent in 1937 as compared to 10.8 per cent in the Southern Province and 28.7 per cent in the Northern Province. Of the amount of £48,100 remitted to Malawi from Rhodesia and South Africa in 1937, the Tonga headed the list with their contribution of £11,800.

Constitutionally, the Atonga Tribal Council was a unique experiment in local African administration, an experiment not wholly decreed by the colonial administration but forced upon it by the initiative and demands of Tonga politics—a further example of the egalitarian concept in Tonga politics. (This is considered more fully in Chapter 13.)

ii THE NORTHERN NGONI

The Ngoni arrived in Malawi in the middle of the nineteenth century. There were two main groups, the northern Ngoni led by the paramount chief Zwangendaba, and afterwards by M'Mbelwa, and the southern Ngoni led by Mputa and afterwards by Chidiaonga and Chikusi. From these two divisions of the Jere and Maseko Ngoni respectively, a number of offshoots settled at different times in the nineteenth and early twentieth centuries in various parts of the country. These branches, from the northern group, include Chiefs Chiwere and Msakambewa in Dowa and at one time Vuso Jere in Nkhota Kota district. From the southern group they are Kachindamoto and Kachere in Dedza district, Masula at Lilongwe, Simon Likongwe at Neno, Kanduku at Mwanza and Bvumbwe in Thyolo district. Two other Ngoni chieftainships in Malawi must be mentioned. These are Zulu and Mlonyeni at Mchinji, offshoots of the Mpezeni paramountcy in present eastern Zambia.

We shall consider the northern Ngoni in two stages: firstly, during the lifetime of Zwangendaba; and secondly in the years following Zwangendaba's death. Zwangendaba lived in present northern Zululand, in South Africa, where his father Hlatshwayo was a famous general serving a powerful chief named Zwide of the Ndwandwe tribe. Zwide was the last of the great chiefs to stand up to the power of Shaka, the great Zulu king who in the 1820s was already a legend in South Africa, famed for his courage as well as for his brutality, a leader of men, bent upon establishing himself as undisputed ruler of the southeastern portion of southern Africa. Zwangendaba, like his father before him, served in Zwide's army as a division commander. When the fortunes of war began to go against him, he fled, like others who wished to save themselves from the wrath of Shaka, taking with him what motley collection of refugees he could gather. In 1822 two leaders of Zwide's army were already in southern Mozambique. One of them, Soshangane, stayed on to become leader in Gazaland; the other, Zwangendaba himself, moved on, crossed the Zambezi on 19

22

November 1835, and after a few stops in northern Mozambique, notably at Mkoko where his famous son, Mtwalo, was born, he camped at the Mawiri River, near present Loudon, on 19 September 1840, a notable day in the history of the northern Ngoni, the hundredth anniversary of which was celebrated with great enthusiasm thirty years ago.

Zwangendaba, his infant sons, his many wives, his followers and his captives, did not stay for more than a few years at Mawiri. The weary chief who had brought his followers nearly two thousand miles had heard of red cattle farther north and it was in search of this that he continued on his march to the chosen land, the land of his dreams, 'Mapupo' in Fipa country on the Malawi-Tanzania border. Here he died around 1848 after having been on the march for over a quarter of a century. This was a remarkable achievement not only because of the distance covered and the victories gained but because of the assortment of peoples welded together in a powerful unit, people of various tribes, Swazi, Karanga, Senga and Tumbuka, whose destinies became linked with the Jere kingdom.

When Zwangendaba died his sons were all minors. The eldest, Mpezeni or Ntuto, who was born in Rhodesia about 1833, was only fifteen years old; Mtwalo was about ten and Mhlahlo (later known as M'Mbelwa) was around eight. Ntabeni, a contemporary and a close relative of Zwangendaba, assumed the regency of the Jere family. Unhappily, the Jere hierarchy was divided. Ntabeni, the regent, supported one group which looked to Mpezeni as the future ruler; Mgayi, another induna of the royal family, supported the younger M'Mbelwa, who to many seemed to be the legitimate successor. In this serious division, a learned and elderly induna, Gwaza Jere, held the balance. He supported the principle of legitimacy based on an intricate village system in which the successor came from the *lusungulu* or right-hand house and never from the *kwa gogo* or left-hand house. The wives of an Ngoni chief were assigned to different huts either to the right of the Queen Mother's hut (she was mother of the reigning chief) or to the left. The lusungulu hut always produced the successor to a vacant chieftainship. Mpezeni's mother, Soseya Nqumayo, had once occupied the lusungulu house during the great march but a report to Zwangendaba that she was attempting to poison him led to the destruction of her lusungulu village. Fortunately, she and her unborn son were saved from this fate. Munene Mgomezulu, who later bore the son named Mhlahlo or M'Mbelwa, assumed this position. And though Mpezeni, M'Mbelwa and Mtwalo (the brother of M'Mbelwa) grew up together, the indunas and headmen knew of the switch of royal huts. When Zwangendaba died, the succession issue led to a split which became unbridgeable when Ntabeni himself died. Ntabeni's son, followers and sympathisers defected and moved away from Malawi towards Lake Victoria. Mapupo, the burial place of Zwangendaba, became deserted, since the other party moved towards northern Malawi.

The second regent, Mgayi, died before re-entering Malawi. This was the signal for yet another dispersal. Zulu Gama moved east of the northern tip of Malawi into the Songea region of Mozambique; Mpezeni moved westwards with his brother, Mperembe, in search of their own fortune. Mperembe later returned to Malawi but Mpezeni moved on until he established himself permanently in the present Chipata district of Zambia west of Mchinji. M'Mbelwa and Mtwalo, still minors, now under the regency of the last surviving senior induna, Gwaza Jere, crossed the Nyika and arrived in the Henga valley in Nkhamanga country about 1855. Having established that there would be no rivalry between the two sons of Zwangendaba, whose mothers were sisters, Gwaza Jere lived to see a son of Zwangendaba being crowned king of the Jere Ngoni in northern Malawi. The installation of M'Mbelwa I at Ng'onga in the Henga valley, near present Phwampa in the Rumpi District, around 1857, marks the end of an important phase in the history of the northern Ngoni.

M'Mbelwa I left the village called Emchakachakeni to which he had been relegated after his father's death as a result of the power politics of the regents, and built his own lusungulu village which he named Engalaweni. He ruled over the northern Ngoni for almost thirty-four years until his death in August 1891 a few months after Protectorate rule had been proclaimed in the Shire Highlands and the southern lake region. During his eventful reign, the Ngoni spanned out into the Rukuru, Kasitu and Lunyangwa valleys; they raided for food and captives whom they attempted to assimilate into Ngoni society. M'Mbelwa lived to see missionaries come into his area in 1882. It was he who approved of their coming. The first mission to be set up in northern Ngoniland was that started by William Koyi and James Sutherland at Hoho village situated at the foot of Njuyu Hill, north of the Kasitu River, about twelve miles from present Ekwendeni. A second station was started at Ekwendeni in 1889 under the Rev. Dr William Angus Elmslie. A third was set up at Hora near the mountain where many people lost their lives in 1880 in the quarrel between Baza Dokowe and Ng'onomo Makamo, remembered in history as the Baza rebellion.

M'Mbelwa I lived through a number of protests, some very violent, against the Ngoni politics of occupation. Among the local people who came under Ngoni domination of one sort or other were the Henga,

24

the Phoka, the Tumbuka and the Tonga. Most of the last were in the villages under the control of the Ngoni induna, one Chiputula Nhlane, whose grandmother had belonged to the same clan, the Nzima clan, as Zwangendaba's mother. As the Nhlanes had of old been invited to the Hoho village in Swaziland to administer justice, so too in the old Hoho village in present Mzuzu, the Nhlanes led by Chiputula were the agents of M'Mbelwa. When Chiputula Nhlane died in 1874, the Tonga whom he had been able to keep in check rebelled and fled to their former lakeside stockades. A determined Ngoni onslaught in 1876 to recapture them in Tongaland was repelled. The Kamanga under Mwendera and Njuma and the Henga under their leaders Kanyoli and Kambondoma followed the Tonga example in 1879. This was in the year that Dr Robert Laws had his first meeting with M'Mbelwa I.

So by 1879 the Ngoni were being harassed from all sides, including missionaries who were looking for a foothold. Further trouble erupted when Baza Dokowe, the grandson of a Nyirongo chief and the son of a Tumbuka lady, who had been captured by the invading Ngoni years before but had worked himself up to a position of minor chieftainship, was reported for supposedly being in possession of elephant tusks which he was keeping away from M'Mbelwa. One tusk, a particularly big one, Baza Dokowe would not part with. Charles Chidongo Chinula, veteran Tumbuka educationist, politician and minister of religion, takes up the story:

> Baza did not want to part with the remaining ivory, and so deter-
> mined to climb Hora, and fight against the Ngoni if they came. Fire
> and smoke, men and women, could be seen on Hora. After two days
> the Ngoni besieged the Mount, and as the besieged needed water to
> drink, they tried to fight that they might reach the water. The Ngoni
> were so strong that very many Tumbuka men and women were
> killed, and many again were taken alive; until Baza and other men
> and women saw that the Ngoni were rushing up the Mount to take
> Baza alive; so by twilight (about 6.30 p.m.) casting the coveted ivory
> into a deep, narrow cave, they went down the Mount to escape.[1]

Coming as this incident did at the tail end of the series of revolts against the Ngoni from 1875 onwards, the quarrel over ivory has been represented as a major Tumbuka rising against the Ngoni. The journal of the Livingstonia Mission, *Aurora*,[2] published in one of its articles: 'The people had been worked up to a point of rebellion, and it was agreed that on a certain day the Tumbuka should rise throughout the

---

[1] *Livingstonia News*, XV, July 1928.
[2] *Aurora*, V, 25, April 1901.

whole country, kill their masters, and repair with the cattle to Hora, where they would combine and make a great raid on the Ngoni.' This report says that the Tumbuka were driven in 1885 to the point of another rising, stimulated this time by the mission preaching of equality.

The Baza Dokowe resistance was an economic not a political rising. It never seriously threatened Ngoni overlordship in the area though it left behind a legacy of distrust among some. The so-called second attempt against the Ngoni in 1885 never materialised. The missionaries were masterful in keeping the peace between the Tonga and the Ngoni. This tight-rope diplomacy was due no doubt to the fact that two strong-willed missionaries were working in different parts: Robert Laws at Bandawe and William Angus Elmslie at Njuyu. Each favoured the area in which he resided but in the end no side was favoured. Contemporary reports and letters pay tribute to M'Mbelwa I, too, for his patience and tact which helped to keep down the war emotions of the younger warriors.

It was not war which prevailed in the long run but diplomacy and evangelisation. Sutherland and Koyi, pioneer missionaries in northern Malawi, died within nine months of each other in 1885 and 1886 respectively, but the fruits of their enterprise were soon to come. The first African converts in Ngoniland were Mawalero Tembo and Makara Tembo, both of whom were baptised in 1890, at Njuyu in the second Hoho village of the Nhlane family. The first women converts were Elizabeth Moyo, wife of Mawalero Tembo and Ann Zivezah Sakara, wife of Chitezi Tembo, a headman of Hoho village. Hoho village, first in Swaziland fifty years earlier, then at present Mzuzu when Dr Laws first met the Nhlane at Kaning'ina in 1879, at Njuyu in 1890 and in 1904 to shift to Dwambazi where the latest Hoho village is, has always been the headquarters of the Nhlane. As the missionaries saw good prospects in the Nhlane family, they pursued them everywhere carrying education into their villages. Yesaya Mlonyeni Chibambo, first Ngoni historian, was himself born in 1887 while M'Mbelwa I was still in office.

The period of M'Mbelwa I's rule among the northern Ngoni extended from 1857 to 1891. When he died, his brother Inkosi Mperembe (also known as Mwamba), the last of the sons of Zwangendaba, acted as regent while the counsellors set about finding a successor. This was the same Mperembe who after a disastrous period of wandering in Bembaland in the company of Mpezeni had returned to Malawi. There were three candidates put forward by different groups and it took five years to resolve the succession question. Some spoke in support of Mkuzo, others of Mzikubola, and a third group canvassed for Chim-

26

tunga. It was the last who was installed as the second successor to Zwangendaba's throne in 1896. Chimtunga was in the nineteenth year of his rule when he was forcibly detained at the then Port Herald (Nsanje) in 1915 for refusing to support the war effort. He was allowed to return as a headman only in 1920. Four years later, when he died, he had still not been reinstated. Chimtunga was never accorded the title of M'Mbelwa. The second in the M'Mbelwa line was Lazaro Jere who had a most distinguished period of office from 1928 to 1959, a period almost equalling that of his namesake M'Mbelwa I.

Much of the acclaim must go to Amon Jere who was born in 1873 and who was installed Mtwalo II on 15 June 1896. He held office until his death on 1 April 1970, a period of seventy-four years, a record unsurpassed in the annals of Malawi history. The author met Inkosi Mtwalo on 7 December 1969. Tall, majestic and magnetic, Inkosi Mtwalo appeared to be in reasonable command of his mental faculties, though he was unable to walk. He spoke fluent English and Zulu. His Tumbuka was halting for he never spoke it freely, preferring to converse in Zulu and English. He was able to rattle off biblical quotations in support of the postulate he put forward that people of old were hardworking and honest. His parting words, sealed by an affectionate hand grip, were: 'God be with you till we meet again.'

What impact did the coming of the Jere Ngoni have on the indigenous people? Reference has already been made to the fact that the Tumbuka, the original owners of the land, were an agricultural people. With this tradition behind them, they were neither armed nor prepared to resist a military conquest of their region. But conquest did not mean complete subjugation. The handful of Ngoni, with their Karanga and Senga headmen and advisers, could not subjugate the Tumbuka-Nkhamanga people of long standing. Tumbuka headmen survived, Tumbuka religion survived and the Tumbuka language was adopted by the military invaders, which was perhaps the greatest cultural survival. It is true that military organisation based on close village structures, absorption of able-bodied captives and military discipline, gave to the Tumbuka-Nkhamanga community a new look. But Ngoni survival was dependent on the continued goodwill of the indigenous population. For over twenty years military dominance and overlordship went unchallenged. But if these twenty years were a period for the Ngoni to consolidate their position, they were also years during which the Tumbuka-Nkhamanga and Tonga peoples re-evaluated their role and made an attempt to reassert their former independence from a military form of state. Their attempt failed; the Ngoni political machinery overcame that of the indigenous polity and an adaptation was made. In return for the acceptance of the Jere paramountcy and divisional Jere chiefs, the village society of the original inhabitants continued to function as of old.

The northern Ngoni continued to consolidate their political position after the revolts of 1875–80. The deaths of Mtwalo I in 1890 and of M'Mbelwa I in 1891 set them back a while. A period of raiding and disorganisation intruded. By 1893 they had collected large herds of cattle as a result of these raids. In that year the disease rinderpest swept through the country and all but exterminated the cattle. The lands, too, strained by overgrazing, drought and poor methods of cultivation, began to be less productive. When Harry Johnston assumed his position as Her Majesty's Commissioner and Consul-General in 1891, he had no desire to cross swords or spears with the Ngoni. He recognised them as a powerful people and promised not to annex their territory or tax them as long as they remained in the area that they then occupied, i.e. between the South Rukuru River in the north and Hora Mountain in the south, and provided that they did not raid or molest the inhabitants outside this area.

By 1904 the terms of the 1891 treaty could no longer be kept. It was impossible for the Ngoni to stay confined within the boundaries stipulated. Surrounded by restrictions, by administrative boundaries under British rule, by increasing land shortage, the old way of life was no longer possible. And also the Ngoni were no longer a military threat or menace, since years of association with the Scottish missionaries had changed their way of life. And if British rule could be extended to their area to bring advantages to it, so much the better. Thus the Ngoni agreed to come under British rule. On 24 October 1904 the Union Flag was hoisted at Hora Mountain by Hector MacDonald, the first British Resident sent to administer Ngoni affairs in the Mzimba district. Sir Alfred Sharpe, the Commissioner at the time, was there too. The Ngoni were promised that the authority of their hereditary chiefs would be upheld; that chiefs would be able to decide minor disputes among their people and that they would receive annual subsidies. On their part, the chiefs agreed to pay tax and to accept the laws of the Resident.

At the ceremony Mtwalo's official *isibongo* or praise singer intoned in Chingoni the praises of Zwangendaba which resounded in the valley of Hora Mountain:

U Zwangendaba was intentionally black, who struggled until the world became light, who realised the importance of Elangeni, the offspring of people who had black faces. When the dawn appeared the rays of the sun shone on Zwangendaba. Bayete, King of Kings, who belonged to the pure royal blood. He could go back to the time in Swaziland where people died in old age only and ate their meat with forks and spoons.

The history of the northern Ngoni, though largely that of its senior ruling houses, M'Mbelwa and Mtwalo, is also the history of other important Jere chieftainships whose solidarity has done much to seal the bonds of political cooperation. The descendants of the sons of Zwangendaba hold sway in the name of M'Mbelwa, the Inkosi Ya Makosi, at Edingeni; Mperembe, at Emcisweni; Mtwalo, at Ezondweni and Mabulabo, at Emfeni. The descendants of the grandsons of Zwangendaba hold office in the names of Chinde, at Euthini; Mzukuzuku, at Embangweni and Mzikuora, at Emchakachakeni. The one Inkosi Ya Makosi and the six *amakosi* all have their separate and their collective histories.

When the northern Ngoni became located in seven regional divisions, the main power of the paramount chief rested in military leadership. No big raid could be undertaken without his sanction and he himself chose the leader of the expedition. Each of the other chiefs had complete civil control over their respective areas but matters affecting the whole area were sometimes referred to the paramount chief. The paramount did not interfere with the other chiefs provided that they paid tributes to him.

Perhaps these chiefs, like many others elsewhere in the country, did not realise the full impact of the 1904 treaty. M'Mbelwa II made bold to tell the Bledisloe Commission in 1938 that what the Ngoni had been promised in 1904 and what they got were two different things.

It is no wonder, then, that in 1906 when tax was demanded for the second year running that the old warrior Ng'onomo Makamo, now minus his ferocity but still sprightly and volatile, led a large crowd of disenchanted Ngoni to the Mzimba Boma and demonstrated their opposition to the tax measure in the words of their now famous song, 'Madondolo'. The women sang: 'Wasamale Boma Umadondolo', and the men added, in their resonant tone, 'Umadondolo!' The women replied: 'O Savela Sayona' and the men punctuated this with 'Umadondolo!'

The words of the song charged the first District Resident, Mac-Donald, with paying more attention to the Boma than to the welfare of the people, that while the position of the Boma flourished that of the people deteriorated. Thus it is not to be wondered at that Chimtunga refused to allow his people and their products to be exploited for the

29

war effort in 1915. For this he lost his chieftainship for ever, and that is how the northern Ngoni were drawn into the arena of colonial rule. They and their political institutions survived it, however, to emerge into independent Malawi as a powerful and loyal element of the Malawi nation. Their nineteenth-century origins and history no longer stamp them as a group apart.

iii THE NGONI OF CENTRAL AND SOUTHERN MALAWI

One of the offshoots of the Jere Ngoni in the nineteenth century originated in the village of Gwaza Jere, the induna of Zwangendaba. Gwaza Jere had his own induna of Senga origin whose name was Chiwere Ndhlovu. We have already noted that in the years following Zwangendaba's death there was great uncertainty in the Ngoni camps; groups fled in all directions, either to avoid extermination or to seek out new lands for settlement. Zwangendaba's military domination over the peoples and the territories he had captured spurred on some of his followers to seek their own areas of influence and control. One such ambitious man was Chiwere Ndhlovu.

During one of these moments of upheaval—possibly after Mgayi Jere, the regent, had died at Chidhlodhlo near the north end of Malawi —Gwaza Jere's induna moved away with a small following when the main Jere group reached the Henga valley. Ostensibly their aim was to spy out the land for this group in which were M'Mbelwa and Mtwalo, the sons of Zwangendaba, together with their other relatives. The head of the so-called scouting expedition was Chiwere Ndhlovu himself but he had with him in his party some Jere women as well as two sons of Gwaza Jere, namely Msakambewa Jere and Vuso Jere. It is possible that Gwaza Jere had secretly approved that his sons should be in the party in the hope that they would one day establish their own hegemony in a safer territory. There is speculation, too, that Chiwere Ndhlovu absconded with the boys to obtain Jere legitimacy and prestige to strengthen his own position. In any event, Chiwere Ndhlovu moved out with Msakambewa and Vuso Jere, then infants, together with their mothers. Traditions state that this party moved southeastwards and that it was soon pursued by an army from the main Jere group. A battle was fought at Ndonda (Kapichila) in Chief Kanyenda's area in the present Nkhota Kota district. Chiwere Ndhlovu's party was victorious.

From Kapichila the group went to Kasungu but Mwase Kasungu would not have them there and so the expedition crossed the Bua River and entered the hilly region of Dowa. The Dowa area was occupied by the Chewa under the chieftainships of Mkanthama and Nyanda.

However, the villages became overpopulated and in course of time the Ngoni under Chiwere moved farther southwards. Here he established his own chieftainship at Kaso hill near Mvera where the Dutch Reformed Church Mission later set up a station under the Rev. A. C. Murray on 28 November 1889. Msakambewa Jere moved away to establish his own village at Kongwe hill near the Lingadzi River twenty miles from Mvera. In this area the missionary Robert Blake started a branch of the Dutch Reformed Church Mission on 16 April 1894. The third important member of this trio, Vuso Jere, also later set up his own chieftainship in the Chibweya area of the present Ntchisi district. Thus from one central point in northern Malawi, three independent Ngoni chieftainships had been set up in another part of the country by the 1870s.

Like the original Ngoni migrants who had left South Africa in the 1820s in search of new lands, this breakaway group had few pure Ngoni members in its community. It had to absorb large numbers of the indigenous people by marriage, by conquest, or by political overlordship. The settlement of three Ngoni chiefs in Chewa country caused them considerable hardship at the beginning when raids and wars disturbed their original peaceful occupation.

One factor had a considerable influence on both the internal and external relations of these new chieftainships, and that was the Dutch Reformed Church Mission stations at Mvera and Kongwe. Chiwere Ndhlovu and Msakambewa reacted differently to them. Chiwere was pleased to have the station in his area at Mvera. Msakambewa, however, was hostile; he complained that the station had been started at Kongwe without his consent; that the missionaries appeared to be in an alliance with the Chewa since their chiefs Kalindan'goma and Kadiwa had approved of the mission, probably for the same reasons that the Tonga were heartened by the presence of the Scottish missionaries at Bandawe from 1878 onwards, namely because Ngoni raids would be subdued and slave-raiding and -trading would stop.

Contemporary reports provide evidence of slave-trading in the Mvera-Kongwe area. One of the missionaries, W. H. Murray, wrote to his father in South Africa on 9 March 1895: 'Slave raiding is just as little a matter of the past as I am and our men are afraid of being caught by M'pemba.' The missionaries at Mvera and Kongwe felt that the government was not doing enough to eradicate it in that area and that the mission itself was running the risk of getting involved both with the local inhabitants as well as with the central administration if it pursued a vigorous campaign against slave-trading. In the same letter W. H. Murray criticised the Administration: 'This silly administration fondly fancies and flatters itself with the thought that [the] slave trade is suppressed on the lake while we know that numbers of slavers are still sent over the lake and river under their very noses and what makes it worse is that they don't seem anxious for information in the matter at all.'

As a result of persistent mission complaints, the government took action at last against Msakambewa in 1900 on a murder charge. When Msakambewa was arrested, his Ngoni headman Kafanikhale caused considerable trouble for the missionaries.

The Rev. Robert Blake was not altogether unsuccessful in getting across his mission teaching. His greatest success was in the area of the Chewa headman, Msyamboza, at Chibanzi not far from Kongwe. Here a mission school was started and Andreya Mphekerere became the first African teacher to take charge. Nor was Blake unsuccessful in the Ngoni territory of Msakambewa and Kafanikhale. The Rev. and Mrs Blake started a school on the station in 1894; a year later two hundred pupils were in attendance and three years later, in 1897, the Rev. Blake had already translated the Bible into Chichewa as *Mbiri Yakale*.

The area of these three Ngoni chiefs, in what may be described as central Ngoniland, came under British jurisdiction in 1896 but only after a period of considerable negotiation and uncertainty. The northern Ngoni were not yet under Protectorate rule and Chiwere Ndhlovu was particularly anxious to protect his adopted land. His indunas and headmen counselled that the missionaries should be expelled or exterminated because it was feared that they were the agents of the administration. The Ngoni could no longer raid into Dzoole's country westwards without receiving admonition from the government Resident at Nkhota Kota. Even when they promised not to raid any more, they still desired to retain their independence. But time was running out. The Protectorate government was busy putting an end to the old order and bringing all chiefs in the country under its political and military control. From his village headquarters at Msongandeu, Chiwere Ndhlovu watched the march of events. British agents and armed troops were in his area and rather than negotiate with them he went into hiding while his indunas and headmen plotted the overthrow of these new influences, mission and government.

From afar, Dr Laws recognised that the only way to prevent a holocaust, a bloodbath, was for the Dutch Reformed Church Mission to keep on the best of terms with the African chiefs, particularly with Chiwere, the most powerful in the area. Chiwere had no objection to talking to the missionaries but he had a real fear: how could W. H. Murray be his friend as well as the friend of the Nyasaland administration which was anxious to take his lands from him and turn him into a slave? Chiwere addressed a secret meeting at which three white missionaries were present and explained his dilemma as well as his strategy:

> When Sitimali Wankulu [i.e. A. C. Murray] came to my land, he came and asked me in a respectful manner if he and his friend could come and live on my land to teach my people. I agreed and we lived happily together. Now he has left for the south and now a strange white man comes in [i.e. Codrington, the magistrate and tax collector at Nkhota Kota] without asking me and I hear he says the land is his and that we have to pay tax to him; but this will just not happen. What I now want to know is this: How will it be if I call up my warriors and drive out the white man who is trying to come in here and we and you should stay on alone in the land? If you say Yes we can clinch the matter here and now.

Of course, the missionaries could not say yes. They had to advise Chiwere that the might of the Protectorate was too powerful to resist. He had better agree to the Protectorate terms of peaceful occupation and administration. In return they pledged their honour and their persons to a promise that Chiwere would not be molested—a promise that was necessary and timely in view of what had happened further south not long before to the Maseko Ngoni ruler Gomani I.

Thus we see that, in the diplomacy of 1895–96, the central figure was Chiwere Ndhlovu, the same induna of the Ngoni who had some forty years earlier led a breakaway group from Mzimba to Dowa. His protégés, Msakambewa Jere and Vuso Jere, princes of the royal Jere line, had accompanied him as infants. Now, when British rule came to their new lands, they also had chieftainships of their own within about forty miles from one another. All three had mission stations too, at Mvera, Kongwe and Chibweya respectively. The arrival of these three men had resulted in the introduction of a new ruling class in Chewa country but Chewa chieftainships, language and customs survived. Except for congestion in certain areas and resiting of villages, the newcomers did not radically alter the traditional patterns of life. However, the missionary work of both the Protestants and the Catholics and the economic and social results of migrant labour contributed in a bigger way to radical change. The full force was more fully recognised in the twentieth century than in the nineteenth.

We must move now to a brief consideration of what may be termed the Mchinji Ngoni in the central region. This area is bordered by Zambia to the west, Kasungu to the north, Mozambique to the south and Lilongwe to the east. The Mchinji Ngoni are an offshoot of the

Mpezeni Ngoni in the present Chipata district of Zambia. Mpezeni, the eldest son of Zwangendaba, broke from the Ngoni in Malawi a few years after his father's death and moved into Bemba country. By 1866 he was already settled in the present Chipata district. When David Livingstone, the first known Briton to reach the country under Mpezeni's influence, was in that area in 1866 he noticed the results of Ngoni raids and found difficulty in getting carriers to take him to Ngoni villages. Mpezeni's country was too good to escape attention. It was thought to have gold deposits; it was healthily situated on good plateau lands; its vast herds of cattle were a fascination to travellers; it flanked several trade routes from the Zambezi and Lake Malawi regions.

Mpezeni's impis raided both east and west, east into Malawi territory of Chiefs Mkanda, Mwase Kasungu and the Maseko Ngoni. All this came to an end when his eldest son, Singu, rose in revolt against the British settlers in his father's territory, in December 1897. Malawi history became involved in a number of ways in this rising. Firstly, troops were sent out from Malawi: five companies of the B.C.A. Rifles, made up of 550 Africans and 100 Sikhs, moved in support of the administration of the then Northeastern Rhodesia. Secondly, a number of refugee groups fled into Malawi, some to return later and others to establish permanent settlements under refugee chieftainships.

The rebellion lasted over a month and the campaigns were hard fought on both sides. On 5 February 1898, Singu was shot after a court martial; four days later his father voluntarily surrendered and was banished to the newly founded Fort Manning. After a year's exile he was reinstated, but he died soon afterwards, in 1900.

It is worth recording that immediately prior to the rising of 1897, Mpezeni, worried by the fact that European traders, administrators and concession seekers were closing in on him, asked the Nyasaland Administration for permission to shift his residence to Nyasaland. This was at a time when the territories of Northeastern Rhodesia and Nyasaland had already been administratively separated, so the request was refused. Seven years earlier, in April 1890, Consul Alfred Sharpe had visited Mpezeni with a view to drawing up a treaty of friendship with him. Sharpe reported on this venture as follows.

He [i.e. Mpezeni] was very friendly, and approved of all I had to say; but Treaties he would not touch, nor the flag. I tried all ways I could think of to bring it about, but without the least effect. He said he was glad to be friends with the Queen, and with all other 'big chiefs'; but letters he did not know anything of, nor of flags. He asked why I should ask [in the Treaties] that he should do various things for us

[English] and for no others. . . . He is under the impression that he is the most powerful monarch in the world, except possibly Mombera; and the suggestion that it would be a good thing for him to have (in case of future war) so powerful a friend as the Queen, created great amusement. . . .[1]

However, by the time Mpezeni died in 1900, the Mchinji Ngoni had already settled in Malawi. One was led by Magwambane Jere, son of a kinsman of Zwangendaba named Lomabela, whose army and followers marched as far as the present Dedza and Ncheu areas of Kachindamoto and Gomani. A famous battle known as Nkhondo ya kwa Mgabi was fought and Magwambane was killed. He was succeeded by his eldest son who assumed the name Zulu I. When he settled at Mchinji he was given land by the Chewa chief, Simpase. The successors of Chief Zulu I have now come down to the fourth line; the present incumbent, Gasiano Masala Jere, was installed in 1968 as Chief Zulu IV.

About three miles from Chief Zulu's village was the headquarters of the second Mchinji Ngoni, Chief Mlonyeni. During the Mpezeni rising, Mlonyeni, son of another of Zwangendaba's kinsman, Somfula, fled to Mzimba to seek shelter with the northern Ngoni. It would appear that his settlement south of the Bua River in Mchinji was before the Mpezeni rising, for when the rising was over he returned to Mchinji.

In the first diary of Kachebere Mission there is an entry dated 12 August 1906, which reads: 'From a rumour going around we learn of the death of old chief Mlonyeni. This old chief has left fifty-four children for posterity, once lived in the district of Mombera far from the influence of British authority from which he wanted to withdraw himself when the country was conquered. . . .' (His successor was Udindani Jere.)

As at Dowa and Ntchisi, the Mchinji Ngoni are settled in a predominantly Chewa society. Most of the villages are Chewa villages under Chewa headmen but there are some distinctly Ngoni villages under Ngoni village headmen. In 1969 in Mlonyeni's area there were over a hundred villages but of these only fifteen were pure Ngoni villages. As a result of the predominance of the Chewa numerically, in Mlonyeni's area the language spoken is Chichewa and the customs, including dances, are Chewa. Intermarriage over the years has tended to wipe out any distinctions between the minority and the majority, and for all practical purposes Mlonyeni's area is Ngoni in name only. Succession to the chieftainship is patrilineal as in the other Ngoni

[1] T. W. Baxter, 'The Angoni Rebellion and Mpeseni', *Northern Rhodesian Journal*, 11, Dec. 1950, pp. 14–24.

societies and Mpezeni is looked upon as the paramount chief of the Mchinji Ngoni.

In Chief Zulu's area, the numerical proportion between Ngoni and non-Ngoni is about equal; the common language is Chisenga with traces of Chingoni. The distinctive Ngoni tribal mark of pierced ear lobes is common here.

The Mchinji Ngoni under Mlonyeni and Zulu in the Malawi-Zambia border region represent a good example of the superficial nature of the boundaries dividing many tribes in Africa. What was once a natural spillover into neighbouring areas is today underlined by political boundaries. This point was stressed by Paramount Chief Mpezeni when he attended the installation of Chief Zulu IV in 1968. He said that the artificial boundaries between the Ngoni of Mchinji and Chipata should not serve as a barrier between the people themselves.

Missions have played an important part in Mchinji, as in the rest of the country. The Dutch Reformed Church Mission was the first to open a station at Magwero in 1899, which was followed by another at Mchucu in 1901, now known as Mchinji Mission. The White Fathers established the Kachebere Mission in 1903 and have since played an important part in educational and religious developments in the area.

We come finally to the last of the Ngoni communities in nineteenth-century Malawi in the central and southern regions. These belong to the Maseko line of the Swazi chief Ngwana, whose sons Mputa and Chidiaonga were responsible for setting up the Maseko Ngoni in Malawi. Though a number of refugee groups scrambled for places, property and persons in the time of troubles which attended the expansionist policies of the great Zulu king Shaka, there is little trace of durable alliances among the refugees themselves. Zwangendaba, Soshangane, Mzilikazi, Ngwana, Nxaba and Sebetwane were among the leaders of fleeing parties who carried with them destruction and conquest into the interior, in an epoch of unrivalled chaos in southern and central Africa.

What Zwangendaba succeeded in achieving we have already noted. The feat of Mputa Maseko was equally great. He led his followers in a separate group, crossed the Zambezi River just west of Tete a short while after Zwangendaba, and keeping in a more easterly direction in order to avoid the Jere Ngoni reached the area of Domwe Mountain to the south of Dedza. Here the wide rolling grasslands of the country made an impact on the Maseko. This was good cattle country. The non-military agricultural and pastoral people who inhabited it also had vast stocks of sheep and goats. Livestock, women and other captives were added to the Maseko community and had it not been for the information that seeped in that Zwangendaba's Jere were not far to the west, Mputa would have stayed on permanently. Having reaped his crops probably in early 1837 he set out further eastwards to get away as far as possible from the Jere Ngoni. Descending from the high inland plateau, Mputa found his further progress blocked by the presence of the lake. He followed the lakeshore until he reached the point where the lake waters enter the Shire River. Here he enlisted the services of the Karonga, Sosola, who lived at that time near Maere a Nyanga at Ulongwe, to get his party and livestock across the wide and deep Shire. Sosola was well paid in cattle for his services.

Once across the Shire the Maseko had to find a permanent home away from the cattle-less country of the Yao and Lomwe. At last, about 1839, the party crossed the Rovuma River and once again found itself in rich cattle country among the Amatengo near modern Songea. Here, about 1850, the Maseko were joined by one of the breakaway groups of the northern Ngoni, led by Zulu Gama. For a few years both Ngoni groups lived together peacefully, but when both leaders died within a short time of each other the successors were less keen on keeping the peace. The Mputa faction was driven out. Led by Mputa's brother Chidiaonga, who acted as regent for Mputa's minor son, Chikusi, the Maseko were once again on the march. After over thirty years of wandering they did not succeed in finding a permanent home and were being compelled to retrace their steps; they finally reached Domwe about 1867 or 1868. Chidiaonga had been harassed by the Yao and the Lomwe and was in no position to enter into local military alliances.

The Karonga, Sosola, remembering the Ngoni fondness for cattle which Mputa had shown thirty years earlier, tried to induce the Maseko to attack the Yao chiefs Pemba and Tambala who had newly arrived in Chewa country. Chidiaonga was more content to be back in the rolling grasslands round Domwe Mountain where he could lord it over the Maravi chiefdoms, themselves pretty much unorganised militarily and an easy prey for Ngoni domination. The local inhabitants were willing to become 'Ngoni-ised'; their women adopted Ngoni customs; their men joined the Ngoni military regiments. If there was one thing Chidiaonga could do well it was military action. For long a war commander at the head of the Njokozera war division, his very name meant 'eater of gunpowder'. Carefully he set about consolidating the Maseko position, sending out expeditions against the Yao in search of cattle. By the time he died, in 1878, the Maseko were dominant both east and west of Ncheu and Dedza, the bulk of their dominance being in the Portuguese territory of today.

For various reasons, the Maseko became divided after Chidiaonga's death. Chikusi succeeded to the paramount chieftainship which had been vacant since his father Mputa had died in Songea country. But there were some who wished to consider Chifisi, the son of Chidiaonga, as the successor of a worthy father, as he was certainly a good warrior and a loyal regent. From this point in time the Maseko were divided under a single paramountcy into two political entities, the lines of Mputa and Chidiaonga. The former was held by Chikusi, Gomani I, Gomani II and, today, Gomani III; the latter by Chifisi, Kachindamoto I and, today, Kachindamoto II.

We have already noted that the Ngoni of Malawi came to the country around the middle of the nineteenth century and settled among the local inhabitants. But three other African groups entered Malawi at about the same time and competed with the Ngoni for areas of influence. These were the Yao, the people of the Jumbe of Nkhota Kota and the Makololo who were brought to the lower Shire area by Dr David Livingstone. It is natural that four external groups converging on to a new country at about the same time should cause serious disruptions.

Let us trace some of these. The Yao under Kawinga from the Mount Chikala area raided as far as Matope. Here the local chief Mpimbi looked about for support against the Yao. Not far from Mpimbi's area lived the Maseko Ngoni who were ready to join hands with Mpimbi's people to keep the Yao away. Thus an alliance was formed and the Yao were driven away.

Soon afterwards trouble broke out in another Yao camp and again the Maseko Ngoni were involved. This time the involvement led to a split in the unity of the Maseko Ngoni. The old Yao Chief Mponda, who then lived where Fort Johnston was later to be founded, died in 1889. A common difficulty now arose: there were two claimants for the vacant chieftainship and the two rival sons of the late Mponda looked around for alliances. Other Yao chiefs were drawn in. The Maseko Ngoni were also approached to take sides and they readily obliged; but they made the mistake of supporting different sides. We have noted that there were two groups among the Maseko, led at this time by Chikusi and Chifisi. The fact that they now supported rival Yao camps could only mean the end of their own unity. It would also mean war before the end would come. In Maseko history two important wars of the 1890s are remembered: the Mwala wa Nkhondo and the Mlomo wa Nkuku, both fought in the present Dedza district.

We have referred to the four incoming peoples whose domestic and foreign politics caused serious disruptions. There was, however, a fifth force which tended to ease the disruptions—the missionaries, who were beginning to operate among the Maseko Ngoni as in other parts of the country. Though the Scottish missionaries were the first to attempt to start a mission station in 1878, it was only fifteen years later that an important step was taken when Dr William Affleck Scott and Mr Harry Kambwiri Matecheta set out to open a station in central Ngoniland in 1893. For Matecheta this was a great opportunity. In 1884 when the Ngoni, among whom he was now going to work, had raided Blantyre and the neighbouring areas, Matecheta and his parents had fled to the Nguludi hills where they had remained in hiding till the raids were over. Now a young man of about twenty-five, Harry Kambwiri Matecheta was being assigned a difficult duty, one which he finally discharged with honour to himself, his church and his country. In his Memoirs, obtained through the kindness and help of the Right Rev. Jonathan Douglas Sangaya, present General Secretary of the Blantyre Synod, Harry Matecheta takes up the story:

It was on a Sunday afternoon when Rev. Dr Scott called me from our dormitory and said: 'We have held a meeting and have decided to send some of you to Ngoniland. Two ladies have been found, Miss Bell and Miss Werner, but we have no males. All want you to go, Harry, will you?' I answered that I would, even though the Ngoni had burned down our maize and our houses in 1884. 'Now I am a Christian and I will go.'

We left Blantyre Mission with Dr William Affleck Scott to accompany me. On 10 August 1893 we arrived at Rivi Rivi where Mr Morgan was. On the following morning we chose a place and chose Nthumbi. The following morning Dr Scott left for Blantyre. There was no one who knew the A.B.C. and there was no government, no roads, only war going on in the year when Gomani was fighting for the chieftaincy when Chief Chikusi died.

I did not find many difficulties because I made friends with the son of Chief Mandala. . . .

In November 1893 the ladies came. Miss Bell, myself and Mr George Pasily taught in a school, Miss Werner went into the villages to teach adults. The trouble was that grown up boys were not allowed to go to school. They were the chiefs' soldiers. . . . But we secured 28 children but after schooling for one month the children demanded pay. . . .

Harry Matecheta went on to become the first ordained minister of the Church of Scotland, Blantyre Mission, and his Memoirs, which will be published some day, throw considerable light on his experiences in Ngoniland and on the failures and successes of missionary enterprise there.

Before the nineteenth century ended, the Maseko Ngoni were established at their headquarters at Lizulu as well as in a number of other places: Kachindamoto and Kachere in Dedza; Masula at Lilongwe; Simon Likongwe at Neno; Kanduku at Mwanza and Bvumbwe at Thyolo. Unlike the Jere Ngoni who were concentrated in a single district, the Maseko Ngoni were spread out over a wider region.

But even if the end of the nineteenth century meant the end of a long road for them, it meant, too, the visitation of a tragedy to the Maseko. Their chief, Gomani I, was shot on 27 October 1896 for what the administration deemed to be seditious behaviour, but which in reality was no more than a vigorous assertion of Maseko nationhood and the right of the paramount chief to rule his own subjects, collect his own taxes and direct his own labour resources.

Gomani had a number of grievances. He was not in favour of the people in his area paying tax, arguing that he had never asked for British protection. He objected to the employment of his subjects by the administration or by the Zambezi Industrial Mission or other employers. On 6 October 1896 he and his indunas called on the missionary in charge of the Zambezi Industrial Mission at Dombole and demanded the release of those who worked for the Mission, suspecting that some of them had been responsible for plundering the goods of the African Lakes Corporation. The demand was refused. That night about twenty-seven villages were burned down on Gomani's orders, with the result that he was arrested by a Captain Ashton. On 27 October Gomani was given a summary trial and ordered to be marched off to Blantyre. Refusing to walk further he was tied to a tree between two places called Dombole and Chiole and shot. Thus another strong Ngoni community was now under effective British rule. This time it was partly because of grievances against missionaries and on the strength of testimonies by missionaries, but fundamentally because the paramount chief believed that the area was his domain. He was not prepared to compromise as M'Mbelwa had done.

With Gomani's martyrdom, the nineteenth century ended for the Ngoni of Malawi. The British administration had established itself over them, except in M'Mbelwa's country. Willingly or unwillingly, the Ngoni had to put up with it. There were other areas in which compromises or adaptations had to be worked out: martial peoples had to merge with non-martial peoples, raiders with agriculturists, patrilineal with matrilineal societies and Chingoni and Chisenga with Chitumbuka and Chichewa. This final adaptation, which infused new blood and vigour into Malawi society as a whole, contributed towards the concept which reached fulfilment with the advent of independence, that of one people and one nation.

CHAPTER 3

Nineteenth-century Islamic influences in Malawi

i THE SWAHILI ARABS OF NKHOTA KOTA

For over five hundred years before the birth of the religion of Islam, traders from the south of Arabia, the Persian Gulf, as well as from India, Indonesia and faraway China, had been dealing with parts of the East African coast, from Somalia in the north to Sofala in the south. Among the items traded were aromatics and incense used in the manufacture of perfumes and medicine as well as in religious ceremonies, ivory, timber, tortoiseshell, leopard skins, ambergris, gold and slaves. As long as supplies were available along the coast these eastern traders had no need to organise interior trade.

Then around the year 975 A.D. a prince from Shiraz in south Persia came to East Africa with his six sons and a fleet of seven ships. Prince Ali ibn Hassan was in search of a new home and was prepared to conquer and to destroy anyone who stood in his way. He built his headquarters first at Malindi, then at Mombasa and finally at Kilwa-Kisiwani, the largest and the most prosperous settlement of all. On the coastal settlements, the Persians and Arabs traded and intermingled with Africans, marrying African women and influencing African culture in the development of a new language, kiSwahili, as well as in dress and religion. As coastal trading influences spread into the interior so did these cultural traits. When the Portuguese came to Sena and Tete in 1531, they found eastern trading communities and settlements already existing in these places. A number of kiSwahili words were already part of the local African languages.

The political power and the economic dominance of the Shirazi Muslims on the East African coast declined within a few years of the coming of the Portuguese in the sixteenth century. But the Portuguese themselves had started off too late in their quest for a durable empire on the Indian Ocean coast and except for their hold on Mozambique they had to give up the rest of the East African coast to the Arabs of Oman. One of the most notable rulers of the Omani dynasty, Seyyid Said, built his new capital at Zanzibar in 1832. He encouraged the opening up of clove plantations, an enterprise which soon made Zanzibar the leading producer of cloves in the world. Merchants from east and west were attracted to Zanzibar; an American consulate was opened in 1837 and a British consulate in 1841, followed by a French consulate in 1844.

These developments in Zanzibar had repercussions in near and distant places. Kilwa and Mombasa lost their importance to Zanzibar, and Bagamoyo on the mainland became the terminus of a great caravan road to the interior lakes. On the Kilwa-Lake Nyasa caravan road Seyyid Said ordered that a number of forts be built to protect his trading interests. The main economic commodities sought by the Arabs were ivory and slaves. Ivory was in great demand in the east and the west for the manufacture of fans, ornaments, billiard balls and piano keys.

As elephants became scarce along the coastal supply centres, Arab traders and their agents of mixed blood pushed into the interior. In 1863 David Livingstone noted that these traders were already west of Lake Malawi trading with the Bisa in the Luangwa valley. When the Livingstonia missionaries landed at Mponda's village at Cape Maclear in 1875 they reported that several Swahili Arabs, or Arabised Africans, were already at Mponda's and that five slave-trading dhows were in evidence as were large numbers of slaves. Mponda was friendly but he made it clear that he was attracted to goods from the coast, especially cloth and guns, and that since his main supply centres were controlled by the Arabs, he was compelled to trade with them. Indeed, Arab influences extended further westwards. In the 1890s, Alfred Sharpe, Acting British Consul, found them in the Lake Mweru region in Northeastern Zambia.

If Mponda's, at Fort Johnston (now Mangochi), was the main slave-trading area in the south, Nkhota Kota was the main slave-trading post in the centre. One of the Scottish missionaries visited Nkhota Kota in 1876 and reported that upwards of ten thousand slaves were shipped annually from this notorious port.

How did Nkhota Kota come under the influence of slave-trading and of the Swahili Arabs? The story begins with one Jumbe Salim bin Abdallah who left his home in Zanzibar between 1833 and 1840 for Nyamwezi country on the East African mainland. After stopping at

Ujiji and Kilwa he travelled by overland route to the east of Lake Malawi. With one wife, a nephew and the son of a friend, he crossed the lake in dhows in the company of his followers and servants, most of whom were slaves.

In the 1840s the Jumbe Salim bin Abdallah arrived at Nkhota Kota with a retinue of slave followers, an impressive display of guns and ammunition and much cloth. He came in peace and friendship and is reported to have told the Chewa Chief Malenga: 'We are traders and wish you to give us permission to trade in your country.' By careful diplomacy he was able to convince most of the Chewa that he meant no harm while at the same time he enlarged his village by acquiring slaves. Soon slaves and ivory were being dispatched to the coast in return for guns, gunpowder and cloth. He built large dhows and sent trade caravans to the coast. This was a new development. Hitherto caravans had come from the east and would return to the coast after a period of raiding and trading. Now with Nkhota Kota as his base, the Jumbe was able to direct trade both east and west of the town, profiting from his favourable situation.

Of course, not all the local inhabitants were happy that a foreign trader had come to settle permanently in their midst. Chief Malenga was blamed by some of his followers for being too friendly towards the Jumbe and it is reported that he lost his life on this issue in a local scuffle. However, the death of Malenga placed the Jumbe in a more favourable position, since it was Malenga who had arranged that Kanyenda of Nkhunga, the overlord of the Chewa in that region, would accept the presence of the Swahili Arabs in Nkhota Kota.

Now the Jumbe proceeded to consolidate his position by further enlarging his village, by appointing trustworthy headmen and by increasing his trading activities. His reputation soon spread both east and west. Traders from Zanzibar and the coast came to Nkhota Kota; some penetrated as far as Kasungu and Marambo.

The first Jumbe was regarded at Nkhota Kota as head of the Swahili Arabs and Zanzibaris, for whom he was the final authority in judicial matters. The Chewa continued to be under the jurisdiction of their traditional rulers and were allowed to do very much as they pleased provided that they did not interfere in the Jumbe's affairs.

There were four Jumbes in the history of Nkhota Kota. The first, as we have noted, was the man who brought his followers to Malawi in the 1840s. He lived at Nkhota Kota for about thirty years. When he died, he was succeeded by a kinsman, sometimes called a nephew, Mwenye Nguzo, who had come with him from his East African home. The second Jumbe did not live for more than a year but left an infant

43

son, Mwene Heri, who as Jumbe IV ruled as the last of the Jumbes for a few months in 1894–95. It was the period of office of the third Jumbe, or Tawakali Sudi, from 1875 to 1894 which was not only the longest but the most important.

As foreigners, the Jumbes had various roles to play. The first was that of representative or *wali* of the Sultan of Zanzibar. Whether officially or unofficially, all the Jumbes felt that this was an important function. Their title was the Sultan of Marimba and they flew the flag of the Sultan of Zanzibar.

The second role was an internal one connected with their relations with the Chewa, the Ngoni, the Yao and the Tonga. There is no doubt that since the Swahili Arabs were in possession of guns and gunpowder, they were useful allies in the local wars of the time. It has been argued that one reason why the Chewa accepted the Swahili Arabs was their fear of the Ngoni. The Jumbe provided guns to Mwase Kasungu and together they were a powerful combination against the common foe. Even the Tonga sought an alliance with the Jumbe in their conflict against the Ngoni. Contemporary mission reports refer to this as well as to the fact that in the 1880s at least one Ngoni punitive expedition was sent to Nkhota Kota, but that it was severely crushed.

We do not as yet know details of the trade relations between the Tonga and the people of Jumbe. But there is sufficient circumstantial evidence to show that there was a trade connection between them. The geographic proximity must have made the Tonga aware of the new goods being introduced by the Jumbe in the form of cloth and guns, as well as the cultivation of rice and the planting of coconut trees at Nkhota Kota. The Jumbe also collected grain in the form of tribute from local headmen; insisted upon a share of all ivory collected in his dominion, and controlled trade caravans passing through his newly-occupied territory. All this could not have taken place at Nkhota Kota without its immediate northern neighbour realising what was happening. There is also the evidence in contemporary reports of military alliances between the Tonga and the Swahili Arabs against the Ngoni.

The Jumbe also played a third, diplomatic, role in forging official relations with the missionaries and with representatives of the British Government who, from 1875 onwards, began to take a keen interest in the country.

The Livingstonia missionaries set up their station at Cape Maclear in 1875 and visited Nkhota Kota within six weeks of their arrival. They described it as the largest slave depot in Central Africa but of course they had not yet visited all of them. They thought that the then Jumbe

44

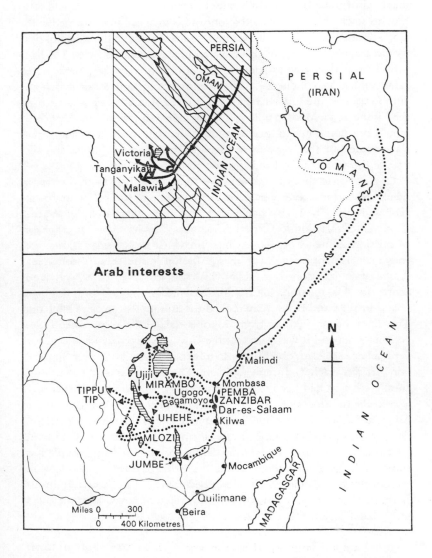

Arab interests

was about forty years old and quite sick. Dr Laws spoke to Jumbe through an interpreter and gathered that he was quite prepared to stop indulging in the slave trade if only the missionaries would help him carry his ivory to the coast in their ships. Four years later when they met again Jumbe III was as friendly to Dr Laws as before. He showed him his stack of ivory, saying that one of his men had just returned with 2,000 pounds of it. What he wanted was cloth and if the missionaries would trade with him much of his troubles would be over. He had problems at that time as some of his headmen, especially those who came under Yao influence, were beginning to agitate against him. Jumbe wanted the missionaries to be on his side but this was against the Livingstonia Mission policy. The missionaries pointed out that they would not take sides in local disputes; that they were opposed to the slave trade but that they were prepared to bring to Jumbe and his people the word of God and the goods of civilisation.

One question that the missionaries themselves had to resolve was: which of the missions would open a station in Jumbe's country at Nkhota Kota? The Livingstonia Mission was prepared to do so but the Universities' Mission to Central Africa was also looking for a sphere of mission influence to reopen mission work in Nyasaland after the tragic experiment of the Magomero Mission in the 1860s. From 1882 Archdeacon Johnson of the U.M.C.A. was in search of a Nyasaland centre for his mission. The U.M.C.A. finally moved onto Likoma Island in 1885 and from there looked for an outpost on the mainland. The lines of navigation from Likoma Island led conveniently to Nkhota Kota and it was here that the U.M.C.A. opened a station on 2 September 1894 with one European missionary, Arthur Fraser Sim and one African teacher, Joseph William. The time was not propitious. Jumbe III who had been in office from 1875 died in July 1894. For a few weeks the affairs of Jumbe's state were in the hands of the British Agent at Nkhota Kota while the people resolved the matter of succession. On 7 September, five days after the opening of the new U.M.C.A. Mission, Mwene Heri, the son of the second Jumbe, was installed as Jumbe IV. Arthur Fraser Sim and the British Agent, Nicholl, were present for the ceremony. Sim described the scene most vividly in his diary. For Sim's own feelings at this time reference may be made to his entry dated 9 September 1894.

Here I am in a large—perhaps the largest and most important town in Nyasaland. Jumbe is dead; long live Jumbe. The original old Jumbe fifty years ago was a coast Arab, conquering the place and enriching himself with the profits of the slave trade. This is a most

46

interesting place. Jumbe, compared with his purely native neighbours, was an enlightened man. He planted many trees, even coconut, thereby breaking down the superstition that coconuts will only
grow near the sea. . . .

The last of the Jumbes of Nkhota Kota did not rule for long. In
December 1894 he was charged with murder and sent off to Zomba to
stand trial. The British Administration stepped in and declared the era
of the Jumbes to be at an end. After his trial Mwene Heri was deposed
and banished to Zanzibar. As from 4 January 1895 Nicholl, the British
Agent, took over the government of Nkhota Kota.

How did the U.M.C.A. missionaries fare at Nkhota Kota? A school
was started in 1895 in a village of freed slaves; however, very few
children came to school. It was only in 1896 that the first nine boys
were accepted as catechumens. These boys were the first to be baptised
as Christians in 1897, almost three years after the mission began. A
year later, the first three women were baptised.

As schools were slow to start so were Christian converts difficult to
get. The Muslims complained of the ringing of the school bell to
summon children to the mission schools. The British Agent thought
this was a fair complaint as both religious faiths had agreed not to
interfere with each other, and he forbade the ringing of the school
bells.

With the passing of time both Christianity and Islam learnt to live
together in peace and mutual respect at Nkhota Kota. To leap into
the future, attention must be drawn to a notable event in the history of
Nkhota Kota when the Archbishop of York, the Most Reverend
Michael Ramsey, visited Nkhota Kota in 1960. The Rev. F. R. Msonthi
presented the Archbishop with an elephant tusk, on behalf of the
Anglican community. And, of course, Nkhota Kota was the venue for
the memorable Malawi Congress Party Convention in July 1960 where
political detainees were reunited after their detention during the days
of the emergency in Nyasaland. The first Jumbe had come to Malawi
125 years before this Convention. After fifty years the last of the Jumbes
was back in Zanzibar. During those years the Jumbes introduced a
new dimension with its attendant good and evil into Malawi history.

Let us look now at the relations between the Jumbe and the British
Administration. When Acting Consul Goodrich visited Nkhota Kota
in 1884 he met Jumbe III. Goodrich reported that in the presence of
about three thousand people, of whom about a hundred were Arabs,
he presented a letter to the Jumbe from the Sultan of Zanzibar and
another from the British Consul in Zanzibar, Sir John Kirk. Jumbe was

friendly and agreed to cooperate, saying: 'All my country belongs to the Seyed [i.e. the Sultan of Zanzibar] and his friends the English.'[1]

The pattern of this pro-British policy was characteristic of the political response of the Jumbes throughout their occupation of Nkhota Kota. No doubt the friendship between the British and the Sultan of Zanzibar had much to do with this. When Consul Harry Johnston visited the Jumbe in September 1889, he too carried a letter of introduction from the Sultan of Zanzibar. Johnston negotiated two treaties with Jumbe: one on behalf of the African Lakes Corporation which promised Jumbe a subsidy of 750 rupees (or about £30) quarterly under certain conditions, and the other a treaty of friendship with the British. On that occasion Johnston reported that Jumbe had raised a force of four hundred soldiers and placed himself at the head of it. According to Johnston, this action turned the general Arab feeling in the lake region as well as in Tanzania in favour of the British. Without it, the British would have found themselves in greater difficulties in attempting to put down the Swahili opposition in northern Malawi. It was in Johnston's interest when he set up his administration in 1891 to divide or reduce the strength of the opposition. One way in which he did this was to ensure that Jumbe III did not join the camps of the opposition, so he was given a subsidy of £200 a year which was partly in compensation for the surrender of customs duties but also in reality a sop to keep Jumbe happy.

Johnston saw nothing bad about the Jumbe, but he saw everything wrong with the Yao. The European missionaries considered both to be agents of Islam; but from the point of view of the European administration one was unnecessarily maligned, the other was incurably bad and had to be purged of its sins. Such were the vagaries in administrative and missionary policies that they were seriously divided on the merits and demerits of Jumbe and his people on the one hand and the Yao on the other. The Administration's view was to be seen in what Harry Johnston felt about the Jumbe:

> I really myself believe that Jumbe, ever since concluding his Treaty with Her Majesty, has honestly striven to put down the Slave Trade in his dominions. He is not always very kindly spoken of by the missionaries, because, being a zealous Mahommedan, he objects to the establishing of a Christian Mission in his town, though he readily permits Mission stations to be erected elsewhere in his country. Consequently, one hears from time to time allegations of the Slave

[1] A. J. Hanna, *The Beginnings of Nyasaland and North-Eastern Rhodesia, 1859–95*, Oxford, 1956, p. 71.

Trade being carried on secretly under Jumbe's rule. I have never been able to find any truth in these allegations. . . . I might conclude by saying that he is the only loyal good-hearted Arab that I know of on Lake Nyasa.[1]

In summary, the period of fifty years between 1844 and 1894 brought a number of influences to Nkhota Kota and the neighbouring regions. A foreign dynasty survived for half a century. It succeeded in introducing aspects of Islamic culture into Malawi. It brought trade goods from the coast and tapped the interior resources of slaves and ivory. It did not align itself actively with the Swahili Arabs of Karonga or with the Bantu-speaking Yao who entered Malawi at about the same time as the first Jumbe arrived, though both these were also associated with Islamic influences. The Jumbes also introduced coconut trees and began rice cultivation. Among the Arabs of Karonga, a Scottish trader reported that three classes were to be found: the Muscat or white Arab; the Swahili or coast Arab and the African who adopted the manners and customs of the Muslims. At Nkhota Kota, the latter two groups were more in evidence.

Of course the religion of Islam was very much evident with the coming of the coastal Arab influences. In 1910, the Governor of Nyasaland, Sir Alfred Sharpe, wrote about this:

Twenty years ago when I first came to know Nyasaland, Muhammedanism was almost non-existent except at one or two spots where it had been brought in by Arabs. Since then, it has spread greatly, particularly during the past eight or ten years. The Yao are the tribe who have adopted Moslem teaching mostly. On the other hand among the Yao to the west of Lake Nyasa, there is hardly any Muhammedanism. . . . All through Yaoland, that is to say from Lake Nyasa to the east coast there is in every village a mosque and a Moslem trader.[2]

But it was Nkhota Kota that made the greatest impact in the import of Islamic influences into Malawi. Its geographical location on an important lake port and trade route gave it an advantage which led to a concentration of population surpassing any other of similar size in rural Africa.

[1] Report by Commissioner Johnston of the first three years' administration of British Central Africa, *Africa*, 6, London, 1894, p. 29.
[2] J. S. Trimingham, *Islam in East Africa*, Edinburgh, 1962, p. 28.

We have already considered the influence of Islam as seen in the religion, trade and politics of the Jumbes of Nkhota Kota. This influence was of east coast origin which, in turn, could be traced farther afield to Arabia, Persia, India, the offshore islands of Comores, Zanzibar and Pemba, as well as to certain coastal towns like Sofala, Kilwa and Mombasa. We have now to look at the spread of Islamic influence into the interior, in the north of Malawi as well as the south.

Let us take northern Malawi first. Here, at the north end of the lake, Swahili Arab traders began to take a closer interest in the country in the last quarter of the nineteenth century. These traders were looking for a new trade route which would give them access to the country of the Bisa and the Bemba, west of the Luangwa River. Before, the traders, who were looking mainly for ivory and slaves, had crossed the lake at Nkhota Kota to do their business. While some of them manned the caravans and took their trade goods from present eastern Zambia across Lake Malawi to Zanzibar, others stayed on in fortified villages among the Senga to collect ivory and slaves and generally to remain as traders on the spot. Having established themselves in Senga country, they began to explore the possibilities of an overland route all the way to the coast. One such route lay in the Malawi-Tanzania corridor in the plateau lands which constitute the present border between Malawi and Tanzania. The country south of the Songwe River was good cattle country. It was fertile, too. Here the Ngonde as well as a few smaller groups lived as simple pastoral and agricultural communities.

This was good elephant country, too, and in the early 1880s a famous elephant hunter, Msakachuma Sichinga by name, began to sell his ivory to a Swahili Arab trader whose name was Mlozi. By stages Mlozi's interest expanded and he decided to set up a trade settlement at Mpata in present Karonga. At about this time another trading interest arrived in Karonga. This was the African Lakes Corporation, commonly known as Mandala. This company, which had started its operation in Malawi in 1878, now opened a branch at Karonga in 1884 under Monteith Fotheringham.

Trade rivalry developed between the Swahili and the Scottish traders. Mlozi began to increase his strength by raiding and trading. He was assisted by a number of Swahili subordinates like Msalemu, Kopa Kopa and Namakukane. He rallied some of the Henga refugees in Karonga to his side and began to harass the Ngonde. What started off as trade rivalry soon became a political issue when the Ngonde appealed to the manager of the African Lakes Corporation for help.

The area of conflict was extended when the Swahili Arab leaders enlisted the help of the Bemba to raid Malawi territory from Chitipa in the north to Chilumba in the south. From 1887 the country was in turmoil as a result of Mlozi's exploits in northern Malawi. The objective no longer seemed to be confined to trade alone. A state of war existed in which a number of interests were involved and a number of parties, too, African as well as non-African, Christian, pagan and Islamic.

In the meantime, British influence began to expand in the area as well. The chairman of the African Lakes Corporation in Glasgow, James Stevenson, donated £4,000 for the building of a road which bears his name. The road was intended to link Malawi and Tanzania through Chitipa and to help in trade as well as in the mission work of Livingstonia and the London Missionary Society. The Livingstonia Mission opened two missions in the area of conflict.

To protect these interests and to repel the influence of the Swahili Arabs, the British Consul at Mozambique, Harry Johnston, arrived at Karonga in October 1889 to negotiate a treaty with Mlozi. The treaty included the following clauses: the Ngonde and other displaced local inhabitants were to be allowed to return to their villages; they were not to be molested again; no new Arab villages were to be set up on the north side of the Rukuru River or to the south of the Stevenson Road; the settlements of two of Mlozi's subordinates, Kopa Kopa and Msalemu, which were already south of the Stevenson Road, were to shift from the south side within a year; the African Lakes Corporation would protect the interests of its allies and any hostile acts on the part of the Swahili Arabs would be dealt with by the company.

The terms of the treaty were not kept; the Swahili Arab settlements not only remained where they were but expanded. Slave-raiding and -trading continued and Mlozi became more defiant as he learnt of the wars which the British Administration was waging farther south against slave-traders. Harry Johnston visited Karonga again in July 1895 in order to negotiate with Mlozi. But Mlozi refused to see him and instead sent Johnston a letter which read: 'The British have closed my route to the coast: very well, I will close their road to Tanganyika.'[1]

Johnston took up the challenge. A force comprising 100 Sikhs and 300 African troops left Fort Johnston under the command of Captain Edwards on 24 November 1895. On 1 December, first Msalemu and then Kopa Kopa were overcome. On 3 December Mlozi's stockade was bombarded and he was captured by a Tonga soldier, Sergeant-Major

[1] H. H. Johnston, *British Central Africa*, London, 1897, p. 135.

Bandawe. The following day he was tried by a council of Ngonde chiefs and hanged.

One may now ask what the designs of Mlozi and his followers were. Were they actively engaged in an Islamic conversion programme or in trade for its own sake? Or were they bent on extending political influence? If so, the timing of Mlozi's arrival in northern Malawi, that is, in the 1880s, did not give him any opportunity of setting himself up without challenges from a number of quarters, including European missions and European traders who were themselves converging on to Karonga at that time. Though Mlozi was married to the daughter of Bibi Siyeni, the head wife of the last of the Jumbes of Nkhota Kota, nothing more may be read into this in the political sense. The testimony of the Ngonde historian, educationist and minister of religion, the late Rev. Amon Mwakasungula, points to trade as the motivating influence. He says that the Arab war which broke out in 1887 was due to the misdeeds of Kopa Kopa whose followers murdered an Ngonde whose name was Fumbuka. This incensed the Ngonde people as a whole and a number of Arabs were murdered in retaliation.

> The man who is assumed to have caused this trouble was Kopa Kopa who was not an Arab but a Yao from Nkhota Kota. He was a trader in search of ivory. He came to Karonga so that he could obtain a boat there as Karonga had become a famous port due to the Mandala settlement at Karonga. He was a Moslem by religion.

Of Mlozi himself, Mwakasungula states:

> Mlozi did not come to fight against the Ngonde but he wanted to establish a station at Karonga so that all his goods could be kept there until it was transported to Zanzibar. But he never wanted any of his companions to be murdered by anybody. It was, in fact, the Kopa Kopa's people who killed Fumbuka [a friend of Mlozi], but since Kopa Kopa was also Mlozi's companion, Mlozi had to defend him, too. Therefore the death of Fumbuka on the one hand and the deaths of several Arab men and women on the other, caused the breaking up of the good relationship between Mlozi and the Ngonde. Since Mlozi had guns, the Ngonde sought Mandala's protection.[1]

The Yao who settled in central and southern Malawi in the mid-nineteenth century were of greater economic, cultural and religious significance than either the Jumbe of Nkhota Kota or the Mlozi of Karonga. The Yao of Malawi who today constitute a very sizeable

[1] A. Mwakasungula, 'Thank You, Scotland' (unpublished manuscript).

52

5. Livingstonia Mission Church at Khondowe.

6. St Peter's Cathedral, Likoma Island.

8. Rev. Stephen Kauta Msiska.

7. Rev. Charles Chidongo Chinula.

9. The last meeting of the Joint Council of Blantyre Mission before the transfer of powers to Blantyre Synod in September 1958.

proportion of the population have not yet had their history thoroughly and satisfactorily investigated.

The Yao, as a single tribe, originally occupied the country between the Rovuma and the Lujenda rivers in what is today Mozambique. There is some linguistic evidence to suggest that some members of the Yao tribe lived at Kilwa-Kisiwani many centuries before. As a result of internal wars, external pressures and natural disasters, the Yao became divided in the course of time into ten major divisions of which only four are to be found in Malawi, namely the Achisi and the Amasaninga in the Fort Johnston area; the Mangoche around Blantyre and the Machinga between Fort Johnston and Zomba.[1]

The first Yao historian, Yohanna Abdallah, in his book *Cikala ca WaYao* (*The olden times of the Yao*), traces the homeland of the Yao to a hill area bearing that name between Mwembe and the Luchilingo River with Mwembe as the capital centre. In fact the Yao lived in a wider area than this and four rivers may be listed as representing their original boundaries: the Rovuma in the north; the Luchilingo in the west; the Lujenda to the east, and the Luambala to the south.

Long before the Yao began to move from this nuclear area into southern Tanzania and southern Malawi, they were already established traders. In the 1730s and the 1740s they were the greatest long-distance traders in east Central Africa, trading with the Malawi people in the southwest and with Kilwa in the northeast. Ivory was the mainstay of this trade and the chief customers were the Portuguese and the Arabs. When the Portuguese were expelled from Mombasa in 1698 the Yao trade was deflected from Kilwa to Mozambique. Here at Mossuril Portuguese, French and Indian traders bought both ivory and slaves from the Yao. Later, Kilwa regained its former importance and the Yao traded both north and south of their nuclear centre.

So the Yao had had a firm foundation in coastal trade for hundreds of years before they came to Malawi in the nineteenth century as refugee settlers. The Wachisi division were efficient blacksmiths who made hoes, axes, knives, razors, mat needles and other iron goods. These they exchanged for other goods with neighbouring people as well as on the coast. They took their hoes, tobacco and animal skins to the coast and brought back calico, salt and beads which they bartered with the Malawi peoples in exchange for salt and cattle.

The existence of iron in Yao country, the skills of the Wachisi blacksmiths, the favourable location of the Yao, straddling the lake on one side and the ocean on the other, helped in promoting their trading

[1] T. Price, 'Yao Origins', *Nyasaland Journal*, XVII, 2, 1964, pp. 12–13.

activities. Iron goods and ivory, at first, constituted their main trading interests but as the Yao were forced to flee in search of new lands for settlement they realised the asset of being in possession of guns and gunpowder. Yao fought against Yao as well as non-Yao. By the 1860s most of the Yao were trading in slaves, in league with the Bisa west of the Luangwa and the Arabs east of the lake. The Yao slavers were now well and truly middlemen. When Dr Livingstone was in Malawi in 1863 he reported that the Yao paid four yards of calico for a man, three yards for a woman and two yards for a boy or girl. Because of this sort of publicity the Yao were all lumped together as inveterate slave traders who had never known anything else. This, as we have seen, was not the case. In fact, the 1860s marked the high-water mark of the Yao slave trade in Malawi.

The Machinga Yao were the first to be squeezed out of their Mozambique homeland as a result of pressures from the Makua as well as the Ngoni. Under one of their leaders, Kawinga, the Machinga crossed the Shire and settled at Kongwe. Here the first Kawinga died. His successor was driven off by the Maseko Ngoni and fled to Chikala. The Machinga pressures in turn displaced other Yao groups and the Masaninga Yao and the Mangoche Yao soon settled in all parts of the southern lakeshore region and the Shire Highlands country under such chiefs as Malemia, Nkata, Malunga, Manjombe, Matenje, Kapeni, Mpama, Matapwiri, Kaduya, Mtirimanja, Njowe, Lundu and Mlumbe.

In the central region, Tambala, Ndindi, Mpemba and Chipoka established their new homes in the present Dedza district. These were by no means all the Yao chiefs who first entered Malawi between 1850 and 1870 but they do represent a sample of the founding fathers of present Yao settlements in Malawi. Some of the leaders had been territorial chiefs in the homeland of the Yao in Mozambique before coming to Malawi in the nineteenth century. Of this category such names as Mataka, Makanjira, Mponda, Macemba, Kawinga and Jalasi come to mind. They were certainly 'owners of the territory' or *asyene cilambo*. But there were others who were headmen and therefore only *asyene muzi* or 'owners of the village'. Some of these headmen went on to become territorial chiefs in Malawi during the flight for safety and shelter or after reaching their new homes. A matrilineal people, the Yao chiefs or headmen counted their wealth by the size of their villages, which were added to by conquest as well as by normal expansion.

Just as the chieftainship of Kabunduli of the Tonga is referred to in traditions and in literature as belonging to both the early Malawi people as well as to the later Mlowoka, so are two Yao chieftainships, those of Makanjira and Bibi Kuluunda, spoken of in both Yao and

54

Chewa traditions. These were interesting chieftainships and throw light on the complex nature of reconstructing pre-colonial history. An important historical problem derives from the migration and settlement information. Did the original migrants into Malawi not come in on both sides of the lake? To what extent did the lake act as a dividing line between peoples who were separated at the north end of it? What relationship, for example, was there between Chitezi, the Chewa chief on the mainland opposite Likoma Island and those on the mainland of Malawi and between Chitezi's kinsman, Mwasi, who was once Chitezi's representative on Likoma Island, and the other Mwasis in Malawi history?

The Rev. Laurence Cisui wrote in 1928 about Chewa–Yao relations:

If only you will ask you will be told everywhere that Makanjira, the Phiri of the Mang'anja people, was the one who beat the Yao. He speaks Yao because he had so much to do in ruling and controlling Yaos that Yao is now almost as his native speech. Yet he is true Mang'anja of Phiri lineage. Sufficient that if you do not clearly know, then question us ourselves, or the chief men of your own group.[1]

This African minister of the Anglican church was reminding his readers to look closely at Malawi history and society. The Makanjira chieftainship, according to the old traditions, belonged to the same family as that of Mwase Kasungu, Makanjira of the Kachulu line in Dowa and Mpinganjira. In very early days, Makanjira's people lived near Ulongwe from where they travelled eastwards and settled at Ngondo in the Mozambique country near Masaninga Hill, an area which had a long trading association with the Malawi people. On one of these trading trips a minor Chewa chief committed an offence with the daughter of a Masaninga Yao chief. In order to punish him, the aggrieved Yao chief sought the assistance of Makanjira's people, who lived in his neighbourhood. When this mission was satisfactorily concluded, the people of the deposed chief accepted Makanjira as their new chief. Because this happened at about the same time that some Masaninga Yao, notably Nkata and Msamala, entered Malawi, Makanjira's chieftainship is bracketed with that of the other Masaninga Yao. A similar confusion, though different in detail, has come down in the history of the chieftainship of Bibi Kuluunda, who was originally a niece of the Chewa chief Makanjira before he migrated into Yao country.

[1] *The Nyanja Peoples* (1928).

A number of other points of difference have arisen from time to time about the historical role of the Yao in pre-colonial as well as colonial times. One of these misconceptions is based on the generalisation that *all* Yao have *always* been slave traders. This, as we have seen, is not the case. Another was that all Yao were implacably opposed to Christianity, the missions and the British Administration. A final misconception was that *all* Yao embraced Islam when the Swahili Arabs went on their long-distance trade trips, thus spreading the influence of this religion along the Indian Ocean coast and inland. Generalisations on these points have no basis in historical fact, although there is an element of historical truth.

Chauncey Maples, one of the most knowledgeable Christian missionaries in Yaoland, who had a profound respect for the Yao as a people, has drawn our attention to another misconception of this sort: that all the important Yao chiefs had agents responsible for preaching and converting. This excerpt is taken from an observation he made in 1893:

> One hears something of the so-called Mohammedan *Mwalimu* or *Waalimu*, as the case may be, at Yao towns like those of Makanjira, Mponda, Mataka, and it might be supposed that their business consists in an active Mohammedan propaganda. The facts of the case, however, seldom bear out this supposition.

He observed that the scribes and clerks of the chiefs as a rule did not teach even the rudiments of reading and writing, still less those of religion.[1]

In the early years of the different Yao groups' settlement in the new lands of Malawi, they had no time or need to pursue an active Islamic conversion programme. What was needed was an unchallenged territory which was big enough and populated enough to cater for their raiding proclivities. Their arrival in the country was badly timed. The Ngoni had just preceded them; the missionaries were to follow them and British protectorate rule was to come soon afterwards. All this happened within the short space of about thirty years. The missionaries were committed to preaching the Gospel as well as the virtues of legitimate commerce. They could not take an active or militant part in eradicating the slave trade. The first Anglican missionaries had made a costly mistake in 1861–62 when they took sides against the Yao. When the first Livingstonia Mission arrived at Cape Maclear in 1875 the Yao chief Mponda gave them permission to settle in his area. They were helped in their negotiations by a relative of Mponda, one Wakotani, who had

[1] From *Nyasa News*, Nov. 1893 in Ellen Maples, *Journals and Papers of Chauncey Maples*, London, 1889, p. 247.

once worked for David Livingstone and who had later been taken to Bombay by him. Similarly, the Yao chief Kapeni granted permission to the Church of Scotland to open a mission in his area in 1876.

But even if these Yao chiefs granted lands to the missionaries, they knew that the mission teaching would be opposed to their slaving practices. To that extent the missions were a nuisance but there was another side, too, which Mponda and the other Yao chiefs saw. The missions were the forerunners of legitimate commerce. Trading companies followed and cloth, beads and other western goods were now available. There was a market, too, for ivory. There was one deficiency in this commercial link: guns and gunpowder were not supplied. This could only come through trade with the coast.

If the missionaries and the Yao tolerated each other, the first Protectorate Government under Harry Johnston was unshakeably committed to wiping out all slave-trading and -raiding. If this was possible by negotiating treaties so much the better. Cecil John Rhodes had given Johnston the sum of £2,000 to enter into treaties with the African chiefs. But if this method failed to buy peace, law and order and an end to slaving activities, a further £10,000 were available to wage wars against the slavers, chiefly Makanjira. In the end, this was the course Johnston chose, one which he sincerely believed was the correct one but for which he was both at the time and later severely criticised.

His own initiation to the Yao could not have been worse. He arrived in Malawi to take up his duties in July 1891. Two days after reaching Chiromo he heard that the Yao chief in Mulanje, Chikhumbu, was busy attacking the coffee planters there. The British had a year earlier negotiated a treaty of friendship with the Chewa chief in Mulanje by which the British Government had pledged its support of the local inhabitants against Yao attacks. An armed Sikh force (Indian soldiers recruited by Johnston) was sent against Chikhumbu while Johnston was still at Chiromo. When this was over the newly-appointed officials set out for Zomba which they reached in September 1891. There was no time to rest before news came in of further disturbances in the south lakeshore area. Mponda was one culprit; Makandanji was another; Zarafi was a third; Makanjira was the fourth; Kawinga was the fifth. A series of wars against the Yao broke out which only ended five years later. The first commander of the armed forces in Malawi, Captain Cecil Montgomery Maguire, was killed in one of these wars on 15 December 1891, barely six months after arriving in the country. Another person who was killed on this occasion was Dr Boyce, an Indian doctor who had been recruited by Johnston at Zanzibar.

These incidents no doubt influenced Johnston's estimation of the

Yao but there is evidence, too, that he had made up his mind even while he was still a consul at Mozambique that the Yao chiefs had to be defeated in war before the Protectorate could become a reality. He was not prepared to deal with them in any other way.

The Church of Scotland missionaries at Blantyre Mission did not agree either with Johnston's philosophy of the Yao or his methods of dealing with them. Johnston felt that the 'robber-chiefs' should be militarily defeated; the Blantyre missionaries believed that the conflict could be averted by opening up talks with them on the traditional basis of *mlandu*.

The head of the Blantyre Mission, Dr David Clement Scott, pointed out what the missionaries would have liked to do in the first conflict which broke out against Chikhumbu at Mulanje. They had offered to mediate and settle the dispute their way. This was refused.

> Our motive in the offer of mediation was two fold. Firstly knowing the difficulties of the case we felt it a necessary thing, that someone with a knowledge of the language greater than newcomers could be supposed to possess, should be there to help to avoid difficulties. Secondly although Chikhumbu is excitable and imperious, some of his men are the finest specimens of Yao we know. We thought it would be an immense pity if anything that could be avoided with a little timely patience and aid, should occur to destroy hopeful and helpful relations with them. . . . It is our opinion that from our experience of native custom and from our relations with Chikhumbu, that what seemed to call for the initial use of force could without much difficulty have been settled by Mlandu.[1]

But a mlandu was just what Johnston did not believe in, unless he was driven to it. In his proposals for the future administration of Nyasaland he had stated: 'I do not think the negro race will be competent to rule itself or others for at least another century . . . .' This was written in 1890.[2]

It is no wonder then that Johnston pursued a belligerent policy in the first five years of his administration until he had won many military encounters, mainly against the Yao who offered the greatest resistance. It was not only because certain chiefs were slave traders that Johnston fought against them but also because they were independent chiefs. He could not accept so many small states within his larger state.

[1] Dr David Scott, *Life and Work in British Central Africa*, Blantyre, Aug. 1891.

[2] *The Zambezian Past*, eds. E. Stokes and R. Brown, Manchester, 1966, p. 357, footnote 3.

This brought him into difficulties with the Blantyre missionaries, with the Foreign Office, and also with the Anglican missionaries of the Universities Mission to Central Africa, whose knowledge of the Yao and experience in Yaoland were second to none. Chauncey Maples of the U.M.C.A. wrote in 1893 about the Yao: 'We do not admit that they are a bad people at bottom. We believe them to be distinctly contaminated by coast influence, which has acted only too surely on their quick receptive natures. . . . We see in the Yao race ground, exceptionally fertile and productive, for the seed we missionaries come sowing.' Chauncey Maples suggested other ways of handling the Yao problem: the buying centres east of the lake should be closed and a firm warning be given to the slave dealers there to stop the practice; trade should be opened up with the Yao on the lakeshore and their supplies of ivory bought. This way the Yao would rather deal with the lakeshore traders than with the Swahili or Indian traders on the coast. In short, the lines of communication with the Yao should be opened up; the wishes of the administration should be pointed out to them and every effort should be made not to antagonise them. The policy of the U.M.C.A. missionaries was that the administration should befriend the Yao and enlist them as soldiers and policemen; the coastal caravans should be taxed heavily; slave dhows should be examined and slaves should be set free, but the dhows should be allowed to run. This way, by gradual yet constant application, the Yao would be weaned away from slaving into more productive activities.

This was not Johnston's way of doing things unless he was dealing with a weak chief like Mponda whose friendship and alliance he could buy over. In his policy of divide and rule Johnston proposed a scheme 'to bind over the more influential men to your interests by small money subsidies'. In practice he did not carry this out with any powerful or influential Yao chief. Mponda was already tottering when Johnston made an ally of him by paying him £100 a year to keep the peace and to stay on the British side. He did this again when he placed a woman whose name was Kumbasani on the throne vacated by the banished chief Makanjira.

Johnston's task in defeating the Yao was made easier by the fact that the Yao never had a paramount chief. The nearest the Yao leaders came to setting up a confederacy against Johnston was in 1892 when under the influence of Makanjira five Yao chiefs joined hands to strike in a concerted action. They failed to achieve any success.

In 1896 when Johnston's main task of 'pacifying' the troubled spots of Malawi was completed, the Yao and other Malawi tribes came under colonial rule. By then they had at long last found a permanent place for themselves in Malawi, a place which they were to adorn by their prowess as fighting men, by their industry as domestic labourers, by their service to both Islam and Christianity, and as scholars and evangelists. They had come as refugees or as migrants but they stayed on to become Malawians.

CHAPTER 4

European interests in Malawi

i THE PORTUGUESE

The Portuguese began to take an interest in Africa over five hundred years ago, for a number of reasons. They wished to increase their geographical knowledge; to open up trade with near and distant places; to find gold and other valuable goods, and also the so-called kingdom of Prester John, a Christian who would help them against the Muslims. They also wanted to find out more about the Muslims and how powerful they were and if possible they aimed to defeat them; to convert people to Christianity; and, finally, to discover new lands for Portugal. These were certainly ambitious reasons for setting out on their voyages of discovery at a time when little was known about the outside world.

As it happened, it was almost a hundred years from the time they first set out for Africa until Vasco da Gama reached India in 1498. Along the way they stopped at the Congo and found a powerful African king in office. Here an interesting experiment began in Afro-European relations. Portugal opened diplomatic relations with the African king of the Congo. Portuguese priests, artisans and farmers came out to the Congo. They even brought out two German printers with their printing press in the same year, 1492, that Christopher Columbus hoisted the Spanish flag in the West Indies. It was a two-way traffic, for some African youth went to Lisbon to study. In 1513, or just about the time when the famous German monk, Martin Luther, was in Rome, two members of the Congolese royal family were also there to see the Pope. One of them, whose baptismal name was Dom Henrique, later became a bishop, the first African bishop to return home and work among his people, in 1521.

This experiment of an equal and dignified relationship was

unfortunately shortlived. The right focus was soon lost. The wrong kind of people and the wrong kind of material interest damned the experiment within less than fifty years. Profit in the slave trade soon superseded other objectives.

While all this was happening, the Portuguese looked out for other areas of influence. They avoided South Africa for a number of reasons, one of which was that the east coast was more attractive. They seized Sofala in 1505 and from this coastal town traded inland towards present Rhodesia. They reported favourably on the wealth of the interior, which included fruit, cattle, ivory and gold. While they explored the overland route from Sofala westwards, Arab and Indian traders continued to use the Zambezi River waterway to trade with the interior. Trade rivalry led to the Portuguese gaining control of the Zambezi. To keep the gold trade to themselves, the Portuguese established trading posts at Sena and Tete in 1531 and a few years later one at Quelimane near the coast so as to guard the entry into the Zambezi River.

From the vantage points at Quelimane, Sofala, Sena and Tete the Portuguese began to spread their influence. An attempt was made to introduce Christianity on the lines of the Congo experiment. The Society of Jesus sent out seven of its members from Goa in 1559 on what has been called the Monomotapa Mission. The leader of the mission party was Father Gonzales Silveira who was then the Provincial Designate of the Society of Jesus at Goa. Three of the seven members reached the headquarters of the ruler of Monomotapa on Christmas Day, 1560. The ruler, Mupunzagutu, and his mother, gave the visitors a good reception, even accepting Christianity themselves shortly afterwards. The Muslim traders were disturbed by this development. They feared for the future of themselves as well as their trade in the Monomotapa country of present Rhodesia. A conspiracy was hatched up and Father Silveira was murdered. Thus religious and trade rivalry combined to put an end to this peaceful contact.

Naturally, the Portuguese Government and the Society of Jesus were upset by this setback and many plans were laid to send a military expedition, but it took ten years before another party could come. By then the Arab trade interest, centred on ivory, was directed north of the Zambezi while the Portuguese interest, centred on gold, was south of the river.

The Malawi people were drawn into these rival camps by accident and by design: that is, because of geographical and political reasons. The Karonga, Mazura, would certainly have sent ivory and other produce to the Portuguese market town of Tete while his kinsman, Lundu, in the lower Shire area could trade at Sena. Whatever the strength or weakness of the traditional bonds between Karonga and Lundu, the fact that they traded with the Portuguese at different points, separated by many miles, tended to create economic rivalry which was afterwards to lead to political disharmony.

Portuguese records in the 1590s are full of reports of troubles with the Zimba people on both banks of the Zambezi. They complained of the disruption of trade caused by one whose name was Tondo. This name may or may not refer to Lundu but it must refer to a Zimba leader of some importance if contemporary writing mentions him by name.

The main Portuguese interest was, of course, in the territory of the Monomotapa ruler. They would do everything possible to defend the interests of the friendly rulers for in doing so their own interests were also safeguarded. One such ruler was Gatsi Rusere who asked the Portuguese for help in 1608 to put down some rebellious subjects. The Portuguese volunteered 75 of their number and 2,000 of their slaves and others. They succeeded in getting some 4,000 Malawi warriors, too, from the Karonga Mazura. Here was a grand alliance: the Karonga Mazura; the Mwene Mutapa, Gatsi Rusere and the Portuguese. In 1623 the Mwene Mutapa died and his ally Mazura crossed the southern bank of the Zambezi in an attempt to take over the lands of the Mwene Mutapa. He came back with much cattle and gold but little else.

Nor did the Karonga Mazura's designs end with the failure of his mission to conquer the lands of Mwene Mutapa. He turned now on his former ally, the Portuguese. The Portuguese writer, Antonio Bocarro, tells us what was happening in 1635:

This King is at peace with the Portuguese, and he used to keep it better than today, before he was so powerful, because since he has defeated, with our help, a Kaffir King called Rondo, with whom he was fighting, he thinks of making war against us; it is said that some Portuguese have been killed in his lands by his order, and he wrongs us at every occasion.

Thus by 1635 the Portuguese were in trouble with the Karonga Mazura. This king had put down his subordinate, Lundu, and had expanded his territory right up to the Indian Ocean coast opposite Mozambique. Bocarro writes that Karonga now wanted to be designated an 'emperor' like Mwene Mutapa.

It can be seen, therefore, that the Portuguese were by no means having it all their own way in Central Africa at this time. They were not interested in political conquest but in trade. Religion, too, except for its few grand moments in the Congo earlier on and at the court of Mwene Mutapa in 1560–61, was not a strongly motivating factor. Religion and politics would combine in the nineteenth century to create a new situation, but this will be considered later.

For the present, it was only trade that set the pace. In 1608, the very year in which the Mwene Mutapa, Gatsi Rusere, asked the Portuguese and the Karonga Mazura for help, the King of Portugal ordered the Viceroy of India to organise the exploitation of the gold and silver mines of Monomotapa. The plan was big: a few forts were to be constructed; five hundred soldiers would be placed on the Zambezi; an official was to be appointed with the imposing title of General of the Mines of Monomotapa. This commercial plan does not seem to have worked because most of the Portuguese desired war instead of peaceful commerce. The African king of Monomotapa was not slow to retaliate when he noticed acts of duplicity, such as when the Portuguese at Tete weaned one of his sons away from him in an effort to cause the father trouble.

In the midst of all this one Portuguese nobleman, Gaspar Bocarro, left Tete in March 1616 to find an overland route to the east coast so as to reach Portugal without the knowledge of the Portuguese in Mozambique. Accompanied by twelve slaves he left Tete, crossed the Zambezi, and after two days of travelling in the direction of Malawi, he bought a thousand bracelets from Chief Inhampury in an area famous for copper and reached the capital of the Karonga, Mazura, which he described as a place a day's journey from Lake Malombe. The Maravi king and Bocarro exchanged gifts. Mazura entertained him for fifteen days and then sent him on his way with three guides. At Malombe he obtained three more guides. In his own account of the journey, Bocarro writes that he heard of the great 'Nyasa' or lake nearby but did not visit it. He crossed the Shire at the south end of the lake and then travelled northwards in the present Malindi or Makanjira area east of the lake. This he described as still being Mazura's country. Farther on there was Chicoave, a vassal of Mazura. He crossed the Luambala River, entered the valley of the Rovuma and reached the sea near Kilwa-Kisiwani.

This was a remarkable trip. In all he travelled something like eight hundred miles in fifty-three days. He passed through the territories of three paramount chiefs but was not detained for a single day by wars or other disturbances. At about the time when the Thirty Years War was about to break out in Europe between Catholics and Protestants, a single white man crossed through strange African lands without being molested. The Bocarro expedition is a remarkable historical event during the middle ages of Malawi history. Though Bocarro failed in the main objective of his journey, namely to reach Portugal, his report is nonetheless a valuable document. It was published twenty years afterwards. Eight years after Bocarro's trip, a Catholic priest at Sena, one Luis Mariano, wrote a report to his superior at Goa, describing aspects of the interior of Malawi. The Portuguese were now becoming more interested in the area north of the Zambezi and wished to know more about trade prospects, especially about the existence of gold and silver mines. Luis Mariano does not give any evidence that he himself journeyed to Malawi but the report was certainly based on reliable testimony. Whether the information was obtained from Africans or from Portuguese travellers or both is not clear. He writes of a powerful chief whose name he spells as 'Massi' and another farther inland whose name he spells as 'Rovenga'. These must refer to Mwasi and Luhanga. Here follows an excerpt from this letter dated 1624:

From Tete begins the overland route for Maravi, which is the headquarters of the kingdom of Muzura, and which is, for persons travelling without much baggage, a journey of six or seven days I am informed, 60 or more leagues distant to the north-north-east, and so Maravi must be approximately a little north of, or at the same latitude as, Quelimane. From Maravi to the lake is only half a league, and so almost all who went to Muzura saw it, but few examined its characteristics. However, I found someone who was able to specify to me the direction of its axis, which he said was in part N.N.E.–S.S.W., and in part north–south, both of which are very convenient for being able to travel from there to the lands of Prester John, and it stretches a good distance more to the south within Maravi, from which end the River Cheri leaves, at first very smoothly and with only a little water, and later, because of the many rocks over which it passes, it becomes rough and unnavigable. Maravi lies between the lake and the Zambesi, on whose bank is a densely populated land with which the Portuguese trade, as does Muzura. But there are two principal kings: one is Massi, which is 15 days journey from Maravi along the lake and the other is Rovenga, a further 15 days distant, . . . it is much better to travel through the land of these Rovengas, who have not left their homeland at the extremity of the lake which stretches such a great distance.[1]

To the Portuguese of Luis Mariano's day, Maravi was the name of a

[1] Camillo Beccari, *Rerum Aethiopicarum Scriptores Occidentales*, XII, Rome, 1912.

territory or state under the rule of the Karonga. It was for them an important overland route to the interior, a link to as far afield as Ethiopia where the so-called 'lands of Prester John' lay. Luis Mariano's letter also refers to the other interest the Portuguese had in Malawi, that is trade. A Portuguese report of 1609 states that provisions for their trading post at Sena were obtained from the fertile lands of the Shire valley: 'From it come nearly all the provisions consumed in Sena, such as rice, millet, sweet potatoes, pigs and fowls. . . . [The Shire] is navigated by the Kaffirs and residents of Sena who carry on commerce from one part to another.'[1]

How did the Portuguese promote commerce in the areas of their influence? They did not have sufficient manpower in Africa to do it themselves and in any case during the early years of their settlement the few Portuguese men concentrated on military and church matters. In 1686 the Portuguese Viceroy in India granted the exclusive right to trade in the area between Diu in the Persian Gulf to Mozambique in the south to an Indian firm. With trade monopoly went certain administrative privileges such as the administration of justice. The Indian monopoly holder chose Jesuit priests to act as judges. However, whenever the traders got into difficulties, the Jesuit judges were also implicated. In 1759 the Jesuits were recalled and a few years later, in 1777, the trading privileges of the Indian traders were withdrawn. This did not mean that the traders left the area. As late as 1882 the British Consul at Mozambique, O'Neill, reported that they were 'in sole possession' of trade on the Portuguese coast line, penetrating far into the interior by river and caravan, exchanging Indian and European wares for local produce which included ivory, copper and animal skins.[2]

The organisation and extent of internal trade in which the Portuguese were involved, either as administrators or as participants, needs further investigation. As gold was the chief attraction they concentrated on the region south of the Zambezi. But they had their designs on the north, too, for future exploitation. For one thing, an unhindered overland route, helped by interior waterways provided by rivers and lakes, would secure mineral and commercial exploitation. Fears of being cut off from the interior became real in the eighteenth century. In 1795 the British occupied the Cape. The Portuguese were shaken by this act and felt that any further British expansion northwards would cut off Portuguese Angola from Portuguese Mozambique. For this

[1] G. Theal, *Records of South-Eastern Africa*, VII, Cape Town, 1964, p. 278.
[2] H. E. O'Neill, *Royal Geographical Society Journal* paper, 1882; W. B. Worsfold, *Portuguese Nyasaland*, London, 1899, pp. 37–40.

reason an expedition set off from Brazil under Dr Lacerda in 1796. The object was to get to the court of the African ruler Kazembe in present northeast Zambia. This expedition is described in *The Lands of Cazembe*, translated into English by R. F. Burton. Lacerda died at Kazembe's without meeting the king. In June 1831 another Portuguese party set out from Tete to visit King Kazembe. This expedition had hopes that the king would allow the party to travel westwards from there as far as Loanda. The objective, again, was to spread Portuguese economic interests and to exploit the wealth this part of the world was reputed to have. None of these attempts bore any important fruit. After almost three hundred years in Africa they had not succeeded in entrenching themselves in the interior.

Even the coastal settlements were in a bad way. In 1870, Sofala, the first Portuguese settlement on the Indian Ocean coast, had not a single Portuguese resident. Fear of attacks from the African chief, Mzila, had caused the Portuguese to shift their headquarters to a nearby island which had a military strength of 129 persons. At Quelimane there were 85 troops; at Sena, the centre of considerable trade at one time, there were only 4 Portuguese residents in 1875. It was a military post with only one soldier. At Tete, the capital of Portuguese Zambezia (that is, the Zambezi area), there were 118 soldiers; at Zumbo, their farthest post on the Zambezi, there were 21 soldiers.

In the third quarter of the nineteenth century, then, the Portuguese hold on their Zambezi settlements was precarious. This hold was to be further shaken when new people entered the area at about that time—Dr Livingstone's Kololo and the Scottish missionaries. These arrivals were to stir the Portuguese from their slumber; and a new period of imperialism dawned when the Portuguese made one last effort to assert their age-old claims to the Zambezi region and the hinterland. Malawi was involved in this rivalry and these claims.

The system of Portuguese land grants known as *prazos* should be mentioned at this point. To encourage white settlements in their territories, the Portuguese Government introduced a system of land grants in the eighteenth century by which Crown lands or prazos were allotted to Portuguese-born women on condition that they married Portuguese men. These conditions, as well as a whole host of others, including the size of the prazos, were soon ignored. Originally set down as areas roughly ten miles by one mile, prazos were soon in holdings of hundreds of miles. One such prazo holder was a native of Portuguese India who came to Sena in 1853 and within ten years was appointed commander-in-chief of the Portuguese settlements of Manica and Quiteve.

Another, whose descendants were more involved in Malawi history, was one Paul Marianno, also a native of Portuguese India. The first Marianno came out to the Quelimane district in 1824 as a military man. He soon began to trade in gold dust and ivory and ran a plantation of his own. The second Marianno led a military expedition against the Mang'anja chief Massangano in the lower Shire area in 1854. From the lands conquered in this expedition some fifteen miles up the Shire River near the present Nsanje district, Paul Marianno II built a stockade at Shamo. Here he built himself a fine brick building and reinforced his power with over seven thousand muskets and four brass guns. From his base at Shamo, Marianno became one of the leading slave traders. In 1860 he assumed the African name of Matakenya. He and his brother Bonga defied the Portuguese in whose name they had first come to Zambezia and even raided the town of Sena. Sought now by the Portuguese, Marianno and his brother moved northwards into the Malawi region and settled near Mount Mulanje. Here the Mang'anja people accepted Marianno as their chief. His subjects were now called the Massingire and his influence extended both east and west of the Shire.

This period of Malawi history is a fruitful area for further research. Who were the people who called themselves the Massingire? How was the traditional system of government by chiefs modified to provide for the recognition of the intruder Paul Marianno or Matakenya? Was it a military system of government?

Fortunately, some written records on this period exist, supplied by the missionaries who came to Malawi in the nineteenth century. Dr David Livingstone's Zambezi expedition of 1858 came face to face with the upheavals created by Matakenya and his followers. Matakenya in fact offered Livingstone an alliance against the Portuguese. He was to do the same when the Universities' Mission to Central Africa came out to Malawi in 1861. Livingstone was convinced that he could count on Matakenya not attacking the ships and the property of the British. Paul Marianno II or Matakenya died in September 1863. We are told that one of the members of the U.M.C.A. expedition, Horace Waller, even contemplated taking over the leadership of the Massingire people when Matakenya died, but of course this must be seen in the context of the difficulties the U.M.C.A. were going through at this time and their search for a new mission site.

The story of the Massingire does not end in 1863. It will be followed through in a later section. It is mentioned here to draw attention to the state of Portuguese economics and politics in Zambezia in the 1860s. The conclusion cannot be escaped that the Portuguese were now a spent force. Their settlements were in ruins, their commerce at a standstill. Slave-raiding and -trading could no longer be the mainstays of imperial survival. Ever since the Congress of Vienna met at the end of the Nap-oleonic wars to redraw the map of Europe and to make plans for future peace, the slaving activities of European powers abroad had come in for serious criticism. The slave trade had been outlawed in the British Empire since 1807; slaves had been set free in the British Empire as from 1 December 1834. Though Spain and Portugal had been slow in following the lead given by the other European powers, they could not continue to ignore the example.

The exploits of Paul Marianno and his descendants were both an embarrassment and a nuisance to the Portuguese in Zambezia, especially when British missionaries were on the spot to give publicity to the shortcomings of Portuguese policy in Africa.

In the 1860s the Portuguese were faced not only with the slaving activities of the rebellious and defiant Matakenya. They were confronted also with British inroads into their 'dominions'. Since 1505 when Sofala had been first occupied, they had lorded it over the Zambezi area unchallenged seriously by any European power. In 1817 a treaty with Great Britain had recognised the Portuguese occupation of the Indian Ocean coast lands from Cape Delgado in the north to Delagoa Bay in the south but there was no mention of the interior. However, in the 1870s the interior suddenly assumed an importance that had never existed before. The days of Portuguese monopoly in fact were numbered and an Anglo-Portuguese imperial contest would have to be waged for the control, occupation and development of the lands north of the Shire-Zambezi confluence.

Before we consider these new developments, let us summarise the earlier phase of Portuguese interests and activities in the Zambezi area (Zambezia). Religious activities and motives occupied a very small part of the main objective. It is true that the Society of Jesus made an effort to introduce Christianity in the court of the Mwene Mutapa but with the murder of Father Silveira this hope faded. A military force was sent to punish those responsible but a few hundred soldiers could hardly achieve this. In any case, since the Portuguese main aim was not political conquest but trade in gold, there was little point in antagonising trading partners. It must be remembered also that Portugal and Spain had made a political union in 1580, so that Portugal no longer had the freedom of individual action. The religious wars of Europe, rather than the economic exploitation of Africa, dictated much of contemporary policy.

That the Portuguese knew about Malawi long before the coming of Dr Livingstone and his successors cannot be denied. In fact, Dr Livingstone was himself greatly annoyed when the Portuguese writer Dr

Jose de Lacerda wrote a book in 1867 whose English title was *Examination of the travels of Doctor Livingstone*. This was a reply to the doctor's own book, *Missionary Travels and Narrative of an Expedition*. In his rebuttal of Dr Livingstone's claims, Jose de Lacerda states that the Portuguese were familiar with Barotseland and Makololo land long before Livingstone; that they knew the cataract 'Mosivatunya' before Livingstone and that it was audacious of him to baptise it 'Victoria Falls'; that they also knew of the lands of Kazembe before Livingstone; that two of their subjects were the first to journey from Angola to Mozambique; that the Shire highlands and the Lake Nyasa regions were places which the Portuguese had penetrated before Livingstone and that they had not settled there because they already had their settlements on the Zambezi. Of Livingstone's claims on behalf of the British missionaries, Jose de Lacerda is contemptuous: 'Protestant missionaries may perhaps be expert in history, mineralogy, geographical sciences ... and to those who pay them they render more valuable services as explorers for industry or commerce than they do as truly sincere apostles for the Gospel and humanity, but what is the final result?'

The final result was to be left to the subsequent contest between Portugal and Britain, and the quarrels between Lacerda and Livingstone were only the first blows exchanged.

ii ANGLO-PORTUGUESE CONFLICT FOR THE CONTROL OF MALAWI

We have seen how the rivalry between the Portuguese and the British began to build up towards the last quarter of the nineteenth century. This was due, in part, to increasing activity from British Protestant missions in Malawi, which was in its turn a result of the work and writings of Dr David Livingstone. On his first journey from Loanda to Quelimane, which he completed on 20 May 1856, Livingstone did not come to Malawi but travelled down the Zambezi. On his first visit home in 1857 he spoke to ordinary people as well as to government officials about the prospect of opening the Zambezi to European commerce. There was one snag to this: the Zambezi passed through Portuguese territory so that their goodwill was necessary for the success of any Zambezi scheme. The Portuguese were prepared to give him limited help as long as their reputation and interests were not at stake.

By the time Livingstone reached Lake Malawi on 17 September 1859 he had learned a lot. He discovered that some chiefs like Tengani in the Chikwawa area were not on friendly terms with the Portuguese, particularly because of their slaving activities. He reported that the Malawi lands he had seen had good soil, especially for cotton and sugar. Commercial prospects, too, were good. With the growth of lawful commerce, slave trading would be reduced and eventually exterminated.

Livingstone saw two pillars for the operation of his scheme. These were Christianity and commerce, both of which had to be launched at the same time. During his lifetime attempts were made to get these pillars of progress constructed. A Scottish medical student by the name of James Stewart put forward a scheme in 1860 to start a mission in the Zambezi valley to develop cotton cultivation and to carry on Christian teaching. He tried to get the Free Church of Scotland and some businessmen at Glasgow, Manchester and Liverpool interested, but without success. Anglican missionaries attempted to start a mission at Magomero in 1861. In two years time this turned out to be a tragic failure and to Livingstone's great disappointment it was closed down.

These were only temporary setbacks, for there were some favourable auspices. The Suez Canal was opened in 1869 making it possible for ships from Europe to reach the east coast of Africa in quick time. In 1872 a monthly mail service was started from Aden in the Red Sea to Durban via Zanzibar. With postal and naval communications improving so rapidly, the prospects for inland commerce also became bright. The telegraph line reached Mozambique and Lourenço Marques in 1879. Thus Lisbon was no longer cut off from her overseas possessions. Interior water communications provided by such rivers as the Zambezi and the Shire as well as lakes like Malawi and Tanganyika improved trading prospects. The economic and political climate was right. All that was needed to launch the enterprise was the emotional momentum. This was provided by the news of Livingstone's death in 1873, the manner of his death in a remote part of Central Africa, the devotion of his faithful African servants who carried his body to the coast for transportation to Britain and the glory of a Westminster Abbey burial. Scottish missionaries, businessmen and philanthropists were quick to take advantage of this. The first Scottish mission party reached Cape Maclear in 1875; this was the Livingstonia Mission. A year later the Blantyre Mission was founded. In 1878, the Livingstonia Central Africa Company, later to change its name to the African Lakes Company and finally the African Lakes Corporation, was started. The combination of Christianity and commerce that Livingstone had lived and died for was now a reality.

How would all this affect the relationship between Britain and Portugal? Many things had happened since the 1860s which would affect their relations in Central and southern Africa. For one thing diamonds were discovered in South Africa and gold in Matabeleland. Both the British and the Boers of South Africa were interested in these places. In this economic rivalry the port of Lourenço Marques in Delagoa Bay assumed an importance it had never enjoyed before. The problem for Portugal then and for a long time to come was simply this: should she interest herself in what was happening in the interior so that the economic development of her Mozambique territory could be enhanced? Would economic development not eventually undermine her political sovereignty in Mozambique?

In the end, the answer given by Portugal was clear: it was more interested in its national prestige than in economic development. This attitude is exemplified in a statement made by the Portuguese foreign minister in 1889:

> Portugal, who conquered India and created Brazil, has a past exceeded by that of no other nation. That past gives her the right to ensure her hopes of a new and brilliant period for her nationality. Africa alone can guarantee it to her. When she defends her rights in that continent, she defends her future.[1]

Her future, in this light, was placed in some doubt when British Protestant mission stations were opened at Blantyre and Livingstonia, plus the business firm of the African Lakes Company. The survival of these enterprises depended upon the use of the Zambezi River to transport people and goods. According to Sir Travers Twiss, one of the most eminent British jurists of the nineteenth century, any nation which held both banks of a navigable river had an absolute right to exclude all other nations from using the river. The Portuguese refused to allow other nations to use the Zambezi as of right. They could only do so after negotiating treaties.

In 1876 H. B. Cotterill, the son of a Scottish bishop, asked the British Foreign Office to obtain permission from the Portuguese Government for him to carry trade goods on the river. This application took about a year to be considered. In the same year, 1876, the Portuguese granted to two of their own merchants a monopoly to place steamers on the Zambezi and Shire Rivers for a period of thirty years. The British Government did not protest because it did not realise then the seriousness of this move.

Internal developments in the lower as well as the upper Shire were soon to remind the British Government of its fairly heavy involvement in the area. One was the arrival of the Kololo from Barotseland. Living-

[1] P. R. Warhurst, 'Portugal's Bid for Southern Malawi', *Malawi Past and Present*, eds. B. Pachai, G. W. Smith and R. K. Tangri, Blantyre, 1971, p. 49.

Portuguese and British imperial interests

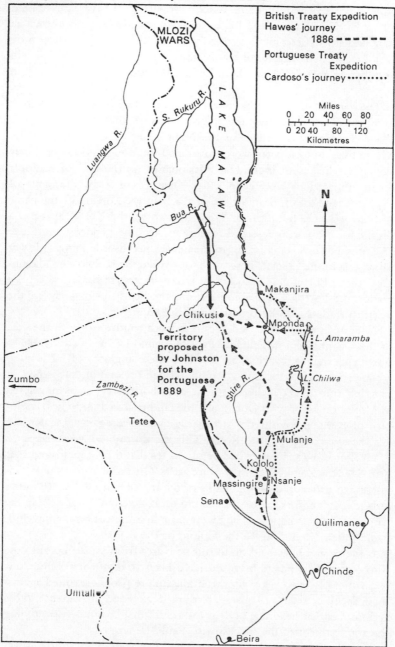

stone had brought 140 of them on his first trip and had left them at Tete while he was away in Britain. When he returned in 1858, he recruited a new batch in Barotseland led by Moloka and Kasisi (also known as Ramakukan). These numbered only 16; of these, only 2 were pure Kololo. When Livingstone left Malawi on 19 January 1864 he said goodbye to these settlers whom he had brought to a new country in 1858.

The handful of Kololo became a force out of all proportion to their numbers. They took over the chieftainships of the Mang'anja; made alliances with the Yao; fought the Ngoni, and gave shelter to those whose lives and property were threatened by foreign invasions. They also quarrelled with individual missionaries or traders, for example during the serious conflict in 1884, when a Kololo by the name of Chipatula and a European artisan of the Blantyre Mission by the name of Fenwick were both killed. What was worse, the Kololo also had a dislike for the Portuguese and for anyone who befriended them.

A number of events began to create serious disorders in the lower Shire area in the 1880s. These were to involve the Kololo, the Massingire (those Portuguese subjects to whom reference has already been made), the Portuguese Administration, the Scottish missionaries, the Scottish traders and the British Administration.

Since 1864 the Kololo had begun to push southwards into the area of the Massingire now ruled by Paul Marianno IV, who was unable to push back their advance. This lost him the confidence of his leading *capitaos*, who after various attempts to get rid of him succeeded in handing him over to the Portuguese authorities. He was murdered at Mopea on his way to Quelimane to stand trial in 1881. The Massingire now asked for direct Portuguese assistance against the Kololo advances towards the Ruo River. This the Portuguese were happy to grant. For some years they had begun to see that they were losing their grip over the Zambezi and the Shire areas. On 12 May 1882 the Portuguese flag was raised on the banks of the lower Shire River at Pinda's village. Massingire territory bordering on Kololo lands was now in the hands of the Portuguese. They were now in Shire country, a development which did not please the Kololo or the British.

If they could have held on to this new area from the Zambezi to the Ruo River their position would have been strengthened immensely. Unfortunately, two years later, the Massingire people revolted against them for these main reasons: collection of taxes and interference in the appointment of headmen and in the traditional customs surrounding the appointment of the successor to Paul Marianno IV.

The Massingire rising of 1884 affected everyone living in the lower

Shire and the lower Zambezi areas. Rebels attacked European trading posts, stole the boats of the African Lakes Company and found themselves not only in a war with the Portuguese but with all countries whose commercial interests were affected. Some of the refugees fled into the Kololo villages and asked for their help. Had it not been for the Scottish missionaries who advised against it, the Kololo would have become involved.

Though the rising was crushed it had serious repercussions all around. The African Lakes Company, fearing for its future business interests, entered into treaties with the Kololo chiefs by which these chiefs were promised British protection (an obligation which the British Foreign Office disavowed in 1885). The British Foreign Office and the Scottish missions used the rising of 1884 to draw attention to the corrupt Portuguese Administration. The Portuguese became suspicious of the roles of the British and the Kololo, blaming them for the disturbances in their territory. Finally, the Massingire people themselves cherished hopes that the British would give them protection as they had given the Kololo, but their hopes were frustrated when the Anglo-Portuguese treaty was drawn up in 1891. Most of their lands fell within the Portuguese sector.

The Portuguese won the battle against the Massingire but not the war for imperial overlordship in the Shire region. They had to change their tactics there. One line of action was to win the Yao over to their side. A start had been made many years before when the Yao and the Portuguese became trading partners in slaves. Guns from the Portuguese towns of Ibo, Angoche and Quelimane found their way into Yao hands. Even when slave trading began to be looked upon with disfavour in the 1880s, the Yao still carried on with it. Except for Chief Chikhumbu of Mulanje, the other Yao chiefs were more friendly to the Portuguese than to the British.

After the Massingire rising the Portuguese took steps to strengthen their alliance with the Yao. In 1886 Lieutenant Cardoso visited Chief Matipwiri in Mulanje. Trading caravans heading for Quelimane usually stopped over at Matipwiri's village. From here Cardoso went to the area of Chief Makanjira at the south end of Lake Malawi. Here he signed a treaty with one of Makanjira's men named Kwirazia. Makanjira did not approve of this and expelled Kwirazia for having taken such a step.

While the Portuguese were negotiating with some of the Yao, the British Consul at Mozambique, Captain Hawes, decided to play the same game and called upon the Yao chief Mponda. He gathered that the Portuguese had already made overtures to the present chief's father a year before without success. Hawes proceeded to the Maseko chief, Chikusi, and got his agreement not to raid Zomba and Blantyre where British plantation and mission interests had been established. Hawes was happy to report that Makanjira's was not as yet a Portuguese sphere of influence.

These moves on the part of Portuguese and British officials to sign treaties with African chiefs illustrate the European diplomacy of the time. The one party had often to call a bluff to keep the other out. In 1888 the Portuguese announced that a 'civilising mission' would be sent to the lake region comprising about three thousand men who would be carrying some twelve hundred guns. This was to be followed by another such expedition to be led by Major Serpa Pinto. The Portuguese now made it clear that they were not content merely with controlling the Zambezi and the Shire. They wanted the control of the interior as far as Lake Malawi. Now the British Government was prepared to negotiate. Harry Johnston was sent to Lisbon for this purpose. Johnston's starting point was that it was his duty to build an empire, not merely to protect the interests of the Blantyre missionaries. He was prepared to say that the Portuguese could extend their territories into Nyasaland as far as the mouth of the Bua River. Likoma Island should remain British because of the mission station there; the Portuguese would have to forget about their grand design of an unbroken Portuguese territory from Angola to Mozambique. Instead, they would have to grant a strip of territory from the Zambezi northwards, west of the Luangwa, so that British expansion from Cape Town to Tanganyika would be possible without Portuguese interference or obstruction.

But Johnston had to convince the Scottish missionaries first.

The Free Church of Scotland, the owners of Livingstonia Mission, reluctantly accepted the agreement. Bandawe, their headquarters, was north of the proposed Portuguese line. The Established Church of Scotland, who owned the Blantyre Mission, was, however, outraged by this proposal. They asked Lord Balfour to express their unflinching opposition to this deal. We have an account of what happened when Lord Balfour spoke to the British Prime Minister, Lord Salisbury, about this:

'My Lord,' he said, 'my Scottish friends don't like the Portuguese terms.' 'Neither do I,' was the reply. 'I don't want your Scottish friends to accept them. I want the Portuguese to know that I, too, have a strong public opinion behind me, and I am sending their Government a warning that they must not go too far.' The hint was taken. The campaign in Scotland was intensified. Representative meetings were held in the principal towns, and a memorandum signed by eleven

76

thousand ministers and elders was taken to London and presented to Lord Salisbury. 'My Lord,' said Dr Scott, 'this is the voice of Scotland.'[1]

It was indeed the voice—or the conscience—of Scotland that prevented this deal from going through. Had it not been sounded so strongly in 1889, half of present Malawi would have been Portuguese territory. By a coincidence, this was the first of a number of events in 1889 that finally prompted the British Government to extend a protectorate over Nyasaland. Let us consider the others.

In May 1889, Harry Johnston met Cecil John Rhodes in London on the eve of setting out for Mozambique to take up his position as British Consul at Mozambique. Rhodes wrote Johnston a cheque for £2,000 to make treaties with chiefs north of the Zambezi River. The idea behind this was to win over those chiefs who had no treaties already with the Portuguese and thus make a claim to prior spheres of influence. These treaties were to be kept a secret until the opportune moment. Rhodes' offer of financial help was a powerful argument in pressing forward the British claims in the area. The British Treasury was always hamstrung by financial difficulties and no colonial official ever had the freedom of committing the Treasury to expenses it was unable or unwilling to meet. As it turned out, it was the money from Rhodes' company that kept the British Administration going for nearly five years.

In April 1889, D. J. Rankin, one-time artisan at the Blantyre Mission, discovered a new entrance to the Zambezi through the Chinde mouth, 300 yards wide and with a minimum depth of 18 feet. The significance of this discovery was that by using this entrance it would be possible for men and goods to enter the Zambezi River without touching Portuguese soil. The A.L.C. now announced that it would use one of its shallow-draft steamers to settle the question of free navigation. We have already referred to the legal argument relating to the use of a river both of whose banks fall within the territory of a single power. In addition, however, there was a further unresolved question. Would the Portuguese allow arms and ammunition to be carried through the Chinde mouth? They had already placed a ban in 1888 on arms and ammunition being shipped by the A.L.C. for use in the Mlozi war in Karonga. This ban was only removed when the British Government threatened to use force.

The third significant event of 1889 was Serpa Pinto's expedition to the Shire and Nyasa areas, and the fourth was the reaction of the Kololo to this expedition and to the African Lakes Company which to them was in league with the Serpa Pinto expedition.

[1] W. P. Livingstone, *A Prince of Missionaries*, London, n.d. pp. 51–2.

On 19 August 1889, Acting British Consul John Buchanan wrote to Serpa Pinto advising him that the Kololo country and the Shire Highlands north of the Ruo River had been placed under the protection of the Queen and asking him not to proceed with his expedition with an armed force; it would disturb the peace in Kololo country as well as the friendly relations between Britain and Portugal. Serpa Pinto could not accept this directive. He could not accept, either, that the British had any reason to champion the cause of the Kololo, who were not their subjects.

Buchanan and John Moir of the A.L.C. were determined that the Kololo should fire upon the Portuguese expedition if it was determined to proceed into prohibited areas. The expedition did proceed and in fact attacked the first stockaded village of the Kololo at Balalika. Buchanan wrote to Serpa Pinto on 21 September 1889 telling him that the Kololo, Yao and Machinga countries were now placed under British protection. He went on to say: 'This country is, by your ill-advised action in a most disturbed state, which I have been doing my best to allay; but the King of the Maviti [meaning Chikusi] having sent his Chief Captain to inquire into the reported invasion of the Makololo country by the Portuguese, tends to keep the war feeling alive . . .'[1]

Buchanan was trying to impress upon Serpa Pinto that if he proceeded further he would have not only the Kololo and the British to contend with but the Ngoni as well—a good example of the use of diplomatic bluff.

Mlauli, the paramount chief of the Kololo, did not himself fall for any bluff. He did not even sign a treaty of friendship with Buchanan. Buchanan reported as follows: 'Some evil influence has been at work with Mlauli and playing upon his superstitious belief represented to him that his acceptance of the British flag necessarily means his giving up his country and all sovereign rights.'[2]

Buchanan might call this reaction 'superstitious'; Mlauli felt something different, a real fear of the motives behind the treaty-making campaigns. It was only when he had been persuaded that the Portuguese were advancing that he put up a British flag in his village at Balalika. At night it was stolen by a party of Portuguese from across the river at Mpassa.

Mlauli was furious. He wrote to Buchanan as follows on 16 October 1889:

I want to speak, saying did you not at that time cheat me, saying 'When you have accepted the flag, the war will not come to take it.'

[1] *Accounts and Papers*, 1890, 51.   [2] Warhurst, *op. cit.*, p. 58.

But today they have stolen the flag, they have taken it, it is with the Portuguese. But my heart says, now I shall go and attack them; have they not stolen my flag. I shall attack them. I am going just now. Further, I want you, Mr Consul Buchanan, and Mr Mauvala [Mr Moir] to come here quickly. If you delay you will find me already gone, and the steamer certainly shall not pass. . . .[1]

His fellow chiefs Masea and Katunga supported him in a letter to Buchanan sent twelve days later: 'You said, "Let the war come, and capture us the Makololo Chiefs." The Portuguese say so, but Masea and Katunga are tired. Mr Buchanan, why did you not come down to speak with us as you had arranged? But the war belongs to the white people, and you deceive the chiefs.'[2]

The Kololo chiefs touched upon the pulse of the matter: they were being used as pawns in the game. The Portuguese claimed that they were invited by the British to attack the Kololo (in fact Simpson, agent of the A.L.C., had asked for their help to reopen the Shire to navigation); the British told the Kololo that acceptance of the British flag would automatically frighten off the Portuguese. Whom were the Kololo to trust? Masea and Katunga saw through all this: it was all a white man's war.

Both Lisbon and London took advantage of the developments in the lower Shire area. Meetings were held and press reports carried inflammatory reactions. The governments concerned exchanged notes at the highest levels. On 26 December 1889, Lord Salisbury sent a strong despatch to Lisbon saying that 'Archaeological arguments . . . are not relevant'; that Portugal had not done a thing in two centuries to govern, to civilise or to colonise. In the meantime British missionaries and traders had opened up the country; British protection had been extended to the people of Lobengula in Matabeleland and Mashonaland and to the Kololo. On 2 January 1890 he warned again that the British would not tolerate any Portuguese expansion into their dominions on the Shire and the Nyasa. These places were under British protection. Towards the end of that year a number of British ships were alerted in the Atlantic and the Indian Oceans. War between Britain and Portugal seemed imminent.

There was no doubt as to who would give in. The Portuguese ordered their forces to withdraw south of the Ruo and from Mashonaland in January 1890. What followed this was a year-long period of negotiations before the final Anglo-Portuguese treaty was signed on 11 June 1891. The confluence of the Shire and the Ruo became the

[1] *Accounts and Papers*, 1890, 51, p. 283.   [2] *ibid.*, p. 285.

dividing line between the British and Portuguese territories in southern Malawi. The Portuguese lost any territory they hoped to acquire north of it; the Kololo lost theirs south of it. The treaty marked the end of an epoch for Portugal; it marked the beginning of an epoch of British Protectorate rule in Nyasaland which officially began a month before this treaty was signed.

When all the issues involved in this Anglo-Portuguese conflict are considered and weighed one cannot disagree with the judgement of the Kololo chiefs Masea and Katunga: the struggle was one between white people; the blacks were pawns in the game.

CHAPTER 5

The British in Malawi

i THE ADVENT AND ORGANISATION OF BRITISH ADMINISTRATION

There were three steps by which the British Government announced a protectorate over different parts of Malawi. On 19 August 1889, John Buchanan, Acting British Consul, wrote to Serpa Pinto, leader of the Portuguese expedition to Malawi, telling him that the Kololo living north of the Ruo River were placed under British protection. When the Portuguese insisted on rejecting this claim, the British took the second step when Buchanan declared a British protectorate over a wider area which he described as 'Makololo, Yao and Machinga Countries'. This was on 21 September 1889. The third step was taken on 14 May 1891 when the territories adjoining Lake Malawi were added to the regions adjoining the Shire River.

The first Commissioner and Consul-General, Harry Hamilton Johnston, arrived at Chiromo in July 1891. He and his staff travelled up the Zambezi and the Shire Rivers in two gunboats (H.M.S. *Herald* and H.M.S. *Mosquito*) which were placed on these rivers by the British Government. Johnston was himself not new to the country. He had already visited it in 1889 and 1890 as Consul at Mozambique. On these occasions, as in 1891, the head of his African staff was Ali Kiongwe whom he had engaged at Zanzibar years before. His European staff in the first days of Protectorate rule was made up of three persons: Lieut. Sclater of the Royal Engineers, Alexander Whyte (a botanist, collector and natural historian) and Captain Cecil Maguire of the Indian army.

For the purpose of keeping law and order in the country, Captain Maguire recruited seventy volunteers from the Indian army. Of this number, forty were Sikhs and thirty were Muslim cavalrymen. Most of the horses died because of the tsetse and the cavalry force had, therefore, to be returned to India. The Indian soldiers came initially for a two-year period. When the first period was up, Johnston asked that a new batch be recruited. This time the number was increased to two hundred.

Harry Johnston was given four main instructions to carry out: firstly, to strengthen the Protectorate; secondly, to advise the chiefs on their relations with each other as well as with foreigners; thirdly, to secure peace and good order and lastly, to check the slave trade.

To carry out his instructions he needed men and money, both of which were difficult to come by. Having started off with a staff of three Europeans and twenty Africans and a little over a hundred soldiers all told in the first days of his administration, Johnston could do little more than add a few more as the months went by. There was a good reason for this and that was shortage of funds. The only money provided by the British Treasury was the salaries of the British officials. The rest had to come from elsewhere. Cecil John Rhodes had promised that his company would provide £10,000 a year when the question of Protectorate rule was first considered in 1889. In actual fact the subsidy provided by Rhodes' company up to 1 July 1895 was about £17,500 annually.

Why was Cecil John Rhodes ploughing so much money into Nyasaland? He had his eye initially on the economic exploitation of the country. In 1889 his company bought off £20,000 worth of shares in the A.L.C.; four years later it swallowed up the A.L.C., buying off its liabilities and assets, one of the biggest of which was its considerable land holdings in Malawi—an issue we shall consider later. What Rhodes wanted after 1893 was preferential treatment for his company. He informed Johnston about this in the following words: 'for the future it must be understood that the Chartered Company alone has the right to acquire, subject to the approval of Her Majesty's Government, concessions of land and minerals both within and without the protectorate.'

It was to Johnston's credit that he did not concede this without prescribing certain safeguards: he insisted that the Administration should have enough lands for expansion; that Africans should be paid a fair price for their lands; that their lands were not to be sold to Rhodes' company without the consent of the African inhabitants, and that all disputes would be settled by Johnston himself.

The reason why Johnston did not place Nyasaland in the lap of Cecil Rhodes and his chartered company was not because of his own policy but because of the protests of the planters and the missionaries. They did not want another Rhodesia in Nyasaland.

82

By 1893 the land position in Nyasaland was as follows: one-fifth belonged to planters, traders and missionaries; one-fifth belonged to Rhodes' British South Africa Company; one-fifth belonged to the British Crown, and the final two-fifths belonged to the Africans. What Rhodes wanted was the opportunity of buying off the one-fifth share belonging to the Crown as well as the two-fifths of the African inhabitants. If he had succeeded, Africans in Malawi would all have become tenants on their own lands, a frightening prospect.

This country was first called the Nyasaland districts, then British Central Africa Protectorate and in 1907 the Nyasaland Protectorate, and interest in it developed rapidly. In 1891 there were 57 Europeans in the country. When Johnston left in 1896, the number had increased to 300. In 1891, the export trade was valued at just under £40,000. In 1896 it was just over £102,000. From four steamers on the rivers in 1891, the number increased to seventeen in 1896. In 1891 there was about one mile of road in the whole country over which a vehicle could be driven: that was between the Blantyre Mission and the African Lakes Company stores at Mandala. By the end of 1896, 390 miles of road had been constructed for vehicles. In 1891, 1,600 acres of land were being cultivated by Europeans; in 1896 it had risen to 5,700.

All this means that the early Administration had got off to a reasonable start within five years. Many things happened: wars were fought to bring the resisting tribes under British rule; lands were sold; taxation was introduced; a customs office was set up; a postal service was introduced. There were six main sources of revenue: postage; hut tax; customs; licences, stamp duties and sale of Crown lands.

The form of government introduced between 1891 and 1896 may be described as direct rule. There was a central administration headed by the Commissioner and Consul-General who was assisted by a Deputy Commissioner and Consuls; after that came Vice-Consuls, followed by a number of administrative officials including a Secretary to the Administration, a judicial officer. There were also a postmaster-general, a medical officer and twelve District Collectors, one each for the twelve districts formed in 1896.

The most important officials were undoubtedly the Collectors. Most of them had what were called 'judicial warrants' and could thereby hold courts as magistrates. There were two kinds of courts: one for non-Africans and the other for Africans. The latter were presided over either by those African chiefs who were authorised to do so by European judicial officers who were deemed to be functioning as substitutes for the African chiefs. These officials were usually the Collectors, whose other duties were to collect customs duties and hut taxes, to act as policemen and magistrates, and to supervise the administration of justice among the African people. In all civil matters, the Collector was the highest official in his district. When one considers the manifold nature of their duties, their youth and inexperience when first coming out to Africa, one cannot but marvel at the fact that the system worked at all.

Capital punishment could only be carried out on Europeans after the minutes of the trial had been submitted to the Supreme Court which was then in Cape Town. Capital punishment on Africans tried in the African courts could only be carried out after the minutes of the trial had been submitted to the head of the administration in Zomba.

Until 1907, the head of the administration of the British Central Africa Protectorate was the Commissioner and Consul-General. The first was Harry Johnston; the second was Alfred Sharpe. There was no parliament.

The first parliament in the country came into existence in 1907 by the Nyasaland Order in Council of that year. Now there was to be for the first time an Executive Council and a Legislative Council. The Executive Council was to be made up of the Government Secretary, the Treasurer and the Attorney-General, as *ex-officio* members. The Chairman, now styled the Governor and Commander-in-chief, was the head of the Administration. Nyasaland's first Governor was Sir Alfred Sharpe.

The Legislative Council was made up of the Governor, the three *ex-officio* members of the Executive Council together with three nominated members who were not government officials. These nominated members, who until 1949 were all European members, were usually drawn from among the planters, traders and missionaries. African interests were deemed to be represented by the missionary members. The first such member was the Rev. Alexander Hetherwick of the Blantyre Mission. Missionaries have played an important part in the history of the Legislative Councils of Malawi. They took their tasks seriously as mouth-pieces of the voiceless Africans. From early days they complained of the burden of the hut tax; they spoke against the law permitting labour migration from the country; they drew attention to the evils of the *Thangata* system on private estates; they protested against the excessive sale of African lands. They were not always understood by Johnston and his administrators. Their motives were often questioned. Johnston called them a group of unofficial opposition members and even once advised that two of the leading members of the Blantyre Mission should be deported. They were too much of a nuisance to him.

Johnston and his successors should not be held wholly blameworthy for the defects in their administrations. They were, after all, only agents of a government which was not prepared to spend much money in the country in any case. A few officials were called upon to do far more than their time or qualifications allowed. For example, by 1896 law, order and defence were left in the hands of 1,300 persons, of whom 1,100 were Malawians. Revenue was collected by twenty-seven officials; communications throughout the country were left to four officers who were expected to find what help they could. If the early Administration had shortcomings, these were due more to the parsimony of the British Government than to the apathy of the local man in charge. Of Harry Johnston a contemporary remarked: 'If he did not satisfy everyone, he left good administrative results behind him.'[1]

ii NINETEENTH-CENTURY MISSIONARY ENTERPRISE

During the second half of the nineteenth century many groups of people entered Malawi, for example the Swahili Arabs, the Yao, the Ngoni and the European missionaries. Of these four groups the only one we have not considered as yet are the missionaries.

The first mission station to be set up in Malawi was that of the Universities' Mission to Central Africa, more popularly known as the U.M.C.A. The site chosen for it was near the Magomero stream not far from where the Nasawa Young Pioneer base stands today. The first camp was set up in 1861 under Bishop Mackenzie. The area was not a healthy one. Why, then, was it chosen? One reason given at the time was that it was on the slave-trading route. This would enable the missionaries to help in the fight to abolish this dreadful trade in human beings. Another reason was because the missionaries wanted to keep close to the lake in case they had to look for a northern outlet and inlet, since it was not clear whether the Portuguese would allow them to use the Zambezi waterway. In addition, the attitudes of African chiefs like Tengani and Mankhokwe were not clear. The Anglican missionaries sought to keep their options open, to be almost equidistant between the port of Katunga's in Chikwawa and the lake.

This ill-fated mission survived at Magomero for two years, then shifted its camp to the highlands of the lower Shire where it was not welcomed by the African chiefs. The founding bishop and a number of his co-founders died and the new bishop, William Tozer, led his

[1] J. Stewart, *Dawn in the Dark Continent*, London, 1903, p. 238.

mission to Zanzibar in 1864. Livingstone's dream that Christianity and commerce would combine to introduce civilisation was shattered during his own lifetime and virtually before his own eyes. He regretted Bishop Tozer's decision, even to the extent of calling it an act of cowardice. The verdict of history leans more in support of Bishop Tozer. European missionaries had not yet found the answer to the dangers of malaria and dysentery; the shortage of food and medical supplies, and the problems of participation in African politics, especially their alliance with the Mang'anja against the Yao slave traders. They had yet to learn that friendly persuasion was more effective than the gun; that it was more desirable for the foreigners to be neutral than to take sides; that African missionaries would be more effective agents of evangelisation in the long run. For these reasons the U.M.C.A. shifted to Zanzibar, not to run away from the difficulties and challenges of mission work but to recuperate from the tragedies and to learn from the mistakes of the first experiment. The history of the first three years of the U.M.C.A. in Malawi lies not so much in what it achieved but in what it failed to achieve. The mistakes made as the pioneering mission were to be helpful to others as well as themselves in later years.

The U.M.C.A. never abandoned Malawi permanently, and from its base in Zanzibar it planned its return. Among the many missionaries who tried to find a suitable locality in Mozambique territory and eventually in Malawi, the names of Chauncey Maples and William Percival Johnson stand out. It was Johnson who finally saw that if the U.M.C.A. had to return to Malawi, it should have a steamer of its own to serve the lake area. The steamer would serve to link the mission stations on the east of the lake; it would provide means of contact with the west side of the lake; it could act as a floating training college for teachers for the various stations. Thus it was that in August 1885 Likoma Island was chosen to be the headquarters of the U.M.C.A. mission station to serve the lake area. A month later on 17 September the first steamer of the mission, the *Charles Janson*, was launched at Matope, where it had been assembled. Ten years later the mission started its first station on the west of the lake at Nkhota Kota. Over thirty years after making its first appearance on Malawi soil the U.M.C.A. was back, this time to stay permanently.

One of the lessons that the mission had learnt during its first years in Malawi in the 1860s was that if it hoped to succeed in its work it had to involve Africans actively at an early date. When the first school started at Likoma Island, the mission depended entirely on African teachers from Zanzibar for all the school work excluding Scripture and singing. A boarding school for boys was started. The first European

86

schoolmaster at Likoma was only appointed after eight years, that is in 1893. The average number of boys in attendance during the first few years was forty, drawn mainly from the east of the lake extending as far as Monkey Bay and Nkope to the south. One pupil came from as far away as Liwonde. Some of them were sent to Zanzibar for further schooling and on their return joined the mission as teachers and evangelists. During the first ten years Swahili was the chief medium of instruction; English and Chinyanja were used less. The first batch, in 1885, of African teachers who left Zanzibar for service with the U.M.-C.A. in Malawi and the lake region was six in number. The party was delayed at Nsanje for over a month because the lower Shire was in a state of upheaval following the quarrel between a European trader named Fenwick and a Kololo chief named Chipatula. At last the party moved on to Matope, where they embarked on the *Charles Janson* for its first trip from Matope to Likoma Island. This was a most historic occasion for several reasons.

One of their number, Augustine Ambali, who went on to become an ordained minister of the U.M.C.A., recalled the experience of the first teachers in the following words:

When we started school we had not anything to teach the boys with, no A.B.C. cards, no book of any kind, and we took to writing A.B.C. cards, on the skin of a goat, and we cut out letters in an old paper and pasted them on pieces of a box which we had pulled to pieces and we had some numerals, too; and we had no house to make school in and we taught the boys under the trees.[1]

The same may be said for the first U.M.C.A. school to open at Nkhota Kota in March 1895. There was no school building or shelter for preaching when the first batch of boys and girls, about one hundred in number, gathered to attend the first classes. Four years later the first boarding school for girls—a most enlightened development for the nineteenth century—was started at Nkhota Kota. Likoma Island had led the way by starting the first girls' boarding school in 1896.

Before the nineteenth century was out the U.M.C.A. had a whole number of schools in the east, the west and on the lake itself. When St Michael's College was founded on 29 September 1899 it represented one of the greatest achievements of the U.M.C.A.

Though education and evangelisation are more properly developments of twentieth-century Malawi, the beginning made in the nineteenth century by the U.M.C.A., in spite of all the initial setbacks, was a most significant one and in many ways vindicated the policy of Bishop

[1] *Central Africa*, 401, May 1916, p. 135.

Tozer of 1864 to withdraw from the scene of battle in order to live to continue the fight another day.

Five other missions also had their permanent beginnings in the nineteenth century. They were the Livingstonia Mission of the Free Church of Scotland (1875), the Blantyre Mission of the Established Church of Scotland (1876), the Dutch Reformed Church Mission (1889), the Zambezi Industrial Mission and the Nyasa Baptist Industrial Mission (1892). These were all Protestant missions. Permanent Catholic missions only came to Malawi in the twentieth century.

Dr Livingstone had been bitterly disappointed when the U.M.C.A. shifted to Zanzibar, and so looked to the Free Church of Scotland to start a mission on the shores of Lake Malawi. Six months before his death in 1873 he wrote: 'The spirit of Missions is the spirit of our Master—the very genius of His religion. A diffusive philanthropy is Christianity itself.'[1]

Businessmen from Glasgow took the lead, followed by Edinburgh with Aberdeen and Dundee in the rear. These Scottish cities braced themselves to honour the memory of the man who had probably done more than any other Britisher to draw attention to the evils that prevailed in Central Africa. In a little less than six years £21,000 was subscribed, enough to keep the mission going for that number of years. On 12 October 1875, the *Ilala* steamed into Lake Malawi after between 700 and 1,000 Africans had carried its parts from Chikwawa to Matope, a distance of about seventy miles, where it was assembled.

Chief Mponda gave the Livingstonia Mission permission to settle anywhere on his land. The missionaries chose Cape Maclear as their temporary site because it had a good bay, was sheltered from winds, and appeared to be a healthy place quite free of mosquitoes. On a few of these points the missionaries were mistaken but the worst difficulty lay in the fact that the place was poorly inhabited for the mission to achieve what it had come out to do, namely, to preach the Gospel, to train the young to read and write and to make itself self-supporting by developing legitimate trade. With such people as a carpenter (George Johnston), an engineer and blacksmith (John Macfayden), a second engineer and blacksmith (Allan Simpson), an agriculturist (Alexander Riddell), a seaman (William Baker) and an ordained minister (Dr Robert Laws), the Livingstonia Mission was well equipped to achieve its objectives. In one area, like the U.M.C.A., it had to recruit Africans especially to do the job, and this was teaching.

A year later, in 1876, four African teachers and artisans were brought

[1] George Smith, *Livingstonia Mission of the Free Church of Scotland at Lake Nyassa: A Six-Years' History and Appeal*, Edinburgh and Glasgow, 1881.

88

out from Lovedale in the Cape Province. For varying lengths of time over the next decade William Ntusane Koyi, Mapas Ntintili, Shadrack Ngunana and Isaac Wauchope played an important part in the development of the mission's work. But the first notable Malawian to make headway was Albert Namalambe, the Mang'anja attendant of one of the sons of the Kololo chief, Ramakukan, who had come in 1876 to serve his young master. Namalambe became the first convert of the Livingstonia Mission as well as the first Malawian teacher at Cape Maclear, a role he fulfilled for many years even after the mission shifted its headquarters to Bandawe (1881).

By 1886 there were three schools—an extremely slow growth rate of one school about every four years. But in the next five years after 1886, thirty-two schools sprang up or about six every year. Again, like the U.M.C.A., the Livingstonia Mission came to see that its work could best be extended through the agency of the Africans themselves. Dr Robert Laws prepared a confidential report in 1892 in which he touched upon the cost of mission work. He wrote: 'it costs as much to send an artisan from Scotland to Livingstonia as to pay the salaries, for one year, of ten native agents at the highest rate; or of twenty and thirty of our junior teachers at lower rates as at present in force in our Mission.'[1]

The question of finance was a matter of some concern when one considers that by the end of the nineteenth century there were 80 mission schools, 209 African teachers and an average of over 7,000 pupils in attendance. The Livingstonia Mission, with headquarters now near the Khondowe stream near the top of Nyamkowa Mountain, had spread its influence and its institutions from Mwenzo in the north to Cape Maclear in the south; from Bandawe in the east to Ngoniland in the west. Before the nineteenth century expired it had produced its first African certificated teacher, Charles Domingo.

Something should be said as well about the Blantyre Mission in the nineteenth century from the date of its official establishment on 23 October 1876. Henry Henderson and Tom Bokwito did a fine job of selecting a good site on Chief Kapeni's land. The good start had a bad ending and there were many disasters in the first five years due largely to the type of instructions given to the Blantyre missionaries by their overseas committee and to the quality of the persons sent out, so that a fresh beginning had to be made. There was no ordained minister for over eighteen months at one stage. The young persons sent out were

[1] Memorandum regarding the organisation and development of the Livingstonia Mission by Robert Laws, 1892, The Livingstonia Mission Papers, 1875–1900, loaned by Professor George Shepperson.

asked to start a Scottish colony, and also to assume civil jurisdiction over the Africans, a task they performed with such enthusiasm that they were either dismissed or recalled in 1880 when reports filtered through to Scotland. It is wrong to say that missionaries of the right calibre were straining to get out to Africa to serve the Blantyre Mission. The Assembly of the Foreign Mission Committee noted a pertinent point in 1877 when it asked: 'Is it not a matter of humiliation that no one has come forth from the ordained ranks of the Church to go to Blantyre?'

Money, too, was scarce; the expenditure during the first five years almost always exceeded the revenue. Through a combination of factors, then, the first five years in the history of the Blantyre Mission were dark ones. It was only when Dr David Clement Scott arrived in 1881 to take charge that a new and bright beginning was made.

Dr Scott saw the missionary as the bearer of the Gospel as well as of modern culture, by which he did not mean purely European culture but modern in the context of a worldwide standard. His head office had instructed him to promote religious work only and to ignore commerce and the related areas of education, technical training and development of trade. Scott favoured an 'industrial' civilising mission because such a programme would strengthen African culture.

From the outset Scott preferred to work with African evangelists rather than with European missionaries. Three Africans became his ardent colleagues: Joseph Bismarck, Rondau Kaferanjila and Donald Malota. In the course of time to these were added others whom he selected for further education at Lovedale in South Africa or in Scotland. In 1894 there were seven, all of whom were ordained deacons. These included Thomas Masea, Harry Matecheta and John Gray Kufa, who were all destined to play important roles in later years. His colleagues and planters did not favour this development or alliance as they called it. Charges were levelled against Scott. Even the *Central African Planter*, founded in 1896, criticised him for working so closely with the deacons. 'The fact is,' it wrote in April 1896, 'no native can, or will for years to come, be able to fulfil even in a moderate degree, the place of a European.'

Scott did not agree. His view on all this was clearly expressed in a report of 1894: 'We are true to our responsibilities, both as regards those who send us, whether that be the standards of our Church or those unwritten laws of love and faith of the people, and as regards those to whom we are sent. We only ask for the Liberty necessary for the fulfilment of responsibilities.'

A Commission of Enquiry was set up into Scott's conduct of the business of the Blantyre Mission. Though found 'not guilty' of the charges levelled, for instance concerning his policy towards African colleagues, there were overtones of censure as *The Scotsman* pointed out. 'Not guilty; but don't do it again.'

Dr Scott resigned his post for health reasons in 1898 but his term of office showed how difficult it was for a radical missionary to win support in the nineteenth century. One other such radical was Joseph Booth who came to Malawi in 1892 and founded the Zambezi Industrial Mission and the Nyasa Baptist Industrial Mission, as well as a number of other missions in later years. At Mitsidi he took to coffee cultivation, an enterprise in which he involved African cultivators so that they could better themselves economically. He insisted that Africa should be held in trust for the Africans; that Africans should uplift themselves through the formation of a union of African Christians.

By April 1893, 35,000 acres of land were under cultivation in the two missions he had started; a million coffee plants had been put in. His labourers were paid four shillings and sixpence per month in calico while other employers paid an average of three shillings per month. At one time between four and five thousand labourers hailing from a number of tribes worked on his mission lands, the idea being to submerge group loyalty to a larger African loyalty.

Other European missionaries as well as the government suspected Booth's motives. The former complained that he was drawing away their converts and their labourers; the latter that he was subverting the government by advocating his 'Africa for the Africans' programme.

What annoyed Booth was that many of his own people held very narrow views on the African. For instance he cited a letter from a European planter in Natal which was published in the *Natal Advertiser* on 5 September 1896:

> My experience of natives convinces me they are a bad lot. They must be kept down with a strong hand. Attempts to Christianize them have proved worse than useless. The school Kaffir almost invariably turns out a blackguard. Our legislature ought to reassert the right of every white man to whollop his own nigger. I would not now give a single penny to the cause of missions.[1]

Booth countered that his African policy was that Africans should run their own missions under European supervision; that educated Africans should be allowed to hold equal positions; that a training institute should be set up to prepare them for their positions. The point

[1] Joseph Booth, *Africa for the Africans*, Baltimore, 1897, p. 35.

Booth stressed was that the African was inferior in opportunity only.

In his nineteenth-century radicalism and optimism, Joseph Booth anticipated the arguments that were to be submitted by Africans themselves in the early years of the twentieth century. If his protégé, John Chilembwe, sounded the loudest cry, it was by no means the only cry on the mission fields. Mission enterprise in Malawi in the nineteenth century was in many ways more formative than in the twentieth not only because problems were identified but because future lines of development were thought out, thus enabling the twentieth century to complete the work that was begun in the nineteenth.

One mission must be singled out for its emphasis on rural development, since all the others considered the priority to be educating people to assume new roles in the schools, in the workshops, in the hospitals, in the civil service and in the churches. This unique mission was the Dutch Reformed Church Mission which opened at Mvera in 1889 from where it expanded to Kongwe, Nkhoma, Mchinji and into eastern Zambia. It stressed the need to set up village industries and to promote agriculture. When a visiting commission, the Phelps-Stokes Commission, came to the country in 1924 it noted that this mission led the others in promoting village industries.

Instead of elaborate woodwork shops and . . . industries, which almost compels the Native to practise his craft in European employment, the work at Nkhoma is planned to fit the men and women to become home workers. Nowhere in Nyasaland has the Commission seen a finer exhibit of home industries. Here were specimens of wood and iron work, bark cloth, wool and linen—weaving, basket and mat work of at least twenty kinds; leather work, including bootmaking, sandal and harness making, the treatment of the skins of animals, soap and oil making, bricks and tiles, machine and hand sewing, and many other kinds of village industry.

Not that the other missions ignored village industry. They did not stress it to the same extent as did the Dutch Reformed Church Mission. The reason for this lies largely in the background of these missionaries and the ideologies which prompted their work.

Thus in nineteenth-century Malawi there were six European missions which introduced and expanded their work in the interest of uplifting the people of Malawi. Their basic concern in general was school education and the teachings of Christianity. Beyond this they differed in their emphasis and their outlook to marked degrees. The objective was one but the ways of achieving it were many and varied.

The African response to mission education was to be left to the twentieth century.

Since the name of Joseph Booth comes up again and again in early mission history in Malawi, some additional information on him will not be out of place. He was born in England in 1851 of humble parentage. At the age of twenty-six he migrated to Australia where he did sheep farming for about ten years. Towards the end of this period he began preaching the Gospel to atheists and sceptics and became committed to spreading the teachings of Christ. It was to do this that he came to the then Nyasaland in August 1892 accompanied only by a nine-year-old daughter. This little girl, Emily Booth, wrote a book fifty-eight years later called *This Africa was Mine*, in which she describes her experiences. This excerpt recounting the sort of thing that happened during her early days in the country is taken from it:

> Father was despairing of ever being able to find a dependable boy, when out of heaven's blue the right boy came to find us. His name was John. He was a very black boy with very white teeth and a gleaming smile. John's English was limited. But at a mission school somewhere, he had learned to speak and to write a few English words. On a scrap of paper he brought to Father a pencilled note . . . 'Dear Mr Booth', the note read, 'you please carry me for God. I like to be your cook-boy.' Thus did our dear black boy John come into our lives. . . . He was so kind and true—so thoughtful and unselfish. . . . John had come to us of his own choice. He had heard of Father as being a kind, white man and he had heard of our need for a house-boy. He came to give help as well as to receive it.[1]

The boy referred to was, of course, the famous John Chilembwe whom Joseph Booth was to take to the United States in 1897.

By any standard, Joseph Booth was a friend of the Africans—as he was of mankind as such. His concern for his fellow men, especially the Africans with whom he was now thrust, gained tremendously by his association with John Chilembwe as it did from a whole host of personal experiences. From Booth's own writing we get some idea of what he felt about his early experience of African understanding. He reached Mitsidi towards the end of 1892. Here he was to establish the Zambezi Industrial Mission in the valley of the Michiru Mountain, a scene he described as one of 'imposing majestic grandeur—the silent guardian of the scene before us'.

Booth wrote of his arrival:

[1] Emily Booth Langworthy, *This Africa was Mine*, Stirling, 1950, pp. 39–41.

In or about the close of the year 1892 I reached this spot, weary, sickly and weak. My little daughter was with me. A great tree stood where the house now stands. A drenching rain was falling. Several Angoni men were sheltering under a grass roof they had constructed on the boughs of that tree. They had made a fire there and were crouching round to keep warm. . . . Yet these men out of their good nature got up instantly and insisted that myself and little child should sit round the fire while they stood round close to the trunk of the tree in the rain to get what shelter they could.[1]

This was Booth's initiation to missionary work. It does emphasise the uniqueness of missionary experience that contributed to a variety of responses.

[1] Joseph Booth, *op. cit.*, pp. 6–9.

CHAPTER 6

Land policies in Malawi

i TRADITIONAL LAND PRACTICE

Land in Malawi may be defined today as customary land, public land and freehold land. Of these three kinds of lands, customary land accounts for just over 86 per cent of all the land in the country. The President of Malawi is the trustee of all customary land but its distribution and inheritance are regulated by traditional custom.

Next in size to customary land is public land which accounts for nearly 12 per cent of the land space. This land is used or set aside by the government for certain buildings or projects or for future development plans.

The third category of land is the smallest. This is freehold land or land which is held in private ownership, and today it covers just over 2 per cent of the land area. But this was not always the case in the colonial days; nor was land always defined in this country as customary, public and freehold. Customary land was first described as traditional land and after 1936 as Trust land. Public land was referred to as Crown land in the colonial days.

Land has always featured as the most important single attraction in colonial affairs. Sometimes it was the situation of the land which attracted attention; at other times it was the wealth of the land, either agricultural or mineral or both. Since land generates wealth and wealth generates conflict, land forms the basis for both competition and conflict. The history of land policies in Malawi clearly shows that much of the history of this agricultural country was really the history of land matters, complicated by different concepts of land occupation. In Europe, for example, private ownership confers on the title holder the right to consider and to use the land as his private property, combined with the right to sell or lease his property as he wishes.

In African society, according to customary law, the land does not belong to an individual or group as such. It is there as a gift of the gods to occupy and to cultivate under certain conditions. It is not ownership but useful occupation that is the guiding principle.

In traditional African society the smallest political unit in respect of land distribution was the village. Here the central position was occupied by the village headman among whose duties it was to allocate land and to settle land disputes. The headman was not the 'owner of the land' (the *mwini wa dziko*). He was merely the warden. When an area of land was first occupied by a settlement group from outside, as was the case when the Karonga of the Chewa tribe brought his people to settle in Malawi, the leader would look upon the unoccupied lands as places where he and his subjects could settle. He would then distribute land for settlement among his important relatives or kinsmen. The relatives would in turn pay tribute to the founding leader or chief. Thus *mtulo* (tribute) was paid or given to the one higher up whose generosity made land available for settlement. The tribute was given in various forms: sometimes in foodstuff, other times in services like working in a chief's garden. Material gifts such as ivory or the skins of leopards and lions were also given. Thus land was given out or occupied under a system of rights and obligations. The recipient had the right to cultivate the land and enjoy its fruits, in return for which he paid tribute in material goods, in services and in his loyalty to the chief. The chief had the obligation to arrange for the peace, prosperity and abundance of his subjects.

The distribution of land either at the level of the chief or of the village headman was a systematic affair. In Chewa society, for example, the chief had a number of advisers called the *amulumuzana a fumu*, selected by himself. In land disputes the chiefs called in their village headmen (the *aphungu a fumu*) who in turn sought the assistance of lesser headmen.

Land allocation was a serious business. Ownership according to the western concept was not vested in the chief or in his subordinates. Instead of ownership one should in fact substitute the term guardianship or trusteeship. Instead of individual or communal rights one should speak of rights deriving from occupation and cultivation of land. For as long as land was occupied and tilled it could not be taken away. But if the occupier left his land permanently or abandoned it he could not claim any rights over it on his return.

In short, land was a sacred unit of traditional life. The dead chiefs had an interest in it, the living chiefs had an interest in it; the occupants had an interest in it and the unborn generations had an interest in it.

Where the interests ranged over so wide and continuous a circle, it was untraditional and improper for anyone to disturb the cyclic pattern. The idea of selling land according to western concepts was not part of traditional society. In any case, no one had the right to sell what did not belong to him. The granting of land for occupation and cultivation was different from the practice of selling land for private or personal gain.

When Europeans entered Malawi from 1875 onwards to do mission work or to trade, the whole business of land guardianship and occupation was altered because of the conflict of cultures. Missionaries, traders and companies competed with one another for traditional lands. Various means were used to obtain it. Various explanations were given too. When trade goods or calico or beads, copper wire or trinkets passed hands, and the chiefs received them, it is inconceivable that the chiefs realised that the newcomers would hold on to the land as their permanent and private property, since the concept of permanent and private property did not exist. It could not be understood overnight with the sudden influx of foreigners.

Whatever explanations were given and whatever goods were handed over for the right to occupy certain lands, these dealings were reduced to treaties by the Europeans. The treaties with missionaries did not cause trouble, for the missionaries who obtained lands from Mponda or Kapeni or the Jumbe of Nkhota Kota or from anyone else, did not do so to exploit the land for private profit. With the traders and planters it was different, since they obtained considerable quantities of land.

The African Lakes Corporation, for example, founded in 1878, obtained a grant of land from Chief Kapeni of about seven thousand acres. Of course, boundaries were not defined with any exactness beyond that of listing natural landmarks. This was but one of many tracts of land it was to obtain throughout the country, some of which were later approved by the British Administration while others were refused.

The first individual to obtain a large grant in Blantyre was John Buchanan who had come out to work for the Blantyre Mission in 1876 but who, after some trouble with the mission authorities five years later, branched off into private enterprise. He obtained 3,065 acres in Michiru for a gun, thirty two yards of calico, two red caps and several small items of that sort. A Pole by the name of Steblecki obtained 2,701 acres in present Limbe while a hunter called Harry Edwin Pettitt got some 80,000 acres in Thyolo which today covers almost all of the tea estates in the Thyolo area.

These acquisitions introduced a new element in land occupation. When British rule was extended to Malawi in 1891 the deals had to be investigated. At the same time the British Government was interested in gaining its own foothold in the country. The easiest way to achieve this was by entering into the treaty race itself to keep out other European powers as well as to obtain land concessions from chiefs. With the exception of one treaty only (that with Chief Chipoka in the Ruo River area) these British Government treaties were of two kinds: the first, numbering sixty-three, were those of friendship only; the second set, of which there were eighteen, were definitely worded in such a way as to grant land rights to the British Crown, but these covered a very small part of the country. Most of the Malawi chiefs, that is those who entered into the sixty-three other treaties, did not cede land rights to the British Government at first.

The coming of Protectorate rule brought many complications in land matters. Questions such as these had to be asked. Did the chiefs understand what they were doing in their dealings with individual traders, companies, hunters or even with the British Administration? To what extent were the original treaties valid? What would happen if the original European treaty holders quarrelled among themselves over land matters? What would happen if the chiefs disputed the land claims at a later stage? Who would be the judge in the disputes and how was one to say who was right and who was wrong?

The African Lakes Company made a proposal in June 1891. It had been forced, it said, to enter into treaties with African chiefs in 1885 in a hurried attempt to keep the Portuguese out. In these treaties it had forestalled everyone else by being the first to take action. Since its action had saved Nyasaland for the British, the company should be rewarded. But since the chiefs, through ignorance, had entered into other treaties without the company's knowledge or approval, the company would now refund to the chiefs half the purchase price of the lands so obtained from them in the treaties of 1885. If the British Government had accepted this fantastic proposal it would in fact have recognised the African Lakes Company as the paramount chief over all other Malawian chiefs. The missionaries, naturally, opposed this ridiculous claim and the Government rejected it.

The Government had to find a solution of its own which would be fair to all the parties concerned. With the coming of Europeans land laws were changed. Traditional practice had to accommodate western ideas. The biggest single problem facing the administration of Harry Johnston was how to merge the concepts of Europe and Africa.

ii EARLY LAND POLICIES OF THE PROTECTORATE
GOVERNMENT

When Harry Johnston took over the administration of the then Nyasaland, the country had over twenty-five million acres of land. Some of
this, as we have already seen, was now owned by Europeans who
claimed to have bought their lands from African chiefs. Johnston was
not sure whether the lands so obtained were justly and honestly acquired. He thus set about examining each purchase and used five
principles to guide him in the difficult exercise of establishing whether
a so-called purchase was genuine or not. These were as follows: the
rights of Africans in their own country should be protected; the
existing villages and plantations created by Africans before the land
was 'sold' should remain undisturbed even after the sale; there should
be sufficient space available for the existing villages and plantations to
expand; acquiring land for speculation purposes was to be discouraged;
and finally, the Protectorate Government should have sufficient Crown
lands of its own in order to develop the country.

Armed with these five guiding principles, Johnston and two of his
senior officials set about examining each land claim. The British Government now assumed the position of being the only authority in the
country who could sanction the sale of lands. Any land sale entered into
before 1891 would only be validated if Johnston approved of it. They
visited the actual sites and had to satisfy themselves that six important
points were met before they could approve of the sale. These were as
follows. Did the seller have the right to sell? Was there more than one
valid claim to the same land? Did the seller understand what he was
doing and did he receive fair value for his land? Were the interests of
the British Government safeguarded in the treaties of sale? Was it clear
that existing villages and plantations were not being disturbed? Were
the boundaries stated in the treaties the same as those of the land now
deemed to be bought?

It stands to the credit of Harry Johnston that he did set out in a
determined and fair way to examine all claims. The task was a very
difficult one. It took over two years to examine every claim. Some of
them he approved as they stood; a few he rejected outright, while
others were reduced in size. One claim in Mulanje submitted by an
individual planter was reduced from 44,000 acres to 4,000 acres. Another claim submitted by a trading company to a large part of a district
which it claimed to have bought for the equivalent of £5 in cash was
rejected. A third claim, the largest in the country, covering all lands
between the South Rukuru River where it enters the lake at Mlowe and

the Songwe River in the north, was granted to the African Lakes Company who later transferred it to the British South Africa Company. This tremendous grant covering almost the whole of the present northern region contained 2¾ million acres of land, which remained the property of the British South Africa Company until 1936 when the land was given up to the Nyasaland Government in return for sole mineral rights in the area. It was only on 1 July 1966 that the company finally gave up to the Malawi Government its mineral rights as well.

By 1894 Johnston had approved sixty-nine land claims. The total extent of land involved was about 3¾ million acres or about 15 per cent of the land area of Malawi. Thus, in the first three years of British rule in Malawi, the Government agreed to allow 15 per cent of the land in the country to belong mostly to Europeans. For each approved claim a title deed was issued, called a certificate of claim. One clause which appeared in all the certificates of claim was called the non-disturbance clause. It stated that no existing villages or plantations should be disturbed or removed without the permission of the Commissioner and that no new villages or plantations should be set up without the consent of the landowner.

Let us examine what all this meant in actual practice for the thousands of people who happened to be living on lands which were sold to Europeans. Those persons who were actually living on the lands at the time they were sold were allowed by law to live on as before without having to pay any rent to the new landowner, but they were to remain in the same villages. New villages could only be started if the owner agreed. The biggest weakness in the arrangement was that no one counted the number of people who were allowed by law to live freely on the land. This could certainly have been done at the time and much trouble would have been avoided. Because this was not done and no figures were kept it was difficult to prove who could live free and who could not.

This oversight played into the hands of the landowners. As time passed the original occupants of villages were forgotten; some moved off to new villages; others died and their descendants could not be identified. Newcomers from Mozambique, chiefly the Lomwe, arrived; husbands joined their wives on the villages which were exempt and soon old and new became confused; those exempt from rent and those liable for rent lived and worked side by side. The non-disturbance clause became a dead letter.

The easiest way out for the landowners was to charge everyone rent. Of course, the landowners were not in need of tenants who paid rent

H.H. Johnston's first land settlement, 1893 (adapted from original)

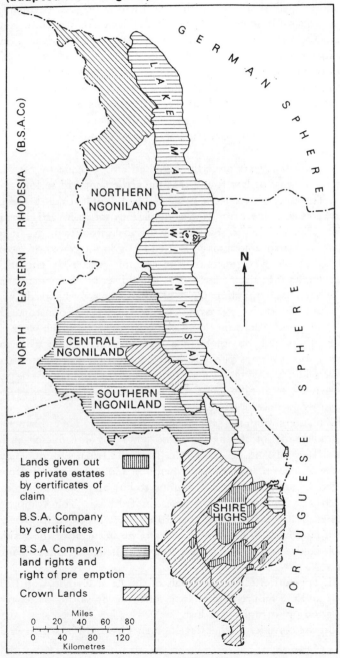

in cash. They were interested in tenants who would pay their rent in labour, that is *Thangata*.

This was against the law with regard to the original occupants of villages and their descendants, but it was legal for newcomers. One estate manager demanded rent from everyone in the form of two months' work in the rainy season and the matter was taken to court. Judge Nunan ruled that it was illegal to charge rent in the case of the original occupants; it was wrong, too, the judge argued, to say that the original occupants should have stuck to their old gardens and villages. They needed room to practise shifting agriculture. They needed something like eight acres per hut for subsistence farming and for future expansion.

Thus only ten years after the land settlement made by Sir Harry Johnston a court of law found that the settlement had serious weaknesses. Those who were to be protected had now lost that protection. In the years to come many land commissions sat to investigate problems, most of which went back to the original mistakes made. In 1903, 1920, 1946 and 1952 commissions tried to undo the errors of the past. Their proposals were various. For example, the 1903 commission recommended that all private estates should set aside one-tenth of all undeveloped land totalling eight hundred acres or upwards within three miles of Zomba, Blantyre, Chiromo and Fort Johnston. These were to be divided into blocks of eighty acres each, which were to be further subdivided into plots of eight acres each; these were to be rented at four shillings per plot. This commission also found that far too much land was lying idle and recommended a land tax of one penny or more per acre on all undeveloped land in excess of ten undeveloped acres for every developed acre.

The planters opposed the recommendations. They blamed the Government for interfering with land tenure by introducing an individual system of land occupation in place of a tribal system. They argued that they were in competition with the Government and also with educated Africans who were beginning to buy up plots ranging in size between fifty and a hundred acres in freehold. The compromise suggested by the planters was that if they were prepared to give eight acres of land each to heads of families of 20 per cent of the residents on their lands, they should be free to exact Thangata from 80 per cent of the rest.

Their opposition to the proposals of the Land Commission Report of 1903 and the failure of the Government to press the matter meant that a good opportunity was lost.

Before we consider further developments it would be worth while to consider one of the criticisms made by Judge Nunan: that there was too much undeveloped land in the country and that it should be taxed.

One of the strongest arguments mentioned for allowing land sales to Europeans was that such a step would lead to development of agriculture and to the opening up of export trade in such form as to bring considerable revenue to the local administration. But after fifteen years of land occupation by Europeans, statistics told a different story. Little more than 1 per cent, on average, of the vast estates were developed. One company developed only 3,000 acres out of 160,000 acres, or just under 2 per cent; another developed 5,000 acres out of 367,000 acres; while the estates which were later to be involved in the Chilembwe rising developed 500 acres out of almost 160,000 acres.

The explanation for this is not that labour was not available. There was plenty of labour. The inducements were lacking. We have figures for 1913 which show that in the Zomba district 18,000 Africans lived on private estates. They were all available for labour services at the right and proper reward. In Blantyre the number was 47,000. These figures underline the enormity of the labour resources which were right next door to the plantations. However, most of the landowners looked upon their holdings as sources of future revenue and were consequently not in a hurry to develop the country.

In addition to the difficulties of legal interpretation of rights on the lands sold, there were other aspects of the life of Africans on many of the estates. For instance, for years many of them lived under the threat of eviction if they failed to come up with labour service. Then again, life was hard on the estates. The Rev. Stephen Kundecha told the commission which enquired into the causes of the 1915 rising:

Long ago they [i.e. the Africans] all had their proper homes which they chose by themselves. These were good places of good soil, and from where they received good crops from their ordinary labour. But since the new circumstances of the new life [i.e. Kundecha's way of referring to the coming of Europeans and the sale of lands] replaced itself in the country, these old homes have been mostly deprived and they now have replaced themselves instead in the barren places they did not think before.

According to Kundecha, the best lands were now taken up. Kundecha saw other difficulties, too. When the African produced tobacco or cotton he got 1d. or 1½d. per pound for his produce compared to the 3d. which the European planters received. Wages were deferred or underpaid; hours were long; treatment of individuals was far from satisfactory.

The Rev. Harry Matecheta, another knowledgeable contemporary, told the commission what he thought about Thangata on the private estates.

The Thangata which is done in Plantations is not Thangata at all, it is compulsory labour. And the labour certificate [i.e. a document which qualified an African to pay the lower tax rate since he had worked for a European for at least one month in a year] is the same as the Thangata, a difficulty put upon the natives, the natives admit it for fear and for nothing else, they know that if they refuse they will be punished, they say this is *Nkhondo* (war), what can we do.[1]

'What can we do?' The Jackson Land Commission asked very much the same question in 1920; so did the Abraham Commission in 1946. Sir Sidney Abraham came to the root of the matter when he wrote: 'I have reached the conclusion that the only solution is the clear cut one of getting rid of the status of resident native and leaving him free to quit the estate or to stay on terms satisfactory both to himself and the landlord.' The remedy seemed simple. The trouble was that the Protectorate Government took a long time to put it into operation.

iii THE INTRODUCTION OF AFRICAN TRUST LANDS

In 1925 the East African Commission visited countries in East and Central Africa. In its report on Nyasaland it proposed a land tax of $\frac{1}{2}$d. per acre after the first 500 acres. This way it was felt that landlords would be discouraged from owning very large estates and that they would sell to the Government what was surplus to their immediate requirements. The lands so obtained could then be converted into African trust land or be sold or leased to new settlers or to progressive Africans.

Governor Sir Charles Bowring, who was in office from 1924 to 1929, did not agree with the method of taxation to re-acquire land. He felt that this would be unfair on the estate owners who had been in undisturbed possession of their lands for so many years and had paid tax on the whole of their holding. His views are contained in the following report which he submitted to the British Government in London:

If the land is required by Government it should, I consider, be acquired by direct and open action as part of a considered native affairs policy. Again I do not consider Nyasaland a suitable country for settlement by a large number of small land holders. It is in my opinion essentially a country for development by large companies.

[1] C.O. 525/66, folio 325, 9 July 1915.

... Nyasaland is not a suitable country for European colonisation where children can be brought up to take their part in the development of the country and in time to establish their homes there. Nor do I view with favour the establishment of a number of small native individual landowners on what are at present the freehold estates in the more settled Districts. The transition from communal to individual land tenure must be gradual and will require to be very carefully watched.

Governor Bowring's views are interesting. He did not believe that pressure should be brought to bear upon the estate owners to give up part of their lands. This should be done by friendly persuasion and by negotiation. He saw that the development of Nyasaland was dependent upon the contribution of large companies and felt that the time had not come to encourage small African individual land holdings.

At the time when all this was being discussed, that is around 1926, Africans who lived on private estates belonging to Europeans numbered about one-tenth of the entire African population. But this was an important tenth, living and working in the most valuable and productive parts, which involved about 15 per cent of the whole land area.

Instead of steps being taken to acquire land for African settlement, a law was introduced in 1928 by which every adult African was required to pay rent to the landlord unless he offered to work for wages. If he offered to work for wages, the landlord could give him work or a plot of land on which to grow economic crops which the landlord would then buy from him.

From whichever way one looks at the law of 1928 the advantages rested with the landlord. The only protection for the African residents was that if they failed to meet the terms of the law they were to be given six months' notice to quit the estates; these notices were to be served only once every five years and then to not more than 10 per cent of the Africans resident on any particular estate. These were very minor benefits in the whole situation. The larger problem of getting land back for settlement was not tackled. It is not to be wondered at, then, that trouble broke out on estates near Blantyre in 1943 and at Thyolo in 1945 and again in 1953.

While 10 per cent of the African population lived on 15 per cent of the land area there would continue to be troubles on estates. Today the extent of freehold land has been reduced from 15 per cent to just about 2 per cent and an old problem has been solved. But this took a long time to come about and was due more to the initiative and foresight of the independent African government than to the care and concern of the former Protectorate government. By 1960 some 500,000 acres of land had been repurchased by the Government.

Nevertheless, there is one development in land policy that stands to the credit of the Protectorate government. This was the creation of Native Trust Lands in 1936. The origin of this went back to 1913 when Governor Sir George Smith requested each District to prepare maps indicating three kinds of lands in its area: these were referred to as 'native reserves', 'Crown lands' and 'European areas' or 'private estates'. The aim was to ensure that there was sufficient land in every district for each of these three categories. Though the information was obtained no action was taken to make legal provision for these three divisions.

By 1919 it was clear that land was becoming scarce. The large companies refused to sell or lease their undeveloped land. Those lands situated within easy distance of Zomba and Blantyre were in great demand. The added attraction now was the possibility that the railway would be in close proximity and this would itself enhance the value of land. The scarcity of land drove some European applicants to ask for lands which were already marked out as reserved for Africans. In the same year the Acting Lands Officer noted that the increased shortage of land was contributing to labour migration from this country. He spoke of 'the likelihood of Africans leaving the Protectorate as they see the land gradually getting further and further under the control of private owners'.

In spite of the knowledge that this was happening and that the scarcity of land was one of the important causes of unrest in the country as well as of labour migration from the country, the Protectorate government took no active steps to remedy the position by legally proclaiming certain lands for African occupation only.

In 1933 a moment of crisis dawned. This originated in the law of 1928 in which there was a provision that up to 10 per cent of the African residents could be ordered to leave the private estates at the end of the first five-year period, that is in 1933. It now occurred to the Protectorate administration that if overnight thousands of Africans became landless and homeless there could be trouble. The Administration had now to consider what other accommodation was available for displaced persons. There were three possibilities: firstly, the displaced persons could settle rent free on nearby Crown lands; secondly, they could settle anywhere else they chose to where land was available; and, thirdly, they could join existing village communities which would soon be declared as African lands under the management of a Native Trust Board.

It was this urgency that caused the Administration to look around for lands which could be set aside to meet the crisis which was expected in 1933. In the event, the fears and panic were unfounded. There was no mass eviction of African residents on the European estates. The landowners explained that they did not wish to exercise their option to evict undesirable residents; they said that they pitied the Administration since this action would create problems for which it was not prepared. In reality, the landowners were aware of the need to keep their residents happy and on their lands so as to guarantee long-term labour and, therefore, economic prosperity.

It was only in 1936 that African trust lands were legally instituted. All lands which were not already sold or which were not Crown lands were to be reserved for Africans only. They could not be sold or leased to non-Africans except after consultation with native authorities. The Governor could bypass the native authorities if he was acting on behalf of African interests. This was not generally understood by the African people. With a painful history of land tenure behind them the African chiefs and people now assumed that the pendulum had swung in their favour with the introduction of African trust lands and that none of these lands could be alienated without the consent of the native authorities concerned. The question of who could or could not dispose of African trust lands became a bone of contention. The educated members of the African community who expressed their views in native associations and afterwards in the Nyasaland African Congress felt strongly that lands should be looked upon as belonging to the African people. They did not want the mistakes of the past repeated when chiefs had signed away African lands without realising what they were doing. Their view now was that the British Protectorate government in Nyasaland had no right to sell or lease African trust lands without African consent. When in the 1940s the government decided to set aside a portion of the African trust lands in Lilongwe for the purpose of establishing the Lilongwe Agricultural Research Station to conduct experiments in tobacco cultivation, the native authority concerned, his headmen as well as the village people affected, approved of the government proposal. The Lilongwe branch of the Nyasaland African Congress and Chief Mwase objected. Their ground for objection was not that the proposed research station would not be beneficial to the Africans but that in approving of the alienation of African trust land for this purpose, the native authority concerned had not taken the trouble to inform the ordinary people what the scheme was all about and also that the government had deemed it sufficient to deal with the native authority only. The President-General of the Nyasaland African

Congress went so far as to say that the chiefs failed to obtain public opinion before making a decision to alienate African trust land. In such a case they had no business to give their approval.

Internally there was a further difficulty in connection with the allocation of trust lands. What happened if a chief was envious of the progress planned by an African on his plot of trust land? The chief could refuse permission to allocate, or having given his permission could make life difficult for him. A land commissioner recommended in 1946 that the best way to get out of this difficulty was to make it clear that applications for the use of African trust lands could be made by Africans as well as non-Africans and that each application should be considered on its merits.

It is pertinent here to ask whether it was desirable that the occupation of African trust lands (known today as customary lands) should be on customary lines alone which recognised the use of land but not its individual ownership. While allocation and occupation on customary lines constituted an important part of the whole, it was by no means the only way to administer land. As early as 1894 Harry Johnston had reported that many progressive Africans wished to possess personal property comprising about twenty acres on which they could grow cotton and other crops. In 1920 the land commission reported on this very point in the following words:

> There is already a desire among natives for the individual ownership of land, and this is becoming stronger in proportion to their general progress. We think it is one to be in every way encouraged among those natives, comparatively few as yet, who are sufficiently advanced. We regard the individual ownership of land as one of the main starting points of the native's progress, enabling him to separate from the communal village society and to lead a life of individual responsibility. Through it we look for improvement in the methods of native agriculture and for greater economy of the soil. Fixity of tenure is the best incentive to these and is what the native greatly desires.[1]

It was in keeping with this expectation that the Malawi Government introduced new land legislation in 1967 by which customary land may be transformed into private ownership so that individuals may have a greater stake in the development of their own lands. As the smallholding agricultural schemes in tea, cotton and tobacco develop throughout the country and as the experiment of the Lilongwe Land Development Project as well as the land settlement schemes in the

[1] *Report of the Land Commission, 1920*, p. 9.

lower Shire, Salima, Kasungu and other places gets under way, a radical transformation will take place in land use and ownership. In a predominantly agricultural country land is the greatest asset. If individuals are to make their best contribution to national development the land laws of the country must make it possible for them to view this asset as a valuable and rewarding commodity.

CHAPTER 7

Economic issues in Malawi

i TAXATION AND LABOUR

The issues of taxation and labour are often confused in a consideration of the early colonial history of Malawi. There is a good reason for this. When taxation was introduced there was a shift from subsistence economy to cash or wage economy in order to earn money for the payment of the annual tax. In some cases labour laws were introduced to provide suitable conditions for the payment of taxes; in some cases employers were empowered to pay the tax on behalf of their employees and in return were entitled to exact labour payment. In some cases a lower rate of tax was payable if an African employee worked for at least one month for a European employer. All these rules and regulations were introduced at different times but the objective was the same, namely, to provide the Government with revenue to administer the country and to provide the best conditions under which European enterprise could make maximum use of the abundant labour supply in the country.

Where these two issues of taxation and labour merge it is difficult to separate them. Nevertheless, for the sake of convenience, let us begin with taxation, by which I mean tax paid annually to the state by direct means by individuals or by occupants in a residential unit like a hut, or on income earned.

When British administration got under way in 1891, finance was a big problem. Cecil John Rhodes' company, the British South Africa Company, came forward with £17,500 a year to help the Nyasaland administration. In addition, £10,000 was paid into a special fund to defeat the Yao slave dealers, mainly Makanjira. The arrangement ended as of July 1895 as a result of a dispute between Harry Johnston and

Cecil John Rhodes. Henceforth, the British Government took the place of the company in subsidising the local administration. Johnston tried hard not to depend upon outside sources of assistance, but he had no choice since there was very little money available locally.

When trying to arrive at the amount of direct tax that should be levied, Johnston took his cue from the practice of the Portuguese in the area adjoining the British sphere. The Portuguese levy ranged from six shillings to twelve shillings annually. They collected tax from every person: from men, women, and children. Johnston worked out a compromise of six shillings per adult male in 1891. This was called the poll tax. It could be paid in money, in produce, in livestock or in labour.

The six shillings poll tax on every adult male African came into effect in 1892 in all the districts between the lake and the lower Shire where chiefs had entered into treaties agreeing to pay tax. In some cases Johnston had to convert the poll tax into a hut tax where it was clear that a number of male adults living in a single hut were unable to pay the tax separately. For the purposes of taxation a fourteen-year-old was deemed to be an adult.

From the beginning the introduction of taxation gave rise to local difficulties and dissatisfaction. African chiefs complained that it was too high. The Scottish missionaries complained on various grounds: they were suspicious of the influence of the British South Africa Company which was providing so much of the revenue and they wondered whether Johnston was not manipulating local administration to suit the plans of the company. One of the Blantyre missionaries expressed his fears in the following words in a letter to his head office in Edinburgh: 'If he [i.e. Johnston] can lift ivory and taxes when and where he pleases in the interest of the British South Africa Company, we demand on behalf of the natives some independent power to watch their interests.'[1] The missionaries also objected on the point of earlier promises given. When the mad race for treaties between the Portuguese and the British had been on, British agents had made promises to African chiefs that whereas the Portuguese would tax the people, the British would not. These were the verbal promises that had not always been reduced to written form. We have documentary evidence of this in a letter written by Dr Hetherwick of the Blantyre Mission to the Rev. Archibald Scott in Edinburgh on 12 July 1892. The entire letter is devoted to taxation matters and it refers to what happened in August and September 1889 at a meeting between British representatives and African chiefs at Blantyre. Dr Hetherwick wrote:

[1] A. C. Ross, 'The African—a child or a man?', in *The Zambezian Past*, eds. E. Stokes and R. Brown, p. 338.

The chiefs were told on that occasion that the Portuguese were threatening to come up, and that they would impose heavy taxes on them in addition to other forms of oppressive government. The English, as they knew, imposed no taxes on natives. Whom would they prefer—Portuguese or English? The universal reply was, of course, that they preferred the English. On this understanding they signed a treaty agreeing to hand over their territory to no other Power without the consent of her Majesty's representative. . . . I was present when a similar treaty was made with Malemya in Zomba. The chief asked Mr Buchanan, 'Did this treaty mean taxation?' Mr Buchanan assured him that it meant no taxation, only 'friendship'. The chief thereupon appended his mark to the document.[1]

A further objection raised by the missionaries was to the manner of collecting the tax: villages were burned down if chiefs or ordinary people raised the slightest demur. In addition, tax offenders were not imprisoned but despatched to estate owners or company managers to work for a specified period. In later years tax offenders were often marched down hundreds of miles from the northern and central regions to work in the Shire Highlands.

The last objection was to the absence of consultation with the African people. In the final analysis, the missionaries were prepared to disregard the broken promises but they pleaded for a fair and manageable amount and for consultations or *mlandu*. On this latter point, the Blantyre Mission newspaper, *Life and Work*, carried the following editorial in November 1891:

> We ask too for a constitutional mode of dealing with the native life around us. We ask that the authority and influence of the native chiefs in the country be recognised and their counsel sought in dealing with the people. The African, if he is anything, is constitutional—no change or step of importance is taken without first open 'mlandu' in which the opinion of all is fully sought and expressed.

Johnston's reply to these charges was that it was incumbent on the African chiefs to arrange for a contribution towards the costs of administering the country; that is, in return for the protection that was now being accorded them; that no African chief was forced to enter into this arrangement provided he was able to manage his own internal affairs without assistance from the administration; that chiefs were paid 10 per cent of the taxes collected in their areas as a subsidy and as

[1] F.M.C. no. 13/1892, A. Hetherwick to A. Scott, Convenor of the African Sub-Committee of the Church of Scotland (National Archives, Zomba).

a recompense for loss of tribute. Three chiefs were paid more than the 10 per cent of tax collected for special reasons. The Yao chief Kanga was paid a subsidy of £40 per annum for giving up his right to levy dues on caravans passing through the Michesi mountains in Mulanje; Mponda was paid £100 a year for the loss of revenue on merchandise passing in and out of the lake; the Jumbe of Nkhota Kota was paid £200 a year for transferring to the administration the right to levy customs duties in his area.

On this occasion, as on others, Johnston was prepared to compromise. He informed Hetherwick: 'As at present there is very little money in the country, the Administration is ready to accept the said taxes in produce, building material (grass, timber, lime, bricks, etc.) or livestock, or in labour at the rate of one shilling and six pence a week.'

In view of the discontent and dissatisfaction felt locally from various quarters, the Foreign Office in London sanctioned the six shillings poll tax in 1891 conditionally and asked Commissioner Johnston to withdraw it if the experiment failed.

By 1892 it was clear that the six shillings poll tax was too high and that too few people were able or willing to pay it. For example, in the eight districts in which it was collected in 1892 only £200 a month was realised in June, July and August. Clearly, a change had to be made if better results were desired. Johnston took note of this and on 12 June 1893 he informed the Foreign Office of the changes he was proposing:

> It will be seen that in the proposed regulations there is some alteration in the amount and nature of the Native Tax. I propose to make it a Hut Tax and not a Poll Tax, and to levy (for the present at any rate) only 3s. and not 6s. a hut. In time, as the Natives become wealthier, we shall, no doubt, be able to raise the Hut Tax to the original 6s. a hut. I may state that the abovementioned alterations in the method of taxing the Natives have been the result of several conferences held by me at Blantyre, Zomba and elsewhere, in the early part of 1893, at which the Missionaries, Traders, Planters, Officials and Native Chiefs were invited to express their opinions on the subject.[1]

These changes were welcomed, and what was equally significant about them was that they were the result of wide consultations. The point about *mlandu* raised by the Blantyre missionaries was not lost on Johnston.

[1] *Report* by Eric Smith on direct taxation of natives in the Nyasaland Protectorate, and other cognate matters, 1937, p. 7.

The changes came into effect in 1894 when a hut tax of three shillings became payable on 31 December of each year. Failure to pay by 1 March of the following year meant that the hut on which tax had not been paid would become Government property and would usually be destroyed. Chiefs were no longer paid 10 per cent of the taxes collected since the collection of taxes was now the responsibility of the Collector, who was a European official on the administrative staff. Until the end of the nineteenth century the position remained the same.

However, in 1900 there was a slump in coffee production in Nyasaland. The planters blamed this on labour shortage and appealed to Commissioner Sir Alfred Sharpe to raise the supply of labour by two ways, one of which was to raise the tax payable by those persons who did not work for Europeans for at least one month in a year. Sharpe gave in to this demand and in the regulations of 1901 the maximum tax payable was raised to twelve shillings a hut; but there was a rebate of half the tax if the taxpayer worked for a European for at least one month at the current rate of pay, which was three shillings a month on average. The twelve shillings limit existed on paper only; it was too high in 1901. In actual practice the upper and the lower limits were six shillings and three shillings.

In 1911 an interesting provision was introduced whereby the African taxpayer could pay the lower rate of tax if he sold certain cash crops to a European, for example, 120 lbs. of rice or 100 lbs. of tobacco or 36–56 lbs. of cotton. Of course, these crops were then resold by the European at a higher price.

In the tax year 1912–13, the higher and lower figures were raised to eight shillings and four shillings. The Chilembwe rising of 1915 and subsequent events drew attention to the abuses in the rebate system which was in effect a lever for Europeans to extract labour supplies.

In 1921 the rebate system was abolished and a flat rate of six shillings a year took its place. This ought to have been introduced years before. When one considers that in 1901 the tax was six shillings and in 1921 it was still the same one can only imagine the hardship the tax must have brought for those who lived and worked in 1901. As for non-Africans, the Income Tax Ordinance of 1928 provided for a poll tax of £2 per adult male per year. By 1933 the average amount paid in direct tax by Europeans, Indians and Africans was a fair reflection of the difference in income standards. In round numbers, Europeans paid £47 per head of population, Indians £6 and Africans two shillings per year.

It is an old tradition in Malawi for people to go out to work. Movement of labour has taken place within the country as well as to neighbouring and non-neighbouring countries. There have been various reasons for this. Within the country, people from near and distant places came to work on European estates and for business people and trading companies on the Shire Highlands. Places like Blantyre, Zomba, Mulanje and Thyolo attracted labourers. Internal labour migration increased with the introduction of taxation in 1892. Money had to be earned in order to pay the tax as well as to obtain European goods which began to proliferate as missionaries, planters and traders came to Malawi. Movement of labour outside Malawi was an extension of the internal movement and often for the same reasons, that is largely economic. In a consideration of labour migration from Malawi one must not forget the educated Malawians who spread their influence and their talents in various ways and in various countries. In time, the Malawian outside, whether mine worker, office boy, domestic labourer, teacher, priest or trade unionist, earned for himself a good reputation for hard work and for reliability.

Let us look at the internal situation first. The first organised labour force to be recruited from northern Malawi to work in Blantyre was in 1886 when twenty-five Tonga persons set out to work for the African Lakes Corporation. Eight years later this number had increased to 1,400. Clearly, the African Lakes Corporation valued these porters from Tongaland. The reputation of these labourers spread to the neighbouring estates and about 4,000 Tonga were soon in the employ of planters. This number was in addition to the thousands already living in the Shire Highlands and on European estates. The planters favoured labourers whose homes were far away.

At first there were no government regulations concerning recruitment, conditions of labour or the amount of wages to be paid. The first Commissioner in Nyasaland, Sir Harry Johnston, reported on the many difficulties that existed up to 1894. He wrote:

> As a case in point of the mischief which is beginning to arise from the unregulated attempts of Europeans to supply native labour as a speculation, I may mention a case which recently occurred where an Austrian subject named Steblecki went to the west coast of Nyasa and engaged 900 Atonga. He brought them down to the Shire Province, but not being able to obtain the terms that he wanted and being at the end of his resources, he abandoned the men to their own devices and went off to Tshinde. The Atonga, having nothing to

eat, took to raiding some of the villages around Blantyre, and serious disturbances arose. Mr Sharpe had to intervene and has since endeavoured to settle the matter as far as possible by finding employment for these Atonga. At the same time there is very little security that they shall be properly paid, and there is no means of sending them back to their homes. . . .[1]

To take care of these difficulties labour regulations were drafted in the same year to take effect as from 1895. The regulations provided that no labourer from one district could be employed in another district except under an agreement between the employer and the employee entered into in the presence of a magistrate. The duration of employment was not to exceed twelve months at a time. At the end of the period of service every labourer was entitled to a small sum of money called 'conduct-money' or what we would today refer to as his travel money back home. If the labourer worked within one hundred miles of his home he was given two shillings travel money at the end of the contract; if more, he was entitled to one shilling and six pence for each additional hundred miles or fraction thereof. For employment within a district for a period not exceeding one month a written contract was similarly required but no travel money was provided.

In addition, all labourers whether on contract or not were to be properly housed, fed and cared for medically. The rate of wages was not fixed but was left to the fluctuations on the labour market on the principle of supply and demand. There was to be no forced labour; the terms were to be clearly explained to all prospective employees.

The 1894 labour regulations were a sincere attempt by the Nyasaland administration to protect African labourers. In actual practice many things went wrong. As the twentieth century dawned labourers wanted more than a few yards of calico for their labour; they wanted to be paid in cash. The employers, on the other hand, looked to the abundant supply of cheap labour to develop their industries. They wanted this labour mainly in the wet season which was the time when African cultivators too had to till their own lands. When periods of depression struck, the planters blamed the labour laws of the country for the shortage of labour. Their persistent demands compelled the Administration to side with them. We have already noted that in 1901 the hut tax regulations were changed to enable a labourer to pay half the amount of tax if he worked for a European employer for at least one month in the year. On all sides there was a reluctance to pay wages of more than the average of three shillings a month. When Joseph Booth

[1] F.O. 2/66, folios 6–7, Harry Johnston to Earl of Kimberley, 12 Jan. 1894.

10. Seated, left to right : Joseph Kaunde, Thomas Masea, Harry Kambwiri Matecheta, Harry Mtuwa, Stephen Kundecha ; standing, second from left : Justin Somanje ; fourth from left : Joseph Bismarck.

11. Rev. Dr Patrick Augustine Kalilombe.

12. Yotam Bango.

13. Lewis Mataka
Bandawe,
M.B.E.

14. Levi Zililo Mumba.

15. Sir Geoffrey Colby leaving Malawi in 1956.

came to the country in 1892 he worked out a new plan to promote African interests by doubling and even trebling the wages. The head of the Blantyre Mission, the Rev. Alexander Hetherwick, reacted strongly against this. Since the missionaries in general and Hetherwick in particular were guardians of African interests, it is helpful to consider what Hetherwick had to say:

> He [i.e. Booth] commenced inviting our Christian native workers over to his house, and circulated among our printing-staff and others of our native workers a statement stating the terms on which he would employ them, and the wages he would give, these being large to begin with, to be doubled the second year, trebled the third, and so on. These wages were vastly in excess of the current wage paid by the Mission and other employers of native labour in the Shire Highlands. This current wage was recognised by all natives and Europeans alike as a fair and just equivalent for the labour afforded, and must be judged by the extent of native wants and the growth of civilised habits among the native community. To raise the native wages by, in some cases, three or even five times the current price is simply to afford the natives a means to leading an idle life or indulging in degrading debauchery.[1]

Another problem was the recruitment of labour. The planters requested that they should be allowed to form a Labour Bureau, and this was set up in 1901. It became responsible for the collection and distribution of labour among its members, and appointed agents in the districts to recruit labour. These agents, who were often assisted by the official Collectors, tended to overstep their limits and resort to all sorts of dubious practices to obtain labour, and then the Government was also discredited since their administrative officials cooperated with them by handing over tax defaulters to them. Soon the agents were stopped from visiting the districts. The administrative officials then undertook to send labour direct to the bureau.

Before the bureau had been set up in 1901 individual companies carried out their own recruitment. Here again abuses were many. In the Dedza district in 1900 villages and granaries were destroyed in the village of a chief who had told the recruiters that he would not allow a single man to be recruited because of what had happened to others recruited earlier on. Some of his people had died on the way to Blantyre while others never returned to their villages. The matter went to court

---

[1] Memorandum anent the Zambezi Industrial Mission by the Rev. Alexander Hetherwick, 1893, pp. 1–2. Hetherwick Papers, National Archives, Zomba.

since the Dutch Reformed Church Mission complained about the behaviour of the recruiting party.

The mission was not the only one to complain. A. J. Swann, a government official who spent twenty-seven years in East and Central Africa, wrote to the Chief Judicial Officer in Zomba in 1901 blaming the employers for neglecting their labourers and for being callous over their working conditions. He said:

> I was perhaps the only Collector who repeatedly warned the Europeans that there must be a change in their treatment and was practically laughed at or some stupid paragraph was inserted in the *Central African Times*, from a person who thought I desired to clothe the native in lavender.

Swann referred to the plight of the thousands of carriers in the following words:

> During his journeys at Tenga Tenga he was bundled away from Chikwawa, Zomba, Blantyre, Matope, Liwonde at all hours of the day; pushed out on the road with a load, no attention paid as to where he would sleep—on the road, in the bush, in the cold of June, in the rain of December, perhaps with or without his fire and friend, and this on top of 150 miles for a month in order to purchase the right to live in his own house in his own land. Weakness, then sickness, then death. Verdict 'Dead from dysentery. Hill people generally get that way.' Sequel, Collectors get a Report, '69 deaths among your people.'

If there is drama in Swann's description, there is truth in it, too. But not many were prepared to see it. The editor of the *Central African Planter*,[1] R. S. Hynde, was one of those who felt that the Africans in Nyasaland were relatively well off; that in 1896 their wages had increased from 8 yards of calico to 10, 12, 16 and 24 yards; that they were being paid 4d. for their fowls compared to 2d. a few years earlier; that the price of their sleeping mats had increased from 2d. to 8d. He compared the lot of the labourer in Nyasaland with that in Britain and made this editorial comment: 'It is not a kindness to give the native a high wage; in every respect he is better off, materially, than the masses at home, therefore there is no need for the Government to assist him in this way.'

The African himself did not agree. As the twentieth century began he had already entered the economic system of the European. His

---

[1] *Central African Planter*, I, 5, Jan. 1896.

aspirations were increasing and his expectations rising. His disappoint-
ments became keener when these were not fulfilled. In the minutes of a
meeting of the Mombera Native Association in 1921 the following
entry appears: 'The Natives are being brought up from darkness to
light by the Europeans, and they are encouraged in their civilisation to
have also good clothes, instead of wearing skins and bark cloth.' To
introduce them to this and then to hold back wages was to drive them
away from their country so that the aspirations denied at home could
be realised in the neighbouring countries.

iii THE FIRST PHASE OF MIGRANT LABOUR

Up to about 1900 there was sufficient local labour to meet the requirements of the British Central Africa Protectorate, which was what the
country was called from 1893 to 1907. With the growth of the coffee
industry and with the increased demand for labour for the construction
of the Shire Highlands railway in 1904, local labour, however, became
scarce. The scarcity was aggravated because an increasing number of
people were leaving the country to work in the Rhodesias, in South
Africa, in the Belgian Congo and in Tanganyika. Of these centres of
employment Southern Rhodesia and South Africa offered the best
prospects.

One of the causes of labour migration at the beginning was the introduction of taxation and the entry of the African into the wage
economy. Tax defaulters were sent to work for Europeans. When tax
collectors set out to collect tax in the dry season, when conditions were
most suitable, tax evaders or defaulters crossed the borders into
neighbouring countries. To counter this, tax collection was conducted
during the wet season when people tilled their lands. Gradually, labour
migration became a habit even when the necessity to earn tax money
was no longer pressing. Even before taxation had been introduced,
labourers had begun to cross the Zambezi, heading south. It was reported that labourers from north of the Zambezi were already working
in the diamond mines at Kimberley in the early 1880s. But regular
migration dates from 1903.

By this date substantial information was already to be had in the
country about the prospects outside. Tonga labourers, who were
probably more adventurous than many, showed how people could
earn more money outside. With the growth of the cash economy, more
western goods were in demand. The practice of Indian shopkeepers of
allowing credit facilities increased the volume of purchases as well as
the debt into which the unsophisticated purchaser was drifting. A

period of work outside seemed the best method of liquidating debts, purchasing luxury or status goods, earning cash for the payment of *lobola* or bride money and also satisfying one's curiosity about the world outside while at the same time raising one's standards, a point which missionary preaching and teaching never ceased to stress.

Regular labour migration dates from 1903. Many things happened in that year. For one, the British Cotton Growing Association was formed to stimulate the growth and supply of cotton. In Malawi Africans were encouraged to grow cotton and to sell it to the Association. This also meant more employment possibilities on settler plantations. However, this was offset in 1903 by a considerable influx of Lomwe people. In Blantyre alone a Lomwe population of eighteen thousand was recorded in that year. In addition to cotton, tobacco cultivation took a new turn with the arrival of experts to promote the industry which had started on a small scale ten years previously. By 1903 the new tax regulations, which provided a labour inducement by allowing a 100 per cent tax rebate to Africans who worked for Europeans for at least one month in the year, had begun to make an impact on them. The Tonga in the West Nyasa District had staged a demonstration against it in 1902. Clearly it was not a popular measure and the element of veiled forced labour was not lost on many Africans. Finally the land laws and practices of the country received a severe jolt when the Nunan judgement of 1903 in the High Court in Blantyre drew attention to the ways in which some Africans were being deprived of their land rights and privileges, especially the right to live rent-free on certain estates.

While all this was going on in Malawi, there was an increasing labour shortage in Southern Rhodesia and South Africa. South Africa had labour agreements up to 1900 with Mozambique and Bechuanaland (now Botswana) and so had the monopoly of labour in these countries. This drove Southern Rhodesia to look north of the Zambezi for labour. But even the monopoly South Africa had was not sufficient for her purposes. After the Anglo-Boer War ended in 1902, the gold mines of the Witwatersrand had to be reopened but there was insufficient labour. In desperation, the Chamber of Mines looked everywhere in Africa for labour. Over a hundred thousand labourers were needed from abroad. Failing to receive an adequate response in Africa, the Chamber recruited Chinese labourers in 1904. Within three years 54,000 Chinese labourers were imported, but this arrangement proved to be unsatisfactory and inadequate.

Before the Transvaal Government could ask the Foreign Office for labour from Malawi, the mining companies sent out agents there and to Mozambique to recruit labour. Since the agents were able to offer attractive terms and also because the existing conditions in Malawi were not all that good, Africans began to respond and to leave the country. This labour movement was an embarrassment to the Government and the planters as well as the missionaries. As a result of pressure from the Blantyre Chamber of Commerce and Agriculture, the Nyasaland (Malawi) Government introduced a law in 1898 to stop this. Some arguments used by the planters and the missionaries were: the Africans going south would suffer morally, and might take to drinking; domestic life in the villages would suffer as a result of the men's long periods of absence; the Africans were already well off in their home country; the economic prosperity of the Protectorate would suffer if its labour resources were lost or reduced. The administration supported them to the extent, as we have seen, of changing the hut tax regulations to suit the planters' labour requirements, but the Foreign Office was not happy with this, describing it as 'indistinguishable from mere traffic in forced labour.'[1] At this point, in 1903, the Foreign Office agreed to sanction the exportation to South Africa on an experimental basis of up to a thousand labourers, provided that every precaution was taken to safeguard their interests. This labour was to be supplied to the Witwatersrand Native Labour Association (W.N.L.A.), more popularly known as Wenela.

The first batch of people actually numbered 930. They had been recruited exclusively from the low-lying areas of the Lower Shire and Ruo districts because famine and floods in these districts had resulted in serious distress. Many were homeless and on the verge of starvation. Victims of a famine were not the best of labourers to export in an experimental scheme. They were transported by river and by sea to Delagoa Bay; from here they journeyed by train to Johannesburg after receiving medical examination and warm clothing while in transit. They were distributed between two mines named Robinson Deep and East Rand. These pioneers were confronted with serious difficulties. They arrived in midwinter when it can be bitterly cold in Johannesburg. Having never been down a mine before, eighty-five of them refused to do underground work. The mine authorities described their attitude as 'obstructive and insolent' and they were taken to court where they were found guilty and sentenced to imprisonment. The European official who had accompanied the party did not agree with this treatment and in his official report made the following observation:

> I cannot say that I consider the Robinson Deep Company have displayed a desire to treat the experiment of employing British Central

[1] F.O. 2/745, F.O. to Sir Alfred Sharpe, 6 Jan. 1903.

Africa natives in an entirely fair manner. The prosecuting of 85 boys for refusing to go down the mine was both unnecessary and lacking in tact.... They had never seen a mine and they were naturally afraid.[1]

The death rate was high, ranging from 118 per thousand in July 1904 to 135 per thousand in July 1906. In 1904 there was a pneumonia epidemic. It was for this reason that the British Government suggested that they should be given surface work only, which Wenela would not agree to since there was abundant local labour for surface work. However, adjustments had to be made: preference was given to labourers from the higher-altitude areas of Malawi such as Dedza and Dowa who would be better able to withstand the different climatic conditions. In 1906 a further improvement was introduced when it was finally decreed that no labourer from the Protectorate was to be assigned to underground work in the mines.

During this experimental period from 1903 to 1907—when the arrangement was suspended—an estimated 7,000 labourers were recruited by Wenela, of which about one-tenth lost their lives. They were paid 1s. 6d. a day, one-third of which was paid to them in advance to provide for their dependants at home. Wenela paid the 6s. hut tax to the Protectorate government which was later deducted from the wages. The first experiment showed what the advantages and disadvantages of migrant labour were. The worker certainly earned more money but there were physical and psychological strains which called for adjustments; the government revenue in hut tax increased; social strains and stresses were generated as families were separated, old marriages were dissolved and new ones were contracted. There developed, too, that class of men called the *machona* who never returned home. Other results were to follow as the characteristics of migration made themselves felt in both the guest and the host communities. So far we have traced the beginnings only.

The experiment was described by the Government as a success but by the missionaries as a failure. The employers of labour in Malawi viewed with concern the possibility of more and more labourers leaving the country. The new railway works started in 1904 needed 12,000 labourers; the mines in Johannesburg asked for 5,000 more to add to the initial 1,000. A labour crisis would develop if both these demands were met. The African labourer was now caught between two forces: the local employers wanted him to stay; the government was willing to let him go.

[1] B. S. Krishnamurthy, 'Land and Labour in Nyasaland 1891–1914', Ph.D. thesis, Univ. of London, 1964, pp. 250–55.

Workers from the Nyasaland Protectorate did not only venture to the mines of South Africa. Southern Rhodesia was another attraction. Here many local attempts were made to enlist local African labour: a hut tax of 10s. was introduced in 1896; this was increased to a poll tax of £1 in 1901, but still labour was insufficient. One thousand labourers were recruited from both Abyssinia and Somaliland in 1900 but this proved to be a failure and from that year onwards workers from the Nyasaland Protectorate spilled over into the Rhodesias, destined mainly for Southern Rhodesia. At first they moved with impunity but when a hue and cry was raised by local planters and missionaries that the local administration was being negligent, Government took action. It could only regulate and regularise the movement. It could not stop it. In the opening years of the twentieth century migrant labour was already a part of Malawi society and economics.

iv THE LATER PHASES OF MIGRANT LABOUR

During the first phase of migrant labour from Malawi, two developments became clear. The first was the scheme worked out with Wenela. This lasted in the first instance till the end of 1907 and was the first organised scheme in which three governments were involved, namely the British Government, the British Central Africa Protectorate Government and the Transvaal Government.

While this official scheme was in operation, a second development became noticeable; private and unorganised movement of labour was taking place when members of a family or a number of friends banded together for the long march south. Movement was free and the local administration made no attempt to regulate it until 1904 when complaints increased about the Government's lack of concern. Employers of labour in the Protectorate said that the exodus of labour was crippling the local economy; missionaries complained of the hardships experienced in the long and dangerous march and appealed to the Government to stop it or to regulate it.

Having already approved of the first lot of 1,000 labourers for Wenela in 1903, and an additional 5,000 labourers in 1904, the Nyasaland Government was morally bound to give some assistance to the local employers. But to act as a labour supply association for the planters in the Shire Highlands was an embarrassment to the Government, which was accused in the foreign press and in parliament in Britain of practising forced labour. In a strongly worded letter to the chairman of the British Central Africa Company, Commissioner Sir

Alfred Sharpe reminded him that the time had come for the employers to help themselves on the competitive market. He said:

I do not think that I am beyond the mark in saying that 75 per cent of the present labour supply from Angoniland and the Lake Districts would never go to the Shire Highlands. I feel this so strongly that I am very much averse at the present date to modifying, to any great extent, the present system under which natives who have no money to pay their tax and who are willing to work to obtain it are given papers in Angoniland and elsewhere under which they proceed to Blantyre to work for whoever wants them for a month or upwards; as I know that if I discontinued this system the Shire Highlands would at once fall into the condition of having practically no labour at all. And yet who is to blame for this? Clearly and distinctly the labour employers themselves who not only continue the old system of paying three shillings or three shillings' worth of common calico per month to their labourers, but also still neglect to take even the simplest steps to feed their men and to make them comfortable.[1]

There was no point, Sir Alfred Sharpe said, in giving the labourers maize grain. Where were they to grind it? Who was to cook it for them? Would it not be better to give them a daily ration of cooked maize meal or cooked rice and beans? The point was simply that employers should take steps to make conditions of work and rates of pay attractive enough to attract labourers without the intervention of the Government.

What the Government was prepared to do in 1904 was to introduce passes or permits which every person had to obtain from district officials before he could leave the country. The only requirement before such a pass or permit could be issued was that the applicant had paid his tax. At the same time steps were taken to prevent unauthorised persons from leaving the country without permits. Since the usual aim was to get to Salisbury through Zambia, the Nyasaland Protectorate Government got in touch with the Administrator of Northeastern Rhodesia who controlled the entry point at Fort Jameson, now called Chipata. This official gave figures of the number of persons who entered Fort Jameson en route to the mines of Southern Rhodesia as well as the copperbelt of Zambia and the Belgian Congo. By 31 March 1904, 6,126 persons had headed southwards and 3,514 northwards. These figures do indicate that the stream of migrant labour was now flowing fast. The Administrator of Northeastern Rhodesia had this to say about stopping people without permits from passing through:

[1] C.O. 525/5, Sir Alfred Sharpe to Major Wemyss, 22 Dec. 1903.

I am convinced that restrictive measures are impracticable, that these Natives have got into the habit of seeking work south of the Zambezi and will go down in spite of all obstacles short of refusal of work when they get there. Certainly none which we could put in their way would be as insurmountable as those readily faced and overcome by these same people going the same journey a few years ago. They were robbed and murdered going through Portuguese territory, were swindled at the Zambezi ferries and died of thirst and starvation on unknown routes. In spite of this they persevered and now there are practically no difficulties or dangers to be faced. The majority of these Natives come from Bandawe, Mombera's, Fort Johnston and Kota Kota. They appear to know their minds regarding the class of work which they desire and regarding the locality where they wish to work.[1]

In 1904 there were no longer any restrictions on recruitment; the Government kept out of it so that it was simply a matter of agreement between employer and employee. We have just noted that the employees knew their own minds, what work they wanted and where. It was futile to direct them. All things considered they preferred to work outside the country. The pioneers blazed a trail in search of their own El Dorados. Their story and achievements are worthy of note.

There were two main land routes, both passing through Fort Jameson. The first of these passed Feira at the western extremity of the Zambezi near the Portuguese border town of Zumbo, and then continued to Salisbury. The second route headed for Broken Hill in Zambia. Before reaching Broken Hill the migrants stopped at a mine about one hundred miles from Fort Jameson (Chipata) called the Sasare Mine. Here they worked temporarily for between 5s. and 10s. a month before proceeding to Broken Hill where the average pay per month was between 15s. and 25s. for mine work; 15s. for farm work, and between £3 and £5 for domestic labour, chiefly as cooks.

All this was part of the unorganised labour migration. The first organised scheme as we have noted was with Wenela in 1903, which was stopped in 1907. In the same year the Southern Rhodesian Government came through with a request for a thousand labourers for the Rhodesian mines and for a further thousand for farm work in Rhodesia on the understanding that they would be repatriated after twelve months. This was granted in January 1908 on condition that part of the wages would be paid on termination of contract. At the same time Wenela

[1] C.O. 525/2, Administrator, Northeastern Rhodesia to Sir Alfred Sharpe, 7 June 1904.

made its second bid for Malawi labour. Their agent promised to look after the welfare of the workers, to pay their taxes, to hold back two-thirds of their wages until the end of the contract and to repatriate them. The Malawi Governor advised that the terms should be accepted because the workers stood to gain obvious advantages in such a scheme. The strongest argument was that since they would go in any case would it not be advantageous to accept the safeguards which were being offered?

These official agreements of 1908 were shortlived. In 1909 they were withdrawn largely because of missionary opposition to the schemes, spearheaded by the influential Dr Alexander Hetherwick. However, in spite of the withdrawal of the agreed terms, labourers continued to leave the country and to seek employment through Wenela and the Rhodesian Native Labour Bureau (R.N.L.B.). There was no way of stopping it. By 1914, about ten thousand Malawians were working in the Transvaal mines alone and about three times that number in the Rhodesian mines.

In 1935 a commission was set up in Malawi to report on migrant labour, on the effect of this on village life and on the probable future effects on the Protectorate as a whole. The commission found a gloomy picture: 25–35 per cent never returned home; many married foreign wives or entered into irregular unions. It also found that at one time about 120,000 Africans worked outside the country—or one in every four male adults. The commission reported:

> Our investigations have deepened profoundly our individual and collective sense of responsibility. We must confess that, six months ago, there was not one of us who realised the seriousness of the situation: as our investigations proceeded we became more and more aware that this uncontrolled and growing emigration brought misery and poverty to hundreds and thousands of families and that the waste of life, happiness, health and wealth was colossal.[1]

If the trend could not be counteracted and the migration itself controlled, the commission went on to warn that some day 'the Natives will hate administration by white people which has been responsible for such results.' It was as a result of this serious warning that the three governments of Northern Rhodesia, Southern Rhodesia and Nyasaland signed an agreement on 21 August 1936 to help solve the difficult problems of migrant labour. The agreement provided for the issue of certificates of identification; for repatriation after two years of all

[1] C.O. 525/166/44053/1, folio 545, *Report on Nyasaland Emigrant Labour*, 1937.

emigrant labourers; for suitable travel arrangements and rest camps. At the same time Wenela entered the 1936 agreement with an allocation of 4,000 Malawi labourers; this was increased to 8,500 in 1938.

What seemed important in these agreements was that the best conditions were sought for the labourers as well as arranging that the workers would be repatriated at the end of their contracts.

What was the position in 1970? Wenela was still the principal supplier of labour to the South African Chamber of Mines. The Rhodesian African Labour Supply Commission or *Mtandizi* organised labour supply to Rhodesian firms. The third body was the Employment Services Division of the Ministry of Labour of the Malawi Government, which came into being in November 1967 as a result of an international labour agreement between the Malawi and South African Governments. The first part of its service is to provide documentation, medical examination and official transport to the places of employment in South Africa. It also regularises the position of migrant labourers who were in South Africa prior to the Labour Agreement of 1967. The maximum period of employment now is two years, at the end of which every worker returns home. The total number of persons from Malawi employed by Wenela for the South African mines as at the end of 1970 was 92,169; by Mtandizi in Rhodesia, 2,514; and the number of those organised and supervised by the Employment Services Division for employment in South Africa was 10,629. The care, comforts and security of today are a tremendous improvement when compared to the lot of those who blazed the pioneer trail.

CHAPTER 8

Malawians abroad

i THE SECULAR SPHERE

The influence of Malawians abroad has not been felt only on the farms and in the gold mines, the factories or in domestic employment. Malawians have played an important role in central and southern Africa as well as abroad in other capacities. It is with the educated Malawian that we are now concerned. At one time Malawi led the field in Central Africa in the race to produce teachers, evangelists and artisans, largely because of the work of the Scottish missions which placed a heavy emphasis on vocational training. In this the Livingstonia Mission and its branch stations led the way. By 1897 there were ten times as many pupils in the Livingstonia Mission schools as in the Blantyre Mission schools and there were six times as many teachers in the Livingstonia schools. The pastors, the teachers and the artisans produced in these schools were far too many for Malawi to absorb. As late as the 1930s when Levi Mumba persistently pressed the Nyasaland Administration to start secondary schools in the country he was told that there was no point in doing so. There were no jobs in Malawi for her more educated sons. If this was so in the 1930s, the position before had been even worse.

The teachers left first. Their highest educational achievements before leaving were a standard four certificate—or a standard six certificate in rare cases. A few had extra teaching qualifications but all were determined to make good.

What did these teachers achieve outside Malawi? There were so many of them and their achievements were so vast and varied in the context of their day that only a few outstanding examples can be mentioned here. Take the case of Ernest Alexander Muwamba of Chifira village, Nkhata Bay district. Muwamba became a teacher-trainee at Nkhata Bay after passing standard four in 1907. Three years later he obtained the standard six certificate and a teaching certificate. Shortly afterwards he became a headmaster but decided to leave for Zambia. His salary as a headmaster at the time of leaving in 1913 was 12s. 6d. a month. Muwamba's first position in Zambia was that of a clerk at the Bwana Mkubwa Mine. Within a year he was earning £2 7s. 6d. a month, over three times as much as he had earned at home. Besides the money, there were many opportunities for advancement for talented and hardworking individuals. Before the year was out, Muwamba entered the service of the Zambian Government as a clerk and court interpreter. From this point there was no turning back. He went on to become the first African civil servant in Zambia to act as a District Commissioner and one of two Malawians (the other being Thom Manda of Mwaya village, Nkhata Bay) to be the first Africans in Zambia to be appointed to the African Education Advisory Board.

Membership of this Advisory Board indicates that the contribution of some Malawians abroad was not confined to their own material advancement. Alexander Muwamba formed the Ndola Welfare Association. His uncle, Isaac Clements Katondo Muwamba, together with two other Malawians, Jacob Nguluwe and Isaac Nyirenda, applied to the Zambian Government in 1923 to form the Native Improvement Association in Lusaka. The reason they gave to the Government was that they had observed constant weekend quarrels among peoples of different tribal backgrounds who had converged onto Lusaka. Their hope was that the Improvement Association would help to eradicate tribalism. The District Commissioner of Lusaka, commenting on this application, wrote:

> It is very difficult, indeed foolish, to be dogmatic about any native's character, but my own opinion of Isaac Clements Muwamba is that 'get on' he must; he is intensely ambitious, he has a brain always at work and he is at present imbued with a keen desire to 'improve and civilise' himself and all around him.[1]

There were many like Alexander Muwamba and his uncle Isaac Muwamba who left the country as teachers and branched off into other occupations. Take another representative example, Nophas Dinneck Kwenje, in 1970 Acting General Manager of Malawi Press. Educated at the Henry Henderson Institute, Kwenje became a headmaster before he left the country for new pastures. He spent thirty years in Southern Rhodesia, a full and fascinating time during which he worked as a

[1] S2/71/23, National Archives, Zomba.

teacher, a driver, photographer, watchmaker, postal clerk, detective-constable, editor of the *Bantu Mirror* at Bulawayo, then its Works Manager, and finally its business manager. He returned to Malawi in 1956 and immediately won a seat on the newly-enlarged Legislative Council.

To take yet another example from the teaching profession, we may look at the career of Wedson Chaluluma Kaunda, in 1970 a magistrate in Blantyre. Kaunda became a teacher for the Livingstonia Mission in 1943 at a salary of £1 2s. 6d. a month. He decided to leave for South Africa and in 1944 found himself working as a clerk in Port Elizabeth, earning £6 a month. Here he watched the operation of politics in a modern city and especially how trade unions worked. It was a small step from this experience to taking the position of Secretary of the Ekwendeni Branch of the Nyasaland African Congress in 1947 shortly after his return from South Africa. In 1952 he became a member of the Northern Province Provincial Council. So far we have considered the role of Malawian teachers abroad who invariably returned to important positions in their motherland. Muwamba was to become one of the first two African members of the Legislative Council in 1949.

There were, of course, many who did not come back but went on to make their contribution in near and distant places. One such, Martin Kaunda, only recently visited Malawi from Zambia where in 1970 he held the distinguished position of Director of Correspondence Studies of the University of Zambia. Brought up in the challenging environment of Likoma Island, Martin Kaunda completed his studies in South Africa where he obtained a Bachelor of Arts degree in 1946 and a University Education Diploma in 1947, an achievement which must probably rank him as the first Malawian to obtain a University degree in Africa. The first two Malawian graduates, Dr Daniel Malekebu of the Providence Industrial Mission and His Excellency Dr H. Kamuzu Banda, both obtained their degrees much earlier but in the U.S.A.

Another Malawian who did not return was the famous trade unionist, Clements Kadalie, who left Malawi in 1915, the very year when young Kamuzu Banda left his mother country to blaze a distinguished trail also. Clements Kadalie, like Alexander Muwamba, hailed from Chifira village, Nkhata Bay. After obtaining a standard six education, Kadalie left for Rhodesia and South Africa. In 1919 he had an unpleasant experience in Cape Town and this prompted him to organise a trade union to protect the interests of non-white workers. World War I had just ended and there was much unemployment and economic uncertainty. Kadalie formed the Industrial and Commercial Workers' Union and became its General Secretary in 1921. Two years later he started his own newspaper called *The Workers' Herald*.

In that same year, Alexander Muwamba, who was Kadalie's cousin, happened to read a letter written in English by Clements Kadalie in the newspaper *Umteteli wa Bantu* and wrote back promptly to his countryman congratulating him on his remarkable achievements in South Africa and complimenting him on his command of the English language. Back came the following reply from Clements Kadalie:

> You will also admit this fact that when we were boys both you and I had a burning desire to ascend the loftiest pinnacle—hence my adventure when I had to choose not to go to Northern Rhodesia to take up a clerical situation there but to proceed southwards fixing my attention if I could cross over to Europe for promoting myself higher. Shortly when I arrived here in Cape Town seven years ago (1916), I did not waste my time with the outside appearance of this great city in Africa but got down to business to fulfil my ambitions. Immediately in 1919 I organised the I.C.U., the first Labour Organisation of the African people. During that time I engaged myself to take studies to advance my education and I am glad to know that you also record my transition with a fuller grasp of the English language.

This letter could well be described as an African testimony of faith and determination. Kadalie was the firebrand of African politics in South Africa in the 1920s and 1930s. In 1921 Kadalie organised a fund for the relief of African victims in a local tragedy. One of those who sent a donation to this fund was General Hertzog who was to become Prime Minister in three years' time. On that occasion, General Hertzog wrote to Kadalie:

> It is for us by our common endeavours to make this country that we both love so much, great and good. In order to do that we must not only ourselves be good and great, but we must also see that there is established between the white and black Africander that faith in and sympathy with one another which is so essential for the prosperity of a nation.

All the time that Kadalie spent in South Africa did not cause him to forget his own country. He had aspirations—like many Malawians at home as well as abroad—to go to the United States to improve his education. When the Muwamba family agreed to finance him he expressed his gratitude for the communal cooperation that existed in African society.

He exhorted his countrymen to educate themselves in order to share in the government. It was a new experience to find an educated person in the early 1920s criticising the conservatism of the traditional rulers. He said:

> The white man is determined to turn the country his own and it behoves us now to be up and doing to culture ourselves in the white man's modern government. To do this our beloved Chifira must produce most cultured and educated men who will participate to agitate for the modern government alongside the white man. What we require is that we should send men to sit as legislators at Zomba where laws are made to govern Nyasaland.

Such things were not being said in the 1920s in Malawi or indeed in most parts of Africa. Kadalie was ahead of his time, as many educated Malawians were, outside their homes, in the schools, offices and churches of Central and southern Africa.

Kadalie died in South Africa on 28 November 1951. He has given us an account of his experiences in a recently published book entitled *My Life and the I.C.U.*, a remarkable book by a remarkable man.

ii THE RELIGIOUS SPHERE

In discussing the role and contribution of educated Malawians abroad we have so far looked mainly at education, government service and politics. Now we shall examine the contribution in the field of religion, which stands out as a factor in Malawi history. Whether one looks upon it as missionary or Christian is not important. What we are considering is the contribution of mission-educated individuals to the promotion of Christianity. Since the early missions were themselves concerned with four sorts of endeavour, namely, religious education, secular education, technical and commercial education and medical assistance and education, some of the products of missionary work themselves became specialists in one or more of these fields. Our present concern is with those who took it upon themselves to promote the Gospel.

The first in this field was, of course, John Chilembwe. He entered the service of the radical missionary, Joseph Booth, in 1892 when the Protectorate Government was just a few months old. The earliest Scottish and Anglican missionaries had been in the country much longer, as had a few traders, planters and hunters. Some of them had made serious mistakes in their dealings with Africans and Joseph Booth was not slow to point this out wherever and whenever he had the opportunity to do so. His religious creed was that the African should be uplifted economically and politically to take his place in the Africa that was his. Religion, important as it was, was only a means to an end.

John Chilembwe was influenced by Booth's teachings, many of which he put into practice in later life. He was influenced, too, by his experience and education in the U.S.A. He left Malawi for America in 1897 and entered the Virginia Theological Seminary and College, an institution for Negroes, in 1898. He spent just two years at this College, mainly in the theological department. At this time in America Negroes received little more than a simple elementary education. Chilembwe's college was of the grade of a junior secondary school. And yet, when he returned to his home country in 1900, he started the Providence Industrial Mission. He had learnt at Lynchburg, Virginia, not to depend upon whites but upon his own people. The name 'Providence' had a strong connection with Negro Baptist organisations in the United States and the Caribbean. The name 'Industrial' had links with Joseph Booth's first mission at Mitsidi, the Zambezi Industrial Mission. The name selected reflects the aims and objects Chilembwe had in mind for his new mission.

For the development of his schools and his religious teachings he brought out Negroes from America, the first being the Rev. Cheek in 1901 and the second, a lady, Miss DeLany, a year later. These persons were sponsored by the National Baptist Convention of the United States and thus we see the interplay of external influences on local development. This was all because Chilembwe had spent two years in America. The role of educated Malawians must be seen not only in what they did abroad but also in the many ways in which their experiences abroad influenced their future activities in Malawi.

The first Malawian to leave Chilembwe's Providence Industrial Mission to study abroad was Daniel Sharpe Malekebu who left in 1905 for the U.S.A. in the hope that he, too, would receive education with the help of the Negro Baptists. In 1917 Daniel Malekebu qualified as a medical doctor at the Meharry Medical College, Nashville, Tennessee, the first Malawian to achieve this distinction. Dr Malekebu proceeded to study theology so as to serve his country as a medical missionary. This he succeeded in doing when he returned permanently in 1926 to reopen and reorganise the Providence Industrial Mission. In mid-1970 Dr Malekebu's work was still going on and the Providence Industrial Mission at Chiradzulu had been under his charge for thirty-five years. In 1967 he went back to the United States to receive the 'President's Award' of Meharry College to mark the fiftieth anniversary of his obtaining his medical degree. It is in the role of a Baptist medical missionary that Dr Malekebu is remembered.

In 1907 two other Malawians left the same district to improve their education and try their fortune in the United States; they were accompanied by Negro missionaries. Their names were Matthew and Frederick Njilima, sons of Duncan Njilima, a progressive businessman and farmer at Nsoni village in Chiradzulu. The father is remembered in Malawi history for his part in the tragic events of 1915. Matthew went to school in Missouri and Frederick in Kentucky. Frederick Njilima applied for an opportunity in 1916 to complete his studies in England but a former Anglican Bishop of Nyasaland, for whom his father had once worked, advised him to join the British Army instead in order to purge himself of his father's sins of 1915. Frederick Njilima joined the Machine-gun Corps of the 18th Reserve of the London Regiment, saw service in Europe, and was awarded a medal for bravery. He was demobilised for health reasons in 1919 and spent some time in a hospital in Cambridge eagerly waiting for the former Bishop of Nyasaland to find him a place at Cambridge University. This failed and Frederick Njilima returned home in the same year to inherit the ruins of his father's home in Chiradzulu. The romantic story of the little boy from Chiradzulu who went to school in Kentucky, and went on to the battlefields of France and to receive a letter of commendation from King George V, illustrates how daring and adventurous Malawians have been. And for all this John Chilembwe's pioneering example deserves credit because it brought to Chiradzulu powerful influences and took from Chiradzulu enterprising Malawians.

Dr Daniel Malekebu is one of the Malawian grand old men of early missionary fame and contribution. The other is the Rev. Hanock Msokera Phiri, nearly ten years older than Malekebu, who was born at Kasungu in the 1880s and went to the Livingstonia school in Chief Mwase's village in 1897. In June 1916 he left Kasungu with the intention of working in the Transvaal mines. He found employment on the Wit Deep Mine in Boksburg and it was there that he was introduced to the African Methodist Episcopal Church. His mind was set on becoming a teacher and since there was no place in the Transvaal where he could teach he returned to Southern Rhodesia and finally found a job as a teacher at the Paris Mission Society school in Livingstone, Northern Rhodesia. But the lure of South Africa took him back to Boksburg where he became an evangelist and then a licentiate of the African Methodist Episcopal Church. He was finally made a deacon by Bishop Vernon, an American Negro, who was then head of the African Methodist Episcopal Church in Africa. Bishop Vernon entrusted Rev. Msokera Phiri with the duty of starting a branch of the African Methodist Episcopal Church in Nyasaland. In May 1924, the A.M.E.C. was started in Chief Mwase's village; this was its foundation in Central Africa. A year later the first schools of this church were started. Of course, the Nyasaland Government was not happy to approve of missions run wholly by Africans. They needed the endorsement of European missionaries before they could be approved. Dr Donald Fraser of Livingstonia was happy to endorse the Rev. Msokera Phiri. After all he *was* a Livingstonia product and there was some reflected glory to be shared. The Rev. Dr Fraser wrote as follows about Mr Phiri:

> I do not think he wishes to teach disloyalty to the Government. His professed aim is to raise the civilisation of the African through the African, which is excellent as an aim. I have spoken to him of the need for cooperation between the races, and he wholly agrees, and speaks most gratefully of our mission to which he owes all.

Later the contribution of the independent schools started by the Rev. Msokera Phiri will be considered. Here we are concerned with him as the founder of the African Methodist Episcopal Church in Nyasaland in 1924.

Another Livingstonia product who succeeded in founding his own church was Elliot Kenan Kamwana. After receiving his early education at Bandawe, Kamwana went to the Livingstonia Mission at Khondowe but he left after completing standard three in 1901 because he was dissatisfied with the teaching and the teachers. He had too much of a questioning spirit for the peace of mind of his Scottish teachers, so for his own peace of mind he left Livingstonia and Nyasaland, worked as a medical aide in a hospital in Rhodesia and finally reached Cape Town in 1903. Here he joined the Watch Tower church and returned to Nyasaland to start a branch of it there in 1906. Like Chilembwe, his contemporary and friend, Kamwana was to become a political missionary because of the circumstances of his time and day. The years 1906 to 1915 were difficult years in Nyasaland. Kamwana's teachings seemed to offer hope to troubled people. In the West Nyasa District, thousands of Tonga were ready to accept the white man's church but the waiting list was a long one; thousands were ready to accept baptism but the Livingstonia Mission had a firm rule that baptism should not be granted in a hurry. Candidates had to wait for their turn and in the meantime join the Catechumen class and the Hearers' class. Kamwana diverted this waiting list towards his church. He needed members. The members needed quick results and relief from their burdens. They wanted a share in the fruits of the civilisation that was spreading. By 1908 Kamwana had over 10,000 adherents. Though he was arrested off and on for preaching sedition, his churches continued to exist, often secretly.

Between 1909 and 1937 Kamwana was placed in prison or in detention at Chinde, Mulanje, Mauritius and Seychelles, islands in the Indian Ocean. He returned home from the Seychelles in 1937 and founded the Watchman Healing Mission at Msuli in Nkhata Bay. There were congregations of his mission in various countries in East, Central and southern Africa.

The European missionaries and the Protectorate Government felt that Kamwana's church and teachings were dangerous and should be banned, but this was not done because it was felt that there were certain virtues that should not be overlooked. The Blantyre Resident wrote a long report on it in 1923 saying that as long as it remained fundamentally a religious body it was a source of strength to the country. He argued that if its members had aspirations to self-government, this, too, was a healthy sign. In the meantime, the Resident went on, matters connected with African tenure of land should be dealt with at once, in order to deflect or combat unfavourable African religious teachings. Higher education should be made available to Africans and the rising generation should be made aware of the necessity for discipline. To achieve this, he suggested that the curriculum of the mission schools should be broadened and the authority of chiefs and headmen should be established and strengthened.

There were two sides to the role of educated Malawians who had travelled abroad and then put their experience and learning into practice in the country. Were they merely elements of subversion, that is mischief-makers and upstarts who seemed to be in a hurry to create a new kingdom of God in Nyasaland? Or were they agents of change caught between two worlds, the western and their own, and between two religions, Christian and traditional, working seriously to harmonise the contradictions? The answer was that they were both.

Take the unfortunate case of Tomo Nyirenda, a Livingstonia-educated Henga who assumed the title of 'Mwana Lesa' or the Son of God. He started his own movement in Northern Rhodesia, baptising his followers by submerging them in water. If a person died, according to Nyirenda, it was only the witch in him that was killed. After a number of tragedies, the matter went before the High Court in Northern Rhodesia and the Mwana Lesa was found guilty and sentenced to death. Fortunately, such instances were rare.

It was to be expected that when different cultures met there would be difficulties at first. Independent churches would be formed; new teachings would be put forward; new interpretations would be made.

136

These will be considered more fully in a subsequent chapter. Some of the returning Malawians brought with them the vision of a new church. One of them was Kamkati Mkandawire, another early Livingstonia product, an old man living in Chitimba in 1970. A standard six product of the Overtoun Institution at Livingstonia, Mkandawire worked off and on in the Belgian Congo. In 1928 he and Robert Sambo of Muhuju started the African National Church. Sambo had earlier been deported from Rhodesia for promoting the aims and objects of Kadalie's trade union, the Industrial and Commercial Workers' Union. Thus a trade unionist and a mine worker who had both spent years outside the country returned home to start a new church. For them this would provide a platform from which to launch themselves into new endeavours, all of which in general were aimed at self-improvement.

There were others, too, for instance John George Phillips and John Wesley Newton, pure European names. Their names point to the influence of the missions. The first operated as a missionary in South Africa, the second in Rhodesia. The first was a Tonga and the second an Ngoni. Both combined their energies to promote the Christian Catholic Apostolic Church in Zion. Both were eventually deported to Nyasaland. For our purposes they are but two of the many adventurous and ambitious Malawians, educated and forward-looking, who looked to religion as an agency of development and change.

CHAPTER 9

Transport and Communications

The history of every country is affected by considerations of transport and communications, which either hinder or help its economic development, so that the best use has to be made of available resources. Political and economic policies have to be based on the realities of a country's endowment in terms of geographical situation and natural resources. Thus Bismarck, the maker of modern Germany, made the best use of a customs union to draw the German states together. Sir Harry Johnston and Cecil John Rhodes had a vision of an open road which would link the Cape to Cairo and promote British imperialism; Malawi's recent railway link to the Portuguese port of Nacala and the projected Tanzam line which will link Zambia to the Indian Ocean are examples of policies and programmes based on a country's problems. Malawi has had its share of these problems, especially since the country is landlocked and has no independent outlet.

The early travellers, traders and missionaries used river transport to get to Malawi from the Indian Ocean. This was done by entering the Zambezi River through one of its many mouths, such as Kongone or Chinde, or by way of the Portuguese port of Quelimane, a few miles to the north of the Zambezi. If a traveller used the Quelimane route he would have to journey up the Kwakwa River until he reached the river port of Mazaro where he would transfer to the Zambezi River. This was a point about one hundred miles from the Indian Ocean. There would have been compensations if this route provided a direct link-up of the Kwakwa and Zambezi Rivers. But this was not so. The journey by boat or canoe for four or five days up the Kwakwa River ended at some marshy lands where goods and passengers had to be offloaded for a three-mile land journey to the river port of Mazaro on the Zambezi River. Here goods and passengers were transferred to the river steamer. From here the onward journey to the Shire River ports of Chiromo and Chikwawa took anything from three to six weeks depending upon the state of repair of the steamer, the level of the rivers and general weather conditions. At Chikwawa (or Katunga's village) goods and passengers were offloaded once again because rapids for the next sixty miles made river transport impossible. Goods were then carried by porters on the next leg of the journey of twenty-eight miles to Blantyre. If goods and passengers were heading for the Livingstonia Mission or for any point on the lake there were some thirty-odd miles of overland journey to Matope on the upper Shire River. From here the mission steamer, *Ilala*, took over the rest of the journey in Malawi up to the northern tip of the lake.

Most of these early transport arrangements were in the hands of the African Lakes Company, founded in 1878, which placed a small paddle steamer called the *Lady Nyassa II* on the Zambezi and lower Shire sections. A few years later it took over the *Ilala* from the Livingstonia Mission, using it as a trading vessel on the upper Shire and the lake. These two steamers were the only means of river transport, excluding small boats, barges and canoes, for years to come. Some ten years later a second steamer, the *James Stevenson*, was added to the Zambezi and lower Shire end and the *Domira* to the lake end. Thus, with four steamers plying the waters of the Zambezi, the Shire and Lake Malawi, water transport provided the main, and often the only, means of transport from Quelimane to Karonga during the first ten years of the missionaries' and traders' arrival in Malawi.

Water transport was considerably improved when a port was opened at the Chinde mouth of the Zambezi River in 1889, so that there was no longer any need to use the cumbersome Quelimane route to get to the Zambezi. At Chinde a block of land was obtained from the Portuguese Government. From here goods were transported up the Zambezi to British territories without any customs duties being levied by the Portuguese authorities. Chinde became an important port. Several European and Indian firms established businesses there in 1890; telegraph lines were constructed linking Chinde with Quelimane, Chiromo and Sena. Travel became relatively more comfortable since it was now possible to reach Chiromo from Chinde, a distance of 180 miles, in between six and eight days.

The first point of entry into Malawi by the river route was Port Herald, now Nsanje, about thirty miles below Chiromo. Chiromo itself, situated at the confluence of the Ruo and the Shire Rivers, had the first customs house in the country as well as the first post office. From Chiromo to Chikwawa the river route was about seventy miles. During the dry season, from July to December, steamers could not make the journey if the water level was below two feet. In the rainy season this was no problem since the average depth was from three to four feet. The unreliability and fluctuations in the level of the water from Chikwawa to Chiromo and from Chiromo to Nsanje drew attention to the need for a railway line.

The steamers of the African Lakes Company discharged their cargo at a point on the west bank of the Shire River in Katunga's village. From here the cargo was carried to Blantyre. There were two other centres of activity on different sides of Katunga's village. Five miles before reaching this village, in the direction of Chiromo, there was a Blantyre Mission station near the village of the famous Kololo chief, Masea, whom Livingstone had brought to the country. Here was located the river steamer which the Blantyre Mission had acquired in 1892, the *Henry Henderson*, named after the founder of the Blantyre Mission. There was something different about this steamer. It was not a commercial steamer but a sort of floating church and school, staffed entirely by African products of the Blantyre Mission, who helped with school work and church meetings. Here also one must mention the steamer of the Universities' Mission to Central Africa, the *Charles Janson*, which also served for a time as an itinerant training college for teachers, a veritable St Michael's College on water.

In the other direction of Katunga's, that is on the Blantyre end, was the Boma at Chikwawa, two miles away. Steamers could navigate four miles above Chikwawa up to the point where the Likabula enters the Shire but after that the rapids started. It was an advantage to stop at Katunga's rather than four miles upstream. As for road transport, the first road was surveyed and laid out by James Stewart, civil engineer, who worked for the Livingstonia Mission. This was a ten-feet-wide road from Katunga's to Matope via Blantyre, sixty miles in all. With very few changes, this was the same wagon and motor road which was laid afterwards by the Government. The first road in the country was the joint enterprise of the Blantyre and Livingstonia Missions. Their mission work could only advance if they had links with the lake and the Zambezi River.

In the rest of the country, also, development was closely tied to the opening up of lines of communications. From the beginning, even the first Commissioner realised that there should be roads to support the waterways. Already there was the road between Katunga and Blantyre. The next plan was to build a road from Chiromo to Matope so as to use

140

Transport and telecommunications

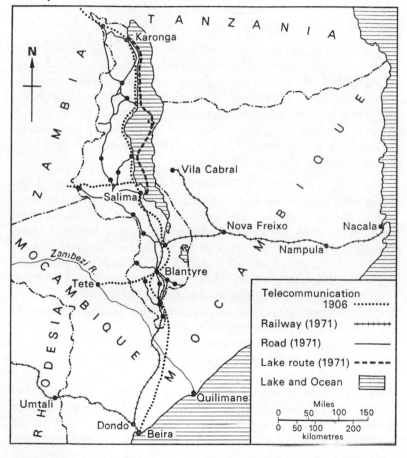

141

a longer overland route when navigation beyond Chiromo became difficult in the dry season. The third important road was between Blantyre and Zomba. This was constructed in 1893 but it followed a different course from the one we now know. The town of Limbe had not yet come into being. The road started from the Blantyre Boma, passed through the Blantyre Mission grounds slightly to the left of the present Chileka road, then to the west of Ndirande Mountain, across the north end of the Lunzu River, on to the present Njuli market, about a mile from which the present road crosses the old one.

Harry Johnston was pessimistic about the feasibility of opening up roads. In 1894 he reported to the Foreign Office:

> Except, however, between the Lower Shire and Blantyre-Zomba, one is not encouraged to spend hundreds of pounds on the making of a carriageable road, because of the presence in various tracts of the tsetse fly, which would render the passage of horses or oxen too risky for them to become constantly used as a means of transport. I fear the only certain and practical way of opening up communications with this country will be by a railway running between the Lower and the Upper Shire.[1]

It was still a long time before the establishment of railways. Meanwhile, more roads were built. The few roads in the south served the traders, the missionaries and the Protectorate administration. There was one famous road in the north, the Stevenson Road. The man whose name is connected with it, James Stevenson, was a Glasgow merchant who was the Convenor of the Livingstonia Committee in Scotland and a director of the African Lakes Company, which already had a branch store in Karonga in 1884. The matter of a road link between Karonga and Lake Tanganyika became a lively issue when the London Missionary Society started mission stations in the then Tanganyika. Some years afterwards the L.M.S. ordered a steamer, the *Good News*, to serve them. In 1881 this steamer was transported in sections by the African Lakes Company along a temporary path. James Stevenson then thought of the good idea of linking the mission work in Tanganyika and Nyasaland. For this he donated £4,000 himself for the venture which could prove to be economically advantageous. It would be easier to get persons and goods across from the north end of Lake Malawi to Lake Tanganyika by way of the Stevenson Road. Construction started in 1881. Only seventy miles of the road were eventually constructed, as the work was hampered by malaria and the outbreak of the Arab

[1] Report of the first three years administration, 1894, *Africa*, 6, London, 1894, p. 40.

War in 1888. The rest of the way to Lake Tanganyika was opened up by porters who used a well-defined track. Nevertheless, a notable attempt was made to link the mission work on two lakes. Even though commercial possibilities were not made brighter by the opening of the Stevenson Road, mission work on the two lakes was well served.

About ten miles west of Karonga, near Mwandambo village in Chief Kyunga's area, one may see a stone cross memorial, about twenty feet in length, on which three names appear: James Stevenson who gave his money for the road; James Stewart, engineer, who died at Mpata in 1883 while engaged on the construction of the road, and that of William McEwan, engineer, who also died at Mpata in 1885 while on the same project.

Telegraphic communications were opened up in the same period. The pioneering company was the African Transcontinental Telegraph Company whose plan was, like that of Johnston's and Rhodes', to link the Cape to Cairo. But owing to construction difficulties the line stopped at Ujiji, the famous town on Lake Tanganyika where Stanley had met Livingstone in 1871. Cape Town was already linked to Salisbury and the Salisbury line was extended via Mazoe, Tete and Chikwawa to Blantyre. This last section was opened in 1894. We have already noted that the Portuguese had a line from Quelimane to Chiromo. By the late 1890s all the big centres of Malawi were connected. The line reached Ujiji in 1903. In Malawi alone there were over seven hundred miles of telegraph wires. The tariff was expensive for that day at 3d. per word for internal telegrams.

All this had happened by 1903, but there was still not a single mile of railway line in use in the country. Railways were essential for future development.

ii THE INTRODUCTION OF RAILWAYS

Though water transport played an important part in the early years of Protectorate rule the drop in water levels from season to season made it difficult to plan development realistically. In the 1880s there was a decided drop in the level of the lake; the Shire River was at its lowest point in sixteen years when Protectorate rule began. For these reasons railway transport was deemed to be necessary. John Buchanan, who had been in the country since 1876, and had become a prosperous planter himself, proposed in 1893 that the country should have a rail link from Chiromo; Harry Johnston gave his support to this in the following year. The big problem was to find the money. Two companies came forward with proposals to build a railway. They were

Sharrer's Zambezi Traffic Company and the African Lakes Company. Johnston submitted their proposals to the Foreign Office. A Departmental Committee of the Foreign Office was set up and it made its report in 1897 to the effect that certain concessions should be granted in return for the construction of a railway. These included a grant of one thousand acres of land together with mineral rights for every mile of railway built; exemptions would be granted to the railway company from import and harbour dues on building material; protection would be granted to the company from competition from another line; the railway was to be the property of the company building it though a clause would be inserted in the agreement making it possible for the Government to purchase it at a future date.

At this stage the Departmental Committee was not sure whether to invite open competition for the construction of the railway, to build it departmentally or to build it under contract. It looked to the surveyors for assistance on all these points. For two years the matter rested with the surveyors. At last, in 1899, their report was published. Their survey covered a distance of 201 miles from Chiromo to the lake via Zomba; the line passed within five miles of Blantyre. They estimated the cost of a 3 ft. 6 in. gauge line to be approximately £1 million or about £4,500 a mile. The cost was high and the Crown agents recommended that the Government should undertake the construction itself. Back came the familiar reply that the Imperial Exchequer was short of funds.

The alternative was to allow a private company to build it on the terms and conditions mentioned earlier by the Departmental Committee of the Foreign Office, namely giving out large grants of land in Malawi to meet the cost. The Crown agents advised the Secretary of State for the Colonies that such a step would be wrong in principle.

While these negotiations were going on the Foreign Office received an attractive offer from one company, which was prepared to build the railway in return for monopoly rights on transport for a limited number of years and exemption from duties on building material. The Foreign Office circulated an offer along these lines among interested companies. The Shire Highlands Railway Company accepted the terms and a contract was signed on 3 September 1901. An exemption was granted from import duties; permission was given to the company to use land, timber and other natural resources free of charge for the construction; a 25-year monopoly was given to the company to run the railway. Armed with these terms the Shire Highlands Railway Company set about raising money overseas for the enterprise. It failed and a year later came back to the Foreign Office for more liberal terms. Would the

144

Government relax some of the more restrictive clauses in the agreement relating to controls over construction details and the right to regulate tariffs? Would the Government agree to a free grant of 6,400 acres of land for each completed mile of railway, preferably land situated near the line of rail?

The Shire Highlands Railway Company argued that only on such terms would it be able to make the project attractive enough for the financiers to take an interest in it. Again the Crown agents opposed the request for alienation of land, the only wealth which the country had. But the Foreign Office gave way and a new contract was signed on 31 December 1902.

The Shire Highlands Railway Company then entered into an agreement with another company already operating in Malawi, namely the British Central Africa Company, to act as their agents in the railway construction. The Crown agents saw complications in this and advised the Foreign Office to deal with the Shire Highlands Railway Company only. Let us look at one of the complications: the manager of the B.C.A. Company, in his capacity as agent of the Shire Highlands Railway Company, requested that his company should be permitted to import certain African trade goods such as calico and hoes duty free. He would use these trade goods to pay the labourers employed in railway construction. There were a number of snags in this application. For one thing, it was illegal according to the labour regulation laws of 1895 and 1903 to pay labourers in calico and hoes. There was a firm insistence that wages should be paid in cash. For another thing, the company would be in a position to undercut other traders who paid duties on their calico and hoes. The application, quite rightly, was refused.

The agreement with the Shire Highlands Railway Company was for the construction of a railway line from Chiromo to Blantyre. The actual construction began early in 1903. Two problems appeared at this time. One was a labour problem; the second was a transport problem. The Railway Company had estimated that it needed between five and six thousand labourers. In 1903 the Government entered into its first contract with Wenela to supply one thousand labourers to the Transvaal mines. This brought the Railway Company into competition with Wenela. Wages increased and labour became more and more scarce. The agents for Wenela offered £2 5s. od. per month and the Shire Highlands Railway Company were compelled to increase their wages to 7s. a month from the 3s. 6d. they paid before.

The second problem was one of transporting building material by water to Chiromo. The level of the Shire was so low that it was evident that some other means would have to be employed to get the material there. One way seemed to be by constructing a temporary railway line from Nsanje to Chiromo. The other argument was that if a temporary line had to be constructed why not make it a permanent line?

This is what the Railway Company wanted. In addition, it asked for 4,000 acres of land for every mile of rail between Nsanje and Chiromo; 100 acres at Nsanje for a terminus and 5,000 acres to be selected in blocks of 1,000 acres each anywhere in the country for mining purposes. If this request had been granted the country would have lost another 125,000 acres of land together with mining rights over 5,000 acres. The consulting engineers advised the British Government to reject the latest proposals as they were far too extravagant. The Shire Highlands Railway Company was told firmly that the extension from Chiromo to Nsanje would have to be built at their own risk; that the Imperial Treasury would not accept any obligation and that no additional land grants would be made. But this refusal gave way ultimately under pressure. Naturally, this decision was not well received by the Railway Company. Many protests were made but the Government remained firm. The Railway Company made capital of the fact that the lower Shire River was not navigable for a few months in the year—it claimed that it was not navigable for as many as seven or eight months in a year. The consulting engineers were of a different opinion. The following excerpt from a letter from the Crown agents to the Secretary of State for the Colonies dated 24 June 1904, explains their concern.

> It will be seen that the Consulting Engineers are of opinion that the Company have exaggerated the difficulties of river transport to Chiromo and that probably there are other reasons for their desire to construct the railway from Port Herald to Chiromo. This indeed is in accordance with the information which has reached us which is to the effect that the B.C.A. Company are doing everything in their power to crush out opposition in the Protectorate.[1]

A serious difference of opinion developed between the British Government and the Railway Company. For one thing, the actual building of the line was in the hands of a commercial company in Malawi which wanted to use its advantage to maximum profit. There were other commercial companies, too, some of which were older, who did not wish to be squeezed out of business. The Government had, therefore, to be careful not to grant too much to one company and yet, since the Government was itself not able or willing to provide the

---

[1] C.O. 525/4, 1904.

funds, it had to be tolerant of the company which did provide the funds. Soon the Colonial Office relented. It was prepared to pay for the extension at last. The Railway Company won by arguing that even if a river was technically navigable it did not follow that it was commercially navigable; that a concession for 42 miles of railway from Chiromo to Nsanje would be sufficiently rewarded by increasing the river traffic from Nsanje to the Indian Ocean, a distance of some 200 miles. The Company argued that the cost over 42 miles should be seen in relation to the advantages over 200 miles.

The Colonial Office gave in to this argument in 1905. For the Chiromo–Nsanje line the Railway Company could take 3,200 acres of land per mile of railway, but the land was to be selected in certain areas only. This figure was half of the subsidy land first agreed upon for the Chiromo–Blantyre line.

Thus it happened that although the original plan was that a railway should be built from Chiromo to Blantyre the actual line was constructed from Nsanje to Blantyre. It was opened to public traffic on 1 January 1908. The original agreement gave the Shire Highlands Railway Company the monopoly on railway traffic for twenty-five years; after this the Nyasaland Government could buy the railway at a cost of £4,750 (K9,500) per mile. There was a clause in the agreement which stated that within five years of the completion of the line to Blantyre, the Railway Company would start with the northern extension of the line beyond Blantyre to the lake. It was the Government's view that until there was a rail link to the lake there would not be meaningful development in the country.

There was another side to it, too. How helpful would it be to have a railway from Nsanje to Blantyre when beyond Nsanje it was difficult for river steamers to come up during the dry season? For several months in the year steamers could only come up as far as the Portuguese port of Villa Bocage, some thirty-nine miles from the railway terminus at Nsanje.

By 1908, when the first railway line opened, the country had a line which did not as yet directly serve the two main waterways, the Zambezi in the south and the lake in the north. Some day these links would have to be forged but for the moment there was the familiar lament of the Colonial Office, exemplified in this despatch of theirs to Governor Sir Alfred Sharpe: 'The fact is that financial considerations prevent us, at the present moment, from embarking on a costly, and uncertain railway policy in this particular Protectorate.'

The railway would have to pay for itself but this could only happen if the import and export trade improved. Already coffee had failed and

147

the planters were turning to tobacco. When the railway reached Limbe in 1908, it began to grow as a tobacco town. The Imperial Tobacco Company opened its factory in the same year. The tea industry, too, expanded its trade with the coming of railways.

For the moment this line of just over a hundred miles cost the country over 360,000 acres of land given by way of subsidy. Problems would arise when the actual land allocation would be made. Where would this land be found? What would happen to the people living on it?

iii THE EXTENSION OF RAILWAYS

We have already noted that the first railway to Blantyre was opened in 1908 and that the Colonial Office of the British Government which became responsible for the affairs of the Nyasaland Protectorate from 1904 incurred an obligation to part with over 360,000 acres of land in subsidies alone. After twenty-five years the Nyasaland Government could buy off the railway if it wished to, at a cost of £4,750 (K9,500) per mile.

In 1910 the issue of subsidy land became a reality. The Shire Highlands Railway Company, through its subsidiary company, the B.C.A. Company, asked for the lands due to them. The Government had already designated blocks of land for them. One was Block B in the Mulanje and neighbouring district. It comprised 98,000 acres in whole numbers. The resident African population was 24,000 living in 7,000 huts in over 1,000 villages. This was the kind of settlement that was earmarked for transfer to the companies which built the railway. It was an embarrassment to the Protectorate Government as well as to the Colonial Office.

The Protectorate Government was always of the opinion that the subsidy lands would be available when required. They had, therefore, taken no trouble to prevent migrants from Lomweland crowding out the lands earmarked as railway subsidy lands. In 1911 Governor Manning admitted this and asked the Colonial Office to hide behind a legal technicality, a clause under the original agreement which read that the subsidy lands would only be allotted 'if convenient'. This would stave off the demands of the Railway Company and in the meantime the Colonial Office could authorise any one of three possible actions: hand over the lands with the African residents on them or after removing them; buy off the Company's land claims; substitute other lands for those earmarked. In the meantime, the Governor asked the Colonial Office to consider paying the Company 5s. an acre for the subsidy lands promised so as to buy off the claims.

16. Mr Ernest Alexander Muwamba (left) and Mr K. Ellerton Mposa, the first African members of Legco, 1949.

17. P. Dayaram.   18. Sir William Tait-Bowie.

19. Members of the Nyasaland Legislative Council.

20. N.C.O.s of the Nyasaland Police, 1926.

The Governor was actually tied to an undertaking to help the Railway Company realise a return of at least 3¾ per cent on its capital outlay of just over £500,000 (K1 million) for the next twenty years. In short, the Colonial Office was making every effort to keep the Company happy by underwriting its profits while at the same time ensuring that it did not overlook its responsibilities as a protector of African interests.

There was a further embarrassment to the Colonial Office. While the negotiations over the subsidy lands due to the Railway Company were going on in 1910 and 1911 there was talk about extending the railway. There was a basic problem over this. If the Colonial Office could not sort out its obligations under the first contract how could it be relied upon to fulfil the terms of a new contract? The Colonial Secretary informed Governor Manning:

> It has been apparent throughout the negotiations for the extension of the Railway that the Company think that they have got us in a bad corner over the subsidy lands, and this belief no doubt stiffens their demands in connection with the extension of the Railway. We have met this attitude by maintaining that, whatever the inconvenience, it is still possible for the Government to allot to the Company the actual subsidy lands specified in the contract; that the rights of the natives settled on the lands are amply secured . . .; and that any disadvantages which might result from handing over those lands with the natives upon them to the Company would be much more serious for the Company than for the Government. . . .[1]

The Colonial Office was calling a bluff. In actual fact it was hard pressed. The Treasury agreed to provide for a maximum of £200,000 (K400,000) to pay the Railway Company for the failure to hand over some of the subsidy lands as well as to guarantee 4 per cent interest on the Company's capital investment of £300,000 (K600,000) for a period of ten years. Half of this money had to come from Protectorate funds and the other half was to be a grant from the British Government.

Thus just two years after the opening of the railways, the British Government realised that it would be a mistake to use land in Malawi to pay for the whole cost of the railways. Some land had been allotted already and actually given over; other land already allotted could not be given over because there were too many Africans resident on it. For this portion of the contract the Government agreed to pay the Railway Company in cash over a number of years. With a little more enterprise or foresight the Government might have avoided the mistake of subsidising railway construction with land grants in the first instance.

[1] C.O. 525/39, Colonial Office to Governor Manning, 9 Nov. 1911.

The next stage was that of extending the line in both directions. In the south, proposals were made to extend the line from Nsanje to Villa Bocage, a distance of thirty-nine miles. From Villa Bocage river steamers and barges could transport goods the whole year round to Chinde. Governor Manning informed the Secretary of State in 1911: 'During [the dry] period the trade of the Protectorate is necessarily disorganised to a lamentable degree, in fact it is temporarily paralysed and Port Herald becomes blocked by large consignments of merchandise which arrive by rail and accumulate there for want of an outlet.'[1]

The Nyasaland Chamber of Agriculture and Commerce, the Legislative Council and the Governor all supported the extension of the line southwards. In fact as early as 1908 the Chamber of Agriculture and Commerce had said that Beira should be the destination, but this was then too ambitious a request. There was Portuguese territory to cross; there was a bridge over the Zambezi to consider. The British Government would only authorise the extension which fell wholly in the British section, that is from Nsanje to Ntumbi. From this point to Villa Bocage in the Portuguese section the Shire Highlands Railway Company could negotiate with its Portuguese counterpart, the Zambezian Railway Company. This the two companies were prepared to do. But a further point arose. What would happen if the level of the Shire River fell at Villa Bocage as it did at Nsanje and Chiromo? The Government wanted a guarantee that the line would continue to be extended if this happened.

This guarantee came from a new company that had become interested in this part of the world. This was the Mozambique Company whose director and general manager was the recently retired Governor of Nyasaland, Sir Alfred Sharpe. This company agreed in 1911 to build a line from Beira to the terminus on the Zambezi at Kaira. It was also prepared to meet half the cost of building a bridge over the Zambezi.

The Shire Highlands Railway Company was then prepared to extend its line to Villa Bocage if the Government would agree to grant a subsidy of £7,500 (K15,000) per annum for twenty years. It did not ask for land because this would have been refused. While the Government was considering these proposals, the Governor of Quelimane stepped in with a proposal that a line should be built from Quelimane to Nsanje rather than from Beira. This would be less expensive, he argued, and in any case would not need a bridge over the Zambezi. The British Parliament, however, approved a Bill in 1912 for the extension of the line to Beira; it was not interested in the Quelimane line.

The effect of all this was that the Shire Highlands Railway Company

[1] C.O. 525/36, 23 March 1911.

was authorised to extend the line from Nsanje to the Zambezi River, a distance of 70 miles, while the Mozambique Company was authorised to build the line from Beira to the Zambezi River, a distance of about 150 miles. At the same time a contract was entered into between the Shire Highlands Railway Company and the Portuguese Government by which the Railway Company obtained a 99-year concession on Portuguese territory; agreement was reached that the railway on both sides of the Zambezi River would be open to traffic in three years, that is in 1915, and that the Zambezi bridge would be built during the same period.

There were three distinct territories covered by this grand plan. The first was the British section north of the Zambezi; the second was the Portuguese section north of the Zambezi; the third was the Portuguese section south of the Zambezi as far as Beira. For these three sections there were three railway companies in operation from 1913: the Shire Highlands Railway Company had responsibility from Blantyre to Nsanje; the Central Africa Railway Company had responsibility from Nsanje to Chindio on the Zambezi river; the Trans-Zambezi Railway Company had responsibility from the Zambezi to Beira.

The first train from Nsanje to Chindio ran on 17 May 1915 but the other side of the line from Beira to the Zambezi only opened in 1922.

Two things remained: the Zambezi bridge was not yet built and the railway had not yet been extended to the lake. There was no conflict of opinion about the bridge: it was necessary and it had to be built. But there was a serious difference of opinion about the railway route for the northern extension. The controversy lasted about ten years. Two routes were suggested by the powerful interests operating in Nyasaland. The first was the so-called eastern route, that is from Luchenza to Fort Johnston via Zomba and Chikala. This was the scheme which the consultants favoured. The second was the so-called central route from Blantyre to Domira Bay via Lunzu. This was the line finally agreed upon. The two main arguments in its favour were that it passed through good agricultural land and that some day it could be joined to a western route from Chipata in Zambia, which would cut through Lilongwe. In 1934 the northern extension stopped at Salima instead of Domira Bay because of the rise in the level of the lake at Domira Bay. Chipoka, some fourteen miles south of Salima, was chosen as the lake port.

On 14 January 1935 the first train passed over the great Zambezi Bridge, $2\frac{1}{4}$ miles long and the longest bridge in the world at the time. It cost about £2 million and took $3\frac{1}{2}$ years to build.

For this as well as for all the extensions both south and north the British Government gave a loan of about £3 million which was later largely waived. The railway development and the concurrent loans represent a most positive contribution by the British Government. The earlier mistakes of allocating large chunks of land in return for railway construction were remedied quickly and firmly.

On 4 July 1970, the rail link from Nkaya junction to Liwonde and from Liwonde to Nova Freixo and Nacala, a port on the Indian Ocean, was opened. The Malawi side of the Nacala rail link covers $62\frac{1}{2}$ miles and cost £$5\frac{1}{2}$ million (K11 million). This marks yet another landmark in the long and often complicated history of railway extensions in Malawi. It gives Malawi its second outlet to the Indian Ocean. Further extensions westwards are bound to come into being some day linking Malawi to her western neighbours as she is today to her eastern and southern neighbours.

CHAPTER 10

Cash crops cultivated in Malawi

i COFFEE

Coffee cultivation was very important in the early years of Protectorate rule. When reporting on the administration of the country during the first three years, Harry Johnston was struck by the fact that there were some two million coffee trees in the Shire Highlands in 1893, and that the export of coffee had risen from about five tons in 1889 to about forty-five tons in 1893. 'It would almost seem,' he said, 'as though the welfare of this Protectorate will be first founded on its coffee plantations.' He had his reservations, though, because the bulk of the trees would only bear in the next few years; there was speculation, too, about how long it would be before the dreaded coffee disease would attack the trees. It had already destroyed the coffee industry in Ceylon. For the first few years, with so many question marks against cultivated crops which were still so much in their infancy, the welfare of the Protectorate, in terms of export commodities, seemed to rest with collected items like ivory and rubber rather than with cultivated crops. In 1891 ivory accounted for 80 per cent of the exports; eight years later it had dropped to 6 per cent and thereafter faded from importance.

Coffee survived for a little longer. The man who introduced it into the country was Jonathan Duncan who tells us how this happened in a letter to the *Central African Planter*, the country's first non-official newspaper, in October 1895:

> In 1878 I was appointed by the Church of Scotland Foreign Mission Committee to proceed to Blantyre. . . . Before leaving, the Foreman . . . of the Royal Botanic Gardens, Edinburgh, gave me the first coffee plants which I tended carefully on the way out, and, with the same care, they were planted in the (Blantyre) Mission Garden. In the

year 1880 we had a small crop off the parent tree, about 1,000 beans in parchment which was all sown up. Four hundred of the seedlings were planted in the Blantyre coffee garden in February, 1881. In 1883, off the four hundred trees, fourteen and a half cwt. of coffee was gathered. . . .

Duncan tells us that in 1879 Henry Henderson brought 56 lbs. of Liberian coffee seed from which only seven plants survived and these took nine years to bear fruit; two other brands, the Blue Mountain and Orange Coffee, were introduced by the Moir brothers of the African Lakes Company.

There were three main centres where coffee was first cultivated: the Blantyre Mission and Mandala in Blantyre, and on the estates of John Buchanan at Mlungusi in Zomba and Michiru in Blantyre. In 1895 coffee cultivation spread to over 100 plantations and over 6,000 acres were under cultivation. The early average yield was around 3 to 4 cwts. per acre. The expansion of coffee cultivation was hampered by labour difficulties and by transport problems. Though Tonga labourers were first recruited by the African Lakes Company in 1885, they were used exclusively for transport work. It was only in 1891 that they agreed to work on the Buchanan plantations in Zomba. Prospects became brighter for the coffee industry from then on. But the absence of good transport facilities made it difficult to transport 2,000 tons of coffee since it had to be done in less than three months. The quality of the first exports of coffee beans received favourable mention by the London coffee-brokers who described it as 'quite as good as the very best Ceylon coffee'. The Nyasaland Coffee Company, a subsidiary of a Ceylon company, was formed in 1895 to exploit the prospects of coffee in Malawi. In that year the coffee output was estimated to reach about 150 tons, with Blantyre as the leading producer with 80 tons. Some of the planters were extremely encouraged and enthusiastic; others, like A. C. Simpson of Ntundulima Estate, Mulanje, were sceptical. Simpson observed in a letter to the *Central African Planter* in 1896: 'We cannot base the prosperity of our coffee industry on any particular plantation or special crop, or on maiden crop, but on the output compared with the acreage in bearing and taking an average for a period of years. . . . We all say, coffee is paying, but where are the exports to show it?'

Commissioner Johnston was worried by the bad publicity being given to Nyasaland's coffee industry by the reports of planters from Ceylon who visited this country and by reports in the local paper as well as in foreign newspapers. He tried to counteract this by producing in the *British Central Africa Gazette* statements by such planters as

Agricultural crops, 1970 Cotton, Coffee and Tea

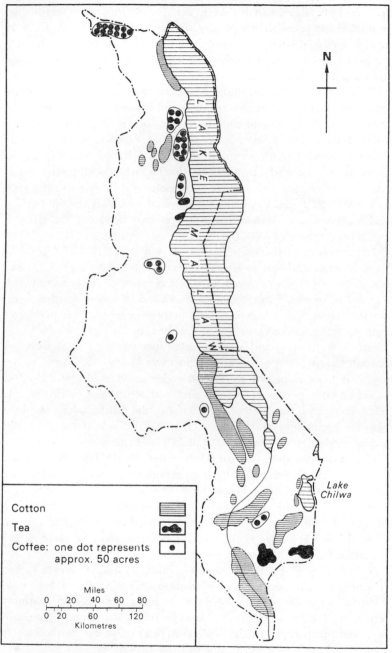

Cotton

Tea

Coffee: one dot represents approx. 50 acres

Miles
0   20   40   60   80

0   20   60   120
Kilometres

Lake Chilwa

N

Solomon Israel of Chipande Estate, later manager of the various estates of the Buchanan brothers, that the returns were reasonable, profitable and promising; a planter who got 20 tons of coffee from 60 acres in an initial attempt had not done too badly, especially since, as it happened in this case, he received an average price of £100 (K200) per ton on the London market.

However hard the optimists worked to present a hopeful picture there were serious difficulties cropping up. Besides the perennial problems of labour shortage and transport, others began to emerge: coffee leaf disease known scientifically as *Hemileia vastatrix* made its appearance. The Government took action by introducing regulations in August 1894 prohibiting the importation of coffee seeds and plants from countries where this disease was known to exist such as Ceylon and India. Pests like the ladybird which ate up the berries, and locusts which devoured the flowers also increased the risks of coffee production.

Nevertheless, in the trade figures of 1893 coffee ranked second to ivory in value and first in terms of quantity. In whole figures, 42,000 lbs. of ivory worth £18,000 (K36,000) was exported as compared with 93,000 lbs. of coffee worth just under £3,000 (K6,000). Further comparisons reveal that tobacco and cotton, both of which were in time to outstrip coffee, ranked nowhere at this time. In 1893 40 lbs. of tobacco worth only £2 (K4) and 400 lbs. of cotton worth £1 (K2) were exported. Except for ivory, whose export was in any case bound to decrease as more elephants were shot, coffee stood head and shoulders above any other economic commodity in the first years of British rule in the country. It was no wonder, then, that the Administration and the planters made every effort to protect, encourage and expand the coffee industry. Sir Harry Johnston included a coffee tree in full bloom in the first coat of arms designed for the British Central Africa Protectorate in 1894, no doubt symbolising the great faith placed in the future of the coffee industry. Johnston made so bold as to say that only a few pounds were exported in the year of his arrival as Commissioner in 1891; when he left the country in 1896, 320 tons had been exported. The amount of land brought under European cultivation during the same period increased from 1,600 acres to 5,700 acres.

Johnston estimated that a planter required a capital of about £1,000 (K2,000) to maintain a coffee plantation of 100 acres. In his book, *British Central Africa*, he devoted twenty pages to a series of imaginary letters in which he attempts to inform his overseas readers about problems and prospects in British Central Africa in case they wished to try their luck in this country. In one of these he writes:

It sometimes seems to me that the bulk of these sturdy pioneers (excellent though the results of their work have been in developing the resources of the country) would, if allowed to govern this land in their own way, use their power too selfishly in the interests of the white man. This I find the tendency to be everywhere where the governing white men are not wholly disinterested, are not, that is to say, paid to see fair play. From time to time a planter rises up to object to the natives being allowed to plant coffee, in case they should come into competition with him, or urges the Administration to use its power despotically to compel a black man to work for wages whether he will or not.[1]

The high price paid for Malawi coffee of over £100 (K200) per ton in 1896 transcended any temporary setbacks. The following year the acreage was increased by about 20 per cent, most of which expansion took place in the Thyolo district. Following the repeat performance of high prices again in 1897, planters increased their coffee acreages in Thyolo, Blantyre and Mulanje; the greatest concentration was between Blantyre and Mpemba on the Chikwawa road. It was here that 16 per cent of the country's cultivated coffee lands were to be found. Other large coffee estates were at Namadzi and Namitembo. The upward trend continued to be recorded when the twentieth century dawned: 17,000 acres were under coffee cultivation. It was unfortunate that this expansion coincided with the growth of the coffee industry in Brazil. In the ten years between 1895 and 1905 Brazil doubled her coffee exports and there was a glut on the world market. Just before the glut, Malawi coffee fetched very high prices—in 1897, between 105s. and 114s. a cwt. These were the highest prices ever obtained. In 1900, 1,000 tons of coffee were exported, accounting for 80 per cent of the total value of the country's exports. Thereafter the decline began to set in. In 1901 coffee accounted for 70 per cent of the country's exports but the quantity dropped from 1,000 tons to 600 tons and the price earned fell to almost half of the former level.

A combination of factors finally put paid to the coffee industry: yields declined and world market prices fell. While the fall in world prices affected coffee producers everywhere, the drop in yields in Malawi itself was due to a number of local factors such as drought conditions, lack of fertilisers, poor quality of seeds and unstable labour supplies. Malawi never recovered from this drastic and rapid decline. A few farmers persevered but by 1915 only 50 tons of coffee were exported and this fetched £5 (K10) a ton as compared with the record

[1] H. H. Johnston, *British Central Africa*, p. 183.

earning of £100 (K200) a ton some years before, that is 5 per cent of the previous income. In 1915 coffee represented 1 per cent of the country's exports; in 1900 it had been 80 per cent. Lingering efforts were made, mainly by those planters who had a few trees still maturing or by those who hoped for the return of the good days. In 1927 16 tons were exported. When this is compared for that same year with 522 tons of tea, 6,905 tons of tobacco, and 826 tons of cotton, a new and different picture appears. Coffee had made its exit, losing its place to tobacco, tea and cotton.

In its short history the rise and fall of the coffee industry had many lessons to teach. Firstly, planters in a new country should not place their hopes on a single crop; the success of local industries depended upon judicious use of land and labour resources, in both of which the early planters made serious mistakes. Greater productivity demanded that the majority of the people, in this case Africans, should be more closely involved in production as producers in their own right rather than as observers and labourers. What remains to be seen is whether the tragic lesson of coffee cultivation gave enlightenment and a new vision to the producers of tobacco, cotton and tea.

ii TEA AND TOBACCO

The introduction of tea cultivation is connected with that of coffee in a number of ways. For one thing, the person who brought out the first three coffee plants from Edinburgh in 1878, Jonathan Duncan, also brought out at the same time the first tea seedling. Though one coffee plant survived, the tea seedling died. Ten years later Dr Walter Elmslie, the Livingstonia missionary, returned from leave in Scotland with more tea seedlings from the same source in Edinburgh, the Royal Botanic Gardens, for the gardener at Blantyre Mission. This was Jonathan Duncan. Tea seedlings also arrived in 1886 from Kew Gardens in London. It is not clear where the tea seedlings from London were planted but it is known that the Edinburgh seedlings were planted by Duncan in the grounds of the Blantyre Mission. Two plants survived and one of them, now nearly a hundred years old, is still to be seen at the Blantyre Mission, a monument to the pioneers older than the church itself. The other connection with the coffee industry comes in the person of Henry Brown who came from Ceylon in 1891 to Malawi to take part in coffee cultivation; initially he was in the employ of the African Lakes Company. Brown opened up the Lauderdale Estate at Mulanje mainly for coffee, but drawing on his Ceylon experience, where tea was beginning to displace coffee, he obtained twenty seeds from the two surviving tea bushes at the Blantyre Mission and planted half of these on the Lauderdale Estate and half on his own estate, Thornwood, a few miles away.

In the issue of the *Central African Planter* dated October 1895, the following entry appears:

> The Lauderdale Estate was first opened up by Mr Brown of Ceylon for the African Lakes Company and some three years afterwards was transferred to Mr Moir. Mr Brown who is a relative of Alexander Brown of Ceylon, the writer of the original Ceylon *Coffee Planter's Manual*, and who is now established at Dunraven some three or four hours south from Mr Moir's place, seems to have opened the estate on the most approved Ceylon methods.

The original tea bushes at Lauderdale are still in existence and in spite of their age give a yield of over 1,000 lbs. per acre. Whereas Lauderdale started off with half an acre under tea, today it has over 1,000 acres.

This was the beginning of the tea industry in Malawi. The other planter who made an early start with tea was John Buchanan who had himself originally worked at the Blantyre Mission with Duncan and others. Buchanan planted tea in Zomba but the low rainfall was unhelpful and it was to Mulanje and Thyolo that the tea planters looked for the success of their pioneering work.

The beginnings were modest. In the early years of the twentieth century the entire area under tea was a mere 260 acres, almost all of which was in the heavy rainfall area of Mulanje district. However, as coffee began to decline tea took its place. The first recorded export of tea was in 1904 when three-quarters of a ton was exported at a value of £40 (K80). In 1966 Malawi exported over 33 million lbs. of tea valued at £4½ million (K9 million).

From Mulanje tea cultivation spread to Thyolo in 1908 where the then owner of Bandanga Estate, Mr Cox, planted the first tea from seeds which he had obtained from the Lauderdale Estate. In the same year, R. S. Hynde, who had come out originally as a missionary at Domasi but later became a planter, and co-founder and editor of the journal, *Central African Planter*, planted tea on his Mudi Estate in Limbe, but later it was abandoned. In the early 1920s of the 4,350 acres under tea 15 per cent fell within Blantyre district which at the time included part of the present Thyolo district. In 1920 about a half million lbs. of tea were exported, the bulk of it going to the United Kingdom, though in 1919 South Africa and Zambia each took 12 per cent of the exports of tea. In 1924 the export figures hit 1 million lbs.; in 1938, 10 million lbs. and in 1950, 15 million lbs.

For a long time tea gave place to tobacco and cotton but the gap was narrowed down each year until tea overtook cotton in 1925 and tobacco in 1955, only to lose first place to tobacco once again ten years later. Tobacco is now the leading export.

Nevertheless, the cultivation and export of tea rank as one of the most important factors in the economic development of Malawi. Unlike tobacco and cotton cultivation, which involved African growers from the inception, tea was until recently wholly in the hands of European planters because of the investment required and also because of production techniques. A lot of thought and effort have gone into it, including the setting up of a Tea Research Association in 1929. This has developed into the Tea Research Foundation which was inaugurated by the President of Malawi in 1966. Three tea research stations in Mulanje and Thyolo are engaged in the tasks of experimentation and improvements.

Since 1962 the Tea Association of Malawi has given its support to the development of the African Smallholder Scheme on the lines of the Kenya industry by the same name. A plan was proposed for cutting up 250 plots near Nkhata Bay and a number of plots in Mulanje and Thyolo to get a smallholder tea industry started. In 1964 plots were acquired and in two years' time 120 acres were under tea in Mulanje alone. As the economic returns become evident, it is likely that tea will be cultivated on portions of customary land, an area of landholding which has not hitherto strongly attracted cash crop cultivators in the way tobacco has.

Though domestic tobacco cultivation goes back many centuries to the years following the arrival of the Portuguese in Central Africa, tobacco cultivation on a commercial scale in modern times among European planters was started by the Buchanan brothers in Blantyre and Zomba in 1889. This was followed in 1893 by the firm of R. R. Stark and R. S. Hynde on their Songani Estate in Zomba. It was this firm that owned and published the *Central African Planter*.

The Buchanan brothers who had estates in Zomba and Michiru advertised themselves in 1895 in this paper as manufacturers of tobacco and cigars. In addition to growing tobacco, they also purchased African-grown tobacco and prepared it for the local market. John Buchanan, who first came to Malawi in 1876, tells us in his book *The Shire Highlands*:

The cultivation of tobacco holds an important place in every garden. The young plants are raised in most cases under the eaves of their huts; and when the rains are well advanced, they are planted out into

Agricultural crops, 1970 Tobacco, Rice and Groundnuts

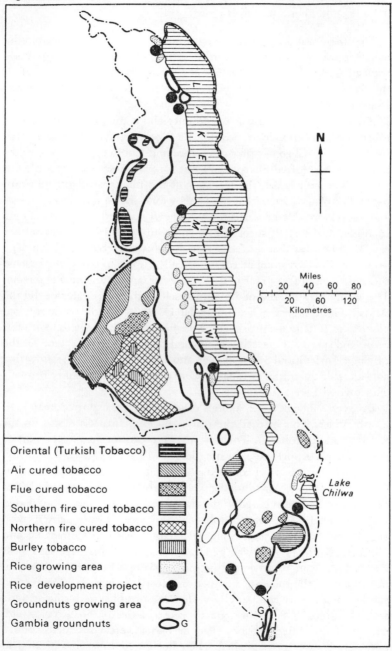

Oriental (Turkish Tobacco)

Air cured tobacco

Flue cured tobacco

Southern fire cured tobacco

Northern fire cured tobacco

Burley tobacco

Rice growing area

Rice development project

Groundnuts growing area

Gambia groundnuts

raised mounds if at the villages, or into fine black loam in some low-lying spot where the soil is moist.

That there was a considerable local market for tobacco is seen in the fact that whereas the first recorded export of tobacco in 1893 was a consignment of just 40 lbs., valued at £2 (K4), the quantity produced in the Shire Highlands in that year was over 3 tons, all of which was consumed locally.

For many years there was uncertainty about the place and value of tobacco as an economic proposition. In 1899 a deputation of the British Central Africa Chamber of Agriculture and Commerce met the Commissioner, Sir Alfred Sharpe, and put forward a scheme by a planter named Solomon Israel, the manager of the Buchanan Brothers Company. The proposal was that Mr Israel would invest money in tobacco cultivation on a large scale for two years to settle the issue of its economic viability. If successful, a company would be formed with a capital of not less that £10,000 (K20,000) for tobacco cultivation. The price that the Government would be called upon to pay if the scheme succeeded was a free grant of 4,000 acres of land to the new company. The Administration did not commit itself to the proposals nor did the British Government react immediately. It was left to individual planters to pursue the prospects as they saw fit. This they did with fair profit and success. Cigarettes, cigars and cheroots were displayed at the Mulanje Agricultural Show in 1898 and a few years later we know that considerable quantities of tobacco were being grown at Henry Brown's Thornwood Estate in Mulanje.

Between 1899 and 1904, 34 tons of tobacco were exported, mainly to South Africa. This marked the real beginning, small as it was, in the export trade in tobacco. Tobacco now represented just 1 per cent of the country's export trade, earning less than £1,000 (K2,000) annually.

Not all the tobacco produced was obtained from large-scale production on estates. African tenants were provided with seeds and after the tobacco had been cured in the traditional method it was purchased and marketed. This 'tenant-tobacco' industry, which started with Hynde and Stark on their Songani Estate, spread to Chiradzulu and Ntonda. While Hynde was general manager of Blantyre and East Africa Ltd, from 1901 to 1918 he pushed forward tobacco cultivation in a big way; the tobacco was then fire-cured or what may be termed smoke-cured. This company was also responsible for hiring experts from Virginia, U.S.A., in 1902 to take charge of the growing and curing of flue-cured tobacco. Proper barns were constructed and a notable advance was signalled when flue-cured tobacco appeared in

1903. In 1907 a number of important developments were noted: there were 2 tobacco factories and 119 flue-curing barns in the country; the Nyasaland Chamber of Agriculture and Commerce was formed; nearly 2,000 acres were under tobacco cultivation and the export figure was close to $\frac{1}{2}$ million lbs. In that year also I. Conforzi was brought out from Italy by the Blantyre and East Africa Company; he opened up estates in Njuli and Lunzu and pioneered the practice of planting tobacco early in the rainy season. Finally, the Imperial and Tobacco Company of Bristol decided in that year to open a buying and packing station in Limbe, a decision which became a reality when its new premises were opened on 31 March 1908 close to the newly opened rail line.

The following year over 1 million lbs. were exported. In ten years the figure reached almost 5 million lbs., one-tenth of which was produced by African cultivators whose commercial areas of operation extended to the central and northern provinces. The four leading districts of African tobacco cultivation in 1925 were Blantyre with 527 tons, Mulanje with 218 tons, Zomba with 193 tons and Lilongwe with 166 tons. With greater African participation legislation became necessary to control production, quality, prices and marketing, for tobacco was now not only being grown on private estates on the old 'tenant-tobacco' basis but increasingly on customary land. The Native Tobacco Board was set up in 1926 to supervise tobacco cultivation on customary land. In that year over 2,000 tons of tobacco were produced on customary land. Lilongwe led the way with over 500 tons produced by over 13,000 registered growers. The tremendous increase in village-grown tobacco pointed one way to the economic growth of the African community. Cotton showed equal promise.

iii COTTON

The cotton industry had been an important local African industry for many centuries. John Buchanan, like David Livingstone before him, gave an eye-witness account of it: 'In 1876 it was quite common,' he wrote, 'to see in villages on the Shire young men and old men busy spinning cotton into thread; and below a shady tree here and there would be an old man weaving a piece of cloth on a loom which he had made himself.'[1]

Though useful as a local industry, the indigenous variety of cotton was deemed to be too short in the staple for export purposes. Before the Protectorate, planters like Buchanan, Hynde, White and Sharrer

[1] John Buchanan, *The Shire Highlands*, London, 1885, p. 127.

had already begun to introduce leading varieties of Egyptian and American cotton and these grew well. A sample of seed cotton was sent to Kew Gardens, London, in 1896 and favourable comment was received. The planters were informed that locally grown cotton could earn almost £40 (K80) a ton and that cotton cultivation could develop into a thriving industry. Johnston's administration not only advised European and African growers to plant cotton but itself carried out experimental work in the Botanical Gardens in Zomba. With the emphasis on cotton as an export commodity cultivation increased. At the same time the importation of European cloth, as Johnston observed, almost destroyed the African weaving industry.

The first recorded export of cotton dates to 1893 when 400 lbs. valued at £1 (K2) were exported. Most of this was grown in the Blantyre district. Progress was slow until the formation of the British Cotton Growing Association in 1902. The object of the Association was to encourage cotton cultivation wherever possible in order to free the British cotton industry from its dependence on the U.S.A. which was increasingly using up its cotton supplies in local manufacturing industries. In 1904 the supplies from the United States were so low that the Lancashire cotton mills were seriously crippled. This led to the granting of a Royal Charter to the British Cotton Growing Association, that is, a monopoly to promote cotton cultivation anywhere in the world in order to obtain raw material for the British industry. In Malawi, the Association advanced capital against growing crops to enable planters to invest in cotton cultivation. Many white planters took advantage of this scheme. The growth of interest in this crop can be seen in a number of developments. In 1901 60 acres were under cotton; three years later the acreage had increased to 22,000. Cotton accounted for 12 per cent of all exports in 1905 and the figure increased each year until it reached a peak of 44 per cent in 1917. In 1916 the Director of Agriculture reported that the cotton industry, both European and African, was the largest in the Protectorate.

While progress was being recorded certain difficulties began to appear. Some European planters switched from cotton to tobacco in the expectation of making larger profits. The British Cotton Growing Association lost considerable sums of money which it had advanced. The Association then decided to make cotton growing an African industry. It set up four ginning factories, the first of which was started in 1910, and a number of buying centres. It also provided cotton seed free of charge for distribution among African growers. When the quality of Malawi cotton deteriorated the Association arranged for good-quality seeds to be sent out from Uganda. It also lent a hand in raising a considerable sum of money towards the extension of the railway line to the Zambezi in order to facilitate transport of local produce.

It was unfortunate that the high level of cotton production occurred at a moment when the effects of war were bearing heavily on the manufacturing industries in Britain and elsewhere. In late 1917 the country produced over 1,000 tons of seed cotton but the Association could only acquire less than 30 per cent of it. It was fortunate that there were other ready buyers otherwise cotton cultivation would have collapsed. The Nyasaland Government itself bought part of the cotton crop from 1919 to 1921. The then Secretary of State for Colonies, Winston Churchill, objected to this practice on the ground that government trading of this kind should not take place without the consent of the Colonial Office. The official view was that the British Cotton Growing Association should be left with the sole right of buying up the whole of the cotton produced. The point was made that the Association could be relied upon to play fair and to maintain the high quality of cotton. The Nyasaland Government could not agree with this. It felt that a price of between 2d. and 2½d. per lb. for no. 1 grade could be improved upon. There was the danger, too, that Africans would begin to lose interest in cotton cultivation because of the wide fluctuation in prices, which ranged from 1d. a lb. to 9d. a lb. for no. 1 grade seed cotton. One way to prevent fluctuations was to grant a monopoly to the B.C.G.A. This was granted as from 1923 when the B.C.G.A. received the sole right of purchasing African-grown cotton on Crown lands in seven districts, an arrangement which was criticised three years later at a conference of Governors of the East African Dependencies who seemed to favour free markets once an industry became prosperous.

There was no doubt that cotton production among Africans was becoming a prosperous industry. In 1904 Africans produced 26 tons of cotton; ten years later the figure had increased to over 1,200 tons. After that it began to fall gradually. The war, low prices, marketing and quality all had something to do with the decline. Better returns from tobacco also had something to do with it. Nsanje and Chiromo were the main production centres. In the central region small quantities were grown in Ncheu; in the north at Karonga.

Of the four ginneries set up by the Association the leading and most up to date was the one at Nsanje; Chiromo came next, while the smallest was at Vua in the North Nyasa District; the Fort Johnston (now Mangochi) ginnery was only purchased in 1914.

The Lower Shire, then, was the leading cotton-producing centre. When things went wrong in that area, production fell noticeably. The area was often struck by extremes of drought and floods and these factors were the most important causes of the fluctuations in production. The year 1914 was particularly bad. Floods struck and in addition the onset of World War I caused the price to fall from 9d. to 5d. a lb. for no. 1 grade.

As well as the Africans, Indian storekeepers in the Ruo and Lower Shire districts took to growing cotton on smallholdings since 1912. In 1915 they accounted for one-quarter of the cotton grown in these districts. The smallholdings were on Crown lands which were leased on annual tenancies.

There was a problem which began to develop at this time in connection with the unauthorised use of Crown lands for the growing of cash crops by Africans. The Chamber of Commerce and Agriculture complained in 1919 that some cultivators were exceeding their limits of eight acres per tax-paying hut and were opening up vast acreages on adjoining lands for the cultivation of tobacco and cotton. In this, the Chamber went on, the growers were financed by Europeans and Indians who afterwards bought up the crops, often at minimum prices. This represented unfair competition since such investors paid no rent, taxes or wages. The Government met this situation by requiring all growers, both African and non-African, who planted large blocks with industrial crops to register their holdings by obtaining regular leases for them.

In spite of its various ups and downs the export of cotton was an important source of revenue. Up to 1910, cotton was the leading export in quantity. The following year it lost its place to tobacco but retained second place till 1935 in which year the export figure of over 8 million lbs. was the highest recorded in nearly fifty years. After 1935, tea overtook cotton which then enjoyed third place in the country's export trade.

Before Federation the story of cash crops cultivated in Malawi was the story of the big three, tobacco, tea and cotton. Mention must now be made of groundnuts which displaced cotton in the period which coincided with the Federation. Like tobacco and cotton, groundnuts had been grown in Malawi as a domestic crop for many centuries. They were first exported in 1904 and within three years accounted for 6 per cent of the total exports. The main production areas were the Lower Shire and M'Mbelwa districts but the crop was grown mainly for domestic consumption. The breakthrough was made in 1952 when 3,000 tons were exported, more than the combined total over the previous fifty years.

Malawi is an agricultural country and it is to her planters and farmers of all races that the country looks for economic growth and development. Companies and individuals have all played their part. Among the first white planters such names as Buchanan, Moir, Sharrer, Simpson, Pettitt, Brown, Hynde, Lindsay, Fotheringham, Duncan, Smillie, Israel, Hastings, Bradshaw, Cleland, Gibbs, Steblecki, Conforzi, Sinderam and Adamson appear among the pioneers. Missionaries, too, have encouraged African participation and economic growth. Pride of place for his radical economic programme must go to Joseph Booth of the Zambezi Industrial Mission founded at Mitsidi in 1892. He encouraged African residents to open up coffee and cotton plantations, offered higher wages and instilled the virtues of self-reliance. He formed the African Christian Union in 1897 and put forward an ambitious scheme which aimed at making the plantations self-sufficient within three years.

The pioneer African planter, Joseph Bismarck, disagreed with Booth's timetabling. Three years, Bismarck felt, were not enough for Africans to achieve self-sufficiency. Bismarck was himself a planter, having bought 50 acres at Namwiri, adjoining Stella Maris on the Chikwawa road, in 1895. To this purchase he added 100 acres in 1901 and on his 150 acres he planted coffee, tobacco and fruit trees. Other early African businessmen and planters were: Kumtaja who cultivated a large estate at Chileka; Donald Malota whose estate of over 100 acres at Nguludi grew coffee and bananas, and Paton Somanje, one-time clerk and head *capitao* for the Buchanan brothers at Zomba, who became a prominent landowner, planter and businessman at Zomba. At Chiradzulu there were John Chilembwe, Augustine Mlanga, Sam Sambane and Thomas Lulanga; at Nsoni, close by, were Chilembwe's colleagues John Gray Kufa, Duncan Njilima and Hugh Mataka, all of whom grew tobacco, cotton and other crops. In the Blantyre district there were Haya Edward Peters, otherwise known as Peter Mlelemba, of Nangafuwe Estate at Ndirande, and Chief Machinjiri at Lunzu. These were among the pioneers who represented African enterprise. They had their business associations, too, like the African Industrial Union, and like their European counterparts who led the way at this time they took to the cultivation of cash or industrial crops. Together they made it possible for Malawi to put her good-quality crops on the world market.

CHAPTER 11

Educational developments in Malawi up to the introduction of secondary education

i THE MISSIONARY CONTRIBUTION

The provision of primary and higher education in Malawi on western lines originated from many sides and was spread over nearly one hundred years. In the forefront of the development was the European missionary contribution; then came the progress recorded since the creation of the Education Department in 1926 and, finally, the changes introduced since setting up the first Ministry of Education in 1961. Between 1926 and 1961 the notable attempts made by Malawian educationists to set up independent schools, the opening of separate schools for Europeans, Asians and Coloureds, all form part of the story.

The story opens with the European missionary contribution which has never ceased to be very important in promoting education, whether secular, religious, technical or industrial.

The first school was started at Cape Maclear by the Livingstonia Mission in 1875. In that year a few boys called in occasionally but there were no African teachers, the missionaries had not yet learnt the language well enough and pupils were hard to come by. However, education on systematic lines commenced in 1876. The second Livingstonia party under Dr James Stewart brought four African teachers and evangelists from Lovedale in South Africa: Shadrack Ngunana, William Ntusane Koyi, Mapas Ntintili and Isaac Wauchope, afterwards known as Isaac Williams. The party also brought along two sons of the Kololo chief Ramakukan from the lower Shire, together with their attendants. These made up the first regular pupils. Ngunana took charge of the school until his death in 1877. In one of his first reports,

168

Dr Laws wrote: 'The School at Livingstonia has two departments—those who come from a distance and are boarded at the station, and those who live with their parents and come to school daily.' In addition to their school work the boarders gave two hours to outdoor work. In 1879 there were 120 pupils on the roll at this first school. Instruction was given in Chichewa and English; the first half-hour was devoted to Bible lessons. Besides learning to read, write and count, carpentry, brickmaking, bricklaying and needlework were taught. In eleven years the number of schools run by the Livingstonia Mission increased to three; African teachers increased to ten; and the pupils increased to three hundred.

After this beginning the familiar story repeated itself in other missions and mission education, whether Presbyterian, Anglican or Baptist, all increased its scope before the end of the nineteenth century. Closely connected with the story of this growth is that of the training of African teachers and evangelists. It was they who had to man the village and outstation schools; it was they who by their example and leadership were to spread the message of development through western education, so that the people should not only fit themselves into the new society that was being formed but make themselves better and more useful members of their own society as well as serve other societies in Central and southern Africa.

In the nineteenth century the pioneer African teachers operating in Malawi were both Malawians and non-Malawians. Some of the latter died in the country while still working, like Shadrack Ngunana and William Ntusane Koyi, the men from Lovedale. Men like Joseph Bismarck, Charles Domingo and John Gray Kufa, who came from neighbouring Mozambique, made Malawi their home. Here they lived, worked and died. Others came from as far afield as Zanzibar in 1885 and were in the party when the first lake steamer of the Universities' Mission to Central Africa was dedicated at Matope on 6 September of that year. These six rank among the unsung men of the nineteenth century: So Songola, Augustine Ambali, Bartlet Kalika, Basil Kamna, Nicholas Farazi and Paul Mambo.

Among the early Malawians who helped to promote education were those who were sent abroad for their studies and preparation. The first were Tom Bokwito and Sam Sambane who had been freed from slavery at Mbame village when Livingstone was taking the first party of Anglican missionaries to Magomero in 1861. They were sent to Lovedale in South Africa and afterwards accompanied the first Livingstonia party to Malawi in 1875. Kagaso Sazuze started his schooling at Blantyre Mission and in 1878 left for Lovedale, where he remained for five years. Other early Blantyre Mission products to go to Lovedale were Joseph Bismarck, Nkolimbo and Sawalangera Evangere. At this time, the Blantyre Mission also sent Henry Cowan Kapito and Donald Malota to Scotland. They were followed there by Mungo Murray Chisuse who returned to take charge of the Blantyre Mission press after his second trip to Scotland. Mention must also be made of Charles Domingo who was brought to Malawi in 1876 from Quelimane by the Livingstonia missionaries and then sent to Lovedale also. Domingo went on to become the first African student to receive what was then equated with a higher teachers' certificate from the Livingstonia Mission in 1897.

It is clear, then, that the early missions made a good start in the nineteenth century establishing and expanding their educational programmes in the country. In order to do this successfully the pioneer missionaries were thoughtful enough not only to train teachers and evangelists locally but also to send them abroad, thereby beginning a tradition which was to grow in the twentieth century when Malawian teachers and church leaders were themselves to act as pioneers of development in various parts of East, Central and southern Africa.

A number of missions opened schools between 1850 and 1875. The Church of Scotland had mission station schools at Blantyre, Domasi, Mulanje and Zomba as well as a number of outstation schools. The Livingstonia Mission had mission schools at Cape Maclear, Bandawe, Njuyu, Ekwendeni, Kasungu, Khondowe, Karonga and Mweniwanda and a large number of outstation schools. The Universities' Mission to Central Africa had mission schools on Likoma Island and Nkhota Kota as well as outstation schools. The Dutch Reformed Church Mission started their main schools at Mvera, Kongwe and Nkhoma while the Zambezi Industrial Mission opened its main school at Mitsidi in Blantyre with branches in the Ncheu district. The Nyasa Industrial Mission opened its main school at Likabula and a branch school at Tholo.

These were the missions which pioneered education in Malawi in the nineteenth century. All of them ran three categories of schools: mission, outstation and village. The European staff were posted mainly to the mission schools, though they often helped to set up outstation schools which they even served when necessary. Though such names as Laws, Henderson, Hetherwick, Murray, Elmslie, Prentice, Fraser and McCallum; Booth, Scott, Johnson and Chauncey Maples do illuminate the pages of Malawi history, women too have played their part.

Dr Jane Elizabeth Waterston arrived in 1879 to serve the Livingstonia Mission. Her work was continued by Dr Agnes Fraser. Then there was Miss Janet S. Beck who came to Malawi in 1886 as an honorary unsalaried missionary and joined the Blantyre Mission a year later. In 1917 she completed thirty years in the service of the Blantyre Mission. Miss Beck and Miss Bell were posted in 1893 to the out-station school at Ntumbi under an African teacher whose name was Harry Kambwiri Matecheta. In the Blantyre Mission journal, *Life and Work*, of December 1893 the following entry appears: 'Letters from Miss Bell give cheering and interesting reports of their progress. It is splendid to work in fresh fields, "far from the madding crowd" and one anxiously waits to see how, and how quickly, the experience gained by years of Mission work takes root in new soil.' Many more were to follow in the tradition of the Waterstons, Frasers and Becks, serving and leaving behind the valuable results of their dedication—persons such as Frederica Mary Klamborowski who came to Malawi in 1912 and died there in 1971 at the age of eighty-seven.

The first school in the country to offer a wide range of subjects and courses in the nineteenth century was the Livingstonia Mission school which was opened near the Manchewe falls on Mount Nyamkowa in 1894 and later named the Overtoun Institution. Here there was an elementary school in which the vernacular language was chiefly used; there was a middle school in which English and vernacular media were used; there was a normal school or teacher training section. In addition, commercial courses were offered to train clerks, storekeepers and telegraphists; medical courses were available to teach students to be medical assistants. There was a theological section to train Africans for the ministry. It was at the Overtoun Institution that promising students from all over the central and northern regions rounded off their education beyond standard three. This was the leading educational institution in its day and it turned out some of the finest products of mission education in the nineteenth century and in the early years of the twentieth century.

Then there was St Michael's College of the U.M.C.A. which was first established at Kanga in Portuguese East Africa in 1899. It afterwards moved to Likoma Island, Malosa and Malindi, where it is today. St Michael's served in very much the same way as the Overtoun Institution in teacher training work, and it too had a wide catchment area.

The leading institution in the south was the Blantyre Mission. Its very varied work reached fulfilment with the opening of the Henry Henderson Institute in 1909. This was for the south what the Overtoun Institution was for the north. When the Dutch Reformed Church Mission opened the William Murray Teacher Training College at Nkhoma Mission, the achievement was the same as what the Presbyterian and Anglican missions had already established in other places, namely institutions where higher technical, industrial, commercial and educational provisions were concentrated at a specially selected centre.

The important contribution of the Catholic missions was made in the twentieth century even though a start had been made in 1890 by the White Fathers who had first arrived the previous year at Mponda's village in present Mangochi. In April 1890 a school was opened for Yao children only. As a result of various difficulties at the time, for instance the conflict raging between the British and the Portuguese for control of the country and the lack of help from sister missions along the coast, this first attempt failed and the White Fathers left for Mambwe in Zambia in 1891. The Montfort Marist Fathers arrived in Malawi in 1901 and opened a mission and a school at Nzama. The White Fathers returned to the country in 1902 to complete what they had begun in 1890. Their work as well as the development programmes of the other missions in the field of education will be considered in the next section.

ii GOVERNMENT PARTICIPATION IN EDUCATION

In the first twenty-five years of mission education in Malawi, there was no single organisation of the different missions where matters of policy could be discussed. The Protectorate government took no part in what was going on since it provided no money for education. What was happening was that piecemeal development was taking place as each mission planned for itself with no directive or guidance from any central body.

Four of the missions made the first move towards a unified system when they met in conference at Livingstonia in 1900. The conference agreed to produce a common educational code. The code was discussed at the second mission conference held in Blantyre in 1904 and was published the following year under the impressive title of *Central Africa United Educational Missionary Institutions*. The code was revised at the third conference in 1910 by which time the missions involved described themselves as the Federated Missions. The members were the Church of Scotland Mission, the Livingstonia Mission, the Dutch Reformed Church Mission, the South African General Mission, the Zambezi Industrial Mission and the Nyasa Industrial Mission.

The code provided for the curricula for five grades of schools and institutions from vernacular village schools at one end to theological schools at the other. In 1910 a Consultative Board was set up comprising Drs Laws and Hetherwick, the Rev. W. H. Murray of the D.R.C.M.

and A. Hamilton of the Zambezi Industrial Mission. It was to this Board, which was the executive arm of the Federated Missions, that matters of general policy were referred. The Government recognised it as a body to deal with while the missions now working together deemed themselves to be sufficiently united to make a concerted appeal to the Government for funds. They had every reason to ask for assistance but the Government was slow in responding. The only reason it advanced for its slowness was that unless there was an educational system to which the missions subscribed it was difficult to apportion government funds in aid. After 1905 that argument no longer existed and the Government announced its first contribution of £1,000 (K2,000) in 1907 to be shared among those missions accepting the education code. The U.M.C.A. was the only European mission which did not subscribe to the code. It did not apply for financial support, preferring to be entirely independent, and thinking that it had enough funds for the work undertaken. In any case this mission did not agree with the need to cater for industrial training. It saw its task as a purely religious undertaking.

The government grant was little more than nominal. It was increased to £2,000 (K4,000) as from 1920 but the grant was even then a small fraction of the total cost. After the end of World War I more attention was paid to educational needs in the colonies and protectorates. Certain international and colonial pressures had much to do with this. The concept of mandated territories impelled the League of Nations to use its organisation in the direction of educational changes. The Phelps-Stokes Fund in the U.S.A., the International Missionary Council, the work of Miss Anna T. Jeanes since 1908, all had a bearing on the changes that were soon to take place. The British Government, marching with the times, set up an Advisory Committee on African Education in British Tropical Africa in 1923 and the following year this Committee cooperated with the Phelps-Stokes Committee which visited Malawi to report on the educational system and facilities. The Phelps-Stokes Committee reported that though Nyasaland had immense possibilities it was 'the poorest Colony in Africa'. One of the reasons for the poverty, it said, was poor internal and external transportation facilities. The report stated:

The second reason for the condition of Nyasaland is in the failure of Government to organize and correlate the splendid educational work of the missions with the various phases of colonial life. Missions have been permitted to struggle alone in their respective fields. Latterly a negligible appropriation has been given to them, but there has been no Department nor Director of Education to confer with the Missions, to encourage them in their work, or to help them relate their influences to each other or to colonial needs.[1]

The report called for the setting up of a department of education together with an Advisory Board on African Education. These recommendations were reinforced by another report the following year, this time from a Commission of the Colonial Office itself. The first Director of Education in Malawi, R. F. Gaunt, arrived in 1926 and an Education Department was set up.

It was because of external pressures rather than internal developments that the first state-organised educational system was introduced in 1926. The Education Ordinance of that year provided for an Education Board, later called an Advisory Committee, to be assisted later by Provincial School Committees but more immediately by District School Committees separately constituted for European and African schools where both existed. The specification for the composition of the Education Board or Advisory Committee was a wide one so as to comprise government advisers, senior civil servants, two representatives each from the larger as well as the smaller missions, representatives of the Planters' Association and the Chamber of Commerce as well as two representatives from the African community. The last provision was only acted upon in part in 1933 when Levi Mumba became the first African to be appointed. He was joined by Charles Matinga in 1937.

The government now set about taking control over education by calling conferences and working out detailed schemes. In 1927 there were 2,788 schools in the country, 4,481 African teachers, 91 full-time European teachers and 63 part-time European missionary teachers. The total number of pupils enrolled was 166,022. The cost of this education was over £41,000 (K82,000) but the government subsidy was just over £4,000 (K8,000), less than one-tenth of the total cost. It is no wonder, then, that at least one mission came out in open criticism of what it considered to be improper interference on the part of the Government. The Bishop of Nyasaland wrote:

The main criticism of the present scheme, which I think everyone who knows the facts must accept, is that the Government is taking a very complete control of Education, and, on paper at any rate, dictating terms and limitations of the most drastic character while still taking it for granted that the Missions will continue to pay for

[1] *Education in East Africa*, ch. 8, Nyasaland, London, 1925.

the greater part of the cost. . . . Where the Government controls to anything like this extent, the Government pays. Here the familiar proverb is indeed upside down: the Government is to call the tune, but the Missions are to pay the Piper.[1]

This was how it was for a long time to come. Government funds in the Protectorate days were extremely limited. The education vote in 1926 was just 1 per cent of the total revenue; ten years later it rose to 4½ per cent and remained at that figure for the next ten years. The real acceleration began with the introduction of the Ministry of Education in 1961; by 1963 the Government was spending 15 per cent of its revenue on education.

One of the most important developments—after the setting up of the Education Department in 1926—was the establishment of a government school for training African supervising teachers. This programme, which provided a special course for selected African teachers and their wives, was aimed at training supervisors who would, after two years of training, be posted to their home areas where they would be placed in charge of a number of village schools. The Jeanes Training Centre opened at Domasi in 1929 after considerable negotiations. It was suggested at first that 'Jeanes departments' be added to the existing training institutions at Blantyre, Nkhoma and Livingstonia, but this idea was turned down for obvious reasons. It would have added to the work of certain institutions and not to others; it would have led to mission controls and promotion of individual mission ideologies.

Named after Miss Anna T. Jeanes of the U.S.A., who established a fund in 1908 to employ special teachers whose task it would be to make the small rural schools of the United States a living part of village communities, the Jeanes programme aimed at improving academic and professional standards but at the same time it emphasised agriculture, health and village industries. The school was to be not an ivory tower for the few but a centre of village life which took account of the society and its environment. The first Principal of the Jeanes Training Centre at Domasi saw five main objects for his training centre: improvement of class-room instruction in reading, writing and arithmetic; the adapting of school subjects to African life and environment; the enlargement of the scope of village school education; the creation of the school as a community centre and the provision of training in homecraft and child welfare for wives of students in training. This was a notable development in a country which was almost 100 per cent

[1] S2/2/38, Minutes of Session of Board of Education, 30 Aug.–1 Sept. 1927, National Archives, Zomba.

rural and which had thousands of village schools and not a single secondary one at the time. When the Government accepted responsibility for the Jeanes Training Centre it guaranteed that the institution would be impartial. It was the first instance of government participation in Malawi in the field of teacher training and indeed in the field of providing a government school.

It must be noted also that in 1929 the Carnegie Corporation of New York voted a grant-in-aid of five thousand dollars for five years provided that the Nyasaland Government invested a similar amount. The five-year grant was extended for an additional two years. However, the Carnegie Corporation not only doubled its grant in 1935 but extended it up to 1938 in order to make a new scheme work. This scheme began in 1934 in Nyasaland, when six selected chiefs and their wives were given a four-month course at Domasi in community development and rural reconstruction; these were, in essence, the main objectives of the Jeanes programme.

By 1937, seventy-five supervisory teachers had been trained. Sixty teachers' wives had benefited from the course while nineteen native authorities, including paramount chiefs, took back to their areas of traditional influence the new ideas and values of the training centre. Immediate improvements were noted in sanitary provisions. For the first time an educational institution provided the various links which brought together the Government, the training centre, the school supervisors, the native authorities, the village schools, teachers, pupils and parents in the villages, an ideal which continues to exercise the attention of educationists and policy makers.

Up till now it was only primary education which was being provided. This did not please the older generation of mission products. Levi Mumba, Charles Domingo, Charles Chinula, Yesaya Zerenji Mwase and Edward Boti Manda, among others, admitted that they were grateful for the education they had received and proved that they were worthy of it. But for the younger and coming generations they asked that higher education be introduced.

iii FURTHER DEVELOPMENTS IN EDUCATION: 1925–1940

In 1925, a year before the establishment of the Education Department, two private schools with boarding facilities were opened for European children. One of these was run by the Montfort Marist Fathers at Limbe and the other was in Sunnyside, Blantyre, and was run by the Rev. Wratten of the Church of England. The following year a similar school was opened at Nkhoma Mission. In January 1927 Mrs M. W. Dally opened a school in Zomba.

The numbers in these four schools were very small. In 1926 there were only 264 European children in the country, of whom 195 were under five years of age. Mrs Dally's school in Zomba started with 11 children; in two years, Rev. Wratten's school had 29 on the roll. These small figures caused a number of difficulties. The question that the Government had to settle was whether it should play any part in these schools either by way of providing subsidies or by becoming involved in the larger issue of building a single big school in Blantyre.

The first of these issues was settled when the Government agreed to allocate £700 (K1,400) as grant-in-aid in 1928. The amount was increased in later years. The second was not easy to resolve. Though the Administration agreed to build a Government Central School as early as 1928 it found itself in grave difficulties over the virtue of spending money which was so urgently required in other directions on such a small number of people. When the Director of Education visited Rev. Wratten's school in 1930 he reported that there were only 26 children on the roll; not one was over twelve years of age. There was 1 child in standard five and 1 in standard four. There were no boarders though the school had boarding facilities. The Director was surprised to find that there were 3 Europeans on the staff for a school with 26 on its roll. Since this particular school received the largest single government subsidy, the Director recommended that government funds might be saved if the Town Council of Blantyre took over the responsibility of building a new school to replace the existing one or if the Town Council undertook to support Rev. Wratten's school. The matter was referred to the Town Council which did not feel justified in using ratepayers' money for one section of the community only.

For its own part the Government wished to be assured that if it did invest in a new school, the numbers would warrant it and that European parents would find it possible to withdraw their children from schools in Rhodesia, South Africa and Europe. Its enquiries led to firm answers that such developments were not likely. One, the District Commissioner for Mulanje, himself the father of two children, had this to say:

There are no children of parents in this district who would be brought back from where they are at present being educated outside the Protectorate and sent to a school in Blantyre. My own opinion, in which more than half the parents seem to concur, and perhaps as a parent I may be allowed to express it, is that it is thoroughly bad, both physically and morally, for children to be educated in this country, and nothing but dire financial considerations would allow me to send my sons to a school in Blantyre.[1]

In view of all this the four private schools continued to operate as best they could with limited government assistance. Neither the Government nor the Blantyre Town Council would undertake to build a European school. In fact, up to 1930, the only schools built by the Government were the Jeanes Training Centre at Domasi, a school for Muslim children at Liwonde and a Police school. The uncertainties about the future of European education in Blantyre were resolved when the Church of Scotland Mission agreed to build a day school at Blantyre and to take over the existing private school. The Government agreed to make a loan of £2,500 (K5,000) and to meet recurrent costs of up to a maximum of £250 (K500) per annum. The agreement was to run for thirty years but could be terminated by either party at the end of any ten-year period. The school opened in 1938. It closed during the Federation when the Federal Government built St Andrews School. The premises are today occupied by the Christian Service Council.

By this time other communities, too, began to clamour for government support. Since 1933 the Anglo-African Association had requested the Government for separate educational facilities but the Advisory Committee on Education could not support it. In 1936 permission was granted to an Indian lady, Mrs Dalvi, the wife of a medical doctor, to open a private school in Limbe for Indian children as well as for children of mixed parentage. A small government subsidy was given to this school which remained in existence for about ten years. It was only in 1943 that the Government finally approved of a separate school for the Coloured community when the community successfully petitioned the Governor of Nyasaland, Sir Edmund Richards, as well as the Advisor on Education to the Secretary of State, Mr (now Sir) Christopher Cox, who was then on a visit to the country. The success of this enterprise was mentioned as one of the factors which contributed to the birth of the Nyasaland Educated African Council in August 1943, the body which later changed its name to the Nyasaland African Congress. The argument was advanced that if other communities could unite in their demands for certain improvements it was time that a national body spoke on behalf of the African community.

In the meantime the Asian community also started further action when two small private schools were started in 1933 by members of the Muslim community in Blantyre and Zomba. The total number for both these schools was thirty-five students. In 1938, the year when the

[1] C.O. 525/138, file 33461/1930, P.R.O.

178

European school opened at the Blantyre Mission, an Indian school was started in Blantyre through the initiative of Mr Osman Adam and Mr C. K. Dharap. The Dharap School was followed two years later by the Osman Gani school at Songani about eighteen miles from Zomba. From then on the idea of starting schools caught on gradually and the next few years saw new schools being opened in Zomba and Limbe. The practice of community self-help with leadership in the hands of a few persons was as evident in those formative years as it is today. Though private schools still exist in Limbe and Blantyre, the most notable of which are the Central High School and the Hazeldean School, admission is no longer exclusive but is open to members of all communities.

The main challenges in education lay not among the minority communities but in the area of African education. Though the main responsibility here rested with the missions there was one delicate sphere in which the missions were helpless and the Government had to intervene: this was in the provision of schools for Muslim children. Statistics collected in 1928 showed that there were 105,000 Muslims in the country, 95 per cent of whom were Yao. The main centres of concentration were Zomba, Liwonde, Fort Johnston (Mangochi), Dedza and Dowa, while most of the non-Yao Muslims—about 4,000 in number—were at Nkhota Kota. In that year the prominent Yao chiefs, notably Kawinga, Jalasi, Kukalanga and Makanjira, notified the Government that they wanted government schools for their children, not mission schools. The Government agreed to begin by putting up a school at Liwonde on an experimental basis. The Education Ordinance of 1927 provided for the admission of Muslim children to Christian schools supported by the Government, but the Ordinance also stipulated that religious instruction should be given in all schools. Hence Muslim children were affected by these contradictory provisions.

Brief mention must be made of the initiative of individual Malawians in the field of education. John Chilembwe opened a school in 1900 at the Providence Industrial Mission in Chiradzulu and a branch school at Kaduya's village in Phalombe. In both these areas he met with stiff opposition from the existing Christian schools run by European missionaries. Then there was Charles Domingo who broke with the Livingstonia Mission in 1907 and started a number of schools in the Loudon area of Mzimba district in the name of the Seventh Day Baptists. Domingo kept up correspondence for many years with Joseph Booth in Cape Town, the one-time mentor of John Chilembwe and early firebrand in Malawi politics. Then there was Hanock Msokera Phiri who returned from South Africa in 1924 and started a church and school in the name of the African Methodist Episcopal Church in the

Mwase and Kaning'a villages of Kasungu. His schools soon spread to other villages as well as to Zambia. Between 1933 and 1934 two ex-ministers of the C.C.A.P. (one of whom was restored two years before his death in 1970), the Revs. Yesaya Zerenji Mwase of the Chinteche district and Charles Chidongo Chinula of the Mzimba district started their own churches and schools. Mwase founded the Nyasaland Blackman's Educational Society while Chinula organised the Sazu Home Mission. Except for Mwase, the rest of these pioneering educationists received grants from the Government for the running of their schools. These grants were always conditional upon acceptable standards being reached, and government inspectors reported on their work from time to time.

It is with the contribution of Levi Zililo Mumba that this section must end. It was he who pressed for better and higher education from the platforms of the North Nyasa Native Association, the Representative Committee of the Northern Provinces Native Associations, the Advisory Committee on Education of which he was the first African member in 1933 and the Nyasaland African Congress whose first chairman he was. When he joined the Advisory Committee, Levi Mumba presented a memorandum on education in which he made the following plea:

> Educate for the employer, educate for service with tribal communities, but MOST OF ALL EDUCATE THE MASSES TO STAND ON THEIR OWN FEET. Give us this chance and I can assure you that within a period of a comparatively few years the response of the Nyasaland African will be surprisingly great.

Levi Mumba was right. The response of the Malawian African was great but the Protectorate was slow to respond. In 1937 the Federated Missions agreed to build a secondary school under the auspices of the Protestant missions if the Government would agree to maintain it. Whatever reluctance there was was knocked out of the Government by the outspoken criticism in the report submitted by Sir Robert Bell in 1939. Secondary education, according to this report, was not only overdue; its neglect had tragic consequences. The Government gave in and £7,000 (K14,000) was voted for secondary education in 1939. The following year the first secondary school in the country, the Blantyre Secondary School, opened its doors. It was a gift from the Protestant missions. The Catholic missions were equal to the occasion and within two years the Zomba Secondary School was in operation. Though long in coming, these steps were a vindication of confidence in the people's deep and abiding love for education.

CHAPTER 12

African administration

i THE PERIOD OF DIRECT RULE

When the former Nyasaland came under Protectorate rule in 1891 the rulers had no intention of involving African chiefs directly in the administration of the country. There were many reasons for this. One was the absence of a single powerful chief or king, like Lobengula in Matabeleland, to deal with. The second reason was the existence of slave-raiding and -trading in some areas, which the new administration decided to crush by military means. The third reason was Harry Johnston's refusal to bring peace by any other way, such as by continued negotiations and by providing attractive alternatives to those peoples who were engaged in human traffic. There *were* alternative ways of meeting the position, and the U.M.C.A. and Scottish missionaries took pains to suggest them to Johnston, without success. Johnston preferred to have a virtual military establishment based on the foundation of a few hundred soldiers from India. The rule began under conditions and regulations which amounted to a state of near martial law.

He began during the first year with a handful of senior European officials, only fifteen in number. The country was divided on paper into four districts at first: Lower Shire, South Nyasaland, West Nyasaland and North Nyasaland. In the next few years they increased until in 1896 there were twelve districts. The districts were the main units of African administration. European officials, named Collectors, were placed in charge. In 1896 there were twelve Collectors and fifteen Assistant Collectors. Their duties were many and varied: they supervised the collection of customs duties and hut taxes; they directed the civil police force and acted as postmasters. And, more important, many

181

of them held documents called judicial warrants which authorised them to try cases involving English as well as African law. In the latter case they were supposed to be operating 'in the name and by the authority of' African chiefs. In all this they were directly responsible to the head of the administration in Zomba. One of the early officials to come to Malawi was H. L. Duff. In his book entitled *Nyasaland under the Foreign Office* he gives us a firsthand account of these early Collectors and their judicial responsibilities.

We have the remarkable spectacle of a score or so of Englishmen, who have received no special legal training at home, administering in a most intimate and homely way, the affairs of nearly a million human-beings of a totally different race, whose own laws, highly peculiar in themselves, have either fallen into desuetude or have been thrown into a state of flux by the sudden transfer of power from their own chiefs to the alien government . . . in all cases . . . which are of constant occurrence in the lives of the natives . . . the authority of the Collector in his District is supreme and his decision final.[1]

There were limitations to their powers, of course, imposed by regulations as to procedures, penalties and appeals, but these did not minimise the grave responsibilities that rested on the shoulders of young and often untrained officials. Within the framework of what was a system of direct rule, these officials did use the services of traditional rulers to settle minor disputes and to assist in maintaining law and order and in the collection of taxes. But these services were obtained on an *ad hoc* basis. Traditional chiefs had no place in the statutory provisions of the administrative system. They were officially regarded as ineffectual, incapable and unnecessary.

This policy of leaving out the chiefs turned out to be a mistake. There were too few white officials and in any case they could never hope to penetrate African society and assume the role of traditional rulers themselves. As early as 1903 the Administration began to question the position. In the Annual Report for 1903–04 it was recalled that in the pre-colonial days chiefs had unlimited powers of life and death; they were able to keep people in order if not by kindness then through fear. In comparison, there was now a lack of discipline; villagers banded into little groups and hived off to start their own settlements. Chiefs were not being useful in judicial work while village headmen could not be entrusted with any responsibility. Within eight years the process of disintegration or dispersion gained momentum and in the Annual Report for 1911–12 the Administration made the

[1] London, 1906, pp. 326–7.

following comment: 'The decay of the power of native chiefs and the tendency all over the Protectorate to the splitting up of villages into small family groups continues.' While the Administration consoled itself with the thought that this tendency was due in great measure to the state of peace and calm which prevailed, it saw the need to re-organise the system so as to employ paid local authorities to assist the District Residents.

It was out of this situation that the District Ordinance of 1912 emerged. Each district was divided into a number of main administrative units, usually seven, each under a principal headman. The qualification for this position was that the person selected should be in good standing with the Government and should have helped the District Resident before in matters relating to district administration. If he had been a chief or headman before so much the better; if not, any ordinary person was eligible for the new office. In actual practice most of the new appointees were the former traditional rulers.

African participation was taken a step further by dividing each administrative unit into village groups under village headmen. There were three levels of responsibility in district administration. At the top was the District Resident; next came the principal headman who together with two councillors selected from village headmen constituted the sectional council. At the bottom there was the village headman in charge of the village area. In actual fact, the District Resident was the 'Big Chief', assisted by handpicked African subordinates whose loyalty to the Government was proven. The duties of the principal headmen were laid down. They were responsible for: order, discipline, reporting of crime; arresting of criminals; cleanliness; control of cattle movement and reporting the outbreak of diseases. They acted as government agents who carried information to the people and organised the required response from the people.

This new system of district administration was not introduced everywhere but in a few districts at a time in order to try it out. The Shire Highlands were specially excluded in the first few years and by the time the Government got round to the Shire Highlands in 1919 various serious flaws in the system had become known: it was difficult to direct that villages be concentrated in units of twenty or more huts, since this interfered with the rights of landowners and tenants. The system was now seen to be unsuitable for private estates as well as for Crown lands. In that year the Chamber of Commerce drew the Governor's attention to some of the defects: principal headmen could not maintain authority over a number of ethnic groups in their sections; village headmen were equally helpless. There was no longer any respect for the old chiefs and this tended also to undermine the authority of landowners and even of the Government. The Chilembwe incident of 1915 did nothing to endear the system to the Government and the colonists. The so-called loyal and paid agents of the Government had failed to report or prevent subversion in certain parts of the country.

The system needed overhaul. A land commissioner reported in 1920 that the introduction of a strong native affairs department was the answer. Governor Smith was of opinion that the powers of the principal and village headmen should be increased so that they could commandeer free labour for local public projects while the District Residents' powers should also be increased in respect of compulsory labour for government purposes and related matters. After twelve years of experiment the Government was now convinced that principal headmen were not reliable enough; that it would be better to strengthen the position of village headmen and to involve principal headmen, village headmen and other useful members in district councils under the District Residents. Necessity drove the Governor in 1924 to admit that the time had come to arrange for greater African participation in the administration of the country. Eleven years earlier, in 1913, a proposal had been made that a Training School for the Native Civil Service should be started. The Governor had then said 'not yet' but 'at some future date'.

Events had now caught up with the Administration. In 1924 a first important step was taken in the direction of greater African participation when District Councils were set up. In that same year the first African, Levi Mumba, was appointed to grade 1 of the Native Civil Service. The 1924 Ordinance provided in principle for the setting up of village and sectional courts for civil and criminal cases in which both parties were Africans. It took a few years before these courts were finally instituted because of the caution of the Provincial Commissioners, appointed for the first time in 1921, and the planters' organisations which were, in any case, opposed to many of the changes that were now being introduced.

The system of direct rule lasted from 1891 to 1932. We have already considered some of its weaknesses. One, which has not been mentioned, should not be overlooked. This was the remuneration given to the agents of the Administration, which in 1918 was fixed as follows. Principal headmen earned a minimum of £3 (K6) per annum and a maximum of £8 (K16) depending on the number of huts; councillors earned from £1 (K2) to £2 (K4) per annum and the village headmen earned 10 shillings (K1) for every three hundred taxes collected. These were by no means attractive incentives.

What, in summary, were the main results of the period of direct rule? Tribal authority declined to some extent. Not all traditional chiefs were appointed as principal headmen and the fact that annual 'tribute' in the form of tax was paid direct to the district official and not through the chief further eroded respect and fear for traditional rulers. The hand-picked replacements were not necessarily better alternatives. What they gained by being government agents did not serve to strengthen their hands in the villages and the districts. They had no powers of their own to make rules and regulations or even to try cases according to customary law. When they did so, it was at the invitation of the District Resident. The increase of their powers, as in 1924 and 1929, had a largely negative effect on society. In 1924 they were empowered to compel people to work in the name of village and district improvement, a power which earned them more enemies than friends. In 1929 section courts were set up with limited civil jurisdiction only, subject to review by the District Resident. The point which rankled most was the complete absence of power and initiative. They were not even cogs in the administrative machinery, only clearing houses. As the Provincial Commissioner of the Central Province informed the Chief Secretary in 1927: 'The old men still think that their duties are purely administrative, that they are only called to the Boma to receive instructions.'[1]

ii 1933–1962

In the story of district administration in Malawi for this period there are three clear phases: the first may be referred to as the time of indirect rule, 1933–53; the second phase saw the introduction of local government on the lines of the British model between 1954 and 1961; the third phase brought local government in line with the aspirations of a self-governing majority.

Up till 1933 no council set up to assist in district administration had any executive, judicial or financial powers. Not a single African court had been established even though enabling legislation had existed since 1929. In all this Malawi lagged behind many African territories. By 1927 it was the only territory in East and Central Africa which had no revenue set aside for African administration of the districts, a provision which was introduced in Tanganyika in 1926 and to a limited extent in Northern Rhodesia in 1929. The virtue of special revenue for

---

[1] T. K. Barnekov, *An Inquiry into the Development of Native Administration in Nyasaland, 1888–1939*, Occasional Paper, 48, Maxwell Graduate School of Citizenship and Public Affairs, Syracuse University, 1967, p. 61.

African administration was stressed in the following words in the Tanganyika Native Administration Memoranda of 1930:

> A Native Administration must have its Treasury, as well as its executive officers and its courts, for experience teaches that it soon becomes of little account if no funds are placed at its disposal out of which it can pay the salaries of its personnel, build its own Court houses and schools, and make its own roads, etc.[1]

The Tanganyika experience was not unique. British administrators had, before this, made use of traditional authority in local government in India, Fiji and South Africa. Lord Lugard found it necessary and helpful to draw chiefs into his district administration first in Uganda and later to a refined and greater extent in Northern Nigeria. After years of experiment Lugard enunciated his doctrine of indirect rule on various occasions, for instance in his book *The Dual Mandate in British Tropical Africa*:

> Here then in my view lies our present task in Africa. It becomes impossible to maintain the old order; the urgent need is for adaptation to the new—to build up tribal authority with a recognised legal standing, which may oust social chaos. . . . The objective is to group together small tribes or sections of a tribe, so as to form a single administrative unit, whose chiefs . . . may be constituted a Native Authority.[2]

Sir Donald Cameron, who had worked as Lugard's Chief Secretary in Nigeria, became Governor of Tanganyika in 1925 and these principles of African administration were consequently introduced in this territory whence their influence spread to neighbouring territories.

Two ordinances were introduced in Malawi in 1933 to inaugurate indirect rule. The first was the Native Authority Ordinance (No. 13/1933) and the second was the Native Courts Ordinance (No. 14/1933). In terms of the first ordinance, chiefs who held positions 'according to the laws of the tribe and the wishes of the people' were recognised by the Government as native authorities either as individuals or as chiefs-in-council, and they had the power to appoint subordinate native authorities in their area of jurisdiction. Governor Sir Hubert Young, to whose lot it fell to introduce the new system, modified the original ideas as enunciated by Lugard and Cameron. The Governor saw the

---

[1] Tanganyika Territory *Native Administration Memoranda*, III, 'Native Treasuries', Dar es Salaam, 1930, p. 1.

[2] F. D. Lugard, *The Dual Mandate in British Tropical Africa*, Edinburgh and London, 1922, p. 217.

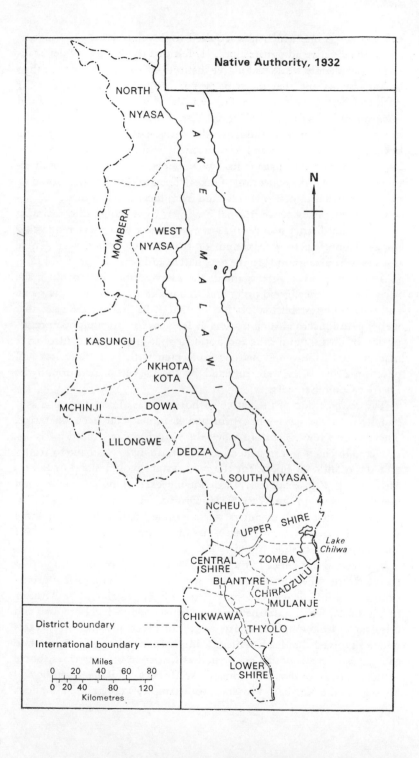

Native Authority, 1932

NORTH
NYASA

L A K E   M A L A W I

N

MOMBERA

WEST
NYASA

KASUNGU

NKHOTA
KOTA

MCHINJI   DOWA

LILONGWE

DEDZA

SOUTH NYASA

NCHEU

UPPER   SHIRE

Lake
Chilwa

CENTRAL
SHIRE

ZOMBA

BLANTYRE

CHIRADZULU

MULANJE

CHIKWAWA

THYOLO

LOWER
SHIRE

District boundary   ---------

International boundary -----·----

Miles
0   20   40   60   80

0 20 40   80   120
Kilometres

new system as one which was required to develop 'local government' rather than 'native administration'. He felt that the process of detribalisation had already weakened native institutions to a greater extent than in Tanganyika and that the tribe was no longer an effective unit for African administration. The Governor's idea of developing 'local government' was further influenced by a shortage of funds and he was not prepared to provide funds for the native authority administration beyond the launching stage. Government would retain control over its own revenue and manage its own services. Government would retain control over the collection of taxes; the native authorities would be permitted to raise their own revenue from local rates or dues.

Under the old system principal headmen were required to maintain peace in the districts; since 1924 they could issue orders requesting unpaid labour up to a maximum of twenty-four days a year. These powers were also granted to the new native authorities. But in addition, two further powers were granted: the native authorities could make rules for the 'peace, good order and welfare' of the people in their area and they could establish a 'Native Treasury'. In practice the rules that were made concerned such matters as licences for brewing beer; registration of births and deaths and non-Christian marriages; control over markets and fishing and matters connected with customary law and practice. Most rules were initiated by the Government through the District Commissioners.

The composition of the native authorities was almost the same as it had been in the days when principal headmen had been operative. There were a few exceptions when the Government refused to recognise certain chiefs but in general a serious attempt was made to recognise the traditional rulers, for the new system would stand or fall on their strength or weakness. Two notable exceptions in composition were to be seen in the West Nyasa District where the Atonga Tribal Council of thirty-two members was appointed native authority; and a European Anglican missionary assumed this responsibility over Likoma and Chisumulu islands.

The second ordinance in the new system related to the setting up of native courts where customary law would be used with as few exceptions as possible. It was necessary that both parties should be Africans in any matter which came before these courts, which had both civil and criminal jurisdiction. The courts were not given jurisdiction in cases which involved the death sentence, imprisonment for life and certain categories of matrimonial cases such as Christian divorce cases. Some of the courts, like those of Gomani, M'Mbelwa, Chikulamayembe and Kyungu in the Northern Province, for example, were granted Grade A status while most of the others in that province were designated Grade B courts, the difference being in the severity of punishment allowed. A few courts had Grade C status. While a Grade A court could impose a fine of £5 (K10), Grade B was limited to £3 (K6) and Grade C to £1 (K2). Similarly, the period of imprisonment allowed for the different courts was six months, three months and one month respectively. Appeals were permitted from a lower-grade court to the one above, then to the District Commissioner, the Provincial Commissioner and finally the High Court. In addition to their work in the field of African law and custom, the native courts were empowered to administer a number of ordinances passed by the Government such as the Native Labour Ordinance, and the Wild Birds' Protection Ordinance.

The system of indirect rule in the districts received a mixed reception. Traditional rulers welcomed it as an improvement in their authority; the European unofficial members of the Legislative Council were divided: the missionary members favoured it while the rest opposed it for diverse reasons such as that the African was unable to assume the increased responsibilities or that the introduction of the system would hinder the possibility of closer union among the territories of Central Africa. A more serious criticism was that levelled by educated Africans who felt left out or neglected. One such African critic wrote in the local African paper, *Zo-ona*:

> There are many today who favour government by Europeans because they know that if they take their case to the Chief's Village Courts the Chiefs will not give just decisions. Many of the Chiefs cannot be trusted in anything, many others are grasping, others quarrelsome. Others again, even though their people entrust them with all the tax money, dissipate it in no time. If there are local disputes in their territory they seize the opportunity for private gain and for trivial offences impose excessive fines. If a relative has a dispute with a stranger the case will not be fairly tried. They are not in touch with the people of their districts.[1]

It was not that the educated elements were left out entirely. Indeed chiefs or native authorities were advised to include them on their councils in the first few years of indirect rule. Further improvements were made when native authority treasuries were amalgamated. By 1940 a number of separate native authorities joined hands in a kind of federation with common councils and common treasuries.

But the question remained: how effective were the native authorities?

[1] C.O. 626/14, *Report on Native Authority Administration*, 1936.

How much participation was there on the part of the educated commoners? To what extent were the native authorities instruments of social and economic development? Lord Hailey, who visited Africa in 1939–40, did not think that they were fulfilling their roles as agencies of change. In 1947 the Colonial Secretary, Arthur Creech Jones, informed the governors of British territories in Africa that the time had come when local government should be streamlined: it should be made efficient and democratic and, what was more, it should be brought close to the common people and be related to their problems. To achieve these objectives, the educated men should be more involved. Actually this involvement was already noticeable in the provincial councils which were set up in 1944–45. Five of the twenty-five members of the Southern Provincial Council were educated commoners while the number was six out of twenty for the Northern Province.

In an attempt to boost district administration and to reach the villages and the educated commoners, group councils and chiefs' councils were introduced in the early 1950s but by that time the Colonial Office had already received a recommendation from the head of its African Studies Branch, Mr R. S. Hudson, that statutory district councils should be set up after the British model. This was introduced in 1953.[1] The system of indirect rule was rejected for various reasons: for one, the native authorities were caught between two extremes. They had to please the ordinary people as well as the Government; they had limited funds; they were not truly representative. Their rate of progress was too slow and the time had come to do more than pay lip service to the concept of partnership.

The District Councils Ordinance of 1953 was non-racial. It was to be introduced in stages; Thyolo was first in May 1954 and three years later there were eleven District Councils. It provided that district councils would take priority over native authorities and assume most of the responsibilities for district administration. African membership was first defined as 50 per cent of the total but the experiment, useful and progressive as it was, came too late to make it durable. In the years after 1953 the Federation issue overshadowed everything else. Elections for district councils were boycotted (the only one that ever took place was at Karonga in 1958) and after 1958 the demand increased to purge the councils of all non-African members. The demand had to be met and in 1960 the native authorities were separated from the district councils. Two years later the first real elections were held and the Malawi Congress Party candidates easily gained control of the councils.

[1] The Nyasaland Local Government (District Councils) Ordinance 48/1953.

For the first time in the history of Malawi, district administration was in the hands of Africans. But the paradox remained that self-determination had been conceded to the people first at national level and only later at district level. In many countries it was the other way round.

CHAPTER 13

African administration: case studies

i THE ATONGA TRIBAL COUNCIL

When the Native Authority Ordinance was introduced in 1933 the Government was anxious to recognise traditional chiefs so that they could be brought in actively to represent the Administration at district level. In some districts, like Mzimba, it was easy to identify the dominant traditional authority, and in most other districts it was possible to do this to a greater or lesser degree. One district, Nkhata Bay, however, presented insuperable problems. The Tonga occupied three main geographical areas, north of the Luweya, south of the Luweya and the western hill regions, which were under a number of chiefs or headmen who considered themselves equals. When the Government created the machinery of appointing principal headmen as their agents in 1912 it took five years for the Tonga principal headmen to be appointed. In 1917, Kabunduli, Mankhambira, Mkumbira, Mlenga Mzoma and Guru were selected for this position by the Administration, not because each of them carried the distinction of being undisputed traditional authorities—this was not the criterion of that time for such appointments—but largely because of favourable recommendations by administrative officers, missionaries and traders. This arrangement was acceptable for the time being because no central or single authority was being sought.

But in 1932 when a new administrative system was being formulated, the question of central authority was put to the Tonga people by District Commissioner O'Brien. The Phiri in the western hill region accepted Kabunduli and the Sisya in the northernmost part of the then West Nyasa District accepted Mbwana; 'but from Nkhata Bay to Dwambazi,' a District Commissioner (H. F. Bingham) noted in 1935, 'a storm of disagreement arose, and past grievances were aired against

192

the old Principal Headmen.'[1] In an attempt to weather the storm, O'Brien set up the Atonga Tribal Council made up of thirty-two members to act as a native authority in the area from Nkhata Bay to the Dwambazi River. The idea was that this would be a council of independent chiefs who would elect their own chairman. A contemporary report tells us that even this was difficult to create. A District Commissioner reported:

> When the Council was formed in 1932 it appears that the Atonga had no idea of the proposed constitution. Each family expected to have its own recognised Court responsible direct to the District Commissioner, once again showing the complete lack of cohesion of these people. The formation of the Council came as a surprise and a shock to most of them, and has been the underlying reason for the length of time that the Council has taken to settle down.

It was not that the Tonga failed to comprehend the position. They did not wish to see their individuality and initiative subsumed in an alien system. The Council was an amalgam of interests bringing together the Phiri and Banda groups; chiefs and headmen who had clearly not seen eye to eye with each other before were now to share a common platform. It was an unholy wedlock. It is a wonder that it lasted fifteen years. Its short existence is nevertheless an interesting chapter in local government.

The position of chairman of the Council was an important one. The first chief to hold this post was Chief Chimbano who served for part of 1933 and 1934. He was elected by his peers, the other area chiefs. Though a maximum of eight village headmen were permitted to be members of the Council they were not allowed to propose or second a motion. When Chief Thowolo was elected chairman in 1934 he succeeded in getting thirteen votes more than his nearest rival. There was no other African institution of comparable importance at the time where contested elections were held in quite the same way. The chairman was elected to office at first for one year but within two years this period was cut by half. The Council did not want to allow any single chief to entrench himself. In the first elections for a six-month term of office as chairman Chief Fuka Mba obtained eleven votes; the successful candidate, Chief Zilakoma, obtained twelve votes. When Chief Majikapotwe became chairman with twenty-four votes in his favour in 1937 it was an exceptional position. It was generally touch and go and votes were often split.

When Chief Mlenga Mzoma was re-elected for the third term in 1935

[1] C.O. 626/14, 1935.

as the representative of the Atonga Tribal Council on the District Education Committee most members felt that this was being manoeuvred by the District Commissioner and that if the chief was not kept in check he would be heading for the position of paramount chief, a situation which would be totally unacceptable to the others. The District Commissioner had a lot of explaining to do to dispel suspicions. Some chiefs used the occasion to suggest that the Council should be disbanded and that each chief should be allowed to have his own council and court. As things stood there was one council and one court for the thirty-two area chiefs. While a third of the membership advocated secession, the remainder were prepared to give the Council a longer trial, but on their own terms. These terms may be seen in the business transacted by the Council and recorded neatly and in good English in the Minute Book of the Council kept by the first Clerk of the Atonga Tribal Council, Dymon Matiya Tembo and his assistant, Eliam Kasambara.

When the secession issue came up at one of the early meetings, on paper it appeared in the following words: 'Council versus certain chiefs who do not attend the Native Authority Court and those who make private meetings in their houses in order to break away from this Council.' These chiefs were charged with 'conspiracy'. In spite of the attempts made to keep the Atonga Tribal Council and the Atonga Tribal Court intact, ten chiefs were allowed to hold their own courts in their areas in 1937 but any dispute which involved other areas would have to come before the Atonga Tribal Court. At first these ten breakaway chiefs were allowed to retain their membership of the Atonga Tribal Council. In 1938 the loyalists in the Council who referred to themselves as the 'Union of 22 chiefs in Council' decided that the disloyal ten could attend Council meetings but would have no voice at these meetings.

In view of these developments the District Commissioner enquired whether all the chiefs would like their own area courts with appeals to the Atonga Tribal Court. The loyalists exclaimed in one voice: 'We wish to march forward not backward,' and they reminded him of what his predecessor had impressed on them six years ago: 'Unity is strength.'

The paradox was that in actual fact there was very little unity in the Council on the most fundamental local issues such as whether or not educated men should be invited to become members of the Council. Like the secession issue, this balked large in Council discussions. The West Nyasa District, later Chinteche and finally Nkhata Bay, has always had voluble characters trained in the missions, the mines and

194

various other places of employment and exposure outside Malawi. Administrators everywhere and traditional rulers at home were divided in their reaction to this voluble sector. On 29 December 1934 the Council voted on the issue of whether or not educated men should be elected to serve on the Council. Twenty votes were cast in favour and a recommendation was accordingly made to the Protectorate Government. The matter was debated off and on for over three years. Finally in 1938 the District Commissioner informed the Council that he could not approve of the recommendation; that the Council was a body of traditional leaders and the educated men could form their own associations and advise the Council through them. It was unfortunate that the issue of educated men came up at the time when the Rev. Yesaya Zerenji Mwase broke away from the Presbyterian Church to start his own church and schools. Chief Mankhambira asked him to leave Sanga because he was a threat to the development of Livingstonia Mission education. The chief was supported by his peers and his action was upheld in all the courts to which Mwase appealed. Traditional power was still a vital aspect of Tonga society for it was at the same time supposed to be operating as a progressive power.

There were various ways in which the Atonga Tribal Council tried to work for the betterment of the Tonga. It recognised the role of educated men even if the Government frowned on them; it supported such local bodies as the Young Teachers' Association of Bandawe which paid the school fees of needy pupils; it gave evidence before the Emigrant Labour Committee of 1935 in which it opposed the principle and practice of contract labour and argued that the tide of emigration could only be reversed if the Government would sponsor local development projects. One other way in which the Government could help was by recognising Africans as landowners with individual title deeds to the land. This would stimulate local participation and development. It opposed the amalgamation of the Central African territories and informed Lord Bledisloe in 1938 that:

> Nyasaland's first duty in the light brought peaceably by the British Flag, is to restore the old relationship of Central African tribes; that Nyasaland's second duty is to glorify God and man and British Crown. Then she will be acquainted with European life and duties which will lead her to have a Parliament of her own.[1]

In speaking of a meaningful future parliament as early as 1938, the Council was forward-looking. Five years later it took another forward step by agreeing to the election of an executive committee of ten

[1] Minutes of the A.T.C., 23 April 1938.

members to hold office for twelve months. The committee was to meet once a month on the first Saturday of the month. Its duties included the control of Treasury expenditure; construction of roads, bridges and other buildings; and the appointment and dismissal of staff.

On 5 October 1943 (the year when the first executive committee was elected), the Council petitioned Governor Sir Edmund Richards—when he visited Nkhata Bay—for compulsory education, a radical request but wholly consistent with their demands along these lines since 1935. But more happened on that day: the dissident group in the Council pointed out their dissatisfaction and grievances. The District Commissioner was enraged by what he described as internal jealousies and presented the Council with a number of alternatives, including that of its own dissolution. Chief Kangoma, the chairman, described the incident as the most shameful in the history of the Atonga Tribal Council and though the Council resolved by a majority of twenty-seven votes to stay in existence, the end was drawing nearer. The Chiefs themselves realised that changes would have to come if the Council hoped to survive. The minutes of 10 January 1944 recorded their intention to choose their next chairman from among the 'wise Chiefs' but when it came to it only eighteen cast their vote out of thirty-two and the new chairman got in with ten votes. For four difficult years the Council continued in existence until it was formally dissolved on 17 February 1948. The Administration gave as its reasons for doing so the internal quarrelling; the status of some of the members; the absence of the educated element. Two years before, a Malawian abroad had written from Zambia pleading for its continuation. 'It may not be amiss,' he wrote, 'to suggest that the Atonga Tribal Council will in future be what the Transkeian Territories General Council—the Bunga—is today. But Rome was not built in a day.' But for the Tonga this unique experiment in local government was now over. It lasted for fifteen years. Why did it fail at last? The first reason is the refusal of the Tonga leadership to accept direction from above. The egalitarian nature of Tonga society which underlined equality with one's peers led to doubts about the role of a superimposed institution or, what was believed to be a sore point, supposed government sponsorship of certain members like the chairman of Council or members on committees such as the Education and Finance Committees. The gulf between the traditional rulers and the educated men of the district was not bridged. Finally, there were grave doubts about the legitimacy of all thirty-two area chiefs to serve as equals on the Council, since some of them were looked upon as mere headmen.

On 24 October 1904 Mzimba District came under protectorate rule long after all the other districts had already been brought under British rule. On that day a treaty was signed between the M'Mbelwa Ngoni and the British Commissioner. It was agreed that a British Resident would be stationed at Mzimba for the first time; that the Ngoni would stop their raiding and accept the new authority. But it was also agreed that the Ngoni chiefs would retain their former traditional positions which included the right to try cases even though this was now restricted to minor disputes. For the first time in district administration the Government accepted the pre-colonial chiefs into the system. Elsewhere in the country this was done in 1912 but with the northern Ngoni it was different. Their chiefs were absorbed into the administrative machinery from the first day of British rule. The senior Ngoni chief, Chimtunga, son of M'Mbelwa I, was to be paid £30 (K60) a year to assist the government officials in their work; five other Ngoni chiefs were to be paid £15 (K30) each. They were Mperembe, brother of M'Mbelwa I; Yohane and Amon Jere, sons of Mtwalo I; Mzukuzuku, brother of M'Mbelwa I, and Maulawo, brother of M'Mbelwa I. Chindi and Mzukubola, sons of M'Mbelwa I, were afterwards added to the list.

The Administration's view on traditional authority elsewhere in the country was that it had broken down and should be replaced by white rule, but this was not the official view with regard to the northern Ngoni. Even though the northern Ngoni chiefs were the first to be directly involved in district administration the arrangement got off to a shaky start and was a source of disappointment and annoyance to the white officials. Cattle raiding went on; quarrels between the Jere chiefs could not always be controlled by the District Resident; the magistrate at Lundazi complained about what he called the illegal behaviour of certain chiefs. In spite of all this, the Government was reluctant to use the opportunity provided by the introduction of the District Administration Ordinance of 1912 to withdraw its treaty arrangements with the Ngoni chiefs. Two years later matters came to a head: the Administration complained that Chiefs Chimtunga and Chindi were encouraging their people to evade payment of the hut tax. The subsidies of these chiefs were promptly reduced. In July 1914 the Governor went a step further and summoned all the Ngoni chiefs to a meeting at Mzimba. They were told that unless they helped the Administration more effectively their subsidies would be discontinued. For their part the chiefs pointed out that lack of employment opportunities and the absence of markets for the sale of their cattle made it difficult for people to find the money to pay taxes. The Governor noted that 'the attitude of the Chiefs appeared to be quite correct' on that occasion. He was to change his mind a few months later. When war broke out later that year the Government needed carriers and supplies of African foodstuffs for the troops. Though a number of districts were cool in their response it was only the area of the northern Ngoni in Mzimba which positively refused to assist. The Government found that the senior chief Chimtunga was to blame. He was banished to Chiromo where he was detained until April 1920. His brother, Mtusane, was deposed a short while later.

This event was the turning point in district administration. The Ordinance of 1912 was at long last made to apply to Mzimba. The treaty of 1904 was now a dead letter. In 1915 the M'Mbelwa district was divided into seven sections, each under a principal headman. The banished Chimtunga was replaced by his brother Mkuzo and the deposed Mtusane was replaced by a non-Jere principal headman, Ben Nhlane. All the Ngoni chiefs were now placed on a basis of equality and were all in the category of paid employees of the Government like every other principal headman in the country. Their former status as standard bearers of the Jere Ngoni was now reduced to that of paid employees of the Administration; their income, too, was reduced to an average of one-quarter of the previous subsidy.

This did not diminish pride in the Ngoni hierarchy and respect for the Jere overlordship in the area. There was no paramount chief as in Zwangendaba's day or in M'Mbelwa's day. The inheritor of M'Mbelwa's mantle spent five years in exile at Chiromo but was not forgotten by his people. When a native association was formed at Mzimba in 1920 it was called the Mombera Native Association. At its first meeting it petitioned the District Resident for the return of Chief Chimtunga. The Government sought and received an assurance from the Mombera Native Association that if Chief Chimtunga was returned he would be no more than a village headman under his brother and that there would be no question of restoring the paramount chieftainship to him. Chimtunga died as a village headman in 1924 and there was an immediate outcry that his son Lazaro Jere should be proclaimed paramount chief. An unauthorised meeting was held in 1926 at which the Jere family and other Ngoni from the Lundazi and Kasungu districts unanimously proclaimed Lazaro Jere as paramount chief even though he was not yet a principal headman. The Ngoni were not prepared to wait for the Government to create a chief. Two years later the Government announced that Principal Headman Mkuzo Jere who had been placed in Chimtunga's position had resigned owing to ill health, but it was obvious that the Government was embarrassed by the Nigon insistence on proclaiming their paramount chief. Lazaro Jere was appointed principal headman but was not recognised by the Government as paramount chief. The Mombera Native Association intensified its demands that the Government should recognise the traditional position inherited by Lazaro Jere and reinforced its case by electing Lazaro as chairman of the Mombera Native Association.

Unlike the position in Tongaland where the Atonga Tribal Council was divided on the question of the role of educated men and traditional leaders, Ngoni society was united in its demands.

When indirect rule was introduced in 1933 the Mzimba District included part of Rumphi and Hewe. Three native authorities were appointed—M'Mbelwa II (Lazaro Jere), Chikulamayembe and Katumbi. It was the largest administrative district in the whole country with a total of over six thousand square miles, two-thirds of which fell within M'Mbelwa's area. M'Mbelwa's traditional administration was enhanced after 1926 when a paramount chief was again recognised by the people. From then on any meeting of the Jere chiefs and their advisers was designated a meeting of the Jere Council. This Council became the M'Mbelwa African Administrative Council in 1933 or the native authority for the Ngoni part of the then Mzimba District. The chairman of the Council or the Inkosi was the paramount chief. His six junior chiefs acted as *amakosana* (minor chiefs) in their respective areas of settlement and were elevated to the rank of subordinate native authorities in 1936. After 1933 the principal headmanship of the Nhlane family disappeared and the section reverted to Mzukubola Jere. Hence local administration now became the exclusive preserve of the Jere hierarchy.

The M'Mbelwa African Administrative Council developed into the most complex native authority in the country. In 1937 its structure included 1 Inkosi, 6 amakosana who were subordinate native authorities, 25 councillors or *izinduna* who were generally educated men, 91 group headmen (*balumuzana*) and 1,017 village headmen (*wenichomizi*). It had a good treasury and a capable clerk, Mr Samuel G. Hara, whose wide experience in government departments in Zambia was of great help in the early years. It was the first native authority to operate a banking account.

Among its local enterprises were a native farm committee of which the Rev. Yesaya Chibambo was secretary; two native authority stock farms at Ekwendeni and Chitara and a ghee industry which yielded over £1,500 (K3,000) in 1939. This last industry was the main African trade in M'Mbelwa's country.

The judicial system was well structured in terms of the Native Courts Ordinance of 1933. M'Mbelwa's court was of grade A status while those of the six subchiefs were of grade B status. Each of the subchiefs headed sectional courts and sectional councils, the business from which normally reached the M'Mbelwa African Council from where it was processed for government action.

In 1948 the system of district administration was further streamlined by the introduction of councils at all levels of settlement. At the bottom of the structure was a village council serving not more than five villages; then came the group council made up from village councils; the third was the councillors' council and then came the sectional councils, with finally the M'Mbelwa Council. Records indicate that good use was made of these councils. Even when further administrative changes were introduced in 1951 by the creation of the Rumphi district to comprise the native authority areas of Chikulamayembe and Katumbi, the M'Mbelwa district administration was not only left intact but improvements were made. The earlier request by the M'Mbelwa Council that the sub-native authorities be upgraded was approved in 1952. At the same time two new sub-native authorities were created, that of Chapinduka Munthali and Kampingo Sibande. The Council was concerned not only with the status of its members but that it should manage its own affairs as the Ngoni had done in pre-colonial times. On 3 July 1952 Inkosi Ya Makosi M'Mbelwa II told Sir Harold Cartmel Robinson who had come to inquire into financial affairs: 'We too are quite willing to be self-supporters, which is a thousand times better than to be always dependants.'

The M'Mbelwa Council survived the colonial period and entered the era of independence as the M'Mbelwa District Council. Throughout its existence it controlled the largest and most complex district administration in the country. Perhaps the best tribute was paid to it by Dr H. Kamuzu Banda when he addressed an emergency meeting of the Council at Ezondweni on 25 August 1960: 'M'Mbelwa Council is a real example of a Council which is not an "Inde Bwana". In every district the D.C. is chairman, but not here where he is a mere adviser. . . . While in other districts Chiefs are mere messengers, in this district the Chiefs have the power to decide what they want . . . .'

CHAPTER 14

The African Church

i THE AFRICAN CHURCH MINISTRY

The success of mission work in Malawi can be gauged from the quantity and quality of the mission products. The artisans, teachers, clerks and civil servants are far too numerous to classify. All of them have made their mark but few have made a greater contribution than the teachers and that exclusive band of outstanding men who were selected to serve the African church. It is with this last group that we are now concerned.

All the Protestant missions recognised that the success of their evangelical work depended upon African evangelists but the degree of responsibility earmarked for them varied from mission to mission depending on what aspects of training were emphasised by each mission. Some missions limited their objectives in various ways, stressing perhaps church work or village development or broad education for a fuller involvement in national life.

In the nineteenth century and in the early years of the twentieth century the churches were controlled by Europeans and these may be referred to as the historic churches, but in the decade before World War I a notable development appeared in Central Africa, chiefly from South Africa where independent churches had been established for some time. A convenient definition of an independent church is that it existed in Africa, was controlled by Africans and operated primarily to serve Africans. However, since this happened later the historic churches must be considered first.

In point of time it was the U.M.C.A. to whose lot it fell to play the role of guinea pigs, make mistakes, pack their bags, rethink their programme and priorities and return to Malawi better equipped. One of the first Africans to catch their eye in Mozambique country was

Johanna Barnaba Abdallah who became a teacher in 1888. Five years later he was made a deacon, an advance familiar for those selected for higher things, and was ordained priest in 1898, the first to be ordained in the diocese of Nyasaland. Most of his priestly work was carried out at the Unangu station in Mozambique territory in the very heart of Yao country. Abdallah's book, *Chikala cha Wayao*, was translated in English by Meredith Sanderson and published by the Government Printer, Zomba, in 1919, five years before his death. In the year when Abdallah was ordained priest, Augustine Ambali, another notable U.M.C.A. product, was made a deacon after having served as a teacher for many years. He was ordained priest in 1906 and was placed in charge of the Msumba station from 1906 to 1917 and afterwards transferred to a less exacting assignment. Father Ambali was made a canon of Likoma Cathedral in 1922 and was the first African to be so honoured. Ambali was the author of the book *Thirty Years in Nyasaland*. He died at his station at Ngoo on the P.E.A. lakeshore where he spent most of his life as a priest. Since the Anglican Church regards ordination as a deacon as a qualification that entitles the holder to be regarded as a practising minister, the dates of the Anglican ministers could well be calculated as from that point: in Abdallah's case the earlier date would be 1894 and in Leonard Kamungu's case 1902.

Though Abdallah and Ambali served the diocese of Nyasaland well, they were not themselves Malawians. The first Malawian priest in the U.M.C.A. was Leonard Kamungu who followed Ambali to St Andrews College, the Anglican theological school at Nkwazi in P.E.A., in 1908 and was ordained priest the following year and was posted to the newly formed diocese of Northern Rhodesia. He died in 1913 at Msoro, probably from poisoning. Kamungu was raised to the dignity of Martyr in August 1969 by decision of the Synod of the Diocese of Malawi. He is remembered on the anniversary of his death which is 27 February.

Eustace Maliswa, Leonard Kangati, Gilbert Mpalila, Lawrence Chisui, Petro Kilekwa and Goodwin Chilombwe are among the other early priests of the Anglican church who distinguished themselves in the service of the African ministry. Lawrence Chisui, who served at various stations, including Nkhota Kota, Matope and Likoma Island, holds the distinction of having served his diocese for fifty-three years.

The products of the Presbyterian churches have been equally distinctive. The head of the Blantyre Mission in 1881, the Rev. Dr David Clement Scott, saw as one of his urgent and compelling duties the need to train Africans to assume positions of responsibility in the mission schools and churches at the earliest possible date. He was often criticised by his European colleagues for pushing this too far and too fast but in a statement he made in 1895 there is evidence that he was at the same time a realist: 'To attempt to force on Africa,' he said, 'the details of church life and organisation at home is, we believe, fatal to true growth. African life must be met in its own way and it will grow on its own lines.'[1]

In the year of the coming of Protectorate rule, seven African church members of the Blantyre Mission stood out and seemed to be the stuff out of which ministers are made. They were John Kuchipuliko, Mungo Murray Chisuse, Thomas Mpeni Masea, James Kamlinje, James Mwembe, Harry Kambwiri Matecheta and John Gray Kufa. Three years later they were all made deacons and were entrusted with mission work responsibilities in the villages around Blantyre. These seven deacons were organised into an African body set up to fulfil the normal functions of a kirk session much to the annoyance of local critics who even vented their feelings in the *Central African Planter* in the following words: 'The fact is, no native can, or will for years to come be able to fulfil even in a moderate degree, the place of a European.'[2] This criticism was not quite true even for that day and Scott attempted to disarm his critics by sending his deacons to take charge of mission work in the 1890s as far afield as Lomweland and Chinde in Mozambique and Ncheu in Malawi. The Rev. Dr David Clement Scott laid a strong foundation for the African church; he retired in 1899. His successor the Rev. Dr Hetherwick made progress by establishing a presbytery the following year to serve the interests of the Mission Council as well as the African church. This was followed by setting up kirk sessions in Blantyre, Domasi and Zomba in which both European and African members represented their various congregations. In 1901 the Nyasaland United Missionary Conference adopted the following resolution: 'That the orderly development, the organisation and establishment of a self-supporting and self-propagating Native Church be a chief aim in our mission work.'

Thus from the beginning of the twentieth century there was a determined drive to involve a greater number of African church members in mission work. The first African church elders of the Blantyre Mission to be appointed to the presbytery in 1903 were Joseph Bismarck, Justin Somanje, Thomas Mbali, John Grant and Stephen Msoma Kundecha. The number of African church elders increased each year and they met under the auspices of the presbytery, kirk sessions and even at conferences

[1] Rev. David C. Scott, *Life and Work in British Central Africa*, Blantyre, Sept. 1895.

[2] *Central African Planter*, I, 8, April 1896.

which they organised. They discussed topics of relevance to themselves and these included matters such as the development of Christian life; church collections; duties of parents; duties of Christians and the inner life of Christians. At this time two elders, Harry Kambwiri Matecheta and Stephen Msoma Kundecha, were selected for theological training. The course began in 1907 and ended in March 1911 when both Matecheta and Kundecha were ordained ministers of the Presbyterian church, the first two to achieve this status in Malawi.

In the meantime the Livingstonia Mission had made considerable headway in the direction of expanding the African church even though no minister was ordained until 1914. Among the early African Christians were men like William Koyi who were brought out from South Africa. The first ordained African minister of the Free Church of Scotland in South Africa, the Rev. Pambwi Mzimba, wanted to come out from Lovedale to serve the Livingstonia Mission but could not be released by his presbytery. In the 1880s and 1890s a number of baptisms took place and from among the early converts came the leading teachers, evangelists and eventually ordained ministers. Albert Namalambe, the first Malawian Christian of the Livingstonia Mission, was baptised on 31 December 1884, almost ten years after the mission had commenced work in the country. Yuriah Chatonda Chirwa, who was one of the first Livingstonia products to be appointed a church elder, was baptised on 21 April 1889. For him the road from baptism to eldership took almost ten years. The first Malawian to complete the theological course at Livingstonia Mission in 1900, Yakobi Msusa Muwamba, had been baptised eleven years before but never lived to see the day of his ordination. His colleague Charles Domingo, who came to Malawi from Quelimane in 1876, was the first African to complete a teacher training course at Livingstonia, in 1897. Together with Msusa Muwamba, he was selected for the priesthood. Like Muwamba, he completed his theological training in 1900. But this was just the beginning of a long road. No African had completed such a course anywhere else in Malawi at that time if one excludes the products of St Andrews College of the U.M.C.A. which was, in any case, then located in Mozambique territory. Two years after completing his theological course Domingo was admitted to what was called 'Trials for Licence' which entitled him to the position of licentiate, that is to a licence to preach but not to serve in the capacity of a full minister. It was in effect the extension of the period of probation and for Domingo it became a really long wait. Four years later he was still at the head of the queue for ordination, though he was now joined by other licentiates.

It was only on 6 November 1907 that Domingo was appointed to take charge of an African congregation in the Loudon area of Mzimba district. The Minutes of the Livingstonia Presbytery refer to this and related issues in the following words:

At the same time as congratulating Domingo, Dr Laws expressed the view of the Presbytery that in the interests of the Native Church and Ministry the African licentiates and, in due course the ordained Native pastors, be for a considerable time under the care and supervision of the European missionaries in whose districts they may be called to labour.

This decision was the cause of much dissension in the years to come.

ii THE GROWTH OF MALAWIAN INFLUENCE

The Livingstonia Mission featured prominently in the training of African personnel in Malawi in every department of endeavour, including the African church. In 1899, when the North Livingstonia Presbytery was formed, two African church elders were made associate members; an African licentiate was appointed in 1903 and two others followed in 1905. But it was only in 1914 that the Free Church of Scotland ordained its first three ministers, Yesaya Zerenji Mwasi, Hezekiah Tweya and Jonathan Chirwa. Even then it was required that these African ministers should be under the tutelage of European ministers for some time to come. One of them got into difficulties on this very point a year after ordination. The Rev. Zerenji Mwasi and the Rev. Dr Turner were both posted to Bandawe. A row erupted about their respective responsibilities and the North Livingstonia Presbytery found, in its own words, 'that Mr Mwasi had failed to subordinate himself to Dr Turner as his position as assistant pastor required'.

This was the kind of difficulty that was bound to arise. Issues such as who should take the decisions in matters of administrative details, including church organisation and funds, had led African ministers in South Africa to start independent churches such as the Tembo Church, the Ethiopian Church, the African Methodist Episcopal Church and the African Presbyterian Church in the last quarter of the nineteenth century. It was to prevent this kind of fission that Dr Laws and others planned a long period of probation after theological training. The Livingstonia Mission was cautious in its choice of sheep and shepherds. Baptism was only granted after a long and rigorous period of church education; ordination was only conferred after a long period of probation after theological training. Thus when the Free Church of Scotland, the parent body of the Livingstonia Mission, celebrated its fiftieth anniversary in Malawi in October 1925 the total number of ordained ministers only stood at ten: the Revs. Yesaya Mwasi, Hezekiah Tweya and Jonathan Chirwa were ordained in 1914; the Rev. Andrew Mkochi in 1917; the Revs. Yafete Mkandawire and Edward Boti Manda in 1918; the Rev. Patrick Mwamlima in 1921, and the Revs. Peter Zimema Thole, Yesaya Mlonyeni Chibambo and Charles Chinula in 1925. A small number as this surely was, it was nevertheless a better figure than that of its southern counterpart, the Established Church of Scotland, the parent body of Blantyre Mission who could only claim to have ordained six African ministers during its first fifty years. They were the Revs. Harry Matecheta and Stephen Kundecha in 1911; the Revs. Thomas Masea, Joseph Kaunde and Harry Mtuwa in 1916, and the Rev. Jameson Kandulu in 1922. Thereafter there was a long gap until 1929 when five more were added to the list.

Meanwhile Presbyterian church organisation finally moved towards a single central body with a local bias and a local designation. This also meant that African church leaders would now play a fuller part in the development of a national church. Since 1900 the North Livingstonia and Blantyre presbyteries had been going in this direction but it was only on 17 September 1924 that the Synod of the Church of Central Africa Presbyterian was constituted when the two presbyteries agreed to this formation. In October 1926 the Nkhoma Presbytery joined the C.C.A.P. This was well timed for only a year before the Nkhoma Mission had ordained its first two African ministers, the Revs. Namon Katengeza and Andreya Namkumba. After the foundation of the C.C.A.P. African ministers were appointed to all the church committees, a necessary preparation for the higher church offices that were gradually being earmarked for them. One of these was not long in coming: the Rev. Harry Matecheta was appointed first African Moderator of the Blantyre Presbytery in 1933.

The advancement of the church was due not solely to the progress and prestige of its African ministry but also to the rank and file in the African congregation and to the work done behind the scenes by numerous deacons and elders not many of whom are listed in the church records. To these unnumbered many the church owes a great debt. One of them was Fidelis Muyeye who was born in 1896 at Ndelama village. Muyeye was in the first group to enter the Mua Catholic Seminary when it opened in 1913. He did not continue with his theological studies but left the seminary in 1918 and began teaching. He was by then a church elder and served to draw the Church, school and community closer and in his humble way was able to attract adherents to the Catholic church. In the same way Adriano Yesaya served the Bembeke parish for many years as a catechist.

The White Fathers came to Malawi temporarily in 1889 and permanently in 1902. The Montfort Fathers arrived in 1901. The first Malawian was ordained into the Catholic priesthood in 1937. (The process had taken about the same number of years as the Presbyterian churches.) The honour went to the Rev. Father Cornelius Chitsulo who went on to become the first Malawian bishop in 1957. Thirty years after the first ordination there were sixty-four Malawian-born Catholic priests in the country, and in 1971 there were seventy. It is therefore correct to say that only over the past generation have African priests begun to assume responsible positions in the Catholic church. A fitting climax was reached when Archbishop James Chiona was enthroned Archbishop of Blantyre on 28 April 1968. The Most Rev. James Chiona was born in 1924 and was ordained priest on 12 September 1954. He was consecrated Auxiliary Bishop of Blantyre in 1965.

Bishop Matthews Chimole, who was consecrated Bishop of Zomba in 1970, was the third Malawian Bishop. He was ordained priest in 1947 and taught for many years at Nankhunda Seminary, near Zomba, after which he studied in Rome and at Antigonish University in Canada. Bishop Chimole is one of many Malawian Catholic priests who are graduates, but present pride of place in this respect must go to his colleague at Nankhunda Seminary, Father Harry Chikuse, who obtained a doctorate in theology in Rome many years ago and subsequently lectured at London University.

If Malawians have come a long way in both the Protestant and Catholic churches the past has been a preparation for the increasing challenges of the future. One of the places where these challenges will have to be met is in the theological colleges and seminaries. The Rev. Stephen Kauta Msiska, a remarkably talented man, is today (1972) in charge of one such leading institution. He was born in 1914 and graduated the hard way from village school to Livingstonia Mission, through teacher training to theological studies after the usual service as teacher and head teacher. This was the familiar road taken by most people on their way to the pulpit. He was ordained a minister at Karonga in 1946. Even then the studies he had embarked on at school and privately years before did not end. In 1948 he was called to teach theological students at Livingstonia and to prepare himself for this role he attended a course of study in Kenya. He was the first African tutor appointed by the Livingstonia Synod to this post, which he retained from 1948 to 1960. He spent a year at New College in Edinburgh and returned in

1962 to join the Nkhoma C.C.A.P. Theological College, working his way up to the principalship of this institution in 1969.

The Rev. Kauta Msiska is a deeply read and a widely travelled man. He has attended many conferences and delivered several papers on religion. One of his more important articles is entitled 'Traditional religion among the Tumbuka and other tribes in Malawi'. It was published in 1969 in the *Ministry*, a theological review journal.

His counterpart at the Kachebere Major Seminary, Mchinji, until June 1972 was Father Patrick Augustine Kalilombe, a very much younger person but endowed with tremendous vitality and intellectual strength. Father Kalilombe was born in 1933 at Mua Mission near Ntakataka in the Dedza district where his father worked in the mission carpentry shop. Father Kalilombe imbibed the mission atmosphere from his cradle days and when he went off at the age of four to the White Sisters Convent at Mua he was in his element. After the various stages of his early education he entered the portals of the Major Seminary of Kachebere to study philosophy and theology. Before completing his studies he was asked to join the Missionary Society of the White Fathers, an assignment which took him to Maison-Carrée near Algiers in North Africa and then on to Tunis and Carthage in Tunisia, all in training and preparation for his membership of the White Fathers' Society. In the end, after years of dedicated scholarship which took him not only into the depths of theology but through the mazes of languages such as French, Arabic, Italian and German, he was made a member of the society, and was ordained into the priesthood on 3 February 1958. In many ways this was only a beginning and more travels in Europe and the Middle East followed: Egypt, Lebanon, Syria, Jordan and Israel. All of this was part of the world of the young man from Kancamba village near Mua Mission; and it was all part of the training that was to lead to his obtaining the Licentiate in Holy Scripture in 1962, the year when he returned home and to service in various parish posts in the diocese of Dedza. He was appointed to the staff of the Kachebere Major Seminary in October 1964. Here he taught various courses in philosophy and theology and emboldened by his intellectual curiosity and strength he sallied forth into new and relevant fields—African studies which comprised elements of history, mainly Central African, ethnology and religious sociology. Father Kalilombe organised a club called the 'African Way of Life Club', which has had an unbroken existence since 1964. He was appointed Rector of Kachebere Major Seminary in 1969 and in early June 1972 was appointed the first African Bishop of Lilongwe, an honour he richly deserves.

Father Kalilombe has published various articles in learned journals, lay and religious, ranging over such wide topics as 'Communism in Africa', 'Adaptation to Modern Africa' and *Bebulo N'chiani?*.

When Patrick Augustine Kalilombe was appointed Bishop of Lilongwe it was more than a success story writ large. It was a vindication of the ability of Catholic mission products of the humble villages of Malawi to take their place alongside their Protestant counterparts who have had a longer innings in the various and varied responsibilities that confront the guardians of the Christian heritage in Malawi. The future of the African ministry, in the custody of such persons as the Rev. Stephen Kauta Msiska and the Rev. Father Patrick Augustine Kalilombe, is safe and assured.

iii INDEPENDENT AFRICAN CHURCHES

While the historic churches, both Catholic and Protestant, have made an important impact on Malawi society, independent churches have also commanded and demanded a place in the story of Christian activity in the country. Basically, the independent churches have been fundamentalist in approach in that the Bible represents for them, too, the basic tenets of Christianity. Where differences have come in these have been motivated by issues of interpretation of Christian doctrine and practice; physical forms of baptism; disagreement over what constitutes the Sabbath; what period of preparation and what nature of training should precede one's admission to the Christian fraternity, and conversely what responsibilities and obligations should rest upon the individual during the entire period of his membership. Various questions have been asked and misgivings expressed by supporters of orthodox Christianity as well as by advocates of unorthodox Christianity. Some have asked questions and expressed their misgivings from within the traditional structure, as Erasmus did in the days of the European Reformation; others have done the same but by standing outside the structure and often by creating their own, as Luther, Zwingli, Calvin and Knox did in the same period. Like their European predecessors, the African voice of dissent was not sounded because of its hatred of the Church, rather from its love for it and regret that certain practices were irreconcilable. It was sometimes unhelpful that the founding fathers of Christianity in Africa came from an alien culture whose exclusiveness and righteousness they often insisted upon.

Points of disagreement arose over questions concerned with beer drinking; the morality of traditional dancing; the recognition of certain traditions and customs connected with coming of age, marriage, birth and death. While some of these issues were reconciled over the years, the Church found one area where reconciliation was not possible: this was over the question of polygamy.

There were casualties in the early years while precedents and adjustments were being worked out and a whole host of things were going on. Some influential men spoke out against the European brand of Christianity. One of the first critics in 1901 was Charles Domingo when he was one of three African representatives from Livingstonia present at a meeting with members of the African kirk sessions of Zomba, Domasi, Mulanje and Blantyre. He had already completed his studies in theology and therefore knew what he was talking about. Though a promising young man, he was never ordained, possibly because of his stand against orthodox practices. Domingo's wife recalled in 1968 that he differed over two main points with the Livingstonia missionaries: one was that he held that Saturday and not Sunday should be observed as the Sabbath day; the other was the treatment meted out to Africans by missionaries who had come 'to teach Africans to have brotherly love of one another in Christ'. Domingo left the Presbyterian church and joined the Seventh Day Baptists. In 1911 he claimed to have over five thousand approved members each in the Mzimba and Chinteche districts. Dissatisfied with the orthodox brand of religion, Domingo looked to Joseph Booth who since 1892 had been advocating a policy of Africa for the Africans and that Africans should learn to fend for themselves. Deported from Malawi in 1904, Booth maintained contact with Africans who expressed dissatisfaction with either church or state. Since Domingo is a typical representative of the African voice of dissent it is worth considering an excerpt from a letter he wrote to Booth on 20 September 1909.

> Nearly all of us of the enlightened Nyasaland do know that you suffer much for the sake of poor African—who is counted by all whites as a 'Black Ink Man'. More do we know that you suffer for the sake of our Lord JESUS CHRIST. Dear Pastor, we ask you earnestly not to stop fighting for us here in Nyasaland. We do not know if there is any man from Europe counted an Ambassador for Africa—chiefly, Nyassaland. There is too much failure among all Europeans in Nyassaland.[1]

Perhaps Domingo was an extremist for his time and his behaviour may be explained by his disappointment over promotion and ordination. But he was not exceptional. A later generation of Livingstonia products whom he had once taught followed in his footsteps. One of

[1] *African Sabbath Recorder*, 1 (obtained through courtesy of Dr H. W. Langworthy).

them was Charles Chinula, one-time headmaster of Loudon Mission station school. Chinula believed that African customs should be purified and preserved rather than neglected and destroyed. He secretly, unknown to the European resident missionary, encouraged his pupils to take part in dances. Ordained minister in 1925, Chinula was defrocked in 1930 on a charge of violating church standards. He was restored to ordinary church membership two years later and busied himself with translating Bunyan's *Pilgrim's Progress* in Tumbuka as well as with composing hymns in that language. Chinula could not conform to the standards and finding himself in trouble again he left the Church. In 1935 he took his independent church, the Eklesia Lanangwa, into a larger independent church which was called the *Mpingo wa Afipa wamu Africa* (The Church of the Black People of Africa). He named his mission the Sazu Home Mission, again, as he stated in a personal testimony to the author in 1967, because he wanted to underline the African or local aspect of his mission station in contrast to the European or foreign aspect of the existing missions. The Mpingo wa Afipa wamu Africa was in reality an amalgam of a number of independent churches in which former members of the Livingstonia Mission took part. The leading light in this independent church was Yesaya Zerenji Mwasi, one of the three first ordained ministers of the Livingstonia Mission (1914) who left the Presbyterian church in 1933 and formed the West Nyasa Blackman's Educational Society in addition to the Mpingo wa Afipa wamu Africa. The fact that they broke away from the Presbyterian church did not mean that they were weak characters, far from it. Charles Chidongo Chinula was one of the liveliest men in Mzimba and stood out among his fellows in education, religion and society. For years secretary of the M'Mbelwa Native Association, Councillor to Inkosi ya Makosi, member of the Provincial and Protectorate Councils, one of the founders of the Nyasaland African Congress, Chinula was no ordinary man. And so it was with Yesaya Zerenji Mwasi whose career almost paralleled that of Chinula in Chinteche.

There were critics from within, too. Men such as the Rev. Edward Boti Banda and the Rev. Yesaya Mlonyeni Chibambo made no secret of the many shortcomings they observed. In the minutes of the Livingstonia Presbytery of 15 July 1921 there is a long and interesting letter from Yesaya Chibambo to the Livingstonia Mission Council of which only an excerpt can be reproduced here:

> The missionary is in Africa for the uplift and improvement of the native. This improvement can better be carried out if the mind of the native and of the missionary are working and designing together.

The members of the Mission Council belong to one race, and are apt to have the same inclination or bias in judging things, i.e. European way of thinking. It is no wonder that when a controversy arises at a meeting where both Europeans and natives are present usually natives take one side and European missionaries also take the opposite side without exception. This takes place simply because the native and the European are not in the habit of getting together to harmonise their thoughts.

Disharmony often existed at the social, economic, religious and political levels. Since religion was only one aspect of community life the other influences cannot be ignored. They often fed the independent churches with ammunition and goaded them to act as platforms to air the manifold grievances of the people. Dr Sundkler, in his book *Bantu Prophets in South Africa*, wrote: 'The independent Zulu Churches may well be regarded as a symptom of an inner revolt against the White man's missionary crusade.' Since so many things were said and done in the name of this crusade it is no wonder that issues connected with land, labour and African administration were also invoked by African reactionaries in their rationale for setting up independent churches and for following certain policies. Shortage of land and attendant problems such as rent, labour tenancy or Thangata and taxation were serious problems in the Shire Highlands where concentration was greatest. In Chiradzulu the Providence Industrial Mission of John Chilembwe was the first notable independent church. Its followers were penalised by the estate for belonging to this church because it was African-run and because they complained about wages, hours of work and ill-treatment. Soon the problems of the workers became the problems of the Church. The church buildings of the Providence Industrial Mission on the estates were pulled down yet on the same estates European-run churches belonging to the Church of Christ were allowed to function. Issues of religion and politics and race soon became interwoven.

Another independent church, the Watch Tower, led by Elliot Kamwana, also assumed religious and political objectives. The dawn of a new age was preached when African leadership and aspirations would at last be recognised. The movement gained tremendous following, mainly in Tongaland, but was successfully put down when the leader was banished to Mauritius and the Seychelles for over twenty-one years. Hauled up before the Commission of Enquiry into the Chilembwe rising in 1916, Kamwana said that he had disagreed with the Livingstonia missionaries who were his first teachers on two basic issues: one was whether baptism should be by immersion or by sprinkling and the

21. Malawi's first African Commissioner of Police, Mr Mc. J. Kamwana, with the Deputy Commissioner, Mr F. B. Chevallier.

22. John Gray Kufa Mapantha.

23. Chief Mwase Kasungu, Nationalist leader, Chairman of the Supreme Council of Action, photographed in 1972.

24. Chief Mtwalo being greeted by President Banda at the Chief's headquarters. Also in the photograph is the Regional Minister for the North, Mr M. Q. Y. Chibambo.

25. Chief Amon Mtwalo Jere with Petros Moyo and the author, 1969. This was probably the last interview granted by Chief Mtwalo prior to the illness which led to his death a few months later.

second was that whereas the European missionaries preached that sin was punishable by eternal damnation he believed that even the sinners would be redeemed by the Second Advent. Here he was in fact pleading for his fellow men who transgressed the law of the European church. There was hope in Christ for them, too.

But while some reactionaries and dissenters pleaded for their fellow men, some individuals broke new ground for personal advancement in power struggles with members of their society, historic churches or with government. Wilfred Good of Thyolo, the founder of the *Ana a Mulungu*, was aggrieved that the Government did not uphold his case in a legal dispute with fellow villagers. 'Look here, Government,' he wrote to the District Commissioner, 'I and my Christian followers, starting from today we shall never pay tax for the British Kingdom. I thought you were servants of God as the Bible says, that is why I was paying taxes, but now I realise that you are not the servants of God.' And all this from a man who was once a respected member of the Seventh Day Adventist Mission at Malamulo.[1]

The variety of the African response in the name of independent churches leads to a confused picture of what it was the founders really wanted. They wanted many things. Among their aims the following stand out: the restoration of the control and interpretation of their religion to Africans themselves; the promotion of the interests of certain individuals, especially those who had quarrelled with the existing order or with individuals in that order; permission for certain practices such as polygamy, beer drinking and traditional dancing; and finally the use of the movement to promote political teachings and organisation.

[1] C.O. 525/176, file 44216/1938.

CHAPTER 15

The Chilembwe rising

i BACKGROUND

At about 9.00 p.m. on Saturday 23 January 1915 a rebellion broke out in Malawi. It took the country by storm because it was so unexpected. It was led by the Rev. John Chilembwe, the head of an independent African church in Chiradzulu. What was the background to the rebellion?

During the first five years of Protectorate rule the British administration had fought a number of battles against those who resisted the new regime. These were successful and British rule began on the bases of treaties and military conquest. The chiefs were not involved in a direct way in the new administration. For the next twenty years there was peace and calm on the surface. The officials in the districts were proud of the stability and cooperation that existed. Minor disturbances did not shake this confidence. Some independent church leaders were placed under detention but their movements were deemed to be minor and isolated. In short, the rulers were of opinion that everything was under control. It is ironical that Governor Sir George Smith sent a despatch to the Colonial Office in London on 23 January 1915 stating that traders and planters who were aliens in the country need not be arrested because he did not think that the aliens could stir up the African population against the British. The Governor gave two reasons for his optimism: 'the general timidity of the native (he is still much perplexed as to what the war means and the dangers which threaten him) and the distances to be travelled. . . .'[1]

On that same day the Chilembwe rising broke out. The Governor's

[1] C.O. 525/61, Treatment of enemy subjects in Nyasaland, 23 Jan. 1915.

reference to 'timidity' was proven wrong. About that time one of Chilembwe's men, Yotam Saidi Bango, was sent by Chilembwe with a letter addressed to the Germans in German East Africa. The contents of this letter have not been traced but a reply dated February 1915 was discovered when Bango was arrested on his way back. In this letter the chief judge at Tunduru gave a garbled account of the war in Europe and ended by referring to a personal message which was entrusted to Bango. Historians will now never know what this personal message was. This incident proved Governor Smith wrong on the second point, that Africans would not travel long distances to further the cause of the enemy. The claim also had no validity because Malawians had been travelling long distances in search of employment long before the rising. Take the case of Yotam Bango himself. He was finally tracked down to a place called Hillcrest in Pietermaritzburg, South Africa, in 1918 where he was found to be in the employ of one Major Tomlinson. Incidentally, Yotam Bango was extradited and given a two-year sentence in March 1919. He was released in August 1920. After working for a year or so in Blantyre, he retired to Nsanje where he died as a cripple in the 1920s, spending the last months of his life in the care of the South African General Mission.

If Sir George Smith was wrong on the two points he touched upon on the very day the rising broke out, he was not the only one who had miscalculated. The Chilembwe rising was due to a series of miscalculations. No senior officer in the Administration had taken note of the complaints that came in from junior officers and from the Catholic priests at Nguludi Mission, which was close to Chilembwe's mission. The Blantyre missionaries, too, discredited the rumours as baseless. As early as July 1914 an African teacher, whose name was Eugenio, in a Catholic school, told Bishop Auneau of the Nguludi Mission that he had heard of a plot against all Europeans as well as against some Africans. This was reported to the Assistant District Resident at Chiradzulu who then went on a tour of inspection in August but found nothing unusual at Mbombwe where Chilembwe's Providence Industrial Mission was. At the Commission of Inquiry the Assistant District Resident was asked how long he had taken over the inspection and he replied that it had lasted about ten minutes! He felt uneasy about the visit and the complaints and probably to cover himself he sent off a letter to his superior at Blantyre. Dated 23 October 1914, part of the letter read as follows:

I haven't heard anything more about him [Chilembwe], but my firm opinion is that there must be something in it and it is no good crying out when any disturbance takes place—as the old saying 'there is never any smoke without fire'. What I should advise is that he should be arrested and sent up to some outstation and to remain there till the war is over, and also his special teachers. I should have much pleasure in arresting him.[1]

This pleasure was ultimately denied to everyone. When Chilembwe was finally cornered on 3 February 1915 it was only his dead body which was recovered.

Chilembwe did not operate in secret only. He sent a letter to the *Nyasaland Times* complaining about African participation in a European war. The letter was published on 25 November 1915 but owing to the operation of the censorship law that particular issue was never circulated.

Let the rich men, bankers, titled men, storekeepers, farmers and landlords go to war and get shot [wrote Chilembwe]. Instead the poor Africans who have nothing to own in this present world, who in death leave only a long line of widows and orphans in utter want and dire distress are invited to die for a cause which is not theirs. . . . We leave all for the consideration of the Government, we hope in the Mercy of the Almighty God, that some day things will turn out well and that Government will recognise our indispensability, and that justice will prevail.[2]

But the Government had its own problems in 1914. The small number of Europeans (in the 1901 census there were 314 and in the 1911 census there were 766) had to defend the country against German invasion from September 1914. They did not have the resources to fight on two fronts. According to the testimony of contemporaries, Chilembwe was summoned to Zomba to talk over his grievances with the Government but he did not go because he feared arrest. David Kaduya, one of the top men at the Providence Industrial Mission, went in his place. Chilembwe's letters were intercepted and as the Governor later reported they were cryptic, wrapped up in scriptural texts. One of his favourite texts he quoted to the Rev. Stephen Kundecha of the Church of Scotland in Zomba was: 'And ye shall know the truth and the truth shall set you free' (St John, chapter 8, verse 32). There were letters, too, from Liberia, probably from a mission of the National Baptist Convention; this fact was enough for some to say that he was planning the creation of an independent African state on the lines of Liberia.

[1] C.O. 525/66, Examination of B. T. Milthorp, A.D.R., 28 June 1915.
[2] G. A. Shepperson and T. Price, *Independent African*, Edinburgh, 1958, pp. 234-5.

The 1915 rising

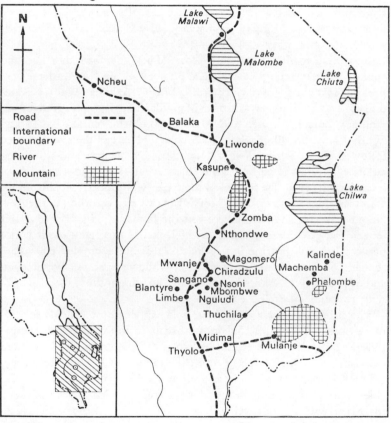

At last the Government decided to take action to deport Chilembwe. On 13 January the Governor of Nyasaland cabled his counterpart in Mauritius with this action in mind. A favourable reply was received two days later and local arrangements were set in train. Even then the arrest could not be made overnight for the main force, including European civilians in the Nyasaland Volunteer Reserve, was up north defending Karonga. A member of Chilembwe's church who worked in the offices of the King's African Rifles in Zomba got wind of information on Friday 22 January 1915 that his arrest was imminent, that instructions had been sent for an attack on Mbombwe, Chilembwe's headquarters, on Monday 24 January. It was this information that precipitated the rising.

According to the statement by Mrs Aida Chilembwe, her husband summoned a meeting at which a number of his ringleaders were present, including John Gray Kufa, Wilson Azimba, Wallace Kampingo, David Kaduya, Daniel Mangulamba, Burnett Kadangwe, Andrack Jamali, Stephen and Andrew Mkuluchi, Yotam Bango and Wilfred Ntambo, all of whom took an active part in the events which followed. One of them, Wilfred Ntambo, born in 1892 and still living at Chileka, told the author about these eventful days in a number of interviews in 1968. He identified the typist who tipped off Chilembwe about the impending arrest as Morris Chikwana. According to the Rev. Ntambo, when Chilembwe received the letter he said: 'Look at this letter. The government wants to catch me. If they take me it is not peace. They will put me in prison.' To this his assembled colleagues replied: 'No, you cannot be taken away while we are here. We must go and offer ourselves. As we have no guns, no ammunition, we shall fight with axes and spears.'

The rising was not well organised. It happened too quickly for this to be possible. Though Chilembwe had been in contact with sympathisers and wellwishers from Ncheu to Mulanje and indeed had sent emissaries over the years to people like Philippo Chinyama in Ncheu, Elliot Kamwana at Mulanje as well as to the African ministers and elders of the Blantyre Mission, and must have confided in some of them, there is no evidence of a well-knit conspiracy to overthrow the Government by force of arms. There is no doubt that a frontal attack must have been considered as a defensive alternative. Much had happened since Chilembwe's return as a minister of religion from the United States in 1900. He had tried his hand at various things: evangelisation, education, business, agriculture. He had tried to get African church leaders together. He had tried, as no doubt his American experience must have prompted him to, to get educated men around him. Here he

218

was at a disadvantage. According to Dr Hetherwick's assessment of the educational attainment of his followers, there were ten who were in the standard four grade, six in standard five and two in standard six, hardly the makings of modern leadership in quantity or quality. He had visions of a better future where justice would prevail, standards would be better and African participation would be greater. There is evidence that in the fourteen years since his return from the United States he had sought to improve the living and working conditions of the rank and file of his people. He encouraged women to wear European-style dresses. The Rev. Stephen Kundecha tells us about this: 'He said that it was not good for those who were well educated like I was, that I should give plain clothes to women, but it was better to give her (my wife) clothes like a lady, in order to show that she was an educated woman.'[1]

He borrowed £50 from a wealthy Malawian around 1909 to set up a business as some of his countrymen had begun to do since 1904 in order to put more money into circulation and in this way to try to reduce the amount of money exported by businessmen with foreign interests and loyalties. He failed in his business enterprise but succeeded in stimulating other people in his area in Chiradzulu to take to business and farming. Most of the ringleaders in the rising owned private property, did cash-crop farming or had small stores. He was the first chairman of the Native Industrial Union formed in 1909, the membership of which represented the cream of the African personalities in Blantyre and the surrounding districts. One of its founding fathers, Ardwell Mlenga, died in 1970 and another, Justin Somanje, died in 1971. Having achieved so much and planned for so much for the future, why did John Chilembwe lead some of his countrymen into rebellion in 1915? Did he do this to throw away his life and his dreams in a single careless deed or was there more to it?

ii CAUSES AND RESULTS

The causes and results of the rising of 1915 may be looked at by analysing four aspects of the person whose name is permanently connected with the event—Chilembwe the man; Chilembwe the politician; Chilembwe the martyr; and finally Chilembwe the catalyst (or the in-instrument of change).

Chilembwe, the man, born around 1870 at Sangano village in Chiradzulu district, belonged on the paternal side to the Chingoli clan of the Yao tribe. This clan was famed in its ancestral home in Portuguese

[1] C.O. 525/66.

East Africa for farming and for making hoes, spears, knives and baskets, techniques which the migrants brought with them when they settled in Chiradzulu in the middle years of the nineteenth century under their Chief Mpama not far from the Mbombwe stream. Chilembwe spent his early years in Chiradzulu with his three sisters and an uncle, Matoga, but later lived with relatives at Chilomoni in Blantyre, where he attended a village school and afterwards had a short spell at the Blantyre Mission itself. His entire life changed when the English missionary Joseph Booth started a mission at Mitsidi in 1892. Chilembwe joined Booth and by so doing launched himself on an adventurous path which took him to the U.S.A. in 1897 where he studied mainly theology at the Virginia Theological Seminary at Lynchburg. Though he was taken there by Booth, it was the negroes of the National Baptist Convention who took care of his stay and education. It was an education in itself to live and travel with Booth, the man who was the first white person to raise his voice and use his pen to promote the cause of African nationalism in Malawi, but to live and study in the United States at this time of extreme difficulties for negroes was an even greater education for him. He was to remember all this when he returned to Malawi in 1900, bought ninety-three acres of land at Mbombwe, and started the Providence Industrial Mission. His early education, experiences and observations were more than ordinary preparations for adult life. They were in effect a preparation for the political role he was called upon to play after his return.

Chilembwe the politician was the inheritor of Joseph Booth's mantle. In this capacity he had to further the aims and objects of the African Christian Union and the petition of 'Africa for the Africans' which Booth had drafted and which Chilembwe supported. These movements aimed at gaining equal rights for Africans as well as Europeans in political, social, economic, educational and religious matters. This was a tall order for the year 1900, and was made more difficult by the fact that Chilembwe was now on his own; the chiefs with their traditional authority behind them did not support him; the educated people, few in number, owed their positions either to the Government or to the missions which employed them. They found his views too radical and often suspected his motives. After all, they had not themselves been to the United States nor had they come under negro influence. They had not joined the African Christian Union or demanded 'Africa for the Africans'. In all these visions Chilembwe was ahead of his time but he took his responsibilities seriously. As head of the Providence Industrial Mission he was placed in the forefront for developing the African church and promoting an African mission. The fact that he had to do this in the Chiradzulu area provided tremendous difficulties for him. His Mbombwe Estate was near the Magomero Estate which belonged to A. L. Bruce. The manager of the Bruce estates was William Jervis Livingstone, a man who by all accounts, European and African, had a violent temper; disliked educated Africans who dressed in European fashion, attended church and sent their children to school. He made no secret of his dislike for John Chilembwe who, he alleged, was a bad influence on the estate workers. He showed his dislike by ordering the demolition of African church and school buildings which belonged to Chilembwe's followers on his estate. This action increased the hostility between the two men. In addition Livingstone resented the fact that his labourers often went to Chilembwe for advice about their many difficulties on the estates. These stemmed from the evils inherent in the Thangata or labour tenancy system of the time. Wages were bad enough in general but often worse on the Bruce Estates. For twenty-seven days in the month labourers toiled from 6 a.m. to 6 p.m. for 1s. (10 tambala) and two rolls of tobacco or 2s. (20 tambala) and one roll of tobacco. Timber for firewood or for building was hard to come by; fines and punishment for cutting down trees and bamboos were severe. Africans were not allowed to wear hats in the presence, near or distant, of Europeans. Shoes were forbidden.

Most of these difficulties existed everywhere on the estates in the Shire Highlands in one form or other and the confrontation between Chilembwe and Livingstone must not be seen purely in terms of personality conflicts. It is true that Livingstone opposed the sale of land to Chilembwe; that there was a serious border dispute in 1911 when the Bruce Estate boundary was extended to include a considerable strip of Crown land; that African schools and churches were forbidden (in fact on the thousands of acres covering the Bruce Estates there was not a single school). Though there were general grievances there were also specific ones and it was largely because of the specific grievances that the Magomero Estates were attacked on the night of 23 January 1915 and three European males lost their lives. This was the extent of European casualties if one excludes injury to two others, one of whom was a Catholic priest in a nearby mission. Women and children were not harmed. One of the children in this human drama was a five-month-old boy at the time. He works today (1972) for an oil company in the Middle East. In 1970 he returned to Malawi and in the company of the author visited his father's grave at Magomero, a difficult pilgrimage but one which he accomplished without the slightest trace of bitterness. After all, his father was not the victim of a personal vendetta but of a political system and age of which he was a part. Anyone could have been singled out to pay the price for the system and practices of the day. It was to fight the system and not a man that Chilembwe made the supreme sacrifice. This system, among other things, required that the black man should fight the battles of the white man and Chilembwe complained strongly against this. While he was in America and after he returned home Malawian soldiers were recruited for serving in Mauritius, Somaliland and the Gold Coast. The King's African Rifles was established in 1903 and it was made up chiefly of Yao soldiers. In 1914 the first battalion of the K.A.R. was made up of seven hundred soldiers, half of whom were Yao. It was easy, therefore, for Chilembwe to learn of their difficulties, especially the problems which faced demobilised soldiers or their widows and children. Mrs Livingstone recalled a special incident which took place in 1914: 'I can remember a band of men coming to Magomero,' she said, 'and asking my husband if they were to pay taxes that year. My husband asked the reason for the question and they replied: "We have no right to pay taxes this year for our men are fighting the white man's battles at Karonga and the Government are seizing more of us." '[1]

This was one of the issues which Chilembwe, the politician, had to take up. It affected his people; it affected his country. It was, to him, wrong in principle that it should be so. His mentor, Booth, had complained about it in his petition of 1899; Chilembwe had complained about it in his letter to the *Nyasaland Times* in 1914 and in a subsequent letter to the Government. All that the Government could see in the complaints was sedition. The Commission of Inquiry set up after the rising took a broader view of its causes. It listed four: firstly, the political notions which had rubbed off on Chilembwe as a result of his association with Joseph Booth and his experiences in the U.S.A.; secondly, the transference of these political notions by Chilembwe to the discontented educated Africans who acted as his assistants; thirdly, the favourable atmosphere created by the outbreak of World War I, including the fact that local troops were concentrated in Karonga; and, lastly, the existence of certain small European and American missions whose teachings ran counter to the ordinary teachings of the larger missions. Chilembwe was implicated in all four of these causes. His own contribution as a politician outlived anything else he was able to achieve.

What of Chilembwe the martyr? It has come down in the increasing amount of literature about this episode that what drove Chilembwe to the deed was a desire to strike a blow and die. This is the fatalistic view

[1] Mrs Katherine Livingstone's reply to the letter to her solicitor, J. Scott, from H. L. Duff, Chief Secretary, 11 April 1916.

which argues that he knew that the odds were loaded against him. Because there was no hope of success, the fatalistic view argues that he wished to strike a symbolic blow at the existing order and die. All this is very difficult to prove. The evidence seems to suggest that if the Administration had taken heed of his complaints about the various local and national grievances, the rising might never have taken place. Since amelioration or positive responses did not materialise, Chilembwe resorted to rebellion in order to counteract his imminent deportation. For some time previously he had been initiating negotiations with kindred spirits in the hope that they would support him in a trial of strength. There was Philippo Chinyama of the African Baptist Church at Dzunje in the Ncheu district, about ten miles to the east of Ncheu Boma. Here this former disciple of the Baptist churches collected around him the support of Chief Makwangwala, Jadali Phiri, the father of the later United Federal Party politician Matthews Phiri, and Nthinda Chinyama, father of the later politician Ralph Chinyama, and others. Nearby in the Chiole area was the African Church founded by Anderson Chimutu. Both Chimutu and Philippo Chinyama came out in support of Chilembwe but their moves were anticipated by the swift action of the District Commissioner at Ncheu and the ringleaders, including Chimutu and Chinyama, were shot there after a summary trial.

A similar rising was planned at Mulanje. A loyalist chief informed the Government that seven men armed with rifles and eight men armed with spears crossed the Tuchila River at about 4.00 p.m. on 26 January, three days after the rising had started. The following day a large meeting was due to be held on Bangula Hill. The ammunition stores of the African Lakes Corporation in Blantyre were raided on the morning of 24 January with very little success. The ammunition supplies on the Bruce Estates were similarly attacked on the first night of the rising. A few followers in the Zomba district tried to throw in their support. But all these attempts were futile only because the plans were not well laid. The timing was not of Chilembwe's choosing. It was sprung on him. There was no planned conspiracy, only a series of panic moves. This was not the way to strike a symbolic blow. When Chilembwe made the move, as the net closed in on him, he hoped that with the support from Ncheu, Zomba, Chiradzulu, Blantyre and Mulanje he would gather sufficient strength to dictate terms to the Government. Because he failed all sorts of explanations have been attempted to show that Chilembwe, the martyr, acted from some weakness. It is true that he was a very sick man physically, suffering from chronic asthma and poor eyesight. The death of a daughter in 1914 had added to his burdens. A district official later tried to show that Chilembwe was mentally deranged. But it was government initiative and strength coupled with the fact that the majority of his people did not support him that contributed to Chilembwe's martyrdom. The government issued a £20 reward for the capture of the ringleaders and it was the act of a Judas Iscariot from Kaduya's village near the Portuguese East African border, where Chilembwe made his last halt, that led to his being shot with his nephew, Morris Chimpere, by eight policemen at noon on 3 February 1915. His body was brought to the Mulanje Boma at 8.30 a.m. the following day, identified by three witnesses and buried in an unknown grave a few miles from the Boma.

Chilembwe died a martyr but not in vain. Governor Smith admitted that the rising introduced a new phase in the history of Nyasaland. After 1915 the shadow of Chilembwe was cast on the private estates, in the missions, in the Legislative Council chambers, in the relations between white and black. Though independence was yet a long way off, 1915 marked the end of the old era. What happened in 1953 and 1959 was a lengthening of this shadow and a reinforcement of all that it stood for. Chilembwe's rebellion was not a mere symbolic blow. It was a real instrument of change, even if it was fifty years ahead of its time.

CHAPTER 16

Political organisations in Malawi

i THE NATIVE ASSOCIATIONS

Between 1912 and 1930 no fewer than nine native associations were formed in Malawi, most of which were limited in name and scope to certain existing districts. There were three notable exceptions. The Southern Province Native Association was founded in 1922 and out of it separate associations were formed for Blantyre, Thyolo and Mulanje in the following few years. The Central Province (Universal) Native Association was formed in 1927 and throughout its existence served the whole of the province. The third exception was a unique experiment of bringing together three associations in a single body, namely the Representative Committee of the Northern Provinces Native Associations, formed in Zomba in 1924 by civil servants from the Northern Province who found themselves living and working in the capital town where the administrative and political decisions were being taken. The earliest associations were the North Nyasa Native Association (1912); the West Nyasa Native Association (1914) and the Mombera Native Association (1920).

All the associations had common aims and objects based on a document prepared by Levi Zililo Mumba, one of the founders of the first association. These were, firstly, to keep the Government informed of African opinion and thus to assist it in its work; secondly, to keep the Africans informed of the laws introduced by the Government and thus to assist them in understanding the objects of such laws; thirdly, to organise public meetings where matters of general or special interest to the African public might be discussed.

The men who formed these associations were first-generation mission products as well as the first generation brought up in the environment of British Protectorate rule. The limitations as well as the opportunities which they provided therefore led to the formation of the associations; in all instances also there were local, regional or national reasons which prompted these men in a new milieu, now marginally spanning the old and the new, to organise themselves as they did.

Take the case of the North Nyasa Native Association which was constituted in 1912. For two years teachers and clerks from Livingstonia Mission had been discussing the need for a representative body to speak in their name. 1912 was a decisive year. Simon Chiukepo Mhango returned from a spell of work in South Africa and advised the educated men to constitute themselves into a body. He was no doubt influenced by the formation in that year in South Africa of the South African Native National Congress, the forerunner of the African National Congress. The educated men of Karonga acted on Mhango's advice and wrote to their counterparts of Mzimba, Bandawe and Livingstonia about their plans. This step was in keeping with the character of the movement, namely that it should be non-tribal in outlook and that it should look to regional cooperation if and when this was possible.

Another important event that year was the introduction of the District Administration (Native) Ordinance in 1912 which enabled the Government to appoint principal headmen to assist it in local administration. The reaction of the educated men was that most of the principal headmen were unfit to act as middlemen between the Government and the Africans because of their lack of education. It was not the intention of the educated men to isolate the principal headmen or be in anyway hostile to traditional authority but really to ensure that the African voice was truly represented and communicated by those who were in the best position to do so. Indeed, progressive traditional rulers were often leading members: Kyungu Peter Mwakasungula was one of the founders of the North Nyasa Native Association; Chief Amon Mtwalo II was one of the founders of the Mombera Native Association in 1920; Chief Chikowi was one of the founders of the Southern Province Native Association in December 1922. When the Chiradzulu Native Association was formed in November 1929 all the chiefs in the district joined about four hundred others of the general public to launch the association. The first chairman of this association was Chief Mpama and his two deputies were Chiefs Malambo and Onga. Thus we can see that it would be wrong to say that the educated men who formed the associations were hostile to traditional authority.

The third influential factor was the support given by two Europeans. One was Dr Meredith Sanderson, a medical officer stationed at Karonga.

Levi Mumba worked with him at the Karonga hospital and gained much from Dr Sanderson's liberal spirit. The other man was Dr Robert Laws of Livingstonia, at whose mission most of the key men were educated. Dr Laws knew in 1912 that when the term of office of the then missionary representative in the Legislative Council, Dr Hetherwick, ended in 1913 he himself was to succeed to that position. When this happened he would be helped in speaking for the Africans if he received advice and briefing from a representative body. Dr Laws supported the move when asked by the Government to comment on it. The final important event that year was a local crisis concerned with resettling Africans from the centre of Karonga in a place some ten miles away because the land was needed for the new Boma buildings.

Thus various influences to a greater or lesser degree led to the formation of the first native association in Malawi in 1912. The associations were properly constituted and run. There were the usual office-bearers associated with organised bodies. Minutes were kept in English and a copy was sent to the District Resident for his information and in case he needed to act. At first the officials worked very closely with the District Resident and, indeed in at least one instance—Chiradzulu—the District Resident was elected vice-chairman. The Mombera Native Association defined its membership requirements as follows: 'The members thereof are to be persons of good knowledge and character. It is also an open question for educated chiefs and Europeans to attend or join it as full members, if they choose to do so.' Every effort was made at the beginning, both in the north and south, to establish that the native associations were in favour of the Government and that their loyalty was unquestionable. Government blessing was sought and kept for most of the initial years. Later, as we shall see, the associations did not see eye to eye with certain officials. At its first meeting the Southern Province Native Association asked its secretary to request the Government 'to give a word of goodwill to the Association to dispel the fears of those who want to join but are inclined to doubt the legality of the organisation'.[1] The Mombera Native Association, whose membership represented the cream of the educated people in the Mzimba district, expressed its loyalty in unambiguous terms: 'The aim of the Association,' it announced, 'is neither directly nor indirectly to subvert the authority of the Government, or of any lawful establishments, nor to induce the community to do so. . . .'[2] And the North Nyasa Native Association, also very richly endowed with talent

[1] S.1./3263/23, National Archives, Zomba.
[2] Minutes of meeting of 7 Jan. 1920.

and education, reinforced its loyalty by dissociating itself from the Chilembwe rising of 1915. It minuted its feelings in the following words: 'The Association regretted exceedingly the rising of John Chilembwe and others inasmuch as they knew that a High Court exists to which appeal could have been made. . . . The rising being a black mark on the natives of the Protectorate. . . .'[1]

The educated men of the native associations were mostly teachers and clerks. Many of them went on to become ministers of religion and businessmen—small retailers or cash-crop farmers, or both. The men at Nsoni in the Chiradzulu district are a good example, though most of them lost their lives in the rising. Some of them organised business associations such as the African Industrial Union in Blantyre and neighbouring districts or the early cooperative concerns in the Mzimba district. As teachers, traders, farmers, civil servants, traditional leaders, and ministers of religion they effectively represented every part of African society. Nothing of any worth escaped their notice. The matters they discussed and made representations on included the difficulties faced by war widows; requests for government loans for the development of agriculture; increased subsidies for education and requests that the Government take over education and provide better schools and secondary education. They also made complaints regarding legislation such as the Dog Ordinance of 1924 which imposed licences and other restrictions on the ownership of dogs, saying that dogs were necessary for hunting. Another cause they took up was Section 129 of the new Penal Code of 1929 which penalised social relations between white women and black men but not between black women and white men. This was taken up so strenuously by various associations as well as by the Representative Committee of the Northern Provinces Native Associations, whose Secretary Isaiah Murray Mopo Jere made special representations against it in Zomba, that the District Commissioner at Karonga was constrained to find a scapegoat in the person of the Rev. Edward Boti Manda. 'This propaganda,' reported the District Commissioner, 'filtered into this District from the Mzimba and West Nyasa Districts and found an ardent supporter (if not originator) in the Rev. E. Manda at Livingstonia. He possesses a copy of the Penal Code, as he subscribes to the Government Gazette, and has had it carefully bound.' The District Commissioner did not feel that the Africans' complaint originated from any moral standpoint but from one of equality and equal rights. This he described as absurd and blamed their education: 'It is a peculiar thing,' he wrote, 'that almost every highly educated native of the Livingstonia Mission is politically minded and

[1] S.1./1481/19, National Archives, Zomba.

race conscious and always on the look out for some stigma.' This was a strange evaluation of a straightforward grievance and though the District Commissioner did describe the legislation as 'a lamentable mistake, unnecessary and unwarranted' his reason for saying so was that it was 'an insult to European women' since 'the bare fact that the morals of white women are discussed by Native Associations is deplorable.'[1]

The native associations did not function purely as instruments of protest. They looked at divorce laws, adultery, cleanliness of the villages, evils of migrant labour, housing conditions for village teachers, improvements to roads and marketing facilities. They discussed price control as well as national political issues. They prepared memoranda for land commissions as well as for commissions enquiring into the feasibility of amalgamating the central African territories. In all these issues they served the important function of acting as the African voice. They initiated many discussions but equally were invited by the Government to investigate certain matters and act as a forum for collecting public opinion. On many issues of local or national import the Government took serious note of the representations made.

These representations were made within the framework of the existing system. There were six guiding principles that Dr Laws had laid down for the associations in 1912 and these had been accepted by the members as well as by the Government. The members had to be educated, of good character, loyal to the Government and approved by the Government; they had to hold their meetings in public and their minutes had to be sent to the highest government officials. All these principles were honoured for many years but in the early 1930s members began to baulk at the restrictions placed on the associations. The West Nyasa Native Association, for instance, began to question the District Commissioner's regular attendance at meetings, because it tended to dampen free discussion. When this association elected a second-grade clerk in the same District Commissioner's office as chairman in 1930, the Government stepped in in support of the establishment, saying that Africans in the civil service were debarred from holding office and that the minutes of the associations would only be considered if they were channelled through the District Commissioner. There was talk, too, of suppressing the associations because some of their members, like the Rev. Yesaya Zerenji Mwasi, were beginning to act as upstarts and revolutionaries. The Government decided 'to pour cold water over them', that is to minimise their importance by looking

[1] S.1./1481/19, Letter from D.C., Karonga, to Prov. Sec., N.P., National Archives, 27 Jan. 1931.

more and more towards traditional authority, the District Councils and indirect rule, rather than to the educated men. But by then the educated men had proved themselves, had made their mark and had staked their claim. The clock could not be turned back.

ii THE NYASALAND AFRICAN CONGRESS AND THE MALAWI CONGRESS PARTY

The first important step towards the formation of a national political body was taken when the Representative Committee of the Northern Provinces Native Associations was formed in Zomba in December 1924. This served as a single mouthpiece for three of the major and senior native associations in the country. The Committee comprised influential African civil servants from the northern provinces who happened to be working in Zomba. They were well placed to make political representations, as they were in the know and had access to senior government officials.

In 1928 the West Nyasa Native Association had a scrape with the Administration over the role of the District Commissioner and the channelling of minutes of the Association. At the same time it passed three resolutions which rattled the Government and made it cool towards native associations. At the crucial meeting of 9 February 1929 schoolteacher S. K. Longwe, as chairman, said that he hoped that the meeting would one day become 'our national meeting'. For the present the Association resolved that all land in the West Nyasa District belonged to the Africans; that no more land should be given to white settlers and that the fishing industry should be encouraged by reducing the dues levied on timber. A combination of factors emerging from this situation caused the Government to move against native associations in general; and the fact that all the associations took similar action against Section 129 of the Penal Code in the same year added to authority's concern. In view of all this the Administration insisted that minutes of the associations had to be routed through the native authorities and District Commissioner before action would be taken. There was one important exception. The Representative Committee was exempted from 20 May 1935. It could deal direct with the Government, and it took full advantage of this by offering to channel to the Government business submitted to it by all native associations. Here lay the modest beginnings of national representation and organisation.

Thus during the 1930s the only effective body among the native associations was the Representative Committee. Though its origins have been traced to 1928, it was in fact established four years earlier.

One of its early documents entitled 'The Representative Committee for Northern Province Native Associations, Zomba. A Record of Effective Work', gives the beginnings in the following words:

> With the arrival in Zomba of several members of associations and others from the Northern Province in search of work, it was decided in December 1924 to form a committee to carry on these duties. Mr Mumba was appointed Chairman and Mr Robert Mandere Nyirenda, who was for many years a branch secretary of the North Nyasa Native Association at Karonga, was appointed the first secretary. The membership was at first only six but this number grew with the years until at one time it reached over 50.

When Robert Nyirenda was transferred to Karonga as clerk and interpreter in 1928, Isaiah Murray Mopo Jere, a member of the Mombera Native Association, was appointed secretary. Both Levi Mumba and Mopo Jere remained at the helm for many years.

It was, however, Levi Mumba's work which earned for the Representative Committee its claim to the position of forerunner to the Nyasaland African Congress. For twelve years secretary of the North Nyasa Native Association, he was appointed corresponding secretary of that body when he was transferred to Zomba in 1924. He was in effect the public relations man who represented the associations to the Government as well as to the outside world. In March 1924 he published an article on 'Native Associations in Nyasaland' in the African newspaper, *Zo ona*. This was reproduced in the *South African Outlook* later that year. In May of the same year he presented a memorandum to the Phelps-Stokes Education Commission which visited Nyasaland and towards the end of the year he presented another memorandum to the East African Parliamentary Commission which visited the country under the chairmanship of W. Ormsby Gore, Under-Secretary of State for the Colonies. For the first time the African case was being put forward by an African who understood the techniques of modern western patterns of negotiation. Earlier in that same year, the Government recognised the role and the qualities of Levi Mumba and appointed him to the level of 1st Grade of the Native Civil Service. He was the first African to achieve this distinction. He was to go on to achieve other distinctions such as being first African member of the Advisory Committee on Education (1933) and first chairman of the Nyasaland African Congress (1944).

It is not generally known that Levi Mumba was sent to South Africa in 1940 by the Nyasaland Government for a period of about three months. During this trip he visited Durban, Lovedale and Cape Town, looked into the educational provisions for Africans and studied the ghee industry, in which he maintained a lively interest while he ran the Veterinary Department in the Mzimba district from 1935 until his death in 1945. While in South Africa he spent a few days in Cape Town with Clements Kadalie, of whom he spoke very highly on his return. Back in Nyasaland, Mumba addressed a number of meetings in 1941 in the Mzimba district, including one at Loudon Mission where he spoke to teachers. At these meetings Mumba advised that the time had come for Africans to have a truly representative political body on the lines of the South African African National Congress. He drew attention to the developments in Blantyre, which Frederick Sangala was going to get involved in, where Afro-Europeans were petitioning for special schools for themselves. The African community should not allow its own case to go by default, said Mumba, through lack of a national body. It must be mentioned that Levi Mumba was in the fortunate position of being able to travel as a member attached to the recruiting unit of the King's African Rifles, which facilitated his contacts with the general public.

While Mumba was doing the spade work in the north, Frederick Sangala and Lewis Mataka Bandawe and others were laying the foundations in the south for the formation of a national body. James Frederick Sangala came to Blantyre from Zomba in 1938 and became assistant secretary of the Blantyre Native Association. At the same time he formed the Parents' and Guardians' Educational Association to protest at the decision by the Blantyre Mission not to admit girls in classes beyond standard three. When in 1943 the Coloured community succeeded in its representations for separate educational facilities, a matter on which Levi Mumba had spoken against years before, Sangala and his friends moved into action to set up a national body. Lewis Bandawe was then senior clerk in the Judicial Department at Blantyre. Sangala was junior to him. Between them they sought the approval of government officials, including the Resident Magistrate and the Senior Provincial Commissioner, for the holding of preliminary meetings, the first of which was held on 19 August 1943. At this meeting, presided over by Lewis Bandawe, the Nyasaland Educated African Council was formed. The term 'Educated' was dropped soon afterwards as it tended to restrict the membership. On Sangala's initiative a circular was published in the *Nyasaland Times* appealing for support from other districts. On Levi Mumba's advice the term 'Council' was dropped as it tended to confuse the new body with other councils then in existence. The introductory meeting was held in Blantyre on 20 May 1944 and the inaugural meeting was held in October of the same year with Levi

Mumba as first chairman; Charles Mlanga as first secretary-general and Isa Macdonald Lawrence as first treasurer-general.

Some Europeans in the country, like W. H. Timcke and M. E. Leslie, as well as abroad, like Senator W. G. Ballinger in South Africa, took an interest in these developments and proffered advice and at least one of them, W. H. Timcke, was prepared to offer financial assistance as well. What was even more remarkable was that Dr H. Kamuzu Banda, then practising medicine at South Shields in England, took a lively and practical interest in what was going on. From the inception he became a life member—and virtually the first life member—of the Nyasaland African Congress. He sent long letters of encouragement and advice to both Sangala and Levi Mumba and with these letters he sent financial assistance, which was then and for long afterwards sorely needed. In a letter dated 21 April 1946, Dr Banda looked ahead to what the Congress might eventually achieve:

> If we organise a strong Congress, the Government will allow us to rule ourselves much more than it is allowing us now. We shall have Africans to represent us in the Legislative Council at Zomba and on Government Boards and Commissions. These Africans will see to it that good laws are passed by the Council and bad ones are not passed. We shall then control our schools, hospitals, internal trade and commerce and shall do many other things that we do not do now.[1]

The Nyasaland African Congress got off to a tragic start: within a few months Levi Mumba and Isa Lawrence were dead; financial and organisational problems appeared; tribalism divided the loyalty of its members. In all their local problems the officials appealed to Dr Banda in England for advice and assistance. Dr Banda suggested that a full-time paid secretary with a permanent office should be responsible for the organisation. He was himself prepared to pay the salary of such an official but the men on the spot thought that the proposals were too far-fetched, a view which they were to regret later on and change. In 1953 a contribution of £200 from Dr Banda financed the employment of two organising secretaries, Mr K. W. Kulujili in the south and Mr K. Mhango in the Central and Northern Provinces. Tribalism reared its head when Charles Matinga, the second chairman of the Congress, chose to take a fellow Yao, Andrew Mponda, then secretary, on an educational deputation to London in 1948 instead of his vice-chairman, Charles Chinula, a Tumbuka who had originally been chosen by Congress. Chinula tried in vain to overtake the Yao team in Cape Town before their departure for Britain. He failed and on 30 April 1948 he

[1] Letter to the Rev. H. M. Phiri.

addressed a pathetic letter to Dr Banda, then in Brondesbury Park, London, drawing attention to the evils at home. Also, funds were mis-appropriated and embezzled. Unsatisfactory leaders were thrown over-board and new ones were tried. In 1950, J. R. N. Chinyama was ap-pointed chairman; in 1954 J. F. Sangala took over; in 1956, T. D. T. Banda. In August 1958, Dr Banda was elected president-general at the annual congress held at Nkhata Bay.

It was from this point that a dynamic advance was registered. The Congress was completely overhauled. Organisation developed from the grass roots upwards. Ordinary villagers, men and women, chiefs, and the youth, were drawn into the movement alongside the educated people in what developed into a well-knit mass movement. The Government stepped in in a hopeless attempt to contain it. On 3 March 1959 a state of emergency was declared and Dr Banda and his followers were arrested. The Nyasaland African Congress was banned. But the floodgates had been opened and the movement could not be held in check. Mr Aleke Banda, recently deported from Rhodesia for his political activities on behalf of the Nyasaland African Congress, with the aid of energetic supporters kept political agitation alive by launch-ing a mimeographed publication entitled *Mtendere pa Nchito*. On 30 September 1959 the Malawi Congress Party was formed with caretaker officials at the head holding the fort until the return of the leaders then in prison in Rhodesia. It started off with a membership of fifteen thousand, which rose to almost twice as many before the year was out. Within a month after the formation of the Malawi Congress Party, a monthly journal appeared as its unofficial organ, entitled *Tsopano*, which was the militant mouthpiece of a determined mass movement. It started in a modest way with a circulation of 1,200. Within a few months the figure increased to 6,000. And on 19 December 1959 the *Malawi News* made its appearance as the official organ of the Party. In its first issue the newspaper explained its position:

> We are waging an uphill struggle against white domination and suppression from the south and colonial agents in Zomba. We have few leaders in our struggle because most of them are in detention. We cannot meet and talk and discuss what we think because of the state of emergency. . . . Yet we want our people to know what we are doing and thinking. . . .

A lot of doing and thinking was going on in Malawi as well as in the prisons of Rhodesia. It represented the fulfilment of a political struggle which had no parallel of the same proportions elsewhere in Central Africa and which certainly served not only to arouse political consci-

234

ousness and activity in Malawi but in other places in this part of the continent. At its conclusion this action brought a fitting finale to a most absorbing development in the political life of the Malawi people—the achievement of political independence.

CHAPTER 17

Constitutional developments

i UP TO 1956

The first European administration in Malawi was proclaimed on 14
May 1891, when British protectorate was declared over the 'Nyasaland
districts'. At the head was the Commissioner and Consul-General,
Harry Hamilton Johnston, who arrived in the country two months
later recruiting a handful of European and African staff along the way
at Zanzibar, Mozambique and Chinde. With him came his deputy,
Alfred Sharpe, a surveyor, Bertram Sclater, with a staff of three non-
commissioned officers, and Alexander Whyte, a sixty-year-old natural-
ist. They were joined soon afterwards by Captain Cecil Maguire of the
Indian army as head of the local army. The first medical man to join the
administration was Dr Sorabji Boyce, a licentiate of medicine and
surgery from Bombay. He was appointed medical officer to the Commissioner and the administrative staff. Before the first year was out
eight other Europeans had joined the staff. Aided by these fifteen ex-
patriates, the Commissioner launched the first administration in
Malawi in the name of the Foreign Office of the British Government
and under the legal provisions of the Africa Order in Council of 1889.

In 1893 the title of the Protectorate was changed to British Central
Africa Protectorate and regulations were issued concerning customs
duties, licences, African labour, land sales, sale of liquor, mining and
manufacturing. Collectors were appointed by judicial warrants to
exercise judicial functions, but the Chief Judicial Officer was only
appointed in 1894. For six years he was the only law officer in the
legal department, and his various duties included acting as solicitor,
notary-public, general law adviser, registrar, administrator, trustee in
bankruptcy, Attorney-General, Director of Prosecutions and judge.

The modern constitution of the Protectorate was introduced in 1902 under the British Central Africa Order in Council. The Commissioner was still head of the Administration with powers as before to introduce ordinances, proclamations, rules and regulations subject to approval by the Foreign Office. A high court was introduced for the first time. Appeals from the high court were to be heard in the court of appeal of the Cape Colony in South Africa. Two years later with effect from 1 April 1904, the control of the British Central Africa Protectorate was transferred from the Foreign Office to the Colonial Office. The official explanation for this move was given in the following words:

the northward expansion of British colonial possessions in South Africa has emphasised the anomaly and inconvenience involved in the existence in adjacent territories of two different systems of law and methods of administration. These will best be harmonised by placing both protectorates in future under the charge of the same department.[1]

While the negotiations for transfer were taking place the question of annexing all British protectorates as colonies was also raised. Various administrative advantages were seen in making them colonies, such as in matters like treaties, jurisdiction over foreigners, extradition and marriage questions and the application of the Army Act. There were only two disadvantages in the proclamation of colonies. In the words of an official minute these were: 'The disadvantages are the effect it would have on foreign Powers at the present juncture, and the fact that annexation entails, *ipso facto*, the immediate abolition of slavery.'[2] The existence of slavery in any form, legal or domestic, was not to be tolerated in any British colony and it was the position in Zanzibar that gave concern on this point. Had it been different Nyasaland might well have become a colony in 1904!

Important constitutional provisions were introduced by the Nyasaland Order in Council of 1907: the designation of the country was altered from British Central Africa Protectorate to Nyasaland Protectorate; the title of Commissioner was replaced by that of Governor and Commander-in-chief; a Legislative Council was set up for the first time made up of Governor, *ex-officio* members (i.e. Government Secretary, Treasurer and Attorney-General), official members and unofficial members. The official and unofficial members were appointed by the Governor. The unofficial members were to hold office for five years.

[1] F.O. 2/885, citing *Morning Post*, 28 March 1904.
[2] F.O. 2/885, F.O. Minutes by 'C.Ll.H.', 7 April 1902.

At the same time an Executive Council made up of the Governor and the *ex-officio* members of the Legislative Council was set up.

The first Legislative Council was presided over by the country's first Governor, Sir Alfred Sharpe. There were three *ex-officio* members: the Deputy-Governor, Major Pearce; the Treasurer, W. Wheeler, and the Attorney-General, C. J. Griffin. There were three unofficial members: the missionary member from the Blantyre Mission, the Rev. Alexander Hetherwick; C. Metcalfe of the British Central Africa Company and A. F. Kidney of the African Lakes Corporation.

The introduction of the Legislative Council did not limit the powers of the Governor. It was he who appointed the members and it was he who initiated legislation. In effect what was introduced in 1907 was the principle of consultation without introducing the elements of constraints on the Governor's position. The Nyasaland Order in Council of 1907 came into operation on 6 July of that year, an auspicious day in the history of Malawi. The first Legislative Council meeting was held on 7 July of the following year.

The interests of the European community were represented by the three unofficial members who were appointed by the Governor himself. The number was increased to six in 1911. Though a number of European associations existed at the time, they were not at first involved in the nomination process. The first of these was the Shire Highlands Planters' Association (established September 1892); the second was the Nyasaland Planters' Association (established December 1892). Both of these finally sank their differences and formed the British Central Africa Chamber of Agriculture and Commerce in October 1895. The next important development was when about seven or eight associations combined in 1928 to form the Convention of Associations for the purpose of submitting names of Europeans, together with the Chamber of Agriculture and Commerce, for appointment to the Legislative Council by the Governor. Among the first persons to be so selected was Mr (afterwards Sir) William Tait-Bowie of the Blantyre and East Africa Company, who went on to serve the Council for eighteen years as unofficial member, during fourteen of which he was the leader of the unofficial members. He also served for eight years as a member of the Executive Council. He was at various times chairman of the Convention of Associations, the Chamber of Commerce and of tea and tobacco associations. When he died in 1949, his successor as senior unofficial member Mr (afterwards Sir) Malcolm Barrow said: 'There has been no one in the history of this country who held for so long a greater respect of all the people of the country than Sir William.'

In 1946 the first lady member joined the Council in the person of

Mrs Mary Tunstall Sharpe, M.B.E., who had come to Malawi in 1919 after having married the second son of the country's first governor. In 1947 Mrs Marjorie Barron (afterwards Mrs F. E. Widdas) became the second lady member. By now the six European members were no longer satisfied with the nomination procedures and made repeated representations for the introduction of a system of direct election. This was finally conceded to them in the constitution of 1955.

In the meantime, Africans and Asians remained without direct or indirect representation. On the Gold Coast, now Ghana, the first African member of that country's Legislative Council, John Mensah Sarbah, was appointed as early as 1889. Closer home, in Kenya, the first African member, E. W. Mathu, was appointed in 1944. However, Kenya had already taken a forward step in 1923 by giving Indians five seats in the Legislative Council. In Malawi, however, both Indians and Africans had to wait till 1949.

The Indians had no political organisation in the country until 1952 when the Nyasaland Asian Convention was founded, followed by the Nyasaland Asian Association. These bodies were formed in response to the issue of federation in Central Africa. Before that Indians in Malawi had been content with their few seats in the town councils and with their own Chamber of Commerce. It was the latter body which was invited to submit up to three names to the Governor from which a single person would be nominated. P. Dayaram became the first Indian member of the Legislative Council, in 1949.

Africans, on the other hand, were granted provincial councils in 1944 and 1945. The membership of the Central and Southern Provincial Councils stood at twenty-five each, twenty of whom represented traditional authority in each case, while the Northern Provincial Council had a membership of twenty. From among the membership of these provincial councils a Protectorate Council of twenty members was established in 1946. This council was invited to submit five names to the Governor in 1949 out of whom the Governor nominated two members to serve on the Legislative Council. The first two African members so selected were Alexander Muwamba and K. Ellerton Mposa. In 1953 African representation was increased to three; Asian representation stood at one and European unofficial representation remained at six.

The 1949 constitution introduced the only significant changes to take place since 1907. For the first time all communities in the country had representatives on the Legislative Council, but it was still an arrangement which favoured one community. The introduction of the Central African Federation in 1953 on the platform of partnership was meaningless until a positive move was made to enlarge African participation and widen its representative base. As things stood twenty members constituted a form of electoral college.

The position was changed in the 1955 constitution which created a common roll for the European and Asian communities; the African community was placed on an entirely different system. European supporters of the constitution argued that it aimed at eliminating the system of separate representation while fostering racial cooperation. Non-Europeans argued that the contrary was true. They said that there were serious discriminatory features in the constitution, for instance, Africans and non-Africans were on totally separate and independent rolls. The franchise qualifications for non-Africans meant in practice that votes for Europeans was ensured because of three factors: a fair number of potential Asian voters were British protected persons who were precluded from the vote which was reserved for British subjects; under the English language qualification (namely, the ability to complete and sign a registration form without assistance) almost 95 per cent of the total Asian population was disqualified; and while European women acquired the vote on their husbands' qualifications, Asian women were required to establish their independent qualifications since their marriages, though monogamous (and recognised as such in terms of the country's law on marriages, divorce and succession), were contracted under a system which permitted of polygamous marriages. The result was that out of 8,490 Asians in the country, only 338 qualified for the vote. Two Asians stood as candidates in the 1956 election: one forfeited his deposit; the other was overwhelmingly defeated. All six non-African seats went to Europeans. Asian representation was finally eliminated. The European population of 6,730 produced 1,866 voters.

What of the African elections in 1956? The three provincial councils, whose membership consisted overwhelmingly of chiefs, were set up as electoral colleges and their members were called upon to vote for five members, two each for the Central and Southern Provinces and one for the Northern Province. Though an improvement on 1949 it was far from popular and was only accepted as a stepping stone. Finally, what of the Executive Council? In 1907 it comprised the Governor and three *ex-officio* members; in 1939 two European unofficials were added on; twenty years later, in 1959, the first two Malawian members were included. But by then the days of gradual change were over. The entire structure of colonial and protectorate rule in Central Africa was tottering. From its ruins more favourable constitutional provisions were salvaged.

The preparation for what was to happen on 6 July 1958 started in a small way in 1949 when K. E. Mposa and E. A. Muwamba joined the Legislative Council as the first African members. In his maiden speech Mr Muwamba recognised how much they were dependent on others for support. He said, 'I should like to say that we shall expect our Chiefs, we shall expect the Provincial and Protectorate Councils, the African Congress and many other institutions and all Africans individually in the territory and abroad who are interested, to help us. . . .' A small step forward was taken when the first five African members took their seats according to the terms of the 1955 constitution. Though indirectly elected, they represented a new force in that they spoke as members of the Nyasaland African Congress. They were J. R. N. Chinyama, M. W. K. Chiume, D. W. Chijozi, N. D. Kwenje and H. B. Chipembere. African membership increased to seven in 1959. In that year, two of the new members, C. M. Chinkondenji and E. M. Mtawali, were elected to the Executive Council. In 1960, when the first constitutional talks were held, of the seven African members of the Legislative Council, three were elected and four were nominated.

When these earlier constitutional changes took place the focus of attention was the much-hated Federation. Records of the proceedings of the Legislative Council in the 1950s and 1960s are replete with criticisms of the Federation. As Muwamba had appealed for the support of chiefs and others in an ordinary situation, so did one of the new members elected to the Legislative Council in 1956 express his determination to enlist support in what was now an extraordinary situation —the fight against the Federation. In the words of one of them:

> The Chiefs of this country and their people will go on struggling for liberation from their federal entanglements until their general object of freeing Nyasaland has been achieved, and they will go on struggling for the establishment of a truly representative Government in this country until that object has been achieved. There will be no surrender, Mr Speaker and there will be no going back.

Though a commitment had been expressed, organisation and leadership were not equal to the occasion and it was to provide these missing qualities that Dr H. Kamuzu Banda arrived in the country from Ghana on 6 July 1958, a day which introduced a new dimension in the political struggle. Out of this struggle a number of constitutional changes emerged. The opening round was the Nyasaland Constitutional Conference which was held at Lancaster House, London, from 25 July to

4 August 1960. It was presided over by Mr Iain Macleod, Colonial Secretary, and was attended by representatives of all interested groups and political parties in the country. The Malawi Congress Party was led by Dr Banda, the United Federal Party by Mr Michael Blackwood and the Congress Liberation Party by Mr T. D. T. Banda. African members from the United Federal Party as well as from the Nyasaland Legislative Council also attended. Nyasaland Asians were represented by the chairman of the Nyasaland Asian Convention, Mr Sattar Sacranie. The conference agreed upon a new constitution: the government was to comprise the Governor, an Executive Council of ten members and a Legislative Council of twenty-eight elected non-official members and five official members of the Executive Council. The Executive Council's ten members were equally divided between officials and non-officials. Of the five unofficial members of the Executive Council, two members were to be drawn from the higher roll and three from the lower roll after the elections of 1961.

The division of the electorate into two rolls was a creation of the Lancaster House talks and it was aimed at taking account of the different levels in the country. First there was a general requirement for all voters: they had to be at least twenty-one years old, and should have resided in the country for two years prior to registration. They had to be British subjects or British protected persons resident in Nyasaland. There were two other requirements for voters on the lower roll: they had to be literate in English or have an income of over £120 or property worth £250 or they had to be literate in any language in common use in the country and be able to provide evidence of having paid tax for ten years (any person of the age of twenty-seven or twenty-eight was deemed to have satisfied the tax requirement if no other evidence was available). Holders of scheduled posts such as chiefs, native authority members, past and present members of district councils, group and village headmen, master farmers, pensioners and ex-servicemen needed no other special qualification to vote on the lower roll.

The qualifications for the higher roll were based on education, income and property: a university graduate was eligible; those with secondary education had to have an income of £300 per annum or property worth £500; those with primary education had to have an income of £480 or property worth £1,000; those with no educational qualification beyond the ability to complete a registration form in English had to earn £720 per annum or have property worth £1,500.

For the first general elections ever to be held in Malawi, 15 August 1961 was chosen as polling day. Of the twenty seats on the lower roll, the Southern Province got eight; the Central Province got seven and

242

the Northern Province got five. Of the eight higher roll constituencies, the Southern Province got five, the Central Province two and the North one. It was also the first and only multi-party election to be held. The parties which contested the elections were the Malawi Congress Party, the Christian Liberation Party, led by T. D. T. Banda (which had amalgamated with the Christian Democratic Party led by Chester Katsonga) and the United Federal Party which had a sprinkling of African support including that of a former chairman of the Nyasaland African Congress and two members of the Legislative Council. There were two independent candidates.

The results were a resounding affirmation of the confidence of the people in the Malawi Congress Party which won all twenty seats on the lower roll and the only two it contested on the higher roll. The United Federal Party won five seats on the higher roll while the last seat on the higher roll went to the independent candidate, Colin Cameron. The Christian Liberation Party was pulverised and its demise marked the end of organised African opposition to the Malawi Congress Party (M.C.P.). For the future it was to be this party alone which had to decide the destiny of the country. For the present, in August 1961 it had control of the Legislative Council, and five seats on the Executive Council were given to M.C.P. members or those supported by it. No other party was represented on the Executive Council, the remaining members being officials of the Government. Dr Banda himself assumed the portfolios of Natural Resources and Local Government while the portfolios of Education, Labour, Works and Transport as well as the position of Minister without Portfolio went to the other four members or supporters of the M.C.P.

By the beginning of 1962 Dr Banda was *de facto* Prime Minister, a position which he sought to regularise in November 1962 at the second constitutional talks held at Marlborough House, London. At these talks a programme of complete internal self-government for Nyasaland was worked out in three stages. On 1 February 1963 the Executive Council was replaced by a Cabinet headed by the country's first Prime Minister, Dr Banda. The other Ministers were eight elected unofficial members of the Legislative Council, all of whom were African members of the M.C.P., while the ninth Minister was the *ex-officio* Minister of Finance, Sir Henry Phillips, specially requested to assume this portfolio by the Prime Minister.

The second stage towards complete internal self-government was enacted on 9 May 1963 when the Legislative Council was re-named the Legislative Assembly and the Cabinet ceased to be advisory to the Governor except in certain matters like public safety and order.

The final stage was the preparation for national independence. This was negotiated in the Butler-Banda constitutional talks held in London in September 1963. Mr R. A. Butler was then the Minister-in-Charge of Central African Affairs. At these talks it was agreed that general elections would be held in April 1964 and that on 6 July 1964 Nyasaland would become the independent state of Malawi. The new constitution provided for a Legislative Assembly of fifty-three members, fifty of whom would be elected on a general roll on the basis of universal adult suffrage—or as it was more popularly called, the principle of 'one man, one vote'. The remaining three seats were reserved for European members on a special roll. There was no separate provision for Asian representation since the Asian representative at the Lancaster House talks in 1960 had announced the community's support for the Malawi Congress Party and had declared that the existing Nyasaland Asian Convention would be dissolved. From that point the Asian community did not aspire for separate political representation.

The general elections were duly held in April 1964. All the candidates of the Malawi Congress Party were returned unopposed. The elections clearly revealed that there was only one political party in the country. This *de facto* position was translated into a *de jure* reality in 1966 when the republic of Malawi became legally based on the foundations of a single party. The decision to make Malawi a one-party state was taken at the Lilongwe National Convention in 1965.

On 6 July 1964 Malawi became an independent state under a monarchical constitution. The British Crown was represented by Sir Glyn Jones, the country's first and only Governor-General. Sir Glyn Jones was the head of state while the head of government was the country's first Prime Minister.

The monarchical constitution was replaced by a republican constitution as from 6 July 1966. The groundwork for this change was prepared by the National Convention of the Malawi Congress Party which was held at Lilongwe 13–17 October 1965. The National Convention comprised 394 delegates drawn from all sections of the Malawi Congress Party organisation, namely the Party's Central Executive, the League of Malawi Women, the League of Malawi Youth, as well as members of Parliament and chiefs. A Constitutional Committee under the chairmanship of Mr Aleke Banda, Secretary-General of the Malawi Congress Party, worked out a republican constitution which was endorsed by the Convention and later approved by Parliament. The Convention nominated Dr Banda to be the first President. This was approved by Act 22/1966. According to the constitution of the republic of Malawi (Act 23/1966), the President is both head of state and

244

26. Osman Adam.

27. Chief Philip Gomani of Ncheu.

28. James Frederick Sangala.

29. Pastor K. M. Malinki.

30. Thornton's grave near Chikwawa. The memorial was put up in 1905 by A. J. Storey.

31. Emperor Haile Selassie (centre) with Prime Minister Dr H. K. Banda and Governor-General Sir Glyn Jones, Chileka Airport, August 1964.

government. At the Annual Convention of the M.C.P. which opened at Mzuzu on 7 September 1970 at which, among other matters, the Party was required to nominate a candidate for the office of President, the Mzuzu Convention 'resolved unanimously that Ngwazi Dr Kamuzu Banda was the people's choice for the office of President and demanded that the Constitution of the Republic of Malawi be amended to provide for Ngwazi Dr Kamuzu Banda to be President for his life time'. This was approved by Parliament in December 1970. The Life President was sworn in on 6 July 1971 at the Kamuzu Stadium.

According to the constitution a subsequent candidate for the position of President must, among other requirements, be of the age of forty-five (reduced to forty in March 1972) and would be nominated by an electoral college comprising members of the national executive of the Party, of the League of Malawi Women and League of Malawi Youth, and of the regional committees as well as by officials of the district committees of the Women and Youth Leagues, members of Parliament, all chiefs recognised as traditional authorities (a term which now replaces native authorities) and chairmen of district councils. During the absence or illness of the President, the constitution provides that the President may by directions in writing appoint three cabinet ministers to be a Presidential Commission. In the event of there being a vacancy or when the President is unable to appoint a Presidential Commission the function of that office will be performed by a Presidential Council consisting of the Secretary-General of the Party and two cabinet ministers who are also members of the national executive committee.

The third general election took place in April 1971. By the terms of a constitutional amendment of 1969 the number of constituencies was increased from fifty to sixty. In addition the President could nominate fifteen members, five Europeans and ten Malawians. Of the sixty elected seats, the northern region obtained thirteen; the central region twenty-five and the southern region twenty-two. Nomination day was 17 April 1971. A special arrangement was worked out for the election procedures, in which about five thousand people out of over two million registered voters participated in the selection process of candidates at district conferences. These conferences which were required to submit a panel of up to five names in order of preference to the President, who was empowered to make the final choice, comprised district officials of the Party and of the League of Malawi Women and League of Malawi Youth, officials of the area committees of the Party and the Leagues, chairman and councillors of district councils, mayors and Malawian councillors, and chiefs and sub-chiefs.

At the time of the dissolution of Parliament on 18 March 1971 there were twelve cabinet ministers, five of whom were members of Parliament. Before 1968 the President could appoint no more than three ministers from outside Parliament. By Act 6 of 1968 this limitation was removed. In terms of the Constitution Amendment Act approved by Parliament on 26 July 1971, cabinet ministers who were appointed by the Life President would be members of Parliament by virtue, and for the duration, of their office as ministers.

CHAPTER 18

The police force and Martyrs' Day

i THE POLICE FORCE

The first official police force was instituted in Malawi after thirty years of protectorate rule. On 5 October 1921 Ordinance 15 of that year was approved and the Nyasaland Police Force was legally formed. On 5 October 1971 the Police Force had therefore been in existence for fifty eventful years and it was natural that this historical milestone should be marked by celebrations as well as by stocktaking. For instance, a booklet entitled *A History of the Malawi Police Force* was compiled by Mr C. Marlow, Assistant Commissioner of Police. It contained a message by the Life President of Malawi and a foreword by Mr P. Long, the then Commissioner of Police.

The story of police services for the country may be set out in four phases: the first phase covered the first five years of protectorate rule; the second, 1896 to 1921; the third, 1921 to 1971, and the fourth is the new phase which began in July 1971.

The first phase was characterised by a series of wars which were waged against slave traders and chiefs who though they were not slave traders themselves were none the less looked upon as opponents of the Administration, since they were either unwilling or reluctant to accept British rule. The Administration was instructed to maintain 'peace and good order' but was not provided with the means to do so. It received a paltry grant of £17,500 per annum from Cecil John Rhodes' British South Africa Company for the first five years. With this the Administration was expected to extend a British protectorate over 36,000 square miles. The first imperative therefore was a powerful police force. For this the head of the Administration looked to India, where his request met with a cool reception at first. The Indian Government was reluctant to allow Sikhs and Punjabis to be recruited for service in the British possessions in Africa but gave way to the urgent and persistent requests. The upshot was that Capt. Maguire of the Hyderabad Continent Lancers was instructed to recruit a force of seventy volunteers from the Indian Army, thirty-nine of whom were Mazbi Sikhs, while the remaining thirty-one were Muslim cavalrymen. They were recruited for two years' military service. They constituted more than half the strength of the entire armed force in Nyasaland, the other half being an English officer and about fifty Zanzibaris and Makua. Johnston, the Commissioner, appreciated the services of the Indian soldiers and when the terms of service of the original batch expired in 1893 he requested that the number should be increased to two hundred. He paid a personal visit to India in 1895 and succeeded in coming to a definite arrangement by which two hundred Sikhs from the Indian army would be employed in regular service for two years at a time in British Central Africa for the next six years.

The second phase opened in 1896 with the creation of a military regiment known as the British Central African Rifles, a term which was changed in 1902 to the King's African Rifles. At the same time the state of the country was such that a distinction could at last be made between the military police and the civil police. The country was no longer in a state of war; the Yao chiefs had been subjugated or expelled; the Arab slaver Mlozi was no more; the resistance of the Chewa of Kasungu ended with the suicide of their chief. And in Ncheu another pocket of resistance ended with the execution of Inkosi Gomani. As from 1 January 1897 each District Collector (later known as District Resident and finally as District Commissioner) was authorised to employ his own police force for the district. A uniform made of strong blue calico was to be worn by district policemen. The cost of the material for one pair of trousers, a jumper and a cap, was just under two shillings at the time of its introduction. This system continued up to 1921.

The responsibility for controlling the district police force as well as organising the entire district administration rested on the shoulders of the District Collectors who were often young and inexperienced, saddled with a variety of complex responsibilities. Quite often many things went wrong with the district police—as with other district matters.

One example, by no means an isolated one, of the excesses of the day is to be seen by describing an expedition undertaken to collect tax in Central Angoniland in 1900. These expeditions were always closely related to labour recruitment as tax defaulters and their relatives were

248

usually commandeered for the labour market. A company representative accompanied by a government official and five askari went on a trip for the purpose of obtaining labourers from among people who had not paid their hut tax. Chief Chimbulanga refused to allow any labour recruitment to take place among his people. Thereupon the askari went to work with gay abandon: whole villages, including *nkhokwe* or food huts, were destroyed. The Dutch Reformed Church missionaries who worked in the area protested that this was not how a government operated. Marlow's book refers to an official report of that day which throws light on how the police operated, considering it to be 'their right to demand fowls, food, beer and even women from the local population'. If this had happened only in the early days it could have been interpreted as teething problems, but as late as 17 March 1921 a mission doctor at Dedza sent a letter to the *Nyasaland Times* which was not published because the editor did not wish to embarrass the Government. In the letter the missionary complained of hut-burning and related matters. He noted that the Africans had rejected the old argument that white rule had brought peace and security, and they consequently had a right to continue living as they had before. The missionary observed:

> They say that there used to be long intervals of peace in the old days whereas now it is a never ending 'nkhondo' [war]. . . . They conclude that they are now practically *all* 'akapolo' [slaves], whereas the slave raiders, of whom the Government has freed them, always left the great majority free.

Similar complaints were repeated in June of that year.[1]

The Administration did take note of what was going on. In 1909 the Civil Police Disciplinary Ordinance was passed in an attempt to punish transgressors.

During the second phase the first two towns in Malawi with town councils of their own made their own police arrangements. Though the Blantyre township had had a Council of Advice since August 1895 it was only in May 1899 that the Blantyre town council began to employ two African constables as policemen at a wage of five shillings per month. When the Mangochi town council was formed on 7 April 1899, it was decided at the first meeting not to have a town policeman or watchman. The reason? It would be too expensive. Two years later, in March 1901, two Africans were engaged to patrol the streets of the town from 8 p.m. to 6.30 a.m. for a trial period of three months at five shillings per month. Reference must also be made to the Nyasaland

[1] S.2/3/21, National Archives, Zomba.

Volunteer Reserve Force which was recognised as a government institution from 1901. It helped during World War I in Karonga as well as in the Nyasaland rising of 1915. In the following year, however, it ceased to operate as a separate unit.

By then the third phase was approaching. Serious re-thinking was taking place on all fronts. The whole concept of protectorate objectives was analysed and improvements were suggested. J. C. Casson, the Superintendent of Native Affairs, pointed out in a report dated 17 December 1912 what was wrong with the basic thinking:

> The opinion is sometimes heard in Nyasaland, as in other parts of Africa, that the native should not be educated: this opinion as a rule emanates from those who look upon the native as an animal merely who should be so trained and instructed as to render him useful in a continual life of hard manual work performed for Europeans.[1]

Many significant changes were thought up and introduced during the period of the governorship of Sir George Smith from 1913 to 1923. A proposal from the Secretary of State in 1920 to annex Nyasaland as a colony was turned down; police seizure of individuals for compulsory labour was discontinued in the same year. At the same time Governor Smith had plans for the reorganisation of the police force. As early as December 1913 a meeting was held of District Residents at which a recommendation was made for the setting up of a national police force. The war intervened and the matter was picked up again at the end of hostilities. The Governor's proposal of 1919, which was accepted, was that the police force should be headed by a Chief Commissioner of Police aided by eighteen other European officers and an African contingent of six hundred. During the initial period the reorganisation would apply to only four of the fourteen districts, Zomba, Blantyre, Mangochi and Mulanje. Though it was only on 5 October 1921 that the reorganisation took legal effect, the first Chief Commissioner, Major F. T. Stephens, arrived in the country in July 1920 to take up his new appointment. He remained at his post until he retired at the end of 1938.

When the third phase began in 1921, district administration was reorganised too, and the country was divided into three provinces for the first time. In that year there were 1,120,000 Africans, 1,486 Europeans and 563 Indians living in the country.

In the first year of the new police force 1,026 convictions were obtained. When this figure is compared with that of 1970, namely 10,435

[1] C.O. 525/47, 'A short history of the educational system (for Natives) of Nyasaland,' 1913.

convictions, it is obvious that the work of the force has increased ten-fold within fifty years. Among the developments in the first decade was the appointment in 1930 of the Chief Commissioner of Police as Principal Immigration Officer as well as the appointment of three Asian Sub-Inspectors.

In the fifty-year story of the Malawi police force, there have been five European Commissioners of Police: Major Stephens, Mr Bithrey, Mr Fraser, Colonel Apthrop, Mr Mullin and Mr Peter Long.

When the fourth phase of the story began on 25 July 1971, the Malawi police force was headed by the first African Commissioner of Police, Mr M. J. Kamwana, who had earlier, in May 1970, been pro-moted to the rank of Deputy Commissioner of Police. Mr Kamwana was born in 1935 and joined the police force in 1953.

Fifty years in the life of an individual is a long time; in the life of an institution it does not feel so long, but the end of it may mark the end of the period of formation and the beginning of the period of consoli-dation. Much had been achieved during this period. The best tribute to this achievement may be recalled in the words of the Life President in his message for Mr Marlow's book:

> It is in essence a story of courageous, loyal and devoted service, given by a Police Force without interruption for the past 50 years. It should serve to reinforce the pride which all members of the Malawi Police rightly take in the privilege of the membership of the Force.

ii MARTYRS' DAY

March 3 is Martyrs' Day in Malawi, a national day to commemorate the march to freedom, to independence and to nationhood. It is a day of thanksgiving to honour the memories of the pioneers of freedom who by their courage, their foresight and their sacrifice made it possible for those who followed to see the dawn of a new age.

The history of every nation is replete with the stories of its martyrs. In Malawi, the events of 1915, 1953 and 1959 are good examples of attempts made by individuals, groups and parties to register their un-compromising opposition to the powers, politics and practices of their day.

What were these powers, politics and practices? In 1915 protector-ate rule was only twenty-four years old in Malawi. Only a single gener-ation had grown up since the Yao leaders Makanjira, Zarafi, Kawinga, Liwonde and others had taken up arms against the Protectorate troops; since Mwase Kasungu had taken his life rather than submit to the demands of protectorate rule; and since Chief Gomani I had been shot for resisting inroads into his domain.

The generation which grew up after this first period of resistance to foreign rule found that the old order was no more while the new order was itself fraught with many difficulties. For those like the European Baptist missionary, Joseph Booth, who were prepared to see, these difficulties were serious. John Chilembwe, who worked for him, saw them too. The unfamiliar cry of 'Africa for the African' was now sounded in a little circle of which Booth and Chilembwe formed the nucleus. When John Chilembwe returned from the U.S.A. in 1900 he saw these problems more clearly, for instance, those concerning the estates. The original occupants of the land had lost their original rights of occupancy when over three million acres of land changed hands in the first few years of protectorate rule; landlords required labour not rent and those who were not prepared to give it were harassed or evicted. There was no security of tenure; there were long hours of work; rolls of tobacco were handed out as wages; schools and churches were not allowed on some estates and fines and floggings were frequent.

Yet Malawian soldiers fought with distinction outside their country in Mauritius, Somaliland and Ghana in wars which were not really their concern. John Chilembwe wrote a letter to the *Nyasaland Times* about this:

Everybody knows that the natives have been loyal to all Nyasaland interests and Nyasaland institutions. For our part we have never allowed the Nyasaland flag to touch the ground, while honour and credit have often gone to others. We have unreservedly stepped to the firing line in every conflict and played a patriot's part with the spirit of true gallantry. But in time of peace the Government failed to help the underdog.

It was only when the Government refused to listen to his complaints on behalf of his countrymen and planned to arrest him and to deport him to the Seychelles that John Chilembwe decided to take up arms against the Government on 23 January 1915. Some people say it was a premeditated blow with months of planning behind it. Let us consider the testimony of one Lupiya Zalela given on 19 February 1915, sixteen days after Chilembwe had been shot and killed:

John Chilembwe sent Johnston Solongolola on Tuesday 19 January to the church at Abraham's village who said that Chilembwe had received a letter from the Europeans and that he [Johnston] must warn the people that the Europeans wanted to kill the natives on Monday 25th January. Johnston said, 'The Europeans are to kill the natives on Monday [25th January]. What shall we do? 'Tis good that we begin war and kill the Europeans before they begin.'

Chilembwe gave up his life in an act which he construed to be an act of self-defence. It was not motivated by a policy of hatred. As an individual he had a lot to lose: his church, his schools, his shop, his family and his friends. He was also planning a trip to Europe and to the United States in early 1914. Would he have given all this up without just cause?

His immediate supporters were also men of means. They had shops and farms at Nsoni in Chiradzulu. Duncan Njilima owned 125 acres of land and 12 head of cattle as well as a store. Two of his sons were being educated in the U.S.A.; he had £54 12s. in actual cash, a considerable sum in 1915. John Gray Kufa had 150 acres of freehold land and dozens of head of cattle. Such people were not soldiers of fortune.

They were educated people, too. Letters were written by Duncan Njilima and John Gray Kufa to their relatives shortly before they were hanged or shot. John Gray Kufa Mapantha wrote to his cousin Johnstone Sazuze, the father of Mr Sazuze of the Malawi Housing Corporation, on 14 February 1915:

Here are my children. I leave them with you and Dr Hetherwick. Please try to come. Please, you will never see me again in this world. We will meet in heaven. Goodbye cousin, God be with you. All documents of the lands at Mlanje and Nsoni were burnt together with the house. You must try to arrange everything, please. I have gone to Father in Heaven. . . .'

It is important to realise that such people have gone down in history for their tremendous sacrifice, though they did not die in vain. The Commission of Inquiry found that there was just cause for the grievances expressed. It recommended various reforms especially in education and in the conditions for African tenants on private estates, a problem which was to cause trouble again in 1953.

The intervening period from 1915 to 1953, as we have seen, saw the rise of native associations and the birth of the Nyasaland African Congress but there was no militancy in these movements and no real involvement on a national scale. Both militancy and national involvement took root as the country braced itself to fight the hated Federation. In this fight the Nyasaland African Congress and the chiefs combined and pooled their resources as well as their respective followings.

The Nyasaland African Congress resolved to conduct a passive resistance campaign against federation. A council of action was set up and this included a number of chiefs. The chairman was Chief Mwase and the secretary was Lawrence Mapemba. The head of the council in Ncheu was Inkosi Philip Gomani II of Lizulu. When the Government deposed Inkosi Gomani trouble broke out at Ncheu; soon afterwards trouble broke out at Thyolo on the estates. Congress advised people not to pay rents, not to observe the agricultural laws and not to take part in the coronation celebrations set for 2 June 1953. An incident on the Mangunda Estate, the main citrus estate in the country, further incensed the opposition. Tempers began to rise and disturbances spread quickly and widely in the southern region. Police reinforcements were brought in from the two Rhodesias and Tanganyika. Strict measures were used including firearms, batons and tear gas. In the disturbances eleven Africans were killed and seventy-two persons were injured.

But all this was a prelude to the main drama which was to open on 6 July 1958 when Dr H. Kamuzu Banda, after forty-three eventful years in South Africa, the U.S.A., the United Kingdom and Ghana, returned to his native land. Dr Banda had come to break up the Federation. To achieve this he mobilised the political resources of Malawi from the grassroots. For the first time in the history of the country Congress resorted to mass appeal.

People rallied to the call of their new leader. Dr Banda began addressing meetings throughout the country in which he electrified the crowds by his dynamic oratory. For the first time since John Chilembwe's rising, the country was in trouble. Public meetings without the permission of the Government were banned. To get some idea of the rising crescendo of African nationalism it should be recalled that in under five months permits were issued for 436 meetings while 31 were refused. In one of his speeches Dr Banda said: 'You have heard of the so-called riots. Well things are hot here. I have the whole of Blantyre and Zomba on fire. Very soon, I hope to have the whole of Nyasaland on fire.'

He was true to his word and the Government stepped in to check the rising tide of opposition. On 3 March 1959 the Government moved to detain 208 of the hardcore leadership in a nationwide swoop at sunrise. The Devlin Report tells us that 'Dr Banda was refused permission to dress but was allowed to put on a dressing gown and he was taken to a waiting Land-Rover. The house was searched, all locks being broken open with an axe or bayonet.'

The arrests were themselves a clear indication of panic in official circles. What was worse about them was the manner in which they were carried out. There were many cases of extreme brutality. Naturally some resisted arrest and were severely manhandled. Rioting and disturbances increased. By May 1959 over one thousand detainees were being held in various parts of the country as well as outside the country. Between 20 February 1959 and 19 March 1959, forty-four men and four women were killed by gunfire; three were killed by baton charge or bayonet thrust; seventy-nine persons were wounded by bullets. All of them were Africans.

The blood of the martyrs was not shed in vain. It nurtured the growth of nationalism and it increased the resolution of the people as a whole to ask or fight for what was justly theirs. If prisons, battlefields and martyrdom are necessary before national independence can be attained, Malawi has had her share and Malawians have made their sacrifice, so that succeeding generations might say with pride and gratitude that as the sun sets on yet another Martyrs' Day the nation solemnly salutes the memory of its martyrs.

CHAPTER 19

Closer union in Central Africa

i EVENTS LEADING TO THE FORMATION OF THE CENTRAL AFRICAN FEDERATION

One of Cecil John Rhodes' dreams was that one day there would be a federal union of southern and Central African territories under the British flag. Though he died in 1902 his dreams were carried forward by others in modified form. One such man was Sir William Milton, administrator of Southern Rhodesia, who led that country's delegation to the meetings in South Africa of the National Convention in 1908 and 1909 which worked out the scheme for the union of the South African states. Though Southern Rhodesia was a mere observer, there remained a possibility that one day it would join South Africa. In the meantime the British South Africa Company, the ruler of Southern Rhodesia, initiated proposals in 1916 to unite the two Rhodesias but opposition from the settler community in Southern Rhodesia frustrated these moves. They were not prepared to join hands with Northern Rhodesia with its poverty and its predominantly African population, at least not yet. So the gaze in Southern Rhodesia was directed southwards once again when General Smuts, the Prime Minister of South Africa, offered favourable terms to them if they would join the South African union. A referendum was held in October 1922 and only 40 per cent of the voters were in favour. That marked the end of any idea to move southwards. Southern Rhodesia received responsible government in 1923 and thereby assumed the constitutional lead in Central Africa.

In that year there were a number of important developments. The British Government announced a colonial policy statement for East Africa through the Devonshire Declaration 'that the interests of the African Natives must be paramount, and that if and when those interests and the interests of the immigrant races should conflict, the former should prevail'. This declaration worried settlers in the two Rhodesias, who began to think that their interests would be best served by amalgamation of some sort. Northern Rhodesia was no longer the poor relative since copper working had begun to show promise. And in South Africa the Afrikaner nationalist, General Hertzog, became Prime Minister in 1924. English-speaking Southern Rhodesians found Hertzog's narrow nationalism unacceptable and this was one other reason for seeking a northern partner. In 1924, also, Company rule ceased in Northern Rhodesia and a British Protectorate similar to that in Nyasaland was introduced. With this the responsibility of the British Government towards the two protectorates in Central Africa increased and the interests of the two protectorates could no longer be separated.

As a reaction to settler interest in combination the British Government appointed the Hilton Young Commission to inquire into the closer union of British dependencies in East and Central Africa. The report was published in 1929 and though a considerable part of it was directed at the East African territories, reference was also made to the Central African area. In his minority report, the chairman, Sir E. Hilton Young, favoured the setting up of three administrative unions in Central Africa: the first, a union of Southern Rhodesia with the European-settled part of Central Northern Rhodesia in the railway zone; the second, the union of Northeastern Rhodesia with Nyasaland, and the third was the creation of Barotseland as a separate African territory. The three other commissioners in their majority report disagreed with these proposals. Though they were inclined to support a closer association of Northeastern Rhodesia, Nyasaland and Tanganyika with the other territories of East Africa, they felt that problems of communications were too serious to make this a workable proposition. As for the alternative of federation, amalgamation or any other form of union of the protectorates of Central Africa with Southern Rhodesia, they rejected it with the following argument: 'The control of a large black population by a small white community [in Southern Rhodesia] is still in an experimental stage, and it would be unwise to add to its burdens until its ability to discharge its present task has been tested for a longer period.' These members used the population ratio as argument. In Southern Rhodesia the ratio was one European to nineteen Africans. If the three territories were united it would become one European to sixty-five Africans.

In 1930 the amalgamation issue was further stimulated by the publication of the Passfield Memorandum which reiterated the principle enunciated in the Devonshire Declaration of 1923. In 1930 the first of various conferences was held attended by members of the Legislative Councils of the two Rhodesias. Prominent at this first meeting was Dr

Godfrey Huggins (later Sir Godfrey and Lord Malvern) whose name has become closely associated with the amalgamation and federation movements in Central Africa.

It must not be thought that support for closer union was developing in the two Rhodesias only. The *Nyasaland Times* supported it on the grounds that it would lead to administrative economy and reduction in taxation. Planters' associations supported it, too, as did the heads of the governments of Southern Rhodesia and the two protectorates. The Prime Minister and the Governors of the territories met in formal conference in April 1935 to discuss closer union in research, customs, communications, education, defence, trade, common currency as well as the possibility of a common Central African Court of Appeal (which was set up in 1939). This was followed by a second meeting in 1936 (the first of many to be held at Victoria Falls) of white parliamentarians and officials. There was a divergence of views at this meeting on the pattern of the closer union. Moore of Northern Rhodesia and Huggins of Southern Rhodesia advocated unification under a single government, which meant amalgamation. Gore-Browne of Northern Rhodesia drew attention to the responsibilities of the British Government to uphold the principles of trusteeship over the African populations of the protectorates. He spoke out for partnership and was the first person to champion this concept during the early talks.

While officials as well as non-officials in Central Africa were moving towards a closer union of the territories, the British Government could not stand by passively in view of its imperial responsibilities, which were chiefly the protection of the interests of the Africans in the protectorates. The Bledisloe Commission was set up in 1938 to reconsider the whole question especially, 'with due regard to the interests of all the inhabitants irrespective of race'. The Commission opposed amalgamation for five reasons. The African policies of the protectorates and of Southern Rhodesia were different and in experimental stages. It was still early to tell which of them would best promote the material and moral wellbeing of the African inhabitants; Africans in the protectorates were opposed to amalgamation. The Europeans were either too few or too inexperienced to administer the combined territories. The three territories had different constitutional status; they were unequal in terms of economic development and financial resources.

Though the Bledisloe Commission rejected both amalgamation and federation it none the less made a number of recommendations on how the three territories could cooperate. One was the creation of an Inter-Territorial Council to coordinate government services wherever possible and to survey the economic needs of the three territories. World

War II intervened and the recommendations were laid to rest until 1945 when the Central African Council was set up. This Council, which was purely consultative, was made up of the Governor of Southern Rhodesia as chairman and four members from each of the three territories. It held its first meeting in Salisbury in April 1945 and was regarded from the beginning as a poor substitute for amalgamation or federation. European representatives from the three territories met for their third unofficial meeting at the second Victoria Falls Conference in 1949 to express their disappointment at the lack of progress and to plan a new strategy. This strategy was to emerge in the name of 'partnership', a political gospel expressed without conviction but intended as a catchword to draw attention to the failure of partnership in any form in South Africa, where the Nationalists under Dr Daniel Malan had come to power in 1948 on the ticket of *apartheid*.

No Africans had been invited to a single meeting, either official or unofficial, up till 1949 to discuss closer union. This omission they criticised very strongly. As early as 1938 the Bledisloe Commission had been informed by Africans everywhere in Central Africa, and certainly quite firmly and frankly in Nyasaland, that closer union in any form or shape was objectionable to the Africans. This view the Commission respected and used as an argument against closer union. On 29 March 1951, Mr James Griffiths, Colonial Secretary, came to Nyasaland to discuss it. This time African opinion was canvassed. At a meeting of the Central Province African Provincial Council held at Lilongwe on 29 August 1951, Chief Mwase addressed him on behalf of the chiefs and people of the country. He said:

When the question of amalgamation came, we rejected it. The report of the London Conference [that is, of officials of the three territories, the Central African Council and of the Commonwealth Relations and Colonial Offices held in 1951] says that there is a Central African Council. Can you tell us, Sir, how many Africans are there on that Council? If there is no African there, therefore, this federation is for Europeans, not for Africans at all. For this reason we hate such federation. We do not want it to press us down. What we want is to have our own self-government in the nearest future. . . . Africans still refuse federation in any form because the experience has shown that federation can only benefit Europeans to have more wealth, more land and more power over Africans, that Africans should remain hewers of wood without any voice in Government. All what is said is only to bluff the Africans, therefore we refuse federation and we shall refuse it even [if] it will mean death.

The strength of African opposition made an impact on Mr Griffiths and he assured them that Nyasaland would remain a protectorate; that African land rights would remain the same; that African political advancement would not be hindered. These assurances were to be discussed later that year at the third Victoria Falls Conference which, unlike the earlier ones, was to have African representatives from the protectorates. The Nyasaland African Protectorate Council was represented by Chief Mwase, Clement Kumbikano and Edward Gondwe, who reiterated their opposition in very clear terms. Mr Kumbikano told the delegates:

I should make it clear that the presence of the three of us at this Conference does not in any way imply that the Nyasaland African population in our country has any other different view on this question than that which they have expressed before the Secretary of State for the Colonies [i.e. Mr Griffiths] during his tour of the Protectorate. That view is total rejection of the proposals and total rejection of federation with Southern Rhodesia.

The total and uncompromising rejection of federation by the African people of Nyasaland shook the optimism of the Europeans in the country and Sir Malcolm Barrow (of Nyasaland) made the significant comment at the 1951 Victoria Falls Conference that while Europeans in the country supported federation they had serious reservations about ignoring African opposition. 'We and others,' said Sir Malcolm, 'have agreed on federation but we shall not agree if we cannot go together with the people with whom we live.'

In the end things turned out differently for various reasons. The report of the London conference of officials which was to form the basis for the coming federation was published in June 1951. The Victoria Falls Conference was convened on 18 September 1951. Many matters went wrong at the Conference. For one thing the African delegates from the two protectorates (there was none from Southern Rhodesia) wanted the *principles* of federation to be discussed; the supporters of federation wanted *details* to be discussed. No positive lead could be given by the Labour Government Colonial Secretary, James Griffiths, in view of the general elections which were pending in the United Kingdom. James Griffiths was in fact a 'lame duck'; less than a month later he became a 'dead duck' when his government was toppled from office. Mr Oliver Lyttelton became the new Conservative Party Colonial Secretary. He threw overboard his predecessor's concept of 'federation only by consent', saying that if Africans could not or would not see the obvious benefits of federation, it would have to be imposed on them. On that very dubious and dangerous principle the Federation was launched.

ii THE CENTRAL AFRICAN FEDERATION: ITS RISE AND FALL

The basis for the Central African Federation was the report drawn up by officials in London in June 1951, which acknowledged the strength of the opposition to federation but argued that if a suitable scheme could be worked out African opinion might be influenced sufficiently to give federation a trial. An acceptable scheme would have to include adequate provision for African representation and adequate protection for African interests. The scheme would have to ensure that services which intimately affected the daily lives of Africans would be left to the territorial governments. Provided these three broad guarantees could be given, Africans might learn to live with and possibly value the virtues of closer union. If African opinion was all that mattered the task of those who framed the constitution would have been so much easier. But the report recognised that there were two other necessary conditions: the wellbeing of the territories had to be promoted and the various governments and legislatures had to be satisfied. In the end it turned out to be an almost impossible task to satisfy everyone.

The conference of officials considered three possible solutions and rejected two of them. Those rejected were, firstly, a scheme to amalgamate the three territories into a single state and, secondly, the creation of a league to which each of the territories would give up some of its powers and functions so that the league could act as a body in possession of delegated authority. Here it was felt that the greatest opposition would come from Southern Rhodesia.

The solution recommended was the federal system with all the necessary safeguards, including an African Affairs Board and a Minister for African Interests. It recommended that the African Affairs Board should be under the chairmanship of the Minister for African Interests assisted by three Secretaries for Native Affairs, three elected European members and three African members. The function of the Board would be to examine all proposed federal legislation before publication to ensure that African interests were not overlooked. If it reported that any proposed legislation was detrimental to African interests, such legislation, if proceeded with, would have to receive the attention of the British Secretary of State. The other safeguard, the Minister for African Interests, was to be appointed by the Governor-General from among the members of the African Affairs Board. Such a Minister would, from his position in the Cabinet, protect African interests further.

The report of the officials was a fair starting point. But in itself it was no more than a recommendation. African fears were not allayed by it because they rightly suspected that the reality of federation would be dictated not by civil servants or technicians but by the politicians. In Central Africa, the Africans had told Griffiths what they thought of federation. In Britain, too, Africans from Nyasaland and Northern Rhodesia were active in opposition. At a joint meeting held in London as early as 27 February 1949, Dr H. Kamuzu Banda and Mr H. Nkumbula had been requested to draw up a detailed memorandum. In their preliminary report they advanced four points against federation at that time: the Africans of Nyasaland and Northern Rhodesia would be deprived of direct political and cultural ties with the United Kingdom; they would be dominated by Southern Rhodesia; the policies of segregation and discrimination of Southern Rhodesia would be extended to the protectorates, and lastly federation would be 'only a thin end of the wedge of amalgamation'.

Local and overseas agitation influenced the debate on the federation in the House of Commons on 4 March 1952 where the voting was 256 in favour and 238 against federation. On 29 April two Africans from Nyasaland (E. K. Gondwe and C. R. Kumbikano) representing the Protectorate Council and three from Northern Rhodesia (G. M. Musumbulwa, P. Sokota and A. K. Walubita) who were either members of the African Representation Council or the Legislative Council expressed their opposition in a letter written to the London *Times*. They boycotted the final London talks from which the draft federal scheme emerged. The only African delegates at these crucial talks were two members of the Southern Rhodesia delegation. Their place and power were more pathetic than effective.

The most serious omission in the draft scheme was the deletion of the office of Minister for African Interests. Thus one of the safeguards recommended by the officials in 1951 was thrown overboard. The other safeguard concerning the membership and functions of the African Affairs Board was also seriously altered: the three Secretaries for Native Affairs were not included and the chairman was *not* a member of the Federal Cabinet. In the report of the officials it had been stated that the Board would draw attention to legislation which was *detrimental to African interests*. This phrase was replaced by the expression '*differentiating measure*'. In the legal world it would be easier to define and to demonstrate something which was *detrimental* but not something which was *differentiating*. For example, a five-shilling annual tax on bicycles, regardless of the owners' race, would be *detrimental* to African interests but would not be necessarily *differentiating* since it would be applicable to everyone regardless of race. In practice it would be the Africans who would be hit hardest since they used bicycles most. Again, that sum of money would mean a larger slice of African income *per capita* than that of any other race. The third safeguard, that of adequate African representation, was conceded because it did not affect the issue of European dominance.

The membership of the Federal Assembly was fixed at thirty-five, of whom six would be Africans. The latter were to be assisted by three Europeans either elected (as in the case of Southern Rhodesia) or appointed (as in the case of the protectorates) to serve African interests. Of the total of thirty-five seats, Southern Rhodesia got seventeen, Northern Rhodesia eleven and Nyasaland seven. In the final Federal Act the African Affairs Board was composed of six members, three Europeans and three Africans. It was given the status of a standing committee of the Federal Assembly. The Central African Federation became operative as from 3 September 1953.

These details and developments did not interest the vast majority of people living in Central Africa. In the protectorates alone there were five million Africans as compared to seventy thousand Europeans. These five million people were thrust into a federation very much against their will. In Nyasaland this will found expression in the outbreak of civil disobedience in April 1953. The Supreme Council of Chiefs and Congress was set up with Chief Mwase as chairman and Lawrence J. Mapemba as secretary. It was this Council which organised and conducted the opposition to federation at home. Six chiefs were sent to the United Kingdom in early May 1953—M'Mbelwa and Katumbi from the Northern Province; Gomani II, represented by his son, Willard, and Maganga from the Central Province; and Kuntaja and Somba from the Southern Province—accompanied by two interpreters. They made one last effort to appeal to the conscience and the justice of the British people. In the name of 120 Malawian chiefs they petitioned the House of Commons for a hearing, but their efforts were rejected. Willard Gomani, now Inkosi Gomani III, who was there at the time, gives us a personal account in the following words:

> We spoke in public meetings in England, Wales and Scotland. The organisations and public financed all our travels. Rev. Michael Scott was especially our great helper all the time we were in England and he cannot be forgotten by the chiefs. British officials refused to see

us but we said that if federation was forced there would be troubles in Nyasaland. . . .[1]

These pleas and prophecies were all rejected and a few months later the much-hated Federation became a reality. What of this reality? The only positive argument ever raised in support of federation was that it would encourage economic advancement. The real position was different. The Federal Government took over the responsibility of raising capital for the territories. In 1958 the Federal Government was allotted 62 per cent of the loans; Southern Rhodesia got 14 per cent; Northern Rhodesia got 18 per cent and Nyasaland got 6 per cent. Nyasaland's share of loans between 1953 and 1958 amounted to just under £2½ million whereas prior to that the amount received under the Protectorate Government had amounted to £5¾ million. In 1959, Nyasaland was still by far the poorest of the three territories with a Gross Domestic Product of £19 a head compared to Northern Rhodesia's £82 and Southern Rhodesia's £89. It was not that capital was not available for investment. In the five years of federation between 1954 and 1959, £805 million were invested in the Federation, most of it channelled to Southern Rhodesia, including the £80 million Kariba Dam project and the siting in Salisbury of the University College of the Rhodesias and Nyasaland which opened in 1957.

Though educational facilities were increased for all races, the disparity in the provisions was glaring. During 1955–56, 50,000 Europeans and 6,000 Asian and Coloured children attended federal government schools at a cost of £126 per pupil. During the same period 800,000 Africans attended government and government-aided schools at a cost of £6 per pupil.

Similar disparities extended to employment opportunities and incomes, housing and health services. In the latter department it is worth noting that there were only three African doctors in the Federation, of whom only one entered government service. In Northern Rhodesia there were five hospital beds per thousand Europeans but less than two beds per thousand Africans. In Nyasaland there were almost eight beds per thousand Europeans but only one bed per thousand Africans. Only in Southern Rhodesia were the provisions almost equal.

Thus it was patently clear in the first five years that partnership as a concept of the Federation had been proved unworkable and that the African fears expressed so freely, frankly and frequently had been well founded. Federation had been given its fair trial but it had proved to be unsuccessful. The African Affairs Board, the only constitutional safe-

[1] Personal communication to the author, 26 June 1971.

guard in the Federal Assembly, had made two atempts to protect African interests. Both attempts had failed.

But the diehard federalists in the European communities sought to save the Federation at least until the review which was due to take place in 1960. Then, they hoped, dominion status would take them away from the meddling oversight of the British Government and leave them free to deal with the recalcitrant African opposition. On the other hand, African nationalists, too, were planning another programme. As 1959 approached the opposition was strained to bursting point. Earlier in 1958 a new federal constitution had come into existence, increasing the number of seats in the Federal Assembly from thirty-five to fifty-nine. The number of African members was increased from six to twelve. The proportion between Europeans and Africans remained constant however. At the same time the first federal franchise law appeared creating two separate electoral rolls, one for general voters and the other for special voters. The general voters got two votes each in the protectorates and three each in Southern Rhodesia. The minimum income qualification for general voters was £300 per annum with a minimum property qualification of £500 together with secondary education. Only a handful of Africans qualified for this vote. The voting provisions guaranteed that the forty-four elected white members would be chosen by predominantly white voters while the eight elected African members would be chosen by the combined vote of white and black voters.

A commission was appointed under Viscount Monckton in 1959 to review the federal constitution. Its report was presented in October 1960. In the last paragraph of its general conclusions the Commission noted:

> The Federation can continue only if it can enlist the willing support of its inhabitants. The wisdom of Solomon himself, were we able to command it, would not suffice to make any constitution work without the good will of the people. We cannot create this good will. Unless both races genuinely wish to make the association succeed, unless they are prepared to understand and to meet each others' point of view, and unless both sides are ready to make some sacrifices, the new forms will do no better than the old. . . .

Viscount Monckton and his commissioners were right. What they were saying ought to have been recognised in 1953 before the unholy and unwelcome Federation had been foisted upon the unwilling African community. Then one of the architects of the Federation had described the partnership as one between a horse and its rider. On 31

December 1963, the horse, after ten years of painful trotting, at last unsaddled its rider.

In Nyasaland itself this vindicated the pledge with which Dr Banda had ended his speech to the All-African Peoples Conference at Accra, Ghana, in December 1958: 'With the rest of Africa, Nyasaland is on the move. Nothing can stay her course. Like the rest of our fellow Africans on this continent, we are determined to be free, to be independent and to live in dignity. Neither Heavens above nor Hell below will prevail against us.' The ten-year experiment of closer union ended in utter failure.

CHAPTER 20

Some famous Malawians

History does not exist apart from the individuals who made it and those who were affected by it. The presence of an important individual in a particular place at a particular time made it possible for his ideas and his influences to affect the course of history. Sometimes these ideas and influences affected the local level only (i.e. the village, the town, the region). At other times these extended to the national level (i.e. the whole country). On rare occasions the international scene was influenced. History is concerned with all these levels and with movements both big and small. The man who introduced the first plough, or co-operative or shop or school or church in a village made a contribution to social change and is as important at that level as one who started a political movement at a higher level. The contribution of individuals to historical movements must be studied in the context of time and place. When the context changes, the emphasis often changes. But what is singularly important is that a changed context should not lead to the omission or neglect of an earlier period. History never exists in a vacuum or starts from nowhere. It is a record of man's continuous journey.

The historical record in Malawi is scattered and incomplete as yet. But within the next ten years it should be possible—and indeed it is absolutely necessary—to clear up the backlog so that the newer biographies which will tell the story of the more recent, and perhaps more colourful, period of Malawi's immediate past may be written up. Much of the material for this is already accumulating. The people as well as the politicians are busy at work in the task of national development. Their contribution and story cannot be described yet with historical exactitude because their work still goes on. Except, therefore, in the historical context of time and place, no further reference will be made in the present chapter to persons actively engaged in public life.

Ideally, biographical accounts of persons who have contributed towards the shaping of Malawi history could be set out in certain neat or convenient categories. Firstly, there should be the biographies of traditional leaders: select members of the Karonga dynasty; the Ngonde leadership; the Mlowoka fraternity; the Jumbe family; the Yao leaders; the Lomwe chiefs; the Makololo men. The form this could take is illustrated by the representative sample on Inkosi Mtwalo II. Secondly, there should be biographies reflecting the contribution of European missionaries. There are already accounts covering a very wide range but only the more prominent missionaries like Livingstone, Laws, Hetherwick, Murray and Chauncey Maples, for example, have received attention. The lesser lights like Elmslie, McCallum, Prentice, Pretorius, the Misses Beck and Klamborowski and a few dozens of all denominations still need to be assigned their rightful place in history. In the third category, the sometimes romantic, other times tragic but always courageous, story of European adventurers should be told. 'From elephant hunter to governor' could well be the title of a study on Alfred Sharpe. In company with him would be included the story of the lives of people like Henry Faulkner who published his own book *Elephant Haunts* in 1868 and who later died in Malawi among Malawians whose community he, and others like him, had entered through marriage or concubinage. Captain Edward Alston, whose diary covering the period 1894–96 is in the National Archives, and A. J. Swann, among others, would also belong to this category. In the fourth category members of the trading community of all races would be featured: traders like Cotterill, the Moir brothers, Eugene Sharrer, A. J. Storey; enterprising African businessmen like Chief Kuntaja, Peter Mlelemba, John Gray Kufa and Duncan Njilima. Pioneering Asian traders like Osman Adam, Amarsi Vithaldas and M. G. Dharap are but a fraction of the flock. In the fifth category place would have to be found for British administrators and civil servants who are too numerous to catalogue. Biographies could also be written about the planters among whom will feature such all-rounders as R. S. Hynde and W. H. Timcke; these would take the story of the Malawian past through a hundred years or so of agricultural endeavours. European politicians from the period of the Legislative Council in 1907, many of whom have been mentioned in this volume, could well constitute a category of their own, even though there would be an overlap between their roles as politicians and as men or women at the same time involved in agriculture or commerce. There should of course be included the African civil servants and rising politicians, the so-called 'new men' like Levi Mumba, Isa Macdonald Lawrence, Lewis Mataka Bandawe, Frederick Sangala and numerous others; African church leaders from Lovedale and elsewhere who lived, worked and often died in Malawi as well as Malawians in churches controlled by Europeans or Africans; and African teachers, both men and women, whose roles as agents of social change cannot be minimised or neglected. Finally, place must be found for the enterprising Malawians abroad. Even if the Kadalies, the Muwambas, the Nyirendas worked and lived elsewhere in Central Africa their historic roles are pertinent to Malawi's history as they and their influences formed so important a part of the Malawi heritage.

Having set out the probable categories more as a manifesto of what has still to be done rather than as an outline of what is envisaged for the moment, selections will now be made at random from some of the different categories.

Amon Muhawi Jere or Mtwalo II

Amon Jere was born in 1873 at Uswesi in Ekwendeni in the present Mzimba district. He grew up at a time when the Livingstonia missionaries were negotiating with the Ngoni ruler, M'Mbelwa I, for permission to open schools in Mzimba. This was granted in 1886 when young Amon Jere was thirteen years old, and his formal schooling began then. He went on to complete standard six and to serve the mission at Ekwendeni as a teacher from 1897 to 1903. He was the first of the Jere line of future chiefs to enter the new world of Christian influence and western learning, traits which were evident in his work and utterances for many years afterwards. As late as December 1969, a few months before he died, as a man approaching ninety-seven years of age he was still able to recall biblical quotations and to speak approvingly of the new influences under which he grew up and with which he was to live for so many years.

But Amon Jere was destined for more than that. When his father, Mtwalo I, died in 1890 the chieftainship was given to Amon Jere's elder brother, Yohane Jere, in violation of the Ngoni laws of succession. Five years later the *izinduna* or headmen in Mtwalo's area gathered at Ekwendeni to elect the rightful heir. Their choice fell on Amon Jere who was duly installed as Inkosi Mtwalo II on 15 June 1896 in the great cattle fold of Engalaweni before the assembled elders and followers of the tribe. A distinguished witness at the ceremony was Inkosi Mwamba, more popularly known as Mperembe, the last of the sons of Zwangendaba, the man who brought the Ngoni migrants to Malawi.

As a teacher at Ekwendeni Mission and as the chief of his people, Amon Jere occupied a most challenging position. He was a representative or agent of two worlds, that of the white man and that of his ancestors. He filled both positions admirably for as long as the roles did not clash.

In 1896 the Christian chief, Mtwalo II, married Emily Nhlane, the daughter of Chiputula Nhlane, a distinguished induna who was himself closely linked by marriage to the Jere family of an older generation. Emily's father had died in 1874. The occasion of his death was to lead to the Tonga rebellion against Ngoni rule. Then Amon had been barely a year old and Emily perhaps not born. Now Amon and Emily were to join two other couples, Jonathan Shonga and Mary Chipeta and Jonathan Chirwa and Jaycee Zazeya Banda, in the first Christian marriages to be solemnised in Ekwendeni Church in 1896.

Amon Jere and Emily Nhlane lived in monogamous union for eight years without any offspring. The village elders urged their chief to marry other wives to ensure the perpetuation of his chieftainship. It was difficult for Mtwalo II to reconcile his Christian with his traditional duty. Finally in 1903 he gave in to the tribal pressures and married again. He was immediately divested of his position as teacher in the mission school. But the missionaries allowed him, as a gesture of their appreciation, to continue to occupy the brick building they had erected for their promising and worthy chief, teacher and Christian soul.

Though suspended from the Church of Scotland, Mtwalo II continued to regard Emily Nhlane as his Christian and main wife. The marriage lasted sixty-six years until Emily Nhlane died on 10 November 1962. Nor did Mtwalo II withdraw from Christianity entirely. He joined the Chipangano church and became an evangelist. He maintained his membership of this church throughout his life. This explains why the Chipangano church had a large following in the Mtwalo area.

Meanwhile on 24 October 1904 the Ngoni came under colonial rule. In a colourful ceremony at Hora Mountain the Union Flag was hoisted by Hector Macdonald, the first British Resident sent to rule the Ngoni. One of the conditions was that the Ngoni chiefs would receive a government subsidy to administer traditional duties. Thus Mtwalo II who lost his mission post in 1903 assumed government service in 1905.

Mtwalo II was a distinguished man. He showed consideration and respect for his elder brother, Yohane, often under deep provocation; he had a benevolent attitude towards commoners; he was concerned for his people and so he migrated from Ekwendeni to the Henga valley in 1914; he supported local African initiative and championed African nationalism. Mtwalo II was tall, strong and talented. He was an excellent Ingoma dancer. He was proud to be an Ngoni but equally proud to be a Malawian.

On 23 June 1956, the sixtieth anniversary of his chieftainship was celebrated at the foot of Hora Mountain. On that occasion, the Governor, Sir Robert Armitage, said: 'As a child Inkosi Mtwalo saw the first Europeans after David Livingstone to enter Northern Nyasaland. He has seen the massing of the Angoni regiments going to war. He has seen the return of thousands of warriors from their great raids as far as the Congo waters.' But Inkosi Mtwalo was to see more than that. He saw the passing of the old and the dawn of the new. When he died on 1 April 1970 he had served as Inkosi Mtwalo II for seventy-four years and had lived for ninety-seven years, a record age.

One human tragedy survived him, since he left behind no children of his own. The Mtwalo chieftainship went to Baiwell Jere, the grandson of Amon Jere's brother, Yohane. The installation of Mtwalo III took place in September 1971 and marked the beginning of yet another chapter in the history of Mtwalo's chieftainship, which Amon Jere did so much to enhance during his seventy-four-year rule as Mtwalo II.

Peter Mlelemba

Among the early Malawian businessmen the name of Peter Mlelemba stands out. To contemporaries he was known by the name which he preferred—Haya Edward Peters. Mlelemba was born in Blantyre about 1880. He went to school at the Blantyre Mission for a few years but shifted after that to the Zambezi Industrial Mission at Mitsidi on the outskirts of Blantyre where he completed his primary education.

About 1905 Mlelemba entered the employment of Eugene Sharrer of the British Central Africa Company, the owner of Kabula Stores in Blantyre. He worked there for a number of years accumulating business skills as well as capital. As he was quick to learn because of his fluency in English and his interest in business he soon looked around for a new venture. This time he launched himself into a business partnership with a white man, Mr Ryalls, the owner of a hotel which still bears his name. The business was that of mining mica in the Kirk range area of Ncheu and Dedza. The business failed and Mlelemba went back to Blantyre. This time he leased a farm, the Nangafuwe Estate, behind Ndirande hill, from the Blantyre and East Africa Company, and entered the timber business. This lease covered an area of 63¼ acres and was for a period of twenty-one years at a rental of £1 16s. 3d. a year. This was entered into on 5 July 1907 and was to be operative from 1 August the following year. In the Deeds Register in the Blantyre office the following entry appears:

Deed cancelled. Lease lapsed and land reverted to B. and E. A. C. Peters expelled from country.

Of course, all this anticipates much of the later aspects of Mlelemba's colourful life. He also grew chillies and tobacco and was soon the leading Malawian businessman in and around Blantyre.

Now Mlelemba was influential enough to drive home his ideas on business and African initiative. He realised that to be successful African businessmen would have to follow the example of their counterparts among the other races. This called for education and for thorough organisation and cooperation. In the first respect, Mlelemba went on educating himself by enrolling with a London correspondence college. He had a flair for speaking English without a distinct accent and with remarkable fluency, a quality which is by no means isolated among Malawians. In striving for the education which was a symbol of progress he committed the error of going too far. Contemporaries have testified without any contradiction that he lived 'like an Englishman', spoke English most of the time, rejected his immediate and extended family and lived on his own. It was common knowledge that his own mother had to enter his house through the rear door. When in the late 1940s he was reduced from riches to rags, he regretted openly the errors of his over-zealous youth.

But, except for his notion of living like a white man, Mlelemba was committed to African upliftment so that more of his own people could live like white people did. One way to do so was by entering business as individuals as well as by cooperation. He formed his own company which was named P.T. Company (which perhaps stood for 'Peters Trading Company'). He went beyond this by helping to found and run the Native Industrial Union which was properly organised with subscription fees and minutes kept in English. The second meeting of this Union was held at Nyambadwe Hill on 15 May 1909. Since this is a biographical sketch it will help to recall the names of the other members who were present. Joseph Bismarck of Namwiri Estate presided; among the others were Thomas Masea, Mungo Murray Chisuse, Nelson Kabweza, Harry Kambwiri Matecheta, Ardwell Mlenga, Cedric Masangano, John Gray Kufa Mapantha, Justin Somanje, Basil Gray and Haya Edward Peters himself. These men were among the foremost Malawians of their time. Haya Edward Peters was elected first joint-secretary of this Union with Mungo Murray Chisuse.

Mlelemba and Chilembwe struck up a lasting friendship. They had similar aspirations. Mlelemba gave Chilembwe a loan of £50 to start a business in Chiradzulu. He conducted his own business with pride, owning a rubber stamp which read 'From H. Edward Peters, Nanga-fuwe, Blantyre, Nyasaland'. In one of his letters dated 7 July 1914, a copy of which he retained, Mlelemba wrote to the Watch Tower Bible and Tract Society in the United States:

> I have a little school of fifty boys and girls, regret I have no Bible training and help. I am a native of this country studying other sub-jects by mail in London in order to help my brethren. The great majority of my people are heathens. I cannot get co-helpers in the Lord's work, still no man having put his hands to the plow and looking back, is fit for the Kingdom of God! . . . please find my two Photos to prove that I am a colored man. I am hard at work in order to lay a foundation for my people. . . .

Whether Mlelemba used the word 'colored' in the American and British sense or in the Southern and Central African sense it is not clear. What is clear is that he was conscious of doing all he could to raise himself as well as his fellow men.

Among his various activities was that of hunting elephants. He made quite a lot of money selling ivory. In this respect he was following in the footsteps of yet another, and older, African businessman in Blan-tyre, whose name was Kuntaja. He was on one of his hunting expedi-tions in Ntengula, in Portuguese East Africa, just beyond Malindi, when the Chilembwe rising broke out. This perhaps saved Mlelemba from a worse fate for he was known to have been a confidant and close friend of John Chilembwe. The letters which passed between them were later discovered.

There is contemporary testimony given by one Sgt-Major Kamakolo of the Third Battalion, K.A.R., that there was a warrant for Mlelemba's arrest immediately after the rising broke out. Some respondents say he was arrested in P.E.A. but released, whereupon he went off to South Africa. Others say that he went to South Africa for his own safety on hearing about the rising. It is clear that he did go to South Africa immediately afterwards and remained there until he was deported in the 1930s because of his involvement in South African politics. The details of this are not known as yet but on his return he did speak of having met Clements Kadalie.

The date of his return is set at about 1933. By now Mlelemba was a poor and broken man but he still had a prison sentence to serve in Malawi and was possibly also under suspicion as a political agitator. His Nangafuwe estates were not restored to him as the entry in the Deeds Register mentioned above indicates and from then until his death in tragic circumstances in Namiwawa on the night of 24 June

1944 he lived on the charity of friends and wellwishers except for a brief period after the outbreak of war when he served as head military clerk at the Blantyre Boma. Though declining he lived on to see the birth of the Nyasaland African Congress in 1943 in which he took a lively interest. He attended the inaugural meeting which must have reminded him of his own Native Industrial Union thirty-five years before.

Not all biographies end in a success story. So it was with Peter Mlelemba who took pride in his other self Haya Edward Peters, a remarkable man with remarkable ideas, even if some of them were a bit strange—like the incident when the first train arrived at Blantyre in 1908. Mr Bandawe, now a very old man, who knew Mlelemba well tells us that he (Bandawe) and his colleague from the Blantyre Mission, Robertson Namate, were at the station awaiting the arrival of the train. Mlelemba and Thomas Masea arrived in a *machilla*. In conversation Mr Lewis Bandawe asked Mlelemba whether he had come to see the Governor, Sir Alfred Sharpe, who was travelling on the train. Mlelemba replied: 'Yes, and also to see whether the home mail has come!' A strange remark for a Malawian but indicative of the sights that Mlelemba had set for himself and his people—the hope that one day he and they would all share in a happier and better world.

If the story of Mlelemba is that of a lone star who cut himself from his family there are other examples where members of a single family provide a broad canvas on which to paint a biographical picture which can be extremely illuminating. To illustrate this point we may tell the story of the Muwamba family from Chifira village in Nkhata Bay.

The Muwamba family

The three persons selected in order of family seniority are Isaac Katongo Muwamba, son of Chief Chiweyu, born around 1890, died in Malawi in 1953; Ernest Alexander Muwamba, son of Yakobi Msusa Muwamba, the first qualified theological student of Livingstonia Mission, born 1892 and died in Malawi in 1970; and Clements Kadalie, son of Musa Kadalie, born about 1893 or 1894 and died in South Africa in 1951.

There are interesting parallels in the lives of all three which indicate the interplay of family influences: they all belonged to the ruling family of their village, either as a son of the chief or as grandsons of the chief. All three were products of the Livingstonia Mission; all three left Malawi as part of the movement which has appropriately been referred to as the Malawi diaspora, that movement of Malawians near and distant, into neighbouring lands and across the seas, which has earned fame in various ways for them as individuals as well as members of a

274

national society. All three spoke English remarkably fluently in spite of their primary school education. For example, when the Prince of Wales visited Northern Rhodesia it was Isaac Katongo Muwamba who was selected to act as interpreter. He worked in Northern Rhodesia from 1912 to 1949 as a clerk in the government service, sometimes interpreting in the High Court, and during the war, from 1939 to 1945, he acted as district commissioner when European civil servants were scarce. Ernest Alexander Muwamba who worked in Northern Rhodesia from 1913 to 1944 accomplished similar feats and had an almost identical career as his uncle. The third member of the family, Clements Kadalie, achieved fame as well as notoriety for his public speaking.

If the parallels are carried further, the fact emerges that all three made a significant contribution to the cause of African improvement wherever they lived and worked. Isaac Muwamba was one of the founders, and chairman, of the Lusaka Native Welfare Association; Alexander Muwamba held a similar position in the Ndola Native Welfare Association; Clements Kadalie was the founder of the Industrial and Commercial Union in South Africa in 1919. Except for Clements Kadalie who narrowly failed to win a seat on the African Representative Council in South Africa, the remaining two returned to their birthplace to fill important positions in the Provincial and Protectorate Councils. Alexander Muwamba went on to become the first African member of the Legislative Council in 1949. Both the Muwambas played their part in the fight against federation as members of the anti-federation delegation to the United Kingdom in 1952.

Kadalie's autobiography is now published, but biographical studies on the Muwambas are still proceeding. The Muwamba family tradition lives on in the younger generation in which a doctor, a chairman of an African businessmen's association and a director of tourism are representative. In the context of this study it serves to draw attention to the fact that while biographies of individuals constitute an ingredient of the nation's history, biographies of families are equally important.

The Malinki family

A second family in Malawi which commands attention is the Malinki family. The founder was the notable Kalinde Morrison Malinki, born at Tete of parents who had been sold in slavery. Though of Ngoni origins the elder Malinki spent his youth in slavery in one situation or another, including a period with Chikunda tribesmen. His mother finally fled to Mwanza with her children and from here moved on to Mpemba, a few miles to the southwest of Blantyre. It was then that the tide began to change for young Malinki. Around 1884 he started attending school at the Blantyre Mission, at the age of about fourteen. He later joined the printing works at the Blantyre Mission but like others at the time, he was attracted to the Zambezi Industrial Mission started by Joseph Booth in 1892. It was here that he met John Chilembwe and Gordon Mataka.

Five years later Morrison Malinki found himself involved in the formation of a body called the African Christian Union. This Union was aimed at promoting African interests in every walk of life. Malinki and Chilembwe were the only two Africans to append their signatures to the document which outlined the aims and objects of this union. Thus as early as 1897 Malinki was already well known and serving his people as a teacher, an evangelist and a politician. By 1900 he had begun opening schools of his own in the name of the Malinki establishment. These schools were based on the principles and pillars of self-help, modern education and Christianity. One of Malinki's earliest mission schools was at Chileka where the international airport stands today.

In his endeavours Malinki stood out as one of the earliest African evangelists and educationists in Malawi. The Negro pastor, Thomas Branch, who came to Malawi in 1902, persuaded Malinki to affiliate with the Malamulo Mission at Thyolo whose name at first was the Plainfield Mission. From 1904 to 1920 Morrison Malinki was inspector of schools of this mission throughout southern Malawi and was then asked to become mission head at Monekera, his home, which is close to the present Chileka airport. Seven years later, in 1927, he was ordained pastor.

According to family traditions, Malinki and Chilembwe were good friends from the days they worked together with Joseph Booth. Their political programmes, however, were based on different concepts. Though both were evangelists, Chilembwe advocated a militant rising whereas Malinki counselled cooperation and persuasion. Because of these differences Malinki did not support the rising of 1915. This did not prevent him from being arrested on suspicion and from being put into leg irons. The soldiers informed Malinki: 'We have arrested you because you have been corresponding with Chilembwe.' Malinki's reply was that he had corresponded with a friend and that was not rebellion. No evidence could be gathered against him and he was released shortly afterwards. He lived to continue with his pastoral duties until his death in 1957.

His eldest son James Malinki carried forward the family tradition and served for ten years as a pastor in the Congo from 1920 and after that in the northern region of Malawi where he started two missions at

Luwazi and Mombera. Pastor James Malinki was awarded the Certificate of Honour by Queen Elizabeth II in 1952 for meritorious work as missionary for over twenty-five years. Now (1972) living in retirement, Pastor James Malinki has contributed his share towards another aspect of nation-building, that is, progressive farming, for which he was awarded a certificate (an Achikumbi Certificate) by President Banda.

Like the Muwamba family, the Malinkis of the younger generation have served or continue to serve in various capacities. One is a director of the Anglo-American Corporation in Lusaka and another is a director of Longman (Malawi) Ltd. There are many teachers, too, among whom ranks the wife of the first African mayor of Blantyre city. A civil servant, an engineer, a chemist and various secretaries carry through the traditions of service introduced by Kalinde Morrison Malinki, a one-time slave in Malawi's distant past.

CHAPTER 21

Some famous towns in Malawi

Many towns have already been mentioned in their historical context as the scenes of trade, political organisation, land disputes, railways, roads and harbours, mission stations and tribal and colonial conflicts. Special studies on towns have already been begun under the auspices of the Malawi Department of Antiquities which has brought out some publications and has more in different stages of preparation.

Every town in Malawi has historical relics and landmarks. For example, in the extreme south of Malawi stands Nsanje whose historical name in colonial times was Port Herald. It has gone down in history as the meeting place of Sena, Mang'anja and Makololo. It was also the meeting place of persons and activities dependent on the Shire–Zambezi river traffic. It has its traditional historic relic connected with the cult of *Mbona*, the guardian spirit of the Mang'anja. How little the force of this cult was appreciated until the recent studies by the Rev. Dr Mattheus Schoffeleers might be illustrated by the fate which befell a 3rd Assistant in the protectorate service who chanced to report on it in 1904. Mr R. R. Racey reported his observations that in 1902 and 1903 the Mang'anja and others were held in a sort of mental servility due to their fear and respect for Mbona; that Mbona's followers, whom he described as the *mbiwi*, believed that Mbona's powers included rain calling and witchcraft, and the ability to turn himself into a snake. Racey visited the headquarters of the cult at Khulubvi thicket. 'It was found,' he noted in a report to the District Commissioner at Chikwawa, 'that there were two villages, one where Mbona lived with his wife, Salima, surrounded by attendants, the other owned by Mbango a chief whose duty it was to act as caretaker.' Racey was shown round by Mbango's son but first he was asked to dress in blue calico or failing that to take off his helmet and boots. This he did and so did his attendants. Racey took up the description in the following words:

The air all about the compound was hushed, tranquil and solemn; the huts lying in the shade of trees appeared not to have been renewed for years; upon my approach a man bearing unmistakeable mental or magnetic power rose to me. . . . All the time a distinct living presence was known to be present but I was not sufficiently clairvoyant to describe the outlines.

What Racey asked for was permission to study the phenomenon. His superiors felt that he was being overcome by the tropical heat and that before he became completely mad he should be invalided home.[1]

As Mbona helped to make Nsanje important so did the missionaries and their enterprises make another town in southern Malawi important. The first important river port was at Chikwawa on the eastern bank of the Shire River less than half a mile from Chief Katunga's village. Chief Katunga, like the other Chikwawa chief, Massea, came from the Kololo settlement in the lower Shire. It was at a place called Thima in Chief Massea's area, not far from the river port at Katunga's, that the Church of Scotland established its first mission station in that part. Because it was in a flood area the mission was transferred about two miles southwards to a place called Mfera. Thus a river port and a mission station served to transform the history of Chikwawa in colonial times. In pre-colonial times its importance was gained from the fact that Chief Lundu of the Karonga dynasty of Chewa rulers resided there. This chieftainship was overthrown by the Kololo incursion and faded into obscurity during colonial rule. It has recently been restored to its former position. As the Mbewe headquarters of Paramount Chief Lundu, not far from the Lengwe Game Reserve, stands as a historical reminder of a distant past, so too do the silent graves of Richard Thornton, Herbert Rhodes, the Rev. H. C. Scuddamore and Dr Dickson tell the story of personal tragedies of a distant past.

If the interplay of various factors in pre-colonial as well as colonial times has influenced the course of the history of the towns in the lower Shire from Chikwawa to Nsanje, similar factors have combined to make Nkhota Kota one of the most interesting towns in Malawi. Known by various names such as Mankhamba and Marimba in pre-colonial times, its present name, according to the town historians, is derived from the zigzag nature of the promontories. At first the centre of Chewa society, Nkhota Kota became the meeting ground of various other influences in the nineteenth and twentieth centuries such as the trade and religion of the Swahili Arabs, the pressures of both the Shaziria and Qadiriya sects of Islam and the Christianity of the Anglican,

[1] C.O. 525/7, Commissioner Sharpe to Colonial Office, 24 Jan. 1905.

Catholic, Baptist and Presbyterian churches. Its historical features include the famous fig tree under the shade of which Dr Livingstone spoke to the traditional leaders, the All-Saints Church Mission ground, the old slave market, the mosques of both Islamic sects, the slave harbour, the Sanduku royal cemetery where the Jumbe rulers as well as other members of their families lie buried. Modern attractions in the town include its natural hot spring, the Mpamantha Rice Scheme, the Thiwi Irrigation Scheme and the famous ivory carver, Bwana Fundi Yatina Chiwala.

The north, too, has its representative towns. In the extreme north-west lies Chitipa which derives its present name from a stream by that name. Formerly known as Fort Hill, the town and district of Chitipa were the traditional home of the Balambya people. Like its eastern neighbour, Karonga, it, too, gained influence from the opening of a branch store by the African Lakes Corporation in the 1880s as well as from the arrival of missionaries. An early important historical influence was the construction of the Stevenson Road to link Karonga with Lake Tanganyika. As a border town Chitipa developed slowly until the circumstances of World War I suddenly infused greater activity. It became an important military base. In the 1940s it became a labour base when the Witwatersrand Native Labour Association set up a camp to recruit labour for the South African mines from this corridor area which tapped the resources from three countries, Malawi, Tanzania and Zambia. This was followed by the setting up of a similar organisation by the Southern Rhodesian Native Labour Bureau (or Mtandizi). The combined influence of Mandala, Wenela and Mtandizi led to the opening up of more stores as well as to the construction of an airfield at Chitipa. The main purpose of the airfield at first was to serve in the shuttling of labourers to and from the town. In 1959 it was the scene of intense African agitation against colonial rule when it was occupied to prevent troops from landing at Chitipa for service in Karonga and elsewhere. Even then the heart of the town was nothing more than the Wenela buildings, the airfield and a small trading centre. At that time only three Europeans lived in the town: the manager of Wenela and his wife and one assistant. This little town is surrounded by scenically beautiful hills, Misuku about fifteen miles to the east and Mafinga about eighteen miles to the south and several others seven miles to the north-west constituting the boundary between Zambia and Malawi. Since independence it has gone on to have a Malawi Young Pioneers Training Base (1964), its first District Commissioner (1965), a customs and immigration post (1966) and a day secondary school (1966).

More has happened in the second of Malawi's two northern towns,

Malawi today

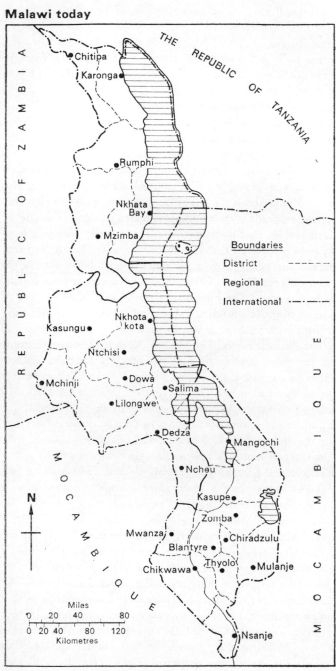

THE REPUBLIC OF TANZANIA

REPUBLIC OF ZAMBIA

- Chitipa
- Karonga
- Rumphi
- Nkhata Bay
- Mzimba
- Kasungu
- Nkhota kota
- Ntchisi
- Mchinji
- Dowa
- Salima
- Lilongwe
- Dedza
- Mangochi
- Ncheu
- Kasupe
- Zomba
- Mwanza
- Chiradzulu
- Blantyre
- Thyolo
- Chikwawa
- Mulanje
- Nsanje

MOCAMBIQUE

Boundaries

District .... — — —
Regional .... ————
International .... —·—·—

N

Miles
0   20   40   80

0 20 40   80   120
Kilometres

281

Karonga. Traditionally the home mainly of the Ngonde people the town (and the district) got its name, according to local testimony, from Karonga, the senior son of Kyungu Mwangonde, who when the first Europeans came to the area ruled over the Ngonde plains from Mwaya in the north to the Mlare lagoon in the south and the Nyika mountains to the west. The Europeans used the name Karonga to describe the Ngonde plains. The early settlers decided to live in the plains in the 1880s, so that they could open a store at Karonga, build the Stevenson Road, and establish a mission station at Mweniwanda on it. These developments encouraged the expansion of the town but also introduced Arab rivalry and competition. Among the historical relics of the past are what remains of Mlozi's (the Arab leader's) stockade. This was located at Mpata about ten miles from Karonga on the Chitipa road. The former stockade is today no more than a garden but as late as 1950 local leaders were able to point to a tall palm tree which was supposed to have been planted by the Arab leader himself. The fortified tree outside the old post office, now the District Council headquarters, and the war graves are reminders of the old and more recent wars which were fought in Karonga. The mission graves as well as the graves of and monuments to those who died in building the Stevenson Road are part of Karonga's past as much as Mbande Hill is the sanctuary of the Ngonde traditional rulers. The town of Karonga features prominently, too, as the place where the first native association in Malawi was started. It had at one time, for all its distance and remoteness, a rich crop of educated men like James Ngelesi Mwalwanda, Mark Mwakabanga Mwambetania, Yaphet Gondwe, Andrew Nkonjera, Reuben Mwenifumbo and others. Its first two ordained ministers were the Rev. Patrick Mwamlima and the Rev. Amon Mwakasungula.

In the story of Malawi's towns Blantyre deserves a place of its own; so do Zomba and Lilongwe as capitals old and designated. In between these, and as well as the few at the extreme ends of the country already dealt with, there are many others of equal importance. At some time or other they were all brought under local administrative constitutions. Blantyre, which will be considered in detail later, had a town council in 1895. Chiromo came next, in the same year. Fort Johnston (now Mangochi) was proclaimed a township in 1899. The first town council was elected on 7 April of that year under the chairmanship of the District Collector, C. O. Ockenden. There were five members in all representing government, naval and private company interests. In 1901 two Asian traders joined the Council. By 1931 the town had no water supply of its own but the trading companies like Sharrer and Mandala had their own wells. There was no petrol pump in the town till 1931 and no town planning had been introduced by that date. The income from rates in that year was £95 7s. 1d. yet the town council could still boast of a saving of £35. Not much seems to have been spent in those days! It ceased to be a township in the 1950s, some say because the employers feared that this would mean paying minimum wages to labourers. It was run by a Rural Area Board from 1954 until its township status was restored in 1966.

Zomba was proclaimed a township in September 1900. In 1922 all the members of the Zomba Town Council resigned in protest at government failure to pay rates on houses occupied by its officials and over a disagreement concerning government responsibility for repairing township roads. In 1923 the Zomba Town Council consisted of two members only: the District Resident as chairman and the Medical Officer of Health as member. From that date it became clear that Zomba could not operate like an ordinary town council. In 1932 its status was reduced to that of a Sanitary Area under a Sanitary Board. The following year it was reconstituted a township but the members of the town council were nominated because of the town's peculiar position.

Port Herald (Nsanje) became a township in 1905 but was reduced to a Rural Area Board in 1935. Lilongwe started off under a Sanitary Board in 1930 and improved its position to become a Rural Area Board. In 1947 it became a township with its own town council. Salima became a township in 1935; Mzuzu was only declared a Rural Area Board in 1957. As the administrative centre for the northern region its importance qualified it to become a township in 1964. Balaka and Dedza which were formerly Rural Area Boards became full townships in 1966.

When Nyasaland received its first Legislative Council in 1907 there were only four town councils in the country. Since the main responsibility of the councils then was to look after the interests of non-African ratepayers it is instructive to remember these councils and their non-African populations. Blantyre had a European population of 200 and an Indian population of 143; Zomba had 96 Europeans and 173 Indians; Chiromo had 72 Europeans and 98 Indians and Fort Johnston had 32 Europeans and 31 Indians. These were tiny numbers of people in little towns, when things were still happening in a small way.

BLANTYRE

Blantyre, named after the birthplace of Dr David Livingstone in Scotland, occupies not only a unique place in Malawi but in Central Africa as a whole because of its associations and its achievements, which have properly been characterised by the three pillars which adorned the life and work of that famous medical missionary and explorer—Christianity, commerce and civilisation. In the Christian sphere the beginning was marked by the work which was begun by Henry Henderson and Tom Bokwito on behalf of the Church of Scotland on 23 October 1876 when the site for mission work was chosen on Chief Kapeni's land. In 1888 the foundations were laid of the building of the Blantyre church. When the church was dedicated on 10 May 1891 the proclamation of the Nyasaland Protectorate was still four days off. In the decade after the inception of the Protectorate other missions, including Catholics, Anglicans and Baptists, added to the religious dimension of the Christian programme.

In the field of commerce the pioneering work was begun by the Livingstonia Central Africa Company (whose name was changed over the years to the African Lakes Company and then to the African Lakes Corporation). This company started operations in 1878 and has survived the changing faces of the country's political and economic life. Its first two-storey building in Malawi, built in 1882, still stands on its original site on the Mandala complex, the popular name for the company. Mandala was followed by other companies, the names or historical bequests of many of which still survive. Among the early concerns were Sharrer's Trading Company; Buchanan Brothers; the Blantyre and East Africa Company and the British Central Africa Company. Its closeness to the river port of Katunga's in Chikwawa before the opening of the railway line to Blantyre in 1908 and its situation in the centre of the agriculturally rich Shire Highlands gave Blantyre the commercial lead in Malawi which it has retained ever since. With this lead many things became possible in succeeding years: the growth of educational institutions which include some of the finest schools and colleges in the country, the Blantyre Secondary School, St Andrew's Primary and Secondary Schools, Chichiri Secondary School, Kapeni Training College, the Henry Henderson Institute, the Central High School, the Malawi Polytechnic and, until the move to Zomba, the Institute of Public Administration, Soche Hill College and Chancellor College of the University of Malawi. Industrially, too, the rise of factories over the last decade is a historical confirmation of the lead that Blantyre has enjoyed.

Its imposing and relatively towering buildings include the Blantyre church, the Chichiri complex of buildings which include the High Court, the Malawi Broadcasting Corporation, the Southern Region Headquarters of the Malawi Police and the Malawi Polytechnic; Development House, Delamere House, Mount Soche Hotel and the

284

Malawi Reserve Bank. These will soon be joined by an increasing number of commercial buildings which match the grandeur of Blantyre's growth. In all this, there is, naturally, a sense of civic pride. For this is the success story of Central Africa's oldest town.

When the beginnings of Blantyre's modern history were being enacted in the closing years of the nineteenth century the town had its share of troubles, too. Contemporary reports speak of daylight robberies from Chikwawa to Zomba, with Blantyre often in the thick of it. There was personal and business rivalry in the town which divided the European element into two parts. One group was led by E. C. A. Sharrer. It had its headquarters at Kabula Hill and spoke through the Shire Highlands Planters' Association which was formed in September 1892. The other group was led by John Moir and had its headquarters at Mandala. This group used the Nyasaland Planters' Association formed in December 1892 as its mouthpiece. Though personal rivalry continued, things began to change in 1894 and 1895, and the result was Blantyre's inauguration into modern times. In August 1894 the African Lakes Corporation opened the first banking department there in the country. In the same year Blantyre was declared a township and in the following year the British Central Africa Chamber of Agriculture and Commerce was inaugurated. These developments were unique not only to Malawi but to Central Africa.

At a meeting held in Blantyre on 14 July 1894 under the chairmanship of the Acting Commissioner, Alfred Sharpe, an agreement to the formation of the Blantyre township was reached between certain property owners and the chairman, acting on behalf of the Government. Sixteen property owners signed the agreement and made a hundred acres available to the township. The first meeting of the Council of Advice of the Blantyre township was held at the court house on 12 August 1895. Those present at this historic meeting were the District Collector, J. E. McMaster (who acted as chairman) and Messrs John Buchanan, J. Gibbs, T. H. Lloyd, Charles McKinnon and R. C. Fulke Greville (who was the town clerk). This meeting noted that its financial reserve stood at £38 15s. and agreed that rates would be collected from 1 July 1896. It resolved, too, to clear the roads of grass and tree stumps and to invite tenders for this job. The question of the inadequacy of water supply was raised. The supply from the Mandala wells was not enough and it was agreed that a few more wells should be sunk. The meeting was pleased to note that a few street lamps, the first in the country, had arrived and that more were expected. (A month later the council was told that there were 55 street lamps in the country and 355 drums of oil to service them.) The meeting agreed that a chairman plus five members would be competent to constitute a quorum and that meetings would be held on the second Tuesday of every month. Thus the first township authority was launched.

The first streets of the town were officially named at the second meeting. The main thoroughfare was named 'Main Street' and the smaller streets were named 'Sclater Road', 'Sharrers Road', 'Stephenson Road', 'Stewart Road', 'Fotheringham Street' and 'Buchanan Street'. One of the early decisions taken was that in order to secure a uniform time in the township a gun would be fired at noon on Friday of each week and on the arrival by train of the English mail.

So far the affairs of the town were in the hands of a caretaker committee. There was no formal constitution. A general meeting of the ratepayers of the town under the chairmanship of the District Collector, Robert Codrington, was held on 10 June 1897 to draw up a constitution. This constitution provided that the town should be known as Blantyre; that the town council should be made up of Europeans only, seven in number to represent missionary, planting and commercial interests; that election should be by open voting or by ballot; Asiatics and Africans who possessed property within the township valued at £100 would be eligible for a vote. For the following year, at least, the word 'European' was defined as 'any white man or man of colour whose education and social position would entitle him to the standing of a Britisher in a British Colony'. On the very sensible basis of one vote for one eligible person the first election to the Council of Advice took place on the same day. (Had it been on a *pro rata* basis calculated on the amount of rates paid, the Administration would have received five votes, the Blantyre Mission thirty votes and Buchanan Brothers seventeen votes!) The first seven elected councillors were James Lindsay, Capt. Daly, P. G. Vertin, the Rev. D. C. Ruffelle Scott, A. Paolucci, D. Beaton and S. Israel. Mr J. W. Kirk was elected town clerk at a salary of £30 per annum. The chairman was the District Collector. The constitution was approved by the Commissioner who agreed to allow the council as much freedom in its local government as the township regulations permitted in return for an undertaking that every decision was to be taken to him for approval. The first meeting of the duly constituted Blantyre Town Council was held on 13 July 1897. Before the first year of the new council's tenure was over a wooden bridge was built over the Mudi River because the Government refused to subsidise a steel bridge and a bitter debate was launched against Indian traders. This debate was sparked off by a group in the council which was opposed to business on Sundays and was also afraid that if no restrictions were introduced Indian traders would invade the township proper. The Commissioner vetoed the motion against trading on Sunday but approved the decision that no new Indian traders would be located 'north of old Mandala road'. On 4 January 1899 Dr Hetherwick introduced a motion that no Indian trader should be allowed to buy land in the township with immediate effect in retaliation against the government decision to allow trading on Sundays. The upshot was that the Administration agreed that the council should set up a separate area for Indian traders but would not go so far as to interfere in private property sales. Hetherwick, however, persisted in the matter of Sunday trading and a subcommittee was set up in early 1900 to ascertain the feelings of residents within a radius of twenty miles. It reported that the majority were in favour of keeping the shops closed on Sundays. The Administration did not accept the findings and requested that a ballot should be taken in the council. This, of course, infuriated some members of the council and an open row developed. Some members now called for the setting up of an enlarged township as an independent body with increased powers. This radical demand was later expunged from the official minutes.

By the time of the outbreak of World War I in 1914 the Blantyre township comprised 126½ acres of land. The biggest property owners were the British Central Africa Company with 46 acres, the Blantyre Mission with 27¼ acres and Buchanan Brothers with 15½ acres. At the same time there were only four Indian property owners in the township: Kalidas with ¼ acre; Osman Adam with ½ acre; Hassam Juma with ¼ acre and Mohommed Hassam with ¼ acre. The total rates earned were just over £200 per annum. As opposed to this modest figure it is worth noting that the valuation of the city of Blantyre for the year ending March 1969 was £24,016,155. It had a population in that year (1969) of just over 120,000.

In 1913 when Sir George Smith arrived to assume his position as Governor, the chairman of the Blantyre Town Council, already designated mayor, was Mr Alexander Hamilton of the Zambezi Industrial Mission. In 1915 the mayor was Mr Claude Metcalfe. In the following fifteen years those who served as mayors were W. F. James, G. C. Duncan, D. Selkirk and William Tait-Bowie. During these years it was a practice to co-opt two Indian members to represent the Asiatic wards.

In 1926, when the fiftieth anniversary of the founding of the Blantyre Mission was celebrated, the Blantyre Town Council had just approved schemes for the town's own water and electricity supplies. For the water scheme which entailed the damming of the Upper Mudi the Government granted a loan of £10,000 payable over forty years. As for the electricity scheme an offer was first made to the council in 1921 by the Shire Highlands Railway Company to supply electricity from the company's own plant. Three years later the company decided to withdraw from the scheme in view of the uncertainties surrounding the future extension of the railway. It was then that the town council decided to launch a municipal scheme of its own. For this it was authorised to raise a loan of £8,000.

Interesting sidelights on the history of the Blantyre Town Council include the election of the first lady member in 1929, Mrs L. G. Ryall; the declaration of the townships of Blantyre and Limbe as mayoralties in 1948; and the amalgamation of the two townships on 31 March 1956. In his report prior to that occasion Mr R. S. McDougall, the County Treasurer of Hertfordshire, England, who made the enquiry and recommendation said, in his concluding remarks in 1954:

> This question is of importance to the whole Protectorate, because the future of Nyasaland is wrapped up in the future of its commercial and industrial centre. The people of Nyasaland will realise that a good commercial centre is a good investment. In some ways Blantyre and Limbe combined is the shop window of the territory.

In 1959 Blantyre-Limbe Town Council was elevated to the status of a municipality. The first Asian mayor was elected, Mr A. Sattar Sacranie, who served from 1963 to 1965. The first African mayor, Mr John Kamwendo, was elected in 1967. On 6 July 1966 the municipality was elevated to the status of city.

In less than a hundred years the oldest township in Central Africa has come a long way. In spite of its expansion and development it still retains a fair measure of the promise, the beauty and the serenity that helped to launch a powerful mission station in its midst on 23 October 1876, a date which rightly marks the birth of modern Blantyre, the present shop window of Malawi.

CHAPTER 22

The story of Malawi's capitals, old and new: 1891–1969[1]

Eight years before the official British Protectorate of Nyasaland, or British Central Africa as it was called for a few years, was established on 14 May 1891 the British Government began to take a keen interest in the political destiny of the territory. It was anxious that another European power should not assume control of the area. There were British missionaries already at work here. There was a humanitarian aspect in this interest. If the work started by David Livingstone to eradicate the scourge of the slave trade which he described as the 'open sore of Africa' could be promoted or advanced by an official British Government or agency the tarnished image of an earlier British involvement in the trade itself would be rectified. With these expectations the British Government appointed Captain Foot in 1883 as its Slave Trade Commissioner accredited to the Kings and Chiefs of Central Africa. Captain Foot used Blantyre as headquarters. Here a European settlement had begun to grow around the Blantyre Mission which was started in 1876. His successor, Captain Hawes, decided to set up his headquarters at Zomba in 1886. The reason for this choice was, as A. H. Mell notes, 'its nearness to the great slave route running from the south end of Lake Nyasa to the Portuguese coast south of Ibo'.

But as there were at least two other such routes further north, there were other reasons for this choice. H. L. Duff noted that Zomba occupied 'a singularly beautiful position on the slopes of Zomba mountain' and in addition there was 'a copious perennial supply of water . . .; the climate is favourable; the soil rich.'

These reasons did not exhaust the possibilities. Harry Hamilton

[1] This article first appeared in the *Society of Malawi Journal*, 24, 1, Jan. 1971. Grateful thanks are acknowledged for permission to use the article in this book. All footnote references have been omitted.

Johnston was the first high official to admit that there were personal as well as official motives underlying the choice of headquarters and that there was serious disagreement over it from the inception. He wrote:

> The choice of Zomba for the Administrative residence had really been made by Consul Hawes, and I was glad to endorse it, because I realised the comparative value of the isolation, and the good effect on one's health of the superb scenery of which my eye never wearied. Although I really only continued what my predecessor had done, I was conscious as the months went by of a sense of hostility in regard to this selection, emanating from Blantyre. That place was pretty, but Zomba was superb. Blantyre was virtually 'safe'. At Zomba during the earlier years of my stay there was a somewhat thrilling sense of danger, attended by a pleasant feeling of security within its defences.

Johnston referred to 'a sense of hostility' with regard to the choice of Zomba as administrative headquarters. This hostility is best explained in the words of R. S. Hynde, founder and editor of the *Central African Planter*, and later of the *Nyasaland Times*, one-time prominent member of the Blantyre Town Council. Hynde commented as follows in the editorial columns of the *Nyasaland Times*:

> The average person thinks that there must be some deep-seated reason why the Government was located at Zomba and not near Blantyre. This unfortunately is not the case. The history of the move is instructive. Consul Hawes, before the British Government took Nyasaland under its protection, located his Consulate at Zomba for personal reasons. He and Mr John Buchanan did not hit it off with the Europeans settled in and around Blantyre, and as Mr Buchanan, who was then a prominent landowner, had his place in Zomba, the Consulate was built there. When Sir Harry Johnston came here and took over the country he also found difficulties with the Europeans and missions, and probably influenced by similar reasons to that of Consul Hawes, he adopted Zomba as his capital. Observe that there was no picking out of Zomba for strategic reasons, or for health reasons, or because it was nearer the line of communications. It was purely a matter of personal idiosyncrasy.

This point is supported by the Scottish missionary, the Rev. Henry Scott, who first visited Zomba in 1890 and later served there as missionary-in-charge. 'It [Zomba] was to be on the main route to the Lakes and not to be too near Mandala and Blantyre.' In addition to these factors, Scott says that Zomba was chosen by Hawes as his administrative headquarters because of its natural beauty, its excellence of water supply and its accessibility. According to Scott the Residency was completed in 1887 and was called the Consulate of Nyasa.

The weight of evidence is clearly on the side of Zomba having been chosen more by accident than by design, more because of the personal feelings of individuals rather than in the interest of the country over whose destiny it was to preside during the whole of the colonial era, even though, as will be shown, there were at least four occasions during this period when serious consideration was given in either official or non-official circles for its removal to another site. The alternative on all these occasions was Blantyre. One ruler thought well of another area and that was, strange as it would seem today, Lilongwe.

But let us look first at Zomba as the choice of the first capital of Malawi. What was it like before Hawes altered its course of history?

Zomba, first occupied in strong numbers by members of the Chewa community, was during the first half of the nineteenth century occupied in turn by the Mangoche Yao who drove off many of the original residents, and later by the Machinga Yao. In course of time the Yao and the Chewa lived together. Here they were joined by the Scottish missionaries who, through the efforts of John Buchanan, started their mission interest in Zomba when Buchanan built his house on a ledge on a hill, on the farther side of the Mlungusi stream, on 5 August 1879. The Rev. Dr Henry Scott, who joined the Blantyre Mission in 1890 and later served as missionary at Zomba at the turn of the twentieth century, had described this date 'as the birthday of Zomba'. The Rev. Scott has left a very graphic account of Zomba as he knew the place in 1890.

The Residence was standing still unoccupied by any European. No other house of any description was to be seen on this side of the Mlungusi stream. On the other side of the stream there was the present house of Buchanan. Here resided a Mr Cameron who was in charge of the coffee estate and who died a few years later of black water fever. He was the only European in the whole Zomba district excepting at Domasi. At this time there was a huge native population. Besides the two principal Chiefs Malemya and Chelumbe, there were a considerable number of influential headmen, such as Kalimbuka, Cherunga, Chenyama, Ibrahimu and Nasinomwe, who had very large villages along the slopes of Mount Zomba. In fact from here right along the slopes of the mountain cliffs as far as the Domasi Valley, there was a continuous series of villages crowded together. These have long since disappeared.

Scott recalls how everybody carried arms in those days: 'I remember distinctly how when the headmen came to church they brought with them their guns and stood them up against the wall during the service.' This was the area which had interested Captain Hawes a few years earlier.

Captain Hawes obtained the site for the Consulate from Chief Malemya to whom he gave, in return for a hundred acres of land, five pounds and trade goods worth £7 15s. 6d., less than £14 in all. The job of building the Consul's official residence was given to John Buchanan of the firm of Buchanan Brothers who tendered as follows on 30 November 1885:

We have now the honour of tendering you our estimate for British Consulate to be built in Zomba including in all two one-storey houses as per plan and specifications with cook-house and servants rooms also goat house, fowl house and byre for the sum of £600 (six hundred pounds sterling) and we guarantee that the workmanship and material used shall be of the best quality.

The Consulate, later known as the Old Residency, was occupied by the Consuls of Nyasaland from Captain Hawes onwards and later by Sir Harry Johnston and Sir Alfred Sharpe. Throughout its existence the Residency has served various purposes. When the Secretariat was burned down in 1919 it served as a substitute and even housed the Legislative Council. It later served as the official residence of the Chief Secretary and other officials till 1948. A year later it was converted to a Government Hostel and continued in that role ever since.

Government House, built in 1901, was first occupied by Sir Alfred Sharpe. It is a coincidence that this official, the first occupant of Government House, was the first high-ranking official to write a favourable report on Lilongwe, a town which was to be selected to be capital-designate sixty years later by the first African occupant of Government House, Malawi's first Prime Minister and later first President, Dr H. Kamuzu Banda. When reporting to the Principal Secretary of State for the Colonies on 7 June 1904 on his visit to the Upper Shire, South Nyasa and Central Angoniland districts, Sir Alfred Sharpe observed that at Lilongwe eight thousand people came to meet him, including every important headman in the western half of Central Angoniland. 'This district,' he wrote, 'is the most populous part of the Protectorate, containing a population, as nearly as can be estimated, of about a quarter of a million. It is the Basutoland of British Central Africa.' Incidentally, eleven years later, another Governor was to underline the strategically favourable location of Lilongwe, a point which Alfred Sharpe first took

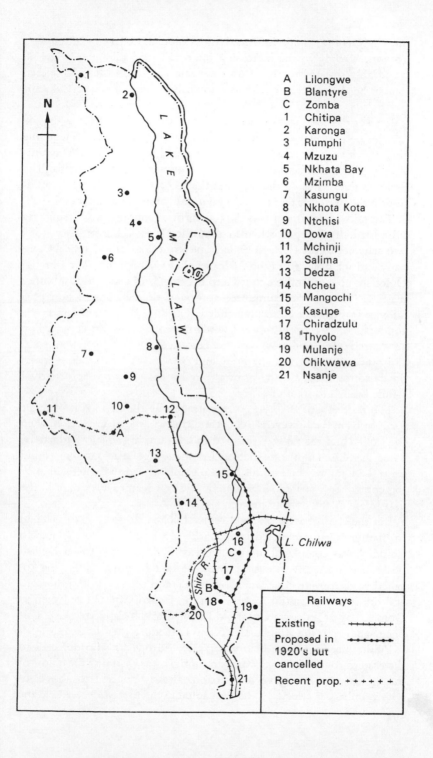

N

A	Lilongwe
B	Blantyre
C	Zomba
1	Chitipa
2	Karonga
3	Rumphi
4	Mzuzu
5	Nkhata Bay
6	Mzimba
7	Kasungu
8	Nkhota Kota
9	Ntchisi
10	Dowa
11	Mchinji
12	Salima
13	Dedza
14	Ncheu
15	Mangochi
16	Kasupe
17	Chiradzulu
18	Thyolo
19	Mulanje
20	Chikwawa
21	Nsanje

LAKE MALAWI

L. Chilwa

Shire R.

Railways

Existing	┼┼┼┼┼
Proposed in 1920's but cancelled	●━●━●━●
Recent prop.	+ + + + +

up. Sir George Smith informed the Colonial Office of Lilongwe's growth: 'Owing to the increasing importance of Lilongwe which is favourably situated for trade on the route to Northeastern Rhodesia, it may be desirable to establish a township there at no very distant future.'

It was still a long way off before Lilongwe could be chosen as the site for the new capital of an independent Malawi. For the present, the rivalry between Zomba and Blantyre remained unabated. The anti-Zomba European faction raised many arguments against Zomba. The first was that it was off the rail link; the second was on the score of ill-health; the third was that it was unfavourably located on a cyclonic belt.

The railway argument was the one most strenuously and frequently submitted. It all began when in 1896 Sir Harry Johnston forwarded two schemes to the Foreign Office, one from Sharrer's Zambezi Company and the other from the African Lakes Corporation. The Foreign Office set up a committee to go into the details of feasibility and other matters. Though the committee approved of the construction of a railway in principle it recommended that an independent survey be conducted as to the best route. The report of the surveyors appeared on 30 March 1899 and covered the favoured route which was from Chiromo to a point near Blantyre and from this point to Zomba and finally to the Lake, a distance of 201 miles exclusive of the proposed 5-mile branch to Blantyre.

The residents of Blantyre were outraged by the implied preference for Zomba in the surveyors' report and this was the first occasion when the capital and the railway featured in the same argument. Ultimately, when the Shire Highlands Railway Company signed a contract to build a 2 ft. 6 in. railway line from Chiromo to Blantyre on 3 September 1901 the controversy abated since Zomba did not feature anywhere in the first phase of the railway project.

But the controversy was soon revived. The first phase (Port Herald to Blantyre) was completed in 1908; the second phase (Port Herald to Chindio) was completed in 1915. It was then that the projected third phase, the northern extension, brought in two possibilities, the so-called eastern route (Luchenza to Chikala and then to Fort Johnston) and the so-called central route (Blantyre, Lunzu, Mpimbi and then to Domira Bay or Indegwere near old Livingstonia at Cape Maclear). This once again split the Zomba and Blantyre factions.

Public meetings were held in 1923 by Europeans who objected to the eastern route of the railway extension. It was then that the editor of the *Nyasaland Times* gave his version, already referred to above, of why Zomba was selected to be the capital in the first place. He held the view that the Blantyre area was preferable because of its greater altitude, better health conditions and because it 'is and always has been nearer the main line of communication'. In Hynde's view, Zomba was unsuitable because its elevation was not as favourable as Blantyre's (3,000 ft. as compared to 3,500–4,000 ft. in Blantyre), thus making the place hot the year round; it was in a mosquito area and, finally, as the nucleus of the settlement was on the side of a hill, road construction was expensive and houses were scattered.

Hynde and his supporters wanted the capital shifted to Chichiri. Interestingly enough, it is in this area that the new municipal buildings of the City of Blantyre will be erected. Hynde described the site of his choice in the following words:

> The site we suggest will get over all these difficulties [i.e. the arguments against Zomba]. It is at Chichiri between Blantyre and Limbe. The Government has about 500 acres of ground between the Mudi and Naperi Rivers, beautifully situated for the purpose, with gentle slopes, and cut clearly by the main road, where a 'pukka' township could be laid out on the most modern ideas with broad roads and side walks.

These proposals were turned down by Governor Smith because his administration could not choose between the two railway routes since both had their supporters and opponents. It took the Administration almost twenty years before it could choose its northern route not only because of its own uncertainties but also because of the delays and financial limitations and apathy of the Colonial Office.

The question, however, remained a live issue in debates on the subject of the removal of the capital, both in Malawi and in Britain. In 1922 it was considered by the Finance Commission: in 1923, 1924 ,1925 and in August 1930 it featured in Hynde's *Nyasaland Times*. The Finance Commission reported in 1922 that on the grounds of health, economy and convenience to the public, the capital should be shifted from Zomba. What is interesting is that the Commission did not recommend that the shift be made from Zomba to Blantyre but rather to some central point further northwards. The relevant section of its recommendation was as follows:

> In regard to the question of the site for the headquarters of Government in relation to the development of the Protectorate generally we agree that in recent years the tendency for development is to move north and it is possible that the main centres of population may move with it. Further, mineral development or amalgamation with

Northern Rhodesia may change the whole orientation of the Protectorate. A survey of the mineralogical resources of the Protectorate has just begun and if a reef were found in the Kasungu district, for instance, we consider that the trading elements in Blantyre would move, wherever Government headquarters might be.

Even if amalgamation of Nyasaland with Northern Rhodesia and the possibilities of mineral exploitation were given as two important reasons why the capital should be shifted northwards, the significant point in the Finance Commission's recommendation was that the centripetal force of Blantyre should not continue to be used as the overpowering reason for considering it as the only alternative to Zomba.

In 1934, with the railway extension along the central route almost complete and the Zambezi Bridge connecting the Nyasaland railway system with the Portuguese line from Beira ready for traffic, the matter of the capital came up for consideration once again. The bridge, which was 2.285 miles long, cost about £2 million and took 3½ years to build, was the longest in the world at the time. The first train passed over it on 14 January 1935. Governor Sir Harold Kittermaster set up a committee comprising K. H. Hall as chairman and J. C. Abraham, H. B. Wilson and A. D. J. Williams as members to consider the matter. In its report dated 7 December 1934, the committee recommended that the status quo should be maintained only because railway development had not reached its optimum at that point. The Committee reported:

> We agree that Government headquarters would most conveniently be situated somewhere on the railway if suitable health and water supply conditions could be found but we do not consider that this country has yet seen the limit of railway construction; for example, the Portuguese have a right to build a railway across Nyasaland and even yet Zomba might find itself on the railway but we are unable at this stage to indicate where a site on the railway should be.

This Committee was not enthusiastic that Zomba should remain the capital but advised that in ten years' time it would be clear which way development was going and it would then be more appropriate for a choice to be made. Sir Harold Kittermaster forwarded the committee's report to the Colonial Office on 15 December 1934, adding his own misgivings about Zomba.

> The extension of the railway to the Lake has already necessitated the removal of the distributing offices and stores of certain departments from Zomba to the railway and it seemed to me probable that definite advantages would accrue by the removal of the Central

Government also. The question has been raised in the past and complaints made by the public of the inconvenience of having the headquarters of Government separated from the commercial centre which was Blantyre and Limbe. I was particularly influenced by a belief that Zomba was not a particularly healthy place and was becoming definitely less healthy. Amoebic dysentery in particular was becoming so prevalent in the station that it could be said to be endemic.

Like the committee he set up, Kittermaster ruled against Zomba but wanted time before being certain of the best alternative. Once the traffic on the Zambezi Bridge increased and the northern railway extension proved itself, the alternatives would become clearer. The local administration recommended that the question of an alternative site for the capital be reviewed later. The Colonial Office was happy to leave it at that in 1935.

During the trial period, war intervened and old priorities were cast aside. When the war ended, new priorities were formulated within the framework of continuing financial restrictions. Economic planning after 1945 was confined to essential projects defined closely and carefully to mean absolutely essential projects. Postwar reconstruction did not normally include a project to start a new capital.

But on 13 and 14 December 1946 Zomba was extensively devastated by a cyclone. A committee was set up consisting of the chief secretary, F. L. Brown, as chairman, and M. P. Barrow and J. M. Marshall as members. The terms of reference of this committee were: 'To examine the advisability of removing the capital from its present site with particular regard to the financial implications.'

The Committee learned that the cost of repairing the storm damage in Zomba would be about £10,000 and that of mounting an antimalarial scheme would be £125,000. It did not find that the expenditure of such sums of money justified the removal of the capital, the cost of which was estimated at £500,000.

On the score of safety too, the Committee, going by the expert advice of the government geologist, could not support removal. The geologist reported that:

there is no reason to regard Zomba as doomed to destruction, but the extraordinarily heavy rainfall has caused considerable damage, the repairing of which must be faced. It should be remembered that the wearing down of a mountain mass is a normal natural phenomenon. Sometimes, as recently, the process is accelerated, sometimes retarded, but it is always progressing. The earth is no dead thing,

297

but one of endless change. The Master Architect is ever pulling down here and building there.

The Committee found that though removal of the capital could not be justified on grounds of safety, health and magnitude of storm damage, there were nevertheless strong reasons why the capital should be removed to the Blantyre-Limbe area. These were proximity to the commercial areas leading to closer cooperation with unofficials; the saving of time and expense (calculated at roughly £3,700 annually) involved in travelling from and to Zomba and the commercial centre of Blantyre and Limbe; removal would lead to better facilities for recreation, shopping and social life; it would place the capital on the railway.

The general weight of the Committee's report was in favour of removal, not for the three minor reasons raised in some quarters (safety, health, storm damage) but in the interest of the larger objectives. Financially, it would involve the finding of an additional £17,000 for the next 25 years, roughly £500,000. But even if removal were not effected in the foreseeable future, the Committee recommended that the following three units should be transferred to Blantyre as soon as possible: P.W.D. Workshops; P.W.D. Transport Section and P.W.D. Medical Stores.

The Committee reported on 22 March 1947 and for the remainder of that year its report was under consideration by officials in the country and in London by the Secretary of State for the Colonies. Sir Edmund Richards, the Governor, told the Legislative Council at Zomba on 2 December 1947 that official reaction to the report would be available at the next meeting of the Legislative Council.

At the scheduled meeting of Legco in 1948 the Financial Secretary moved that the report be accepted in principle but that the immediate steps should be confined to a preliminary survey of the layout of the new site. When this survey was completed and subject to a satisfactory report on the water position, the matter should be reviewed in three years' time 'in conjunction with the general review of the finances of the Post War Development Programme'. The leader of the unofficial members, the Hon. M. P. Barrow, C.B.E., one of the members of the committee which enquired into the matter in 1946, supported the proposal which he described as 'really commonsense'. Mr Barrow recalled the words of a former Chief Secretary who had described Zomba as an 'official zoo'.

When the three-year period elapsed the issue of federation overshadowed every other single issue and it was hardly conceivable that any colonial government would give much or serious attention to an economic proposition as large as that of removing a capital in a country in which it had not in six decades of protectorate rule fostered any serious economic development. What it had done during this period, such as railway construction, was done largely at the expense of the economic wealth of the country, its land resources. Economic development during the colonial era was looked upon as limited development confined to certain elements of the population. In this context it was not difficult to see why certain quarters supported the removal of the capital for different reasons. Some saw in it the lever for a possible merger of Nyasaland and part of Northern Rhodesia in the interest of mineral exploitation. Others saw in it the virtue of harmonious relations between the official and the unofficial elements of the local population. National development in the national interest, that is in the interest of the majority of the population, was not the watchword of the colonial era. It had to await the dawn of independence.

Malawi gained her independence on 6 July 1964. In the same year the new national Government decided to move the capital from Zomba to Lilongwe. This decision was announced in Parliament on 22 January 1965 in a statement by the Prime Minister, the Hon. Dr H. Kamuzu Banda.

Blantyre was considered to be unsuitable as the new capital as it had sufficient commercial and industrial enterprises to be assured of a fairly rapid rate of growth. It was noted that 'any further emphasis in the south could only lead to a lop-sided and inequitable development to the detriment of the Central and Northern Regions'.

The choice before the new Government in 1965 was one between two possibilities. One was 'to perpetuate the existing highly inefficient governmental organisation, divided between Zomba and Blantyre, built up piecemeal over the years and never planned with any thought of the requirements of a capital'; the other was 'to make a new start before the cost became even greater and establish now a modern capital planned to meet efficiently and economically the needs of Government and administration, whilst at the same time stimulating the development of the Central Region'.

In order to help the Government to take the right decision, a firm of consultants, Brian Colquhoun and Partners, was appointed on 27 January 1965. The terms of reference were in two parts. The first part dealt with the possibility of Zomba remaining the capital. In this part the consultants were to: prepare a general assessment of the present condition of Government buildings in Zomba in relation to their economic life and replacement; consider and make recommendations together with estimated costs on what additional accommodation is required in Zomba in order to enable Government business to be prosecuted efficiently, giving due regard to the establishment of a university in Zomba.

The second part dealt with the proposed new capital at Lilongwe and in this section the consultants were required to study site conditions and availability of local material and labour; to prepare a preliminary master plan; and to draw up an overall project estimate.

The consultants worked in haste in order to present their report to the Prime Minister before the arrival of a British Government Economic Mission on 29 June 1965. The report beat this deadline by fifteen days. The consultants reported that the cost of maintaining the national buildings in Zomba and Blantyre and of making extensions and additions over a ten-year period would be £3.6 million. For the new Government buildings at Lilongwe the cost was estimated at £13.5 million. These figures were subsequently revised after a reappraisal by the Ministry of Works of the space requirements and the costs per square foot of all buildings to £3.2 million and £11.8 million respectively.

In conveying his Government's decision to build the new capital on a site on Kanengo Hill, eight miles from the centre of the existing Lilongwe town, the Prime Minister made reference to the usefulness of Zomba as a university town and of the value and suitability of developing the airport at Lilongwe as opposed to the numerous disadvantages experienced at Chileka, when he presented a fuller statement to Parliament in October 1965 on 'The Establishment of a New Capital'.

In the same month a survey was begun at the request of the Malawi Government by H. Hindle, Regional Public Administration Adviser of the Economic Commission for Africa. The survey resulted in a reduction of the forecast of space needs from 358,000 square feet to approximately 240,000 square feet leading to a saving, calculated at the average cost quoted in the Colquhoun Report, of approximately £600,000. Among its twelve recommendations dealing with such details as the building of a hotel and restaurant at the new capital site at an early date, the revision or simplification of existing house plans, the development of Salima and the adjacent lakeshore as a tourist resort, the adoption of East African Standard Time to gain an extra hour of daylight, the requirements of the National Assembly buildings, the Hindle survey recommended that a National Capital Authority be created to manage, control and coordinate all aspects of the proposed capital project.

Having received the Colquhoun Report in June 1965 and the Hindle Report in December 1965, the President of Malawi went on to invite a private firm of consultants to prepare a master plan. IMEX commissioned W. J. C. Gerke, of Withers and Gerke, Town Planning Consultants and Land Surveyors, Johannesburg, and Charl L. Viljoen, Professor of Town and Regional Planning, University of Pretoria, to prepare the *Master Plan for Lilongwe the Capital City of Malawi*. This was published in May 1968. In their summary of the main recommendations and programming, the authors wrote: 'The existing commercial and civic centre of Lilongwe cannot be expanded sufficiently, and a new city centre is to be built about three and a half miles north of the present centre. This will comprise the Government administrative offices, a new civic commercial centre and a city park.' In October 1965 Parliament had been informed that the new capital would be built on Kanengo Hill, eight miles from the centre of old Lilongwe town. The master plan refers to a site three and a half miles away. This will bring the new city closer to the centre of the old town.

With the master plan brought in to supplement the reports and surveys already available, President H. Kamuzu Banda invited Dr P. S. Rautenbach, the South African Prime Minister's Planning Adviser, to report further on the feasibility of the capital project. Strengthened in his immense and deep resolve that his decision was right, the President made a momentous statement to Parliament on 26 March 1968. 'The time has now come,' he declared, 'to do something specific, concrete and tangible on the matter.' This he did by moving a motion 'on the decision of the Government of Malawi to raise finance by way of loans for the purpose of establishing, constructing and developing the new capital city at Lilongwe'. At the same time he announced the creation of the Capital City Development Corporation as 'the agency through which the Government will perform all the physical and practical functions of moving the capital from Zomba to Lilongwe'.

The President announced that in terms of the Malawi Land Act of 1966 as amended in 1967 the whole of Lilongwe district was proclaimed a development area. This meant that the land 'so declared can only be used, or can be used only by anyone under the strict direction and supervision of the Government'.

During the remaining two days Parliament approved the President's motion as well as the Capital City Development Corporation Bill which was moved by the Minister of Economic Affairs, Mr A. K. Banda.

The legal and technical provisions for the capital project were now taken care of. All that was necessary to make it a reality was to find the money. The President had told Parliament on 26 March 1968: 'We have to borrow every pound of it, every shilling of it, every penny of it. From whom? From where? I do not know—so far as I am concerned, from anyone willing to lend us the money.'

Six weeks later, on 6 May 1968, on the occasion of the official opening of Malawi's longest bridge at Chikwawa, the Kamuzu Bridge, President Banda disclosed that he had at last received the money necessary to make a start on the capital project, saying that 'when our traditional friends said they could not help, I said they should not stop me from doing it'. He said that on that very day the South African Government had released a statement indicating their willingness to help Malawi. The amount received was 8 million rand which in terms of Malawi currency was £4,666,666 13s. 4d.

The statement released by the South African Government recalled that on 27 March 1968 the Minister of Finance anticipated the establishment of a 'Loans Fund for the Promotion of Economic Cooperation'. It was from this fund that 8 million rand was made available to the Malawi Government on a long-term loan at 4 per cent interest. The statement added that the loan was intended 'to cover mainly expenditure which cannot be met from local Malawi sources and will be tied to the maximum use of South African contractors and of South African materials in the case of imported requirements'. It added that the South African Government was satisfied that the building of a new capital at Lilongwe was not a prestige project and that it was impressed by the opinion of Dr Rautenbach that the capital at Lilongwe would 'create an important urban growth point in an otherwise predominantly rural region and so help to promote more balanced development of all three main regions of the country'.

When Parliament approved of the New Capital Loan Authorisation Bill, 1968, in June 1968, the loan was duly formalised. President Banda expressed his profound gratitude for the loan and showed how the initial gesture had already begun to open other avenues of support from friendly governments. He told a jubilant Parliament:

> To me personally, to the Government of this country, and our people, the willingness of the Government of the Republic of South Africa to give us financial assistance on the Lilongwe Capital City Scheme in any form, to any degree, to any extent at all, makes that Government in every sense of the word, truly a friend in need who is a friend indeed.

The gesture, the President pointed out, was more than a direct source of help. There were indirect and intangible forms already developing. He said:

> As I stand here now before the House inquiries have been made by representatives of at least three countries and one organisation as to

whether we would be willing to accept assistance in the Lilongwe Project in one form or another or in one particular item or another, in which the countries and organisations which they represent are or might be willing to help us.

Less than a year later the President informed Parliament on 17 April 1969 that preliminary work was already in progress at Capital Hill, Lilongwe, aimed at providing housing and office accommodation for those engaged in carrying out the first phase of the building of the new capital. During 1970 a major contract was let for the construction of offices for the first three Ministries to move from Zomba and Blantyre. Detailed city planning was by then well advanced and work in full swing on the basic urban infrastructure and estate development. The Prime Minister of the Republic of South Africa also visited the site to view progress.

In 1959 and 1960 a number of dreams were conceived during the incarceration of Dr Banda at Gwelo. These were not the fanciful projections of an active mind but the practical calculations of a visionary. In all visions there is an element of uncertainty and risk but Dr Banda's practical and realistic programme represents a calculated risk. He has thought out his plans clearly and carefully, basing them where necessary on expert advice. He has not hesitated to reject the pessimistic view where he has considered this to be ill-conceived. All politicians are judged by the success or failure attendant on their policies. So far, it is abundantly clear that the Gwelo dreams are being translated into practical realities with a great measure of success. The University of Malawi has operated successfully since 1965; the lakeshore road is expanding every year; the new capital project is progressing along calculated and rational lines. It is still early to translate into tangible terms what the full realisation of the Gwelo dreams holds in store for the national development of independent Malawi. One fact is clear: without this realisation development would be severely handicapped. With it, the possibilities of adequate returns for the future wellbeing of the nation as a whole are assured.

CHAPTER 23

Malawi in retrospect: concluding remarks

Over the past six years the most common queries concerning local history that have been raised by persons who were troubled by doubts were: does Malawi have a history? Is there sufficient material to undertake the study and the teaching of this history along ordered and educational lines? It is no longer necessary to give a mere affirmative reply to these queries. The time has come to underline the affirmation and to let the future consolidate it.

The story of Malawi's past goes back to centuries before the advent of Christianity, for the history of the land is that of the people who, regardless of physical differences and cultural attributes, lived in a geographical unit. At one time it was not necessary to define boundaries in terms of national divisions. It was enough if certain natural landmarks like streams, rivers or hills served as signposts so that the owners of the land knew exactly what the limits of their possessions were. In colonial times political boundaries were drawn up, often dividing people of similar ethnic groups. The boundaries have been inherited by modern independent states.

The Malawi of the pre-colonial era attracted settlers in large numbers because of the fertility of the soil, the abundance of water supply and waterways and, what was also useful for a migrating community, the existence of tsetse-free belts which made it possible for cattle and other livestock to enter the country or to pass through it into neighbouring lands. The rivers and the lakes not only attracted settlers but influenced the patterns of migration and settlement. Some migrating groups became divided by the lakes and mountains on their southward movement. While a few re-established their links at a later date, many remained separated. The ethnic affinities among such separated peoples are striking. To say that Malawi and her neighbours are related is to acknowledge this historical development. The significance in this context of the Songwe in the north, the Lake in the east, the Luangwa in the west and the Zambezi in the south is that they are not ethnically limiting.

The boundaries of Malawi's history, whose frontiers are being pushed back and more adequately signposted and recorded all the time, include the prehistoric past when man was a hunter and food gatherer, the proto-historic past when man began making his transition into the next phase, the historic past which saw pastoral farming, agriculture and mining being added to man's earlier activities. The historic past saw, too, the arrival of various African, European and Asian communities who have added considerable grist to the Malawi historical mill.

The products of this mill may be variously described: there was the usual era of man's inhumanity towards man which characterised so much of the history of this continent as well as other continents. The rack and ruin of this era have left their historical legacy, out of which have come the very considerable Christian missionary impact as well as the relative absence of tribal divisions which have been the bane of so much of man's history everywhere. Malawi's history certainly did not begin with the coming of missionaries as is so erroneously supposed, but its later history has been very powerfully influenced by them. This, more than anywhere else in Central Africa, and certainly in very few parts of Africa, directed Malawi's colonial fortunes both through its own ideologies and aspirations as well as in creating these qualities among the indigenous population. The population, the proper focus of Malawi history because of its numerical advantage, has not been a mere weathercock blown by the forces which engulfed it. It has at times asserted itself and consequently made history of its own. Examples of this may be found in every era of the past from the time when natural forces and local peoples were the only challenges to the time when challenges came from outside.

The history of a country involves everyone who happens to be there at any point in time. Though a very small country of 36,145 square miles of land surface today with a lake water area of approximately 9,300 square miles, most of it in Lake Malawi, the history of Malawi is more than that of the people who are indigenous to the land, since the country has a small Asian and European population which is part of the history. The African population has increased from 736,724 in 1901 to 4,020,724 in 1966. During the same period the Asian population (predominantly from the Indian subcontinent) has increased from 115 to 11,299 and the European population (mainly of British descent) has risen from 314 to 7,395. More than three-quarters of the non-African population live in the urban areas of Blantyre, Zomba and Lilongwe and this fact identifies them with the commercial and industrial history of the country. The non-African population constitutes a part of the colonial and post-colonial history of Malawi. In terms of the historical accident of their past most of them are British passport holders; the number of Indian citizens in the country in 1971 was approximately 200 while the number of Malawi citizens among the non-African population in 1971 was under 40.

Historically the non-African contribution has been most conspicuous in the military, agricultural, commercial, industrial and educational sectors. Like the rest of the population they have had to adapt to the changing faces of colonial, federal and national governments and periods. Historical examples show that those who made the adaptation survived while those who were unwilling or unable to adjust succumbed. As in the past so in the future the continuing role of this group will depend on its ability and willingness to adapt to change. In the first coat-of-arms of the country the first Commissioner had embodied his dream that the progress of the country would be founded upon the cornerstones of multi-racial cooperation involving white, brown and black. In the political gospel of independent Malawi, the first President has laid down the cornerstones of unity, loyalty, obedience and discipline. He has also spoken of bridging the gulf of disunity between the races and of cementing the bonds which make for the composition of a non-racial society built on the foundations of these cornerstones. This ideal is, of course, only just a part of Malawi history, since it belongs to the present and to the future when it can hopefully become a fact.

History, like the human mind, has its fringes and its recesses: certain things stand out more conspicuously than others. Some things are seen and remembered for their surface features and superficial values; other things are seen and remembered for their lasting qualities. Among the latter must be ranked the story of man's historic march towards a progressive future. This is not the prerogative of the few but the motivation behind mass action. While history speaks and writes of a few leaders it should also speak and write of the multitudes after whom no streets are named or statues built. In Malawi the masses are the farmers, fishermen and labourers both at home and abroad. For them a meaningful historical development means more farms, more and better roads, markets, boats, transport and employment opportunities. Historically the masses have not been adequately provided for during the colonial period for a variety of colonial reasons originating mainly in

306

the fact that as the country had extremely limited mineral resources and lacked strategic importance the rulers did not consider it a good risk for investment. Nyasaland could not compete with the gold and diamond mines of South Africa and Rhodesia or with the international waterways of the Cape and Suez for the attention of British investors. It was the creation of a flash of the humanitarian spirit without its follow-up. One of the results of this neglect was the rise of migrant labour.

Since the beginning of the most recent period in Malawi's history, the independence era, new plans have been introduced to alter the direction and effects of this neglect. Though labour migrancy continues, better conditions have been exacted and attempts are being made to lessen its flow. This can be done by increasing employment opportunities at home. Since almost 92 per cent of the people live in traditional villages the most gainful employment in a country which is almost wholly rural can only be found in the agricultural sector. Agriculture is being promoted by: the expansion of the Extension Services which include a special farmer training programme; the creation and expansion of a corporation to cater for agricultural development and marketing; the programme for the Malawi Young Pioneers which, in 1971, had twenty-one training bases and seventeen settlement schemes (almost 2,000 Young Pioneers graduate from their training bases every year and about 1,700 are presently located on settlement schemes where they mainly grow cotton, tobacco and groundnuts); the smallholder tea development scheme which started in 1965; and, since 1968, the establishment of settlement projects on a large scale. These latter projects which are financed by foreign agencies include the Lower Shire Cotton Development Project at Chikwawa; the Central Region Agricultural Development Scheme, with its headquarters at Salima, financed by German technical assistance and the Lilongwe Land Development Scheme financed by the World Bank. Added to this, work is going on in related areas like irrigation schemes and fertiliser application. Within the next ten years it will be possible to evaluate the historical results of these developments and projects.

The history of a nation is influenced, too, by internal stability and external respect. Internally, the country has had two brief periods of uncertainty both due to the cabinet crisis of 1964–65. The crisis was precipitated by a power struggle waged by certain cabinet ministers who were disenchanted by the fact that the then Prime Minister, Dr Banda, was in firm command. They had hoped that the Prime Minister could be swayed in any direction they chose. Certain issues were drawn into the arena of conflict as excuses to spark off the crisis. These were

Dr Banda's foreign policy towards South Africa and Portugal; the pace of Africanisation; the salary structure of the African civil service and the charging of a nominal fee for all out-patient treatment at government hospitals. The discontented ministers were either dismissed or they chose to resign. The immediate and subsequent response of the nation was to reaffirm its confidence in Dr Banda's leadership and policies. The armed infiltration led by one of the malcontents in October 1967 failed. Except for the two armed raids of February 1965 and October 1967, the independent state of Malawi has enjoyed considerable internal peace and stability for the rest of the period. In the meantime the rapid calculated rate of Africanisation has redounded to the credit of Dr Banda's policy of localisation only after adequate preparation. The number of senior African civil servants include most of the under-secretaries as well as permanent secretaries. In July 1971 an African Commissioner of Police assumed office. He should soon be joined by an African commander of the army.[1] And in the field of foreign policy Malawi's often declared stand on good neighbourliness and discretional non-alignment has meant that Dr Banda has been able to pursue a policy of realism based on Malawi's internal and external needs. This policy has evoked criticism in the Organisation of African Unity and other bodies but it has also received support in certain quarters. Dr Banda's championship of the policy of dialogue with white-ruled states to the south of Malawi culminated in his remarkably successful state visit to South Africa in August 1971, followed soon afterwards by a similar visit to Mozambique, almost seven years to the day since some of his former cabinet ministers had decried this policy. The visits aroused considerable interest in South Africa and elsewhere and have drawn attention to the pioneering policies of the Malawi leader. The visits have succeeded in unleashing a new force in southern and Central African politics, the fuller results of which are a matter for the future.

In the meantime, as the old chapter of the history of Malawi closes, a new one has begun. Forthcoming features will be the effects of mineral exploitation, particularly that of the Mulanje bauxite; the increased use of hydro-electric power both from within the country and from future possibilities close by; the increased production of

[1] It was announced in January 1972 that further localisation would become operative when Mr B. C. Roberts, the Attorney-General and Secretary to the Office of the President and Cabinet, retired in May 1972. The position of Attorney-General, according to the announcement, would go to Mr Richard A. Banda, Director of Public Prosecutions, and that of Secretary to the Office of the President and Cabinet would be held by Mr George Jaffu, Secretary to the Treasury. (Malawi *Times*, 6 Jan. 1972.)

cash crops and of the manufacturing industries. In all these endeavours, from the lowest to the highest, the historical destiny of the country will lie in its manpower utilisation and efficiency. In this the future will rest in the laps of Malawians themselves. Here, unlike in the army where battles are fought by the young while the peace treaties are negotiated by the old, national development demands the full and complementary cooperation of young and old. As the old chapter closes, in 1971 there were 355,004 pupils in primary schools, 10,937 students in secondary schools; 991 in primary teacher training colleges; 339 in technical schools; 18,811 doing correspondence courses; and 1,003 doing either degrees or diplomas at the University of Malawi. The country spends almost one-eighth of its modest national budget on education. The soundness of this investment is a subject for the historical judgement of the future. But if the past is any guide to go by Malawians of many generations have had an abiding interest in education. And this interest, in turn, has helped to shape so much of the history of the nation.

Bibliography

The most recent publication dealing with the history of Malawi is *The Early History of Malawi* edited by B. Pachai and published by Longman, 1972. The Introduction and the twenty-four chapters have detailed bibliographical references in the footnotes. For purposes of economy it has not been possible to make a selection from these detailed references.

Theses
Edward A. Alpers, *The role of the Yao in the development of trade in East-Central Africa, 1698–1850*, Ph.D., University of London, 1966
J. O. Hoik, *Family law in Malawi*, Ph.D., University of London, 1966
B. S. Krishnamurthy, *Land and Labour in Nyasaland, 1891–1914*, Ph.D., University of London, 1964
Harry W. Langworthy, *A history of Undi's Kingdom to 1890; aspects of Chewa history in Central Africa*, Ph.D., Boston University, 1969
Kenneth J. McCracken, *Livingstonia Mission and the evolution of Malawi, 1873–1939*, Ph.D., Cambridge University, 1967
Roderick J. Macdonald, *History of African education in Nyasaland, 1875–1945*, Ph.D., University of Edinburgh, 1969
Hugh W. Macmillan, *The origins and development of the African Lakes Company, 1878–1908*, Ph.D., University of Edinburgh, 1970
Emily N. Maliwa, *The history of nationalism and intellectual movements in Nyasaland*, M.A., University of Chicago, 1961
Emily N. Maliwa, *Malawi legal history*, M.Phil., University of London, 1967
Emily N. Maliwa, *Status of women iu Malawi*, Ph.D., University of London, 1970–71
Andrew C. Ross, *The origins and development of the Church of Scotland*

mission, Blantyre, Nyasaland, 1875–1926, Ph.D., University of Edinburgh, 1968

J. Mattheus Schoffeleers, *Mbona, the guardian-spirit of the Mang'anja*, B.Litt., Oxford University, 1966

J. Mattheus Schoffeleers, *Symbolic and social aspects of spirit worship among the Mang'anja*, Ph.D., Oxford University, 1968

Samuel W. Speck, *Development of local government in Malawi*, Ph.D., Harvard University, 1966

Roger K. Tangri, *The development of modern African politics and the emergence of a nationalist movement in colonial Malawi, 1891–1958*, Ph.D., University of Edinburgh, 1970

Publications by the Malawi Department of Antiquities
1. P. A. Cole-King, *Mwalawolemba*
2. P. A. Cole-King, *The Livingstone Search Expedition*
3. B. H. Sandelowsky and K. R. Robinson, *Fingira*
4. P. A. Cole-King, *Cape Maclear*
5. G. T. Nurse, *Height and History In Malawi*
6. K. R. Robinson, *The Early Iron Age In Malawi*
7. Various, *Occasional Papers*
8. K. R. Robinson, *The Iron Age of the Southern Lake Area of Malawi*
9. C. A. Baker, *Johnston's Administration*
10. P. A. Cole-King, *Lilongwe*

Final-year history students' seminar papers, University of Malawi, Chancellor College

1968–69

O. Kalinga, *The Rhodesian Constitutional Crisis*

M. A. Karolia, *A Brief Historical Survey of the Indian Community in Malawi*

M. Katayeni, *Taxation in Nyasaland, 1891–1915*

W. S. Khoza, *The Shire Highlands: Aspects of its Importance in Malawi History*

D. M. Manda, *Relationship Between Central Authority and Traditional Government*

C. Z. Mphande, *Some Aspects of the History of the Tonga up to 1934*

M. A. Munthali, *The Issue of Labour in Nyasaland*

W. S. Mvalo, *The Issue of Land in Nyasaland*

M. Y. J. Mwimba, *Concepts of Amalgamation and Partnership in Central Africa*

H. K. Ngoma, *The 1915 Rising in Nyasaland*

D. I. Nkhoma, *The Northern Ngoni—A Political System*

F. J. Buttawo, *Islam in Malawi with Special Emphasis on its Success in Nkhota Kota*

M. M. C. Jinazalih, *The Jumbes of Nkhota Kota and Their External Relations, 1884–1901*

E. B. Kadzako, *The Rise of Nationalism in Malawi*

R. F. Kankondo, *The Ngoni Migrations, Settlement and Political Organisation*

M. Kishindo, *A Survey of Likoma Island from Early Times to 1935*

J. D. Manda, *Independency in the Nkhata Bay Area from 1930 to Current Times*

T. L. J. Mandala, *The Anglo-Portuguese Conflict for Control over Nyasaland*

A. K. Mhango, *The History of the Henga people*

S. Mkwamba, *The Church of Scotland, Blantyre Mission, and the Making of Malawi: an Historical Appraisal*

A. W. C. Msiska, *An Account of Phoka History up to the Coming of the Livingstonia Mission*

G. M. Mughogho, *The Development of Education in the Nthalire (Chitipa District) from the late 19th Century to 1954*

J. W. Nyirenda, *The History of Katote Mission, 1938–1969*

B. M. N. Phiri, *Independent African Churches in Nkhata Bay District*

E. D. K. Simbeye, *A History of the Lambya in Oral Traditions from the Earliest Times to about 1900*

M. A. Wali, *The Nankumba area of Fort Johnston District, a résumé of historical beginnings*

R. P. K. Banda, *Some Reflections on the History of the Tumbuka Proper*

S. A. Bwinga, *The North Nyasa Native Association*

W. L. Dambuleni, *Aspects of early Chewa History with a note on the chieftainship of Chief Chauma*

O. Y. Kayira, *A Survey of the History of the Kayira clan of Northern Malawi*

H. H. Longwe, *An Evaluation of Missionary Activity on the Ngoni of Northern Malawi*

P. Manda, *The Role of Chiefs through changing Administrations—the case of Ngoni Chiefs, Mzimba District*

F. B. Mfipa, *The Decline of the Ngoni of Northern Malawi*

C. Mughogho, *Development of Livingstonia Mission to 1900*

A. C. Musopole, *An Experimeut in Mission Endeavour in Malawi: the 'Civil Jurisdiction' of the Blantyre Mission, 1876–1881*

R. C. Ndiwo, *The Establishment of Chiefs Chiwere, Msakambewa and Dzoole in Dowa District up to 1910*

K. K. Phiri, *The Atonga Tribal Council*

K. M. G. Phiri, *19th Century Economy and Trade in the Marginal Tumbuka–Chewa Area of Malawi*

Index